W9-CSD-998

# C++ Programming
# with MacApp®

# C++ Programming with MacApp

David A. Wilson

Larry S. Rosenstein

Dan Shafer

**Addison-Wesley Publishing Company, Inc.**
Reading, Massachusetts   Menlo Park, California   New York
Don Mills, Ontario   Wokingham, England   Amsterdam   Bonn
Sydney   Singapore   Tokyo   Madrid   San Juan

Many of the designations used by manufacturers and sellers to distinguish their products are claimed as trademarks. Where those designations appear in this book and Addison-Wesley was aware of a trademark claim, the designations have been printed in initial capital letters (e.g., Apple is a registered trademark of Apple Computer, Inc.)

Copyright © 1990 by David A. Wilson, Larry S. Rosenstein, and Dan Shafer

Some of the art in this manuscript is copyrighted by Trici Venola and Kurt Wahlner. Copyright © 1987.

All rights reserved. No part of this publication may be reproduced, stored in a retrieval system, or transmitted, in any form or by any means, electronic, mechanical, photocopying, recording, or otherwise, without the prior written permission of the publisher. Printed in the United States of America. Published simultaneously in Canada.

Sponsoring Editor: Carole McClendon
Technical Reviewer: Curt Bianchi
Cover Design: Ronn Campisi
Text Design: Copenhaver Cumpston
Set in 10.5 point Palatino by Don Huntington

ISBN 0-201-57020-3

ABCDEFGHIJ-MW-9432100
*First printing, July 1990*

This book is dedicated to Alex Munro.

# Contents

# Preface

Shortly after the introduction of our Pascal version of this book, *Programming With MacApp*, Apple Computer began shipping its C++ interfaces to MacApp as well as a C++ preprocessor. It quickly became evident that many Macintosh programmers favored the C++ approach to programming over that of Object Pascal. So many people asked us about the possibility of a C++ version of our book that we decided to put it together.

The essentials of MacApp don't really change, regardless of the language you use to build your programs with the extensive library of routines that is MacApp. As a result, the bulk of this book is nearly identical to the Object Pascal version. The major exceptions to this rule are:

- Chapter 6 has been completely rewritten. It now provides a concise and readable introduction to C++. If you're a C programmer who's never worked with C++, this overview gives you enough information to work with this new version of what has quickly become the most popular programming language on the Macintosh. If you don't know C, you can still learn C++ from this discussion.

- All code listings have, of course, been rewritten in C++. The ensuing discussions of each listing have also been adjusted accordingly.

- The major MacApp application that comprises the final five chapters of the book has been completely redone in C++. You'll find this program is an excellent "style guide" to the effective and most readable use of C and C++ in interacting with MacApp on a larger-scale project than those attempted in earlier chapters.

- Everything in the book has been updated to cover the latest releases of MacApp, its supporting tools, the Macintosh Programmer's Workshop (MPW), and the C compiler as well as the first release of the C++ pre-processor from Apple Computer and the Apple Programmers and Developers Association (APDA).
- Minor typographical errors, formatting problems, and bugs in the Object Pascal version have been corrected.

Like the earlier (Object Pascal) version of this book, we dedicate this work to Alex Munro, infant son of Allen Munro. Allen had the original idea for this book and without him it would not have become a reality. At this writing, Alex continues to struggle with a disease that most adults would find impossible to deal with. We admire the courage and fortitude of this family and acknowledge our deep debt to Allen.

*C++ Programming with MacApp* puts you at the leading edge of Macintosh programming techniques and strategies. We hope this book sets your feet firmly on the path that Apple has clearly marked as the best route to the future of Macintosh software development.

Enjoy.

Dave Wilson
Larry Rosenstein
Dan Shafer

Palo Alto, California,
June 1990

# Acknowledgments

Two people played an especially important role in this book. At the beginning of the project, Neil Rhodes (of Palomar Software) converted many of the MacApp samples from Object Pascal to their initial C++ versions. His expertise in using both MacApp and C++ was invaluable. In the final stages of the book, Curt Bianchi's meticulous technical reviews of each chapter and program listing saved us from literally hundreds of technical errors and typos. Curt made this a much better book than it would have otherwise been. We are not sure if Curt's role in life should ultimately be as a software engineer or a book editor — he is very good at both.

Harvey Alcabes, Steve Burbeck, and Tom Chavez provided years of support and help with both MPW and MacApp. This includes providing beta copies of software and documentation, plus many hours of valuable insights and discussions about the direction in which Apple was taking MacApp in particular, and object programming in general. Jordan Mattson and Tim Swihart provided us with beta copies of MPW and C++, so that this book could be as up to date as possible.

Larry Tesler, David Goldsmith, Curt Bianchi, and Steve Freidrich all provided great technical leadership for the various versions of MacApp. More than that, they helped us understand how to write better MacApp code.

Russ Wetmore, Deb Orton, Lonnie Millet, and Richard Rodseth are some of the other MacApp team members that provided support and technical guidance over the course of this project.

Katie Povejsil of Apple helped us get started in teaching Macintosh programming, while John Ryan and Linda Brown of Apple's Sales

Training and Brenda Buchwitz of Apple's Developer University helped us develop and refine the material used in Apple's programming seminars.

We are grateful for their support and cooperation as we learned by trial-and-error how to present this complex material without putting everyone to sleep. We'd also like to thank the hundreds of students who gave us feedback as they learned how to use MacApp.

Scott Knaster and Kurt Schmucker demonstrated that writing computer books was a sure way to fame, fortune, and a life of leisure. Without these role models, we might have had to keep working for a living. As it is, …

Carole McClendon provided optimism and persistence, single-handedly keeping this project alive when it ran into major delays in its early days. We thank her, and apologize for driving her crazy.

Finally, Joanne Clapp Fullagar's creativity and attention to detail during the editing process made this a much better book, as did Diane Freed's persistence in keeping the production on schedule. Carole, Joanne, Diane, Abby Genuth, and Rachel Guichard have made working with Addison-Wesley a pleasure.

# ▶ The Framework

In Part One, we will explore the framework and background behind object programming in general and MacApp specifically. This Part contains four chapters.

▶ Chapter 1 is an introduction to this book and to our approach to presenting the material. It answers the question of whether this book is for you.

▶ Chapter 2 provides the motivation for you to spend the time and energy to master MacApp. It points out key features and benefits of the MacApp environment, explains what you'll have to do to become proficient as a MacApp programmer, and describes some of the many uses to which MacApp has already been put.

▶ Chapter 3 introduces the basic concepts of object programming, including objects, messages, classes, subclasses, and inheritance. It explains some of the important ways in which object programming differs from more traditional programming approaches.

▶ Chapter 4 focuses on designing applications for object programming environments. It points out some of the basic ideas that will make it easier for you to design object-oriented applications that make efficient and effective use of this technology.

# 1 ▶ Introduction

This book is about MacApp, a programming system from Apple Computer designed to make it easier and more efficient to design and develop programs for the Macintosh computer family than traditional methods and tools have allowed. Thousands of programmers have discovered MacApp and, having made that discovery, have become ardent supporters of its approach to programming.

## ▶ Is This Book for You?

To find out if you can benefit from this book, ask yourself three questions:

- Am I a programmer?
- Am I a C programmer?
- Am I a good programmer?

It is not necessary that you answer yes to all of these questions, but if you can answer a strong affirmative to the first one and at least know what the second one means, you're probably going to find this book quite useful. Let's take a closer look at these three questions in light of what we hope to accomplish in this book.

## ▶ Are You a Programmer?

It was originally hoped that MacApp would be so simple to use that even nonprogrammers could write complete, professional Macintosh applications with it. As it turns out, that is not the case. MacApp greatly simplifies writing programs for the Macintosh, but you should buy this book with the understanding that you must be, or become, a computer programmer. If you know how to program a computer, MacApp will help you write programs for the Macintosh. If you have never written a computer program, this book will help clarify what you are getting into, but it will best serve you after you have learned the fundamentals of computer programming from introductory texts or courses. The Bibliography at the end of the book lists some books for learning about computer programming.

## ▶ Are You a C Programmer?

This book assumes a reading knowledge of the popular C programming language, such as you might get by reading *The C Programming Language* by Kernighan and Ritchie (reference 19). If you have a background in another modern procedural language such as Pascal or Modula-2, you may want to briefly acquaint yourself with the C syntax, or you may prefer to try to get it by osmosis as you read this book.

  This book is based on using C++, a derivative of C developed at AT&T by Bjarne Stroustrup. You do not need any experience with C++, since we will cover what you need to know in this book. In general, C programmers find it easy to learn the basics of C++, but hard to learn many of the details. This is because C++ has many features not found in C. It is a challenge to become a C++ expert, but you will find that mastering the language should make you a better programmer than you could be by using traditional C.

## ▶ Are You a C++ Programmer?

If you are already familiar with C++, we must caution you about our use of object-oriented terminology in this book. MacApp is a library written in Object Pascal, and Apple's MacApp documentation uses Object Pascal terms such as subclass, instance variable, and method. These terms are also used by most of the object programming community, since they are common to Smalltalk, Objective-C, Actor, and other object languages. C++ uses the same concepts, but uses different terms such as derived class, data member, and member function. We decided in this book to use the terminology used by most people in the MacApp and object programming community, rather than the special C++ terms. We will use both terms as we introduce the concepts, so C++ programmers should have no trouble.

▶ Are You a Good Programmer?

You may have been able to answer yes to the first two questions, but the last one is a little harder. Traditionally, programmers judge themselves to be good if they write programs that

- run fast
- take up only a small amount of memory
- take up only a small amount of disk space

These certainly are good measures of a programmer who writes code for a slow personal computer with limited memory and small amounts of slow mass storage.

However, you may have noticed people beginning to measure you with other yardsticks, asking embarrassing questions like these:

- Can you get the program done on schedule?
- Do you program defensively, with complete and consistent error checking and handling?
- Can someone else maintain your program, fixing bugs and adding features, long after you have left the company and moved away?
- Do you create self-contained, modular code fragments that can be easily reused when it is time to write the next program?
- How good is the user interface? If the program is for the Macintosh, the question becomes more specific: How well does your program conform to Apple's Human Interface Guidelines?
- Will your program run on all modern Macs, from the Macintosh Plus, released years ago, to the Macintosh IIfx released in 1990? Will your program run under MultiFinder? Will your program even run under Apple's version of UNIX, A/UX?

Life has certainly gotten more complicated. Traditional programming languages like FORTRAN, Pascal, and C address the traditional concerns of writing small, fast programs, but they offer little or no help in defensive programming, user interface support, or the creation of truly reusable code blocks. These are areas where programming with MacApp has tremendous benefits.

## ▶ How Much Do You Need to Know?

You might be asking yourself, How much do I have to know to use MacApp? Figure 1-1 shows the building blocks of knowledge you will need before you are ready to put MacApp to full use. The shadowed boxes in Figure 1-1 represent subjects that will be discussed in detail in this book. Unshaded boxes in Figure 1-1 point out knowledge you will need to gain from sources other than this book.

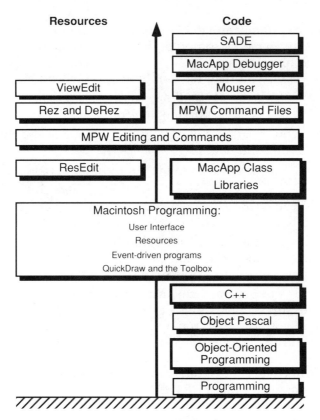

Figure 1-1. What you need to know

Figure 1-2 highlights the specific knowledge about Macintosh's ROM Toolbox that you will initially need. MacApp insulates you from most of the Toolbox, but it is important to understand some of its routines.

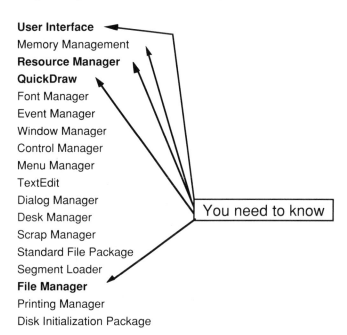

Figure 1-2. What you need to know about the Toolbox

## ▶ Basic Programming Knowledge

As we have said, you should understand the basic concepts of programming — data structures, variables, subroutines, and so on — before you attempt to understand this book or use MacApp.

You need to be familiar with C, and a bit of familiarity with Pascal will also be useful. We will describe Apple's specific implementations of C++ and Object Pascal in Chapter 6.

By the Way ▶ Programmers tend to treat discussions of favorite programming languages with religious fervor. Some C programmers hate Pascal, saying that it is a "toy" language. Some Pascal programmers abhor BASIC, saying that it "causes brain damage." Everybody dislikes Assembler, except low-level hackers, who mistrust all high-level languages. Our philosophy is that programming languages are tools — you simply need to choose the right ones for the job at hand. In this book the right tools are MPW C++ and Object Pascal (since all MacApp source code is in Object Pascal, you'll need at least a reading knowledge of this language as well as C and C++).

## ▶ Macintosh Knowledge

You should be familiar with Apple's Human Interface Guidelines. You should understand how to use resources, QuickDraw, and the portions of the Toolbox highlighted in Figure 1-2 (although you do not have to be an expert). You should understand event-driven programming and the concept of the main event loop around which all Macintosh applications, including MacApp, are built. You should understand the basic structure of a completed Macintosh application, consisting of compiled code in CODE resources, and other resources to support the user interface.

## ▶ What's in This Book?

This book has twenty-five chapters, which are grouped in five parts.

Part One is entitled "The Framework" and provides the framework within which you will be able to place and understand the rest of the book. It discusses object-oriented programming concepts and design issues. Since MacApp is an object-oriented application development environment, a thorough understanding of these basic concepts is essential. Even if you are an experienced programmer, you should plan to read Part One.

Part Two, "Getting Started in MacApp," focuses on the language and environment of MacApp. It explains the basics of using the Apple Macintosh Programmer's Workshop (MPW), which is the editing and programming environment within which you will work with MacApp. Most of the space in Part Two is devoted to discussing MacApp fundamentals: the MPW C++ and Object Pascal languages, the MacApp class library and how its components work, and the construction of your first small sample MacApp program. The section also includes two chapters about Program and User interface design.

Part Three, "Presenting Information to the User," discusses in depth how to design, build, and use views, the visual building blocks of a MacApp application from the user's perspective. It also discusses disk storage of data and the use of lists to manage collections of objects that model your problem domain.

Part Four is entitled "Obtaining Information from the User." It covers the second aspect of interactive program design: the portion with which the user interacts with your program. Here, you'll learn how to handle menus, the mouse, and dialogs.

Part Five pulls all of the pieces together as it discusses "Constructing a Real-World Application." This part not only describes choosing a programming task that's appropriate to MacApp's power and approach, but also how to combine separate, reusable building blocks into a finished application. This section describes how to design reusable classes and how to implement many sophisticated program features.

Finally, we include a bibliography of reference materials on Pascal, Object Pascal, C, C++, object-oriented programming and design, and computer programming.

## ▶ Patience as an Object

You may find object programming somewhat confusing at first. As we point out in Chapter 2, the process of programming with MacApp can seem like "programming in the closet." What you want this book to do for you is to turn on the light in that closet. This is an example of the great "Aha!" theory of learning: You muddle along for a while, mostly confused, when suddenly the light goes on and everything becomes clear. With MacApp, you'll discover that the closet you are in is quite large, so large in fact that one light bulb isn't enough to illuminate all of it. You will probably need to find four or five light bulbs before the whole MacApp universe becomes clear. You will find some concepts coming into focus quickly, while others require a few days of thought and practice before you feel comfortable with them. Be patient with us and we will help you find the light switches. Once all the lights are on, we're sure you'll like your new closet . . . er, room.

## ▶ Joining Other MacApp Developers

There are two organizations that we strongly recommend all MacApp programmers join. The first is the Apple Programmer's and Developer's Association, known as APDA. Membership information for this Apple Computer organization can be obtained from Apple Computer, Inc., 20525 Mariani Ave., Mail Stop 33G, Cupertino, CA 95014.

The MacApp Developer's Association (MADA) consists of over 1,000 people who use MacApp extensively. The organization publishes a newsletter, maintains a presence on electronic bulletin board services, sponsors occasional seminars and gatherings, and sells helpful MacApp programming utilities and sample programs. You can get more information about MADA by writing P.O. Box 23, Everett, WA 98203, or by sending an AppleLink message to "MADA."

## ▶ Summary

In this chapter, we have provided you with information about what you need to know to learn and use MacApp, as well as giving you some guidance about what is in this book and how to use it.

Chapter 2 begins the process of installing and using MacApp and starts the hands-on approach we use as much as possible throughout the rest of the book.

# 2 ▶ Getting Started with MacApp

This chapter makes sure we start our learning experience with MacApp with the same basic ideas and motivations. It has two primary purposes: to define MacApp and to explain why you should learn and use MacApp.

## ▶ What Is MacApp?

MacApp can be accurately described as either an almost complete, generic Macintosh Application ready for you to customize, or a set of reusable libraries upon which to base your program. The definition you find most apt will depend on your experience and your perspective. MacApp is written in a superset of Pascal called Object Pascal that provides support for object programming while still allowing Pascal programmers to feel at home. Apple's MPW C++ includes a complete set of header files to access the MacApp libraries, which remain as Object Pascal source code.

With C++ and the built-in MacApp libraries of objects, you can write complete Macintosh applications that will provide good performance and memory utilization. However, the real benefits come from the built-in support for the Macintosh user interface, sophisticated error checking and handling, program modularity and clarity, and compatibility across the whole Macintosh product line. Furthermore, you will learn to write programs as collections of reusable objects that can greatly simplify the process of writing future programs. Best of all, you will learn how to write complete Macintosh applications in one-half to one-third the time it would take with a traditional programming language.

## ▶ Who Uses MacApp?

MacApp is used by a whole spectrum of applications developers, from R&D programmers inside Apple Computer to university students. Other MacApp users include Apple programmers doing applications development, commercial software vendors, Value-Added Resellers (VARs), manufacturers of plug-in boards for the Macintosh II, and programmers doing custom development for Fortune 500 companies.

## ▶ Why Learn MacApp and Object Programming?

Like any new technology or programming method, object programming requires you to make an investment of time in understanding its ideas and techniques. Most people need only a few weeks to become comfortable with the object approach, but it will probably take a few months for you to feel that you are getting good at it. Since most of us are already busy and we all know that time is money, you may wonder if it is a good investment to take the time to learn a whole new technology. We believe that you should make the investment and that you will see major benefits in the form of increased productivity. We also believe that object-oriented programming is more fun than procedural programming, and that you will enjoy your work (or your play) more if you adopt this new approach.

Much of learning about object programming consists of becoming accustomed to its sometimes peculiar terminology. Words like *object*, *class*, *message*, *method*, and *inheritance* are sprinkled throughout the book. You will get more acquainted with them in Chapter 3. Before we discuss those words, we should address the most basic term of all: *object-oriented programming*. (Noted Macintosh programming expert and author Scott Knaster argues convincingly that tacking the word "oriented" to the end of the word "object" adds no real value. Therefore, he proposes that we call it simply "object programming." We think the suggestion has merit, and we will often follow his advice in this book. But old habits die hard, and OOP is a well-accepted and interesting acronym, so you will still find us using the more common phrase "object-oriented programming" in many places.)

### ▶ Making You a Better Programmer

Learning object programming in general and MacApp specifically will make you a better programmer for the 1990s and beyond. The rules that define good programming are changing rapidly and dramatically.

In the late 1970s, people who wrote personal computer software had two main problems to overcome: computers were slow and had tiny amounts of memory (8 KB of RAM was normal, and 64 KB was about the most that you could find). That meant that a good program had code that executed quickly and was as small as possible.

In the late 1980s, we begin to see new standards being applied. Programmers are increasingly judged on a much larger set of requirements; indeed, program size and execution speed are often unimportant items. Today, your success as a programmer requires that you meet the following set of requirements:

1. *Get the project done on schedule.* MacApp and object programming can facilitate this requirement by making it easy for you to reuse existing code written by you and by other programmers.

2. *Meet the program specifications.* This requirement turns out to have a number of components, each of which can be facilitated by your use of MacApp and object programming techniques. These components include:
   - providing a correct Macintosh user interface
   - using defensive programming techniques to prevent "bombs"
   - including common functions Macintosh users have come to expect, such as Undo and Clipboard support
   - operating on all versions of the Macintosh
   - running under Finder, MultiFinder, and even A/UX
   - making it possible to localize the software so foreign-language versions can be made

3. *Produce maintainable code.* This generally means making it easy to fix bugs and add features. By implication, this means you need to write readable source code that is divided into easy-to-understand modules. Here again, MacApp encourages and facilitates such design. Just by following its rules, you will produce more maintainable code.

Which of these three requirements is most important to you depends on your job. If you are a hobbyist, meeting the program specifications may be most important because your friends and colleagues will expect that. You will learn to appreciate the value of maintainable code the first time you need to fix an obscure bug or add a new feature. If you are a programmer in the management information systems department of a large corporation, or if you are a commercial developer, all three requirements are crucial.

If you make your living writing applications, you will probably experience the most trouble when you miss a deadline for delivering the program. On the other hand, if you have the often unpleasant task of maintaining someone else's code, you will hope that the original authors took the time to write a modular program with clear logic, and well chosen variable and routine names. Unfortunately, most professional programmers find that software maintenance on large programs generally involves many more person-years of effort than writing the original application.

## ▶ C and Pascal Are Not Enough

What has become apparent over the last few decades is that most software technologies do not provide enough help for the programmer to meet all of the needs listed above. A good C or Pascal compiler allows you to write a program that is small and fast. It does not provide enough help with crucial items like supporting a proper user interface, providing an easy way to reuse code, or producing source code that is easily maintainable. Object programming can be of significant help in all those areas, so you can write a professional-quality program in a reasonable amount of time.

## ▶ Features and Benefits of Object Programming

The benefits of using MacApp to write applications for the Macintosh fall into two categories. Some benefits accrue from using object technology. These advantages can be yours if you use Smalltalk, C++, or other object languages quite apart from MacApp or the Macintosh platform. Other benefits derive from the specific support that the MacApp libraries provide for writing programs for the Macintosh. This section discusses some of the features and benefits you will get from using any object programming language. We will focus on features and benefits specific to MacApp in the next section.

## ▶ Object-Oriented Design

Object-oriented program design models the world as a collection of *objects* that interact by passing messages back and forth. This happens to be the same model you learned as an infant: You sent a message to your parent (or, to be more formal, the parent object) when you wanted something. One reason learning traditional programming is difficult for most people is that they must learn to think in a way that is contrary to the normal world; the normal world is not composed of data structures plus algorithms, yet procedural programmers must think in those terms. You will find that designing with objects is more natural and more fun, once you get used to it. It may not be apparent the first time you do it, but it will become clear after you gain some experience.

▶ Readable, Maintainable Code

Most large projects become hard to manage and maintain because their complexity grows faster than the rate at which you add code and features. In other words, a program with ten thousand lines of source code is more than twice as complex as a program with five thousand lines of code. If each feature in the program were contained in a module with a crystal-clear interface, this would not be so. You will see that object programs are generally much more modular and self-contained than traditional programs, so that you can add features by adding new objects and cause minimal change to the existing code.

One computer science catch phrase that you can use to impress your friends at the local users' group meeting is *data abstraction*. This means that objects keep their data hidden from other objects. The only way an object should be able to get information from or about another object is by sending a message. If you're at a party and you meet someone you'd like to call later, you cannot look directly inside his or her brain; instead, you have to ask for the information. This may slow down your social life, but it will help your programming, because the code in one of your modules becomes isolated from the details of the data in another module. If you change the way you do some particular task inside an object, no other object needs to be aware of that fact. Other objects continue to send the same message to your object to get the information they need. We'll consider this important idea in more detail as our discussion progresses.

▶ Reusable Code

Objects are defined in *hierarchies*, inheriting properties from other objects. This allows you to reuse existing, well-tested code in libraries including

- the MacApp class library from Apple
- libraries that you may buy from third-party developers
- libraries that you develop as you program

You will see this in action in every program we examine. Reusing existing code in C or Pascal libraries is something you may already do, but you will find that object programming's code reuse is more flexible and powerful in a number of ways.

## ▶ Programming by Successive Refinement

The preferred method for writing a program using object programming techniques is to develop early versions with relatively few features, each of which is completely implemented and tested. MacApp allows you to write very simple applications in a few hours while still maintaining rigorously correct techniques for memory management, defensive programming, and Apple's Human Interface Guidelines. Programs always behave as expected. You always have something that can be shown without embarrassment; if the deadline sneaks up or changes on you, you can ship a program that works but is merely missing some features.

## ▶ Features and Benefits of MacApp

This section discusses benefits that accrue specifically from using the MacApp libraries to build applications for the Macintosh.

## ▶ Full User Interface Support

Supporting the Macintosh's event- and mouse-driven user interface has been a major obstacle to most developers. If you have ever written a traditional program for the Macintosh featuring something as common as a resizeable window with scroll bars, you know how many hours of studying *Inside Macintosh* were usually required. MacApp provides objects that handle those details with no programming effort on your part, so you do not even need to know when, for example, the user wants to open the Calculator desk accessory, much less write the code to make it happen.

There is also code in MacApp to handle such important user interface details as disabling menu items that are not currently active and deactivating windows that are not in front. You simply use this code without worrying about how it works or understanding its details.

▶ Guaranteed Compatibility

A program written with MacApp can run unchanged on any Macintosh from a Macintosh Plus with a 68000 processor to a Macintosh IIfx with a 68030 processor. It should also be able to run under Finder, MultiFinder, or even A/UX. This means that you will not have to write multiple versions of your program. If you are an experienced user of Macintosh software, you know that most commercial software fails to meet this test, because most software developers do not strictly follow the compatibility guidelines published by Apple's Developer Services. The MacApp programming team follows these guidelines to the letter, and if you do likewise when you add code to MacApp to create your application, then a single version of your program will be usable on the full installed base of Macintosh Plus and later machines.

▶ Making It Easy to Undo

Alas, users do make mistakes. In order for them to recover, you need to make it possible for your users to undo their last actions. Users simply will not tolerate a program that does not bail them out when they accidentally delete the database records for all customers in Ohio. MacApp does not automatically provide a complete, universal Undo capability, but it contains a sophisticated framework to enable you to include one. Providing the Undo capability is usually easy with MacApp.

▶ Debugging Tools

Debugging programs is usually difficult, but traditional debugging tools are even harder to use with object-oriented code because which routines are called is determined at runtime. (We will see in Chapters 6 and 11 why this is the case and what it means for debugging.) Fortunately, MacApp provides a number of high-level debugging tools to make the job much easier. MacApp's Debug menu, Debug window, and Inspector windows usually enable you to find the problem without having to swim in a sea of bits in an assembly-level debugger. Chapter 11 contains more information on debugging and on the MacApp tools to facilitate the process.

▶ Memory Management

MacApp provides optimized routines to allow your program to use memory efficiently. This means, among other things, that the user of your application will be able to open as many document windows as memory allows without you having to worry about heap fragmentation.

## ▶ Error Handling

Users hate programs that crash. To prevent the dreaded bomb from oc-
curring, most Macintosh programmers get anxious every time they
need to allocate memory (there might not be enough), get a resource
from disk (it might not be there), open or save a file (the disk might be
full, the file might already be open, and so on). MacApp provides a set
of powerful and elegant error handling routines that you should use
whenever possible to trap error conditions. These routines are easy to
use: They handle errors, displaying an alert to the user telling what is
wrong (in plain language), and then allow the user to continue to work
in almost every case.

## ▶ Easy Printing

Multiple-page printing, a difficult chore using conventional programming approaches, is extremely easy in MacApp. You just copy three
standard lines of code into your program to define a printable area of a
window and MacApp takes care of the rest.

## ▶ Easy Text Editing

MacApp's text edit building block makes it quite easy to open a window that provides typing, cut, copy, and paste, all with Undo automatically supported. MacApp uses the styled TextEdit routines in the Macintosh Toolbox, which means that each character can have its own font,
size, style, and even color on machines that support Color QuickDraw.

## ▶ Easy Dialogs

The most visually complex windows in an application are usually dialogs. MacApp provides many levels of support for handling dialogs. In
particular, you will find that MacApp supports many special features
not provided by the standard Dialog Manager Toolbox routines. As a
result, dialogs that would otherwise represent major programming
challenges can be created with a few minutes' work in MacApp.

## ▶ What Is Left for You to Do?

If you look back over this long list of benefits, you will see that MacApp does not promise to do everything. It does try to provide easy access to the generic features required by any complete Macintosh application. Table 2-1 lists the functions you are still expected to provide, as well as those furnished by MacApp.

Table 2-1. Responsibilities in MacApp

| *Functions MacApp handles* | *Functions you handle* |
| --- | --- |
| Desk accessories | |
| Selecting menu items | |
| Standard file dialogs | |
| Printing | |
| Standard menu commands | Your menu commands |
| Manipulating windows | Drawing and mouse clicks in content |
| Opening and closing files | Reading and writing data |
| Memory management | Some memory management |
| Error handling routines | Calling MacApp's routines |

In summary, you must provide the things that are unique to your application, such as the text and graphics that go into a window, the routines to write data to your document file on disk, and the actions to be carried out when the user clicks the mouse down in your graphics or text. MacApp has default behavior for much of the rest of what goes on in your program. To be a good MacApp programmer you need to understand MacApp's default behavior and how to change it when necessary. This book will help you to do this.

## ▶ A Real-Life Example

We have presented some so-far unsubstantiated claims regarding the benefits of object programming. In this section, you will see a concrete example of some of the benefits of the modularity provided by programming with objects.

▶ Writing a Paint Program

Imagine that you have just been hired by a commercial software firm. On your first day on the job, you are assigned to write a black-and-white paint program, such as the one pictured in Figure 2-1.

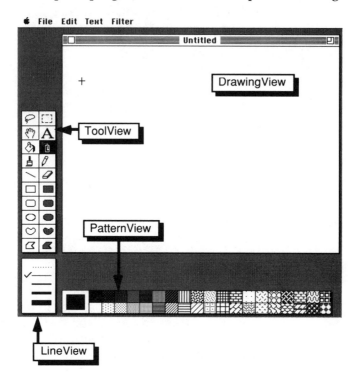

Figure 2-1. A black-and-white paint program

The program has four windows, with a single *view* in each window. In MacApp and many other object-oriented systems, a view is a rectangular part of the window that displays information to the user. For your task, you need to define the following views:

• ToolView that displays a palette of tools that the user can select
• LineView that displays the possible line widths
• PatternView that allows the user to select a choice of patterns
• DrawingView in which the user can draw

Figure 2-2 shows the framework for a traditional C program to do the job, while the beginnings of an object-oriented solution are shown on the right side of the figure. Let's compare them.

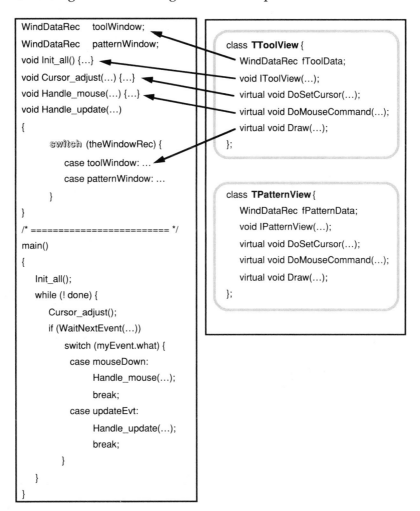

Figure 2-2. The old way and the new way

First, consider the traditional solution, which consists of the following:

- global variables, such as toolWindow and patternWindow, which are structs containing all the necessary information about each window

- the **Init_all** function, which initializes each of your global variables

- the **Cursor_adjust** function, which checks the location of the mouse pointer to see which window it is over and changes the cursor shape as necessary
- the **Handle_mouse** function, which determines in which window the user clicked the mouse and responds as necessary to that event
- the **Handle_update** function, which determines which windows need updating and arranges to draw them

Note that the **Handle_update** function uses a switch statement to handle the different actions required for each window. In fact, you will generally have switch statements in most of these other routines, so that the routines can respond in one way for the ToolView, and a different way for the DrawingView, and so forth. Although the switch statement is an excellent way to implement a structured program, it is nevertheless a major source of difficulty when you add new features — as we will see shortly.

The final part of the traditional solution is the main event loop found at the center of all Macintosh applications. The main program calls the Init_all function once and then spends the rest of its life in the main event loop. In this loop, as all experienced Macintosh programmers know, you must call the **WaitNextEvent** Toolbox routine to determine what the user did, and then call your other routines accordingly. Note that for simplicity, handling of other important events such as activate events and keyDown events is not shown in Figure 2-2.

This program structure can be made to work, but its inherent weakness is that the information and behavior of a given view are distributed throughout the source code, instead of being located in a single module. To write this same program in an object-oriented language, you might start by defining a class of objects for handling each view.

Consider the **TToolView** class definition shown on the right side of Figure 2-2. This encapsulates the data structure (the *fToolData* struct, which holds onto all variables that refer to that view) and the associated routines that operate on that view. These include

- the **IToolView** method (a *method* is a function defined as part of a class) which initializes the *fToolData* struct
- the **DoSetCursor** method, which sets the cursor to the correct shape when the mouse pointer is over the Tool view
- the **DoMouseCommand** method, which handles the selection of a tool when the mouse is clicked in the Tool view
- the **Draw** method, which redraws the Tool view in response to an update event for that window

<table>
<tr><td>Important ▶</td><td>A convention used throughout this book and the MacApp libraries, is that the name of a class of objects always begins with uppercase T, while variables defined in a class have names that begin with lower-case f. The "T" originally stood for Object Pascal Type, while the "f" stood for field of a record. We'll describe classes in detail in the next chapter, and describe the naming conventions in detail in Chapter 6.</td></tr>
</table>

The last three functions are called only when dealing with the Tool view, so they do not have to handle other cases. The advantage of this class definition is that all the data and functions specific to the Tool view are encapsulated and found in only one place in your code. There would be similar class definitions for the Pattern, Line, and Drawing views. Each view need only be concerned with itself, so none of the routines contains the switch statements of the traditional program. We'll show how object programs avoid needing as many switch statements in Chapter 6. To see why this is a good idea, consider the situation shown in Figure 2-3.

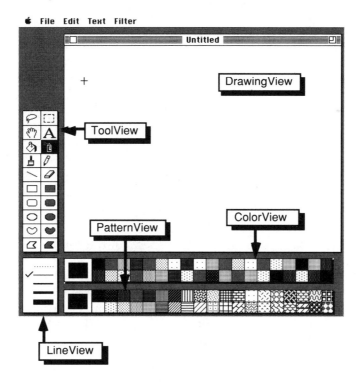

Figure 2-3. Addition of color

▶ Adding a New View

You have somehow finished the black-and-white paint program, but the marketing department has determined that your firm will go broke unless you can quickly deliver a color version of the program. Your boss tells you to start by adding a color view in another window, so that the user can select from a range of available colors. The left side of Figure 2-4 shows the functions that must be changed if you use the traditional approach. Notice that adding this one view to the program affects a large number of functions, in addition to adding more global variables. In all probability, you will have many different switch statements that will need to be modified, adding the case for the color view to each. This creates a major weakness in the program structure, because changes that occur throughout your source code make it much easier for bugs to be introduced and harder to find them. In other words, the program is hard to maintain.

Consider the right side of Figure 2-4, where we add support for the color view to a MacApp implementation of the original paint program simply by adding the **TColorView** class definition, shown in bold. All the information about new data, new routines to handle mouse clicks, and the like is in this class, which makes it much easier to incorporate into the rest of your code. Obviously, we have only sketched part of an actual program, but you will see how this works with real code examples in later chapters. You will see how object programming greatly enhances your ability to add features and fix bugs. You will also see how the capability to reuse code will greatly reduce the amount of code you have to write the first time, which makes maintenance even easier.

## ▶ Changing Your Mind Set

One of the reasons many experienced programmers find learning object programming and MacApp particularly challenging is that MacApp forces them to change some aspects of the fundamental way they think about programming. Rather than bore you with a long dissertation using such exotic terms as paradigm shift and conceptual model, we thought we'd share two visual images that illustrate what we mean. This was first published as part of a longer article entitled "Programming in the Closet," written by one of us (Dave Wilson) for the September 1987 issue of *MacTutor* magazine.

```
WindDataRec    toolWindow;
WindDataRec    patternWindow;
WindDataRec    colorWindow;
void Init_all() {...}
void Cursor_adjust(...) {...}
void Handle_mouse(...) {...}
void Handle_update(...)
{
        switch (theWindowRec) {

            case toolWindow: ...
            case patternWindow: ...
            case colorWindow:...

        }
}
/* ========================= */
main()
{
    Init_all();
    while (! done) {
    Cursor_adjust();
    if (WaitNextEvent(...))
        switch (myEvent.what) {
        case mouseDown:
            Handle_mouse(...);
            break;
        case updateEvt:
            Handle_update(...);
            break;
        }
    }
}
```

```
class TToolView {
    WindDataRec  fToolData;
    void IToolView(...);
    virtual void DoSetCursor(...);
    virtual void DoMouseCommand(...);
    virtual void Draw(...);
};
```

```
class TPatternView {
    WindDataRec  fPatternData;
    void IPatternView(...);
    virtual void DoSetCursor(...);
    virtual void DoMouseCommand(...);
    virtual void Draw(...);
};
```

```
class TColorView {
    WindDataRec  fColorData;
    void IColorView(...);
    virtual void DoSetCursor(...);
    virtual void DoMouseCommand(...);
    virtual void Draw(...);
};
```

Figure 2-4. Changes in the code to add a color view

## ▶ Programming in the Closet

A long, long time ago, in an operating system far, far away, applications programmers wrote code that directed users along a certain path.
As the programmer, you were clearly in control of what happened, so
you gave orders to users, and users did what they were told. If they
did not follow orders, you displayed friendly error messages such as
"Syntax Error 5" and hoped they would shape up.

Then the Macintosh came along, and you were instructed to write
friendly, modeless programs with the operation controlled by the user.
(Incidentally, noted humor writer Dave Barry defines "user" as the

word computer programmers use when they mean "idiot.") You wrote modeless programs by building your application around a main event loop in which you called WaitNextEvent to respond to events caused by the user. This, unfortunately, seemed to many programmers like programming in a room with the door closed. You could not see the user, but when a key was typed or the mouse button was clicked, the Toolbox Event Manager slid a piece of paper under the door that contained the Event Record. You read the piece of paper and responded accordingly. Some programmers who are new to the Macintosh feel a bit nervous with this style because they don't feel in control, but users certainly prefer it because they *are* in control.

What happens with MacApp? You may feel even less secure. MacApp is an expandable generic application, consisting of over seven hundred pages of Object Pascal source code written by some of Apple's best programmers (including one of the present authors). All you have to do is customize the application through the special hooks provided by object-oriented programing, and presto! you have your program.

Are you still alone in the room looking at pieces of paper being slid under the door by the Event Manager? Nope, MacApp is. Where are you? You are in the closet. Most of the time the program runs well without needing your code at all, because MacApp can handle such functions as moving and resizing windows, operating scroll bars, and opening desk accessories on its own. Once in a while MacApp needs you to do something specific for your program, so it opens the closet door, barks at you to "Draw yourself," or "Write your data to disk," and then closes the door again. You must do what you are told and stay out of the way the rest of the time.

## ▶ The Upside-Down Library

Steve Burbeck, a well-known object programming guru, has likened programming with MacApp to programming with an upside-down library. What does that mean? Consider the two situations shown in Figure 2-5. As a traditional programmer, you most likely wrote most of the code for each program but called upon existing library routines to carry out certain tasks. For example, in writing an application for the Macintosh, you would have written the main event loop yourself and controlled when the user chose a menu item or clicked the mouse in a scroll bar. However, you would have called the QuickDraw library routines in the Toolbox to draw graphics in a window or the Window Manager routines in the Toolbox to allow the user to drag a window from one place on the screen to another. With this type of programming you are in charge — not the libraries you use.

Traditional programming:

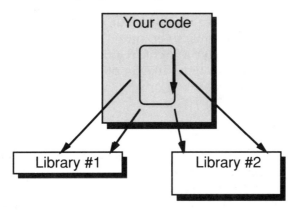

MacApp programming:

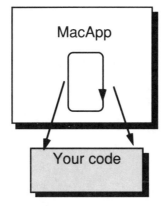

Figure 2-5. The upside-down library

The situation changes dramatically when you use MacApp. MacApp provides a routine to handle the main event loop and handles many events without involving you at all. However, MacApp cannot handle all situations, so your code gets called by MacApp when it is needed. Note that the bottom of Figure 2-5 shows things upside down: Instead of your code being in control and calling library routines once in a while, you see that the MacApp library is in control and calls your routines once in a while.

Thus with MacApp, you are no longer writing an application, but rather writing a few code fragments that customize the generic application written by Apple. Apple's code runs the main event loop and handles most of the events, so be sure to take a good book into your closet because you will have a lot of free time. But first, you need to learn to use MacApp and to think like an object programmer, which brings us to the rest of this book.

▶  ## Summary

We hope this chapter has convinced you of the power and utility of object programming in general and of MacApp as an object programming environment. We have outlined broadly what MacApp handles for you and what you must be concerned with in developing applications in MacApp. As you have seen, MacApp provides a storehouse of functionality that you can use to make creating Macintosh applications much faster and easier than it would be without MacApp's support.

Chapter 3 introduces the basic concepts behind object programming so that you can understand the remaining chapters in the book. It focuses on terminology and design issues that are generally applicable to any object programming environment, not those that are peculiar to MacApp.

# 3 ▶ Object Programming Concepts

In this chapter, we will examine the basic concepts of object programming, providing a framework within which you can better understand the remainder of the discussion in this book. Specifically, we'll focus on defining such terms as

- objects
- messages and methods
- classes
- subclassing and inheritance

We will also talk about how objects work in practice; how the compiler knows about objects and messages and their interrelationships, for example. Finally, we'll discuss the process of learning about object programming and MacApp, providing you with some insights and tips that will make the learning experience easier and more enjoyable.

## ▶ Terminology

As we mentioned in Chapter 1, object terminology is a problem. Smalltalk, Object Pascal, Objective-C and other object languages have popularized the set of terms used above. Although C++ uses the same concepts, it was unfortunately defined using a different terminology. After much soul searching, we decided to use the terminology used by most books and articles about object programming — the one used by Object Pascal and all the MacApp documentation. If you happen to read other books about C++, you will have to perform a mental translation from our terminology to the C++ version. The mapping of the most important terms is shown below. We will review this in later chapters as the need arises.

| *This book* | *C++* |
|-------------|-------|
| Method | Member function |
| Instance variable | Data member |
| Class | Class |
| Superclass | Base Class |
| Subclass | Derived class |

## ▶ Learning Object Programming

Experienced MacApp programmers find object programming to be very natural, reasonable, and logical. Why, then, does it have a reputation for being strange and hard to learn? One of the main reasons is that the terminology is very different from that of ordinary procedural programming. Magazine articles and books are full of phrases like "Now we send the HandleMouse *message* to our *instantiation* of the ListView *class*, and notice that the *method inherits* most of its behavior from the View *superclass*." At this point, the reader's eyes glaze over, after which he or she closes the magazine or book, and goes back to a safe, old-fashioned C compiler.

Some of the object programming terminology is really ungainly (such as the unnecessary word "instantiate" — which merely means to make an object). Most of it, however, comprises perfectly normal English words such as object, message, method, inherit, and class. In this chapter you will see that the words have perfectly reasonable, normal meanings in the context of object programming. In fact, we hope to convince you that programming with objects is not complicated, but merely different from procedural programming, and that those differences will bring you advantages when you write your next program.

## ▶ What Are Objects?

Objects are modular entities composed of their *state* (defined by their internal variables or data) and their *behavior* (defined by the operations that can act on that data).

In any computer program you define certain variables, for example, the amount of money that a customer owes your company. You also typically write subroutines (known as functions in C, or procedures and functions in Pascal) that operate on those variables. In object programming you group together the variables and the routines that operate on those variables into objects.

Objects in MacApp often correspond directly to objects in the real world, which can make program design easy and natural. Real-world objects that you might incorporate into your program include

- customers who buy products from your company
- orders for products they buy
- people in your company
- hardware objects on your computer's motherboard
- the stock market
- a flight simulator

Each of these objects has internal data and behaviors that are based on those data. To the extent that you can mimic those variables and behaviors in your program, you will be using object programming techniques.

Consider the characteristics of the people shown in Figure 3-1. They represent a model of a medium- to large-sized company — a company that requires many levels of management and many people with specialized knowledge. For example, consider the VP of Software Development. That person's internal data might include a list of the programmers in the department and a list of projects underway. The behaviors include the ability to hire new programmers and to decide which projects should be done. But, would it be efficient for the VP to try to write all the code for each project? Not in a large company. Instead, specialists who were skilled programmers would actually write the code. Consider one of these programmer/objects. He or she would have specialized internal data such as a knowledge of the instruction set for the 68030 microprocessor and would have behaviors such as the ability to write 68030 assembly code and then debug and test it. In a large company, you would not expect each programmer to have the same knowledge or behavior as the VP. The programmers would be various kinds of people, with various data and behaviors.

This brings up the first rule of object programming:

Important ▶ **Use specialized objects, each optimized to do certain specific jobs well.**

A small company can get by with one employee; similarly a very small application can be written using only one general-purpose object. Just as a large company needs specialists, a large computer program needs the cooperation of many special-purpose objects. When there are many objects in a program, they must be able to work together to carry out complicated tasks. How do objects work cooperatively? Again, consider the people objects in Figure 3-1. They cooperate by sending messages to one another. A *message* can be defined as a request for another object to do something, and that is how we will define it for object programming. For example, when the VP of Software Development wants Executive Information System software, he might send a message to a programmer, asking the programmer to write this new program. The message would include both the general task (write a program) and specific details (it should have a certain name, be done in a certain time). The programmer might then send a message back to the VP asking for authorization to hire other programmers to help on the job.

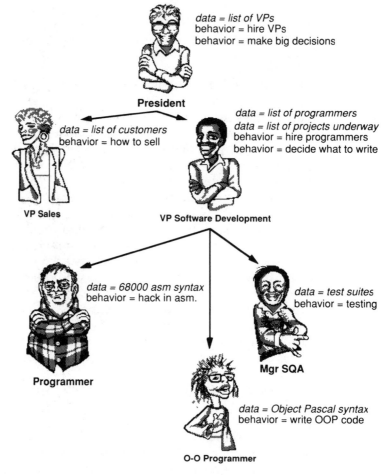

data = list of VPs
behavior = hire VPs
behavior = make big decisions

**President**

data = list of customers
behavior = how to sell

**VP Sales**

data = list of programmers
data = list of projects underway
behavior = hire programmers
behavior = decide what to write

**VP Software Development**

data = 68000 asm syntax
behavior = hack in asm.

**Programmer**

data = test suites
behavior = testing

**Mgr SQA**

data = Object Pascal syntax
behavior = write OOP code

**O-O Programmer**

Figures Copyright 1987 Trici Venola and Kurt Wahlner

Figure 3-1.  People objects running a company

Note that in a well-run company (that is one that practices management by objective), the VP would send a message saying what should be done but not how to do it. The programmer should have the specialized skills and knowledge to decide which development system and language should be used for a given project, which the VP would not need to know. This leads to another rule of object programming:

| | |
|---|---|
| **Important ▶** | A message tells an object what to do. It is then up to the receiving object to determine how to do the job. |

Let's look at another example: the computer on your desk or workbench. If you were to remove the cover and inspect the motherboard, you would see something similar to the Macintosh II system design shown in Figure 3-2. The objects shown include the CPU, the math chip, other specialized chips that control the serial port, and so forth. These chips have internal variables stored in registers and communicate by sending messages over various bus lines. The point we want to stress is that we all use, and are part of, systems that operate by independent objects sending messages to each other.

## ▶ Sending Messages

A message must be addressed to a specific object. A *message* in C++ is the name of a function, with any associated arguments. A particular object is referred to by a variable called, logically enough, an "object reference variable." In Chapter 6 you'll see how to define and create objects. For now, assume we have an object referred to by the reference variable *aBox*. We can send it a message telling it to draw a certain part of itself with this code fragment:

```
aBox->Draw(aRectangle);
//object->message
```

What is the message — is it Draw, or is it the more complete Draw (aRectangle)? Following the model of human communication, where the necessary information would include the area of interest, the message is defined to be the desired behavior and the parameters. Therefore the message is Draw(aRectangle).

What should the object do when it receives the message, or more specifically, by what method should it respond to the message? The *method* is defined to be the function executed by the object in response to a message. That means that for every message, there is an associated response, such as:

```
void TBox::Draw(Rect area)
{
  PenSize(2,2);
  FrameRect(&area);
}
```

The distinction between message and method will become important later, when different objects define different methods to respond to the same message.

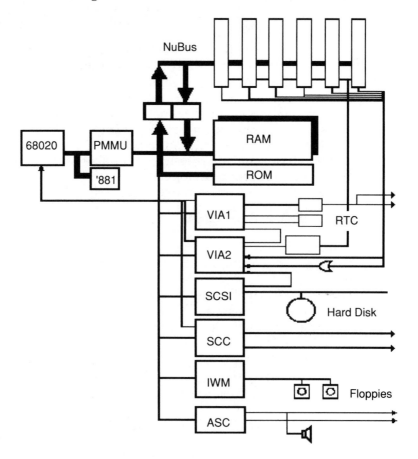

Macintosh II block diagram
from *Technical Introduction to the Macintosh Family*
published by Addison-Wesley

Figure 3-2. Specialized hardware objects

## ▶ Strange Terminology

When you first learn this terminology, you may not understand its usefulness. Programmers with experience in traditional programming often feel that the phrase "call the Draw function" is adequate, but we instead say "send the Draw message." Why do we make things look strange when we could make them look familiar? We do so to help you change your thought patterns — to help you think of your program components as modular objects that know how to do useful things. All you have to do is put them to work by sending them messages. This change in perspective is subtle, but is an extremely important part of learning how to program with objects.

## ▶ Where to Get Objects

Sending a message to intelligent objects sounds easy enough, but how do the objects know what to do? Who writes the methods that give them their intelligence? The answer depends on which objects you use. If you base your Macintosh application on MacApp, then you can use the large collection of objects that are in the MacApp library. This library provides you with over seventy types of objects that know how to respond to hundreds of different messages. All you have to know to use these objects is how to create and initialize them and which messages you can send to a given object.

There are two other possible sources for these intelligent objects. If you want an object almost like one you have in a library but with some customization, object programming provides a particularly elegant way to make one, as you will see later in this chapter. At times, however, you may find that you need an object that is unlike anything you already have. In that case, you have to decide what variables you need for that object and what messages you would like to be able to send that object. Then you must create the object and write the methods, which means writing the functions — just as in procedural programming.

Is the idea of using modular objects that encapsulate their data and functions unique to object programming? Of course it is not. You can make modules composed of data and their associated routines in many languages, including Modula-2, C, Ada, and many versions of Pascal. If that were all that object programming offered, it would still be useful as a design technique, but it would not be as revolutionary as we think you will ultimately find it to be. Beyond modularity, it offers support for writing maintainable, reusable code, which is far more important.

## ▶ Classes of Objects

We define objects as modules that store internal variables and that know how to respond to certain messages. If you are writing an accounts receivable application, you might need an object to represent each customer. This could mean creating hundreds or thousands of objects. All these customer objects would have their separate values for name, address, and so on, but might respond in the same way to the message PrintInvoice. Assume we have five hundred customers in our database. Do you want to have to write five hundred methods called **PrintInvoice**? Since the answer is no, you need a mechanism for grouping all customer objects together so they share common behavior. In C++, as in most object-oriented languages, that is done by defining a *class* of objects. A class is a template for making objects, a bit like a cookie cutter is a template for making cookies. A class in C++ is defined with a class definition:

```
class TCustomer {
   private:
      char fName[255];
      char fCity[255];
      float fAmountOwed;
   public:
      void PrintInvoice();
      Boolean OwesMoney();
};
```

Objects that belong to the same class each have their own instance variables to store the same kind of data and respond to a given message identically. This means that each object of class **TCustomer** has local storage for a name, an address, and an amount owed. But each object will have its own values for those variables. Each **TCustomer** object uses the same **PrintInvoice** method, so you only have to write it once. In Chapter 6, you'll learn the details of defining classes and creating objects from those class templates.

## ▶ Class Diagrams

In this book we are using a documentation technique called class diagrams, illustrated by Figure 3-3. (For a discussion of this technique see "Class Diagrams: A Tool for Design, Documentation, and Teaching" referenced in the Bibliography.) Each shadowed box represents the structure of a class, with the class name in bold letters, the variable names in italics, and the message names in plain text. Class diagrams are useful because they allow you to see the overall structure of your application without cluttering it with the method code. They are used most often at the beginning and the end of a project — at the beginning as a program design tool to help decide what the class structure should be and at the end as documentation to show the program's components.

Class diagrams are also useful as a teaching tool, because they can show code fragments within the total class structure. We will use them extensively in this book. Figure 3-3 shows the code fragments for the messages ICustomer and PrintAddress in the class **TCustomer**.

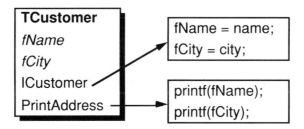

Figure 3-3.  Class diagrams for program design and documentation

## ▶ Subclassing and Inheritance

As all experienced programmers are quite aware, Murphy's Law dominates everything we do. This means that the class of objects you have in front of you may be very nice, but it probably will not behave exactly as you would like. Therefore, you will need a mechanism for modifying or customizing its behavior. The technique for making a new class of objects that is slightly different from an existing class is called subclassing, as shown in Figure 3-4. A *subclass* inherits all the variables and methods of its *superclass*, and thus is defined by how it differs from its superclass.

## ▶ Inheriting Properties

Figure 3-4 shows a class **TProgrammer** with two variables and two methods. To make a special version of the class that adds two methods common to all assembly programmers (**WriteMacros** and **Suffer**), we define **TAsmProgrammer** as a subclass of **TProgrammer**. The **TAsmProgrammer** class *inherits* all the variables and methods of its superclass, **TProgrammer**.

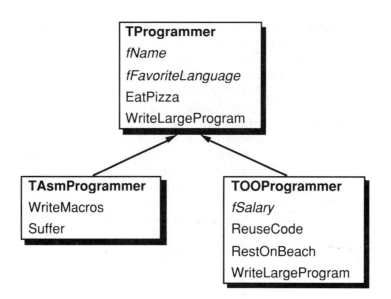

Figure 3-4.  Hierarchies of classes

**By the Way** ▶ | The reason the arrow points upward is that you inherit variables and methods from your superclass, while the superclass code does not even know that the subclass exists.

To be more explicit, a **TProgrammer** object (technically, an *instance* of the class **TProgrammer**) will have data storage for two variables, *fName* and *fFavoriteLanguage*. An instance of **TAsmProgrammer** will also have local data storage for the same type of variables. A **TProgrammer** object can be sent two messages: EatPizza and WriteLargeProgram. By inheritance these two messages can also be sent to an instance of **TAsmProgrammer**, with the added bonus that the messages WriteMacros and Suffer can also be sent.

What is the virtue of subclassing? It is a way to add new methods without affecting the behavior of the original class. This is useful when you want to leave the original class alone, which often happens when it is in a library being used by a number of programs or programmers. Another advantage of subclassing is evident in the **TOOProgrammer** subclass in Figure 3-4.

▶ Overriding Properties

The **TOOProgrammer** subclass, like **TAsmProgrammer**, adds two methods, **ReuseCode** and **RestOnBeach**, but it is different in that it *overrides* the existing **WriteLargeProgram** method and replaces it with a new version. This means you can have two identical messages that invoke different methods. We can send the WriteLargeProgram message to a **TProgrammer** object, and its method executes. We can send the same message to a **TOOProgrammer** object, and a different method executes. This is an extremely powerful capability. It allows you to write generic code. You send the same message to different types of objects, but the resulting behavior will be different for objects of different classes. A method that can be overridden in C++ is called a *virtual function*.

Not only can your code be generic, but the compiler need not know when it compiles your MacApp program what kind of object might be the recipient of a message when the program is actually run. This ability is embodied in the concept of *dynamic binding,* which means that the message and the type of its object can be bound together when the program is run rather than when it is compiled, as is the case with traditional C programs. The ability to use the same message name to apply to two or more potentially radically different behaviors is called *polymorphism* and is one of the main advantages of object programming.

# ▶ Reusing Unique Code

In general, subclassing greatly facilitates code reuse. Once you have written, debugged, and tested the methods for the **TProgrammer** superclass, you can inherit and reuse those methods (and variables) for your subclass without having to recode and test them. You can also add new methods and variables to a subclass as they are needed. You can even substitute a new version of a method in your subclass to override an existing method that does not do exactly what you want.

Object programming provides this opportunity to reuse code by means of subclassing and overriding. However, it may not be obvious why this differs from what good programmers have done for years using libraries of previously tested code. One unique advantage of subclassing is that you get the new behavior you want in a subclass without modifying the original code at all! This means that you could use a **TProgrammer** object and send it the WriteLargeProgram message when you want the original behavior. On the other hand, by creating an instance of **TOOProgrammer** and sending it the same message, you will trigger the new behavior. This allows you to use multiple versions of a code library interchangeably within an application.

## ▶ The Price You Pay

Obviously, you cannot get something for nothing. The price you pay to be able to use multiple versions of the routines with the same name is that object-oriented languages need a special mechanism for determining which method should execute when you send a message to an object. This involves what is known as *method lookup*, or *dynamic binding*.

### Method Lookup

In the example in Figure 3-4, how many versions of the **EatPizza** method are shown? There is only one implementation of this method, so it will execute when you send the EatPizza message to an object of class **TProgrammer**, **TAsmProgrammer**, or **TOOProgrammer**. Life is simple. However, life rarely stays simple for long. We might somewhere in our program find the code fragment:

```
aProgrammer->WriteLargeProgram();
anAsmProgrammer->WriteLargeProgram();
anOOProgrammer->WriteLargeProgram();
```

The property of having many routines with the same name (*polymorphism*) means the compiler often cannot determine at compile time which method should be called, resulting in the need for a *method lookup table* mechanism to find the correct method.

A good object language creates such a table by means of compiler-generated code, so that we do not have to do it or even understand how the compiled code does it. In C++, these tables are called *vtables*, with the letter v standing for virtual.

## ▶ What's Different?

Creating a new class may still feel like programming, because you still define data structures and write functions. If you feel this way, you are correct. On the other hand, you may feel that this is very different from procedural programming. You are also correct. Consider the subtle but important difference in the following example. This is the code fragment that we just discussed:

```
aProgrammer->WriteLargeProgram();
anAsmProgrammer->WriteLargeProgram();
anOOProgrammer->WriteLargeProgram();
```

In object programming, you would most likely keep all your programmer objects in some kind of collection data structure that would allow you to be even more generic; you could write a method something like:

```
ForEachProgrammerOfAnyType(WriteLargeProgram);
```

In this case, **ForEachProgrammerOfAnyType** is an *iterator* method that can be set up to send the same message to every object in the collection. The virtue of this technique is that the receiver of the message determines what to do, by executing the correct method for that object.

Now look at the traditional version of a related code fragment:

```
switch (theProgrammer)
{
   case aProgrammer:
      WriteLargeProgram();
      break;
   case anAsmProgrammer:
      WriteASMProgram();
      break;
   case anOOProgrammer:
      WriteOOProgram();
      break;
}
```

The difference is subtle, but important. In this program, you must determine what kind of programmer you are dealing with before you can call the correct routine. By eliminating the switch statement in the object program, you greatly enhance maintainability. Why? Consider what happens when you want to add another feature later, such as another class of programmers. In the object programming fragment, you would not need to change the code at all. In the traditional programming fragment, you must explicitly add another case to the switch statement. This would not be a problem if there were only one case statement, but typically there are many. For example, you might have one case statement for drawing on the screen, another for window activate events, another for saving to disk, and another for reading from disk. When a new feature is added to your program, you must generally find and modify all those switch statements. The changes are generally much simpler to manage using the object-oriented style.

This is a small advantage in a simple program; its value increases in very large, complex programs. It appears that procedural programs grow in complexity much faster than object programs do when features are added.

## ▶ Programming with Objects

Now that you have been introduced to the components of object programming, there are three techniques to using them in writing your MacApp program: easy, almost as easy, and being creative. In the easy cases you can simply use classes and methods that already exist, such as those provided by MacApp. In these cases, you merely create objects, initialize them (so their variables are set to reasonable values), and then send them messages to put them to work. What could be easier?

If the behavior you need is similar to that of an existing class, it is almost as easy to subclass an existing class of objects. This allows you to add the variables and methods you need. In some cases, it only requires a few lines of code, which makes it almost like the technique just described. In other cases, you may want to change the behavior of a class substantially. Then you have more work to do, primarily by writing new methods. You will see many specific examples of how to do this using the MacApp classes in later chapters.

At other times you need to be creative. You must define new classes of objects, fully defining the variables and the desired behavior. Surprisingly, writing the methods is often easy; what troubles most novices is the design process, during which you must decide which variables and methods you need and which class to sub-class. We'll talk about that process in some detail in the next chapter.

## ▶ The Learning Process

The major obstacle for most programmers in adopting object programming is the learning curve, which typically takes one to six months. With one month of full-time effort, you probably understand the basic concepts enough to begin work on a project, but it may take six months or more before you feel really comfortable with the language, tools, and class library that you are using. Furthermore, it may take a year or more of object programming before you begin to think naturally in terms of objects rather than procedures and become good at writing reusable code. We hope this book will accelerate that process, but it will take time.

## ▶ Obstacles

Becoming an effective object programmer involves major changes in the way you design and build programs, in addition to learning the specific use of MacApp.

### Major Change in Program Design

You will have to decide which classes of objects should be used in each application. You will have to choose the appropriate variables and messages for each class. You will have to arrange these classes in a hierarchy, with some of them defined as subclasses of existing MacApp classes and others created from scratch.

### Major Change in Programming Style

You will have to get used to the fact that in many cases the majority of the code in your application will not have been written by you. You might choose to use MacApp so that windows, scroll bars, menus, and printing are taken care of for you. But the opposite side of that coin is that you are not in control; MacApp is doing much of the work for you. You will generally find that the MacApp methods run the application and call your methods as necessary. To say that this will at first seem weird is to understate the case. But you will get over this and come to appreciate the fact that MacApp does so much of the dirty work for you.

### Learning to Use MacApp

MacApp currently consists of over fifty thousand lines of source code, organized into about seventy classes, some twelve hundred methods, and hundreds of constants, variables, and ordinary Pascal procedures and functions. Fortunately, you only need to become familiar with about five classes and perhaps thirty methods to begin to write applications with MacApp. We will concentrate on these essentials in this book rather than attempting an exhaustive treatment of every detail of MacApp.

### Learning C++

C++ is a complex language. In Chapter 6, we will describe all you need to know about C++ to write programs using MacApp. It will take time to absorb it all, and more time to know when a certain feature should be used. As you become comfortable with C++, you will find it to be very flexible and powerful.

## ▶ Review

The concepts you have met in this chapter may seem a bit unusual. Here are some of the ideas with which you must get comfortable as you learn these techniques.

- You define specialized objects that are optimized to do one job well.
- To get something done, you send a message to the object best suited to do the job.
- The sending object defines what is to be done and sends the appropriate message to another object (or even to itself).
- The receiving object determines how to react when it receives a given message.
- Classes are templates for building objects, but they are not objects themselves. This means, for example, that you cannot send a message to the class **TProgrammer**. Instead you must create an instance of the class and then send that object the message. For example, Bill Atkinson is an instance of the class **TProgrammer**, or, more simply, Bill Atkinson is a **TProgrammer** object.

| By the Way ▶ | In some object languages, such as Smalltalk, everything is an object, which means that a class is also an object, that is, an instance of the class "Class." This concept (technically termed a meta-class) is subtle and can make your head hurt if you think about it too much. Your head will therefore be happy to know that in C++, a class is not an object; a class definition is merely information that the compiler uses to create individual objects. |

However, using object programming techniques has several advantages. To summarize advantages, consider the new ideas one at a time.

- Objects and messages provide an excellent mechanism for encapsulating associated data and functions. This encourages data abstraction, so that an object's variables can be hidden from other objects. This convention encourages you to have methods that allow other objects to access your data. The resulting modularity enhances maintainability and readability.
- Classes provide an easy way to define properties for groups of similar objects, which can save a lot of work.

• Subclassing, inheritance, and overriding capabilities encourage flexible reuse of existing code and allow multiple versions of the same library to coexist. This reuse allows much faster code development, which means that you can actually get the program done on schedule.

Thus, using object techniques, your application gets developed more quickly, has fewer bugs, and is more maintainable.

▶  ## Summary

In this chapter, we have focused on concepts and learning processes. We have learned some of the basic terms and concepts involved in object programming, whether in MacApp or in some other object programming environment. We have also explored the obstacles to learning object programming and how to overcome some of them.

Chapter 4 moves one level deeper into the world of object programming by discussing design issues that you need to address throughout the process of creating object programs in MacApp.

# 4 ▶ Object-Oriented Design: Modeling the Real World

This chapter describes a number of strategies and tactics for designing an object-oriented program. These techniques are generally applicable to programming with any object language, whether it be Object Pascal, C++, or Smalltalk.

## ▶ Where to Begin?

Many programmers find it quite scary to design their first object program, feeling that they don't know where to start. Here are a few easy techniques to get you started.

### ▶ Nouns and Verbs

Try to describe the problem your program must solve in English sentences. Write down the description. Now, identify the nouns; these are a good starting point for class names you might need. Then find the verbs in your description; these are good candidates for the message names.

### ▶ Photography

Another common technique is to imagine photographing a scene that involves the task and then identifying the objects in the scene. Objects you can identify may give some hints about classes you need. Now imagine what these objects can do; these may be the message names.

For example, if you must write a program for managing stock trading on the stock market, you should imagine photographing the floor of the market in New York and photographing investors and stock brokers across the country. (The authors are not financial experts, so you should regard this particular exercise as purely theoretical — a fantasy.) You might see customers placing orders, stock brokers making records of the transaction, and stock options being bought and sold on the trading floor. If you want to model the effects of the economy on the process, then you have to imagine taking a picture of the whole country. You would now see the Federal Reserve bank, which sets interest rates, and the economy as whole with its inflation, unemployment, and other properties. Now use the noun and verb technique to identify classes, variables, and message names. For example, you might, as a first try, make a table such as Table 4-1.

**Table 4-1. Stock market objects**

| Class | Variables | Messages |
|---|---|---|
| Customer | name, date, cash, credit | Pay |
| Broker | name, firm | PlaceOrder, DeliverStock |
| Order | date, amount, value, type | |
| FedReserve | interestRate | GetRate, SetRate |
| Economy | inflationRate, GNP, etc. | |
| StockTrader | | Buy, Sell |
| StockShare | type, amount, owner | Transfer |
| StockOption | faceValue, date | Execute, Expire |

You should not expect to generate a great class design with an approach like this. Your initial goal is to get a design — any design — that you can begin to evaluate. You will then be able to modify and improve that first design using the principles we'll describe below. Most programmers find that their final design bears little resemblance to their initial one, but you have to start somewhere.

## ▶ Think in Terms of Small Methods

Your code will be easier to write and debug if you use many small methods rather than a few large ones. Make sure that your methods have only a single purpose. This approach offers two advantages. First, it is easier to write and debug small methods. Second, it is easier to reuse a class with single-purpose methods, because you can subclass and override any behavior that you want to change without affecting other behaviors you can use unchanged.

For example, consider writing a project management program that requires a graphics display of related tasks. To draw each task in a rectangle, you might define a class called **TTaskBox**, with a **DrawBox** method. You must ask yourself, should drawing the box be one operation, or two? Consider the boxes shown in Figure 4-1(a). If you draw both the rectangular border and the text label with your **DrawBox** method, it will not be difficult. The problem will arise later if you wish to make a subclass that can draw fancier boxes, such as the ones with drop-shadows, as shown in Figure 4-1(b). You must then override the **DrawBox** method, and replace it with a completely new version.

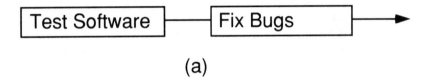

(a)

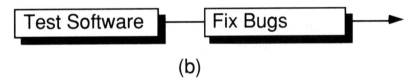

(b)

Figure 4-1. Task boxes in a project management program

As an alternative, consider the **DrawBox** method that follows:

```
void TTaskBox::DrawBox(Rect area, Char* label)
{
    DrawBorder(area);
    DrawLabel(area, label);
}
```

This design allows you to confine the border drawing to one small method and the label drawing to another. Each method is easier to write than if you did all the work in one large **DrawBox** method. Furthermore, you can subclass **TTaskBox**, and override the **DrawBorder** method without having to reproduce the code to draw the text label. Or, you might decide to draw the labels in color or a different location by overriding the **DrawLabel** method only.

**By the Way ▶** | To put the idea of small methods in perspective, one analysis of the Smalltalk-80 source code indicates that its four thousand methods in a typical system average only about seven lines of source code each. That is a remarkably small number, when most of us are probably used to thinking of our ordinary functions as being small even if they require twenty-five lines of code. Our experience is that the code we write when using MacApp has many methods that are less than five lines of code, and many that are only one line. Would you believe that a one-line method tends not to have bugs?

## ▶ Increasing Reusability

There are a number of standard approaches that are commonly used to modify and improve your design once you have started it using the above tactics. They include

- subclass existing classes
- look for common properties
- assemble new classes from existing ones

### ▶ Subclass Existing Classes

Figure 4-2(a) shows a new class that you might design to handle a palette of colors that the user controls with the mouse. It is a perfectly reasonable choice for a class definition, except that it requires you to write the whole collection of methods from scratch. An easier way to do the same thing in MacApp is shown in Figure 4-2(b).

Here the **TColorPalette** class is defined to be a subclass of an existing **TGridView** class that provides most of the necessary behavior. In this example, by reusing an existing class, you need to write only one method, not three methods as in the top example. A method saved is a method earned (or something like that).

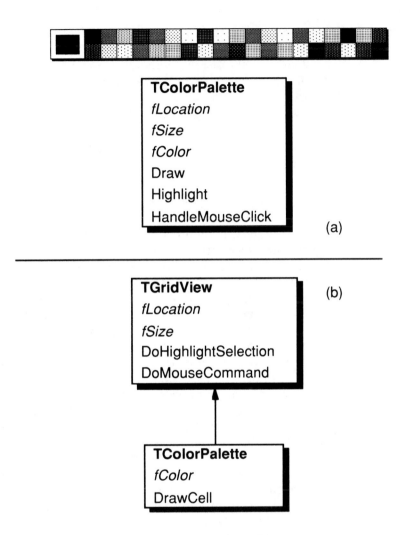

Figure 4-2.  Subclassing an existing class

How often can you use this technique? You will use this in every program to help support the user interface, because MacApp provides many user interface classes. When you are creating the behavior that is unique to your program, you may have a harder time finding an appropriate class to use as a starting point.

| By the Way ▶ | One problem with the technique we just described is that you have to know your class libraries well. Before you could think to subclass **TGridView**, you must know that it exists and know that it has properties that will help solve your problem. This knowledge takes time to learn, and it also requires good documentation of the class libraries. You should be familiar with the most important MacApp classes by the end of this book, but it may take a number of weeks of programming with MacApp to really feel at home with all of the possibilities. |
| --- | --- |

## ▶ Look for Common Properties

Figure 4-3(a) shows some classes that you might develop in an initial design for an object-oriented drawing or CAD program. These classes will work, but a second glance at them shows that there is too much redundancy. Each class has the same messages; an obvious rearrangement is to create a superclass that provides common behavior. This *abstract* superclass, **TShape**, will never be *instantiated*; that is, you will never make an instance of this class, but it provides a common starting point for more *concrete* subclasses. In Figure 4-3(b), you can see a three-level hierarchy that was developed using this technique. Looking for commonality, also known as *abstraction*, reduces the number of variables you have to manage and the number of methods you have to write. The resulting abstract classes are also more reusable in other programs.

In this case, by realizing that **TBox** and **TOval** classes can both use a common **Drag** method, we also provide an intermediate class, **TQuad**, to be the superclass of both **TBox** and **TOval**. Similarly, **TLineShape** can be defined to be the superclass of both **TPolygon** and **TLine**.

How much work can we estimate the technique has saved in this case? Our original design in Figure 4-3(a) showed 4 classes with 12 methods and 14 variables. The new design in Figure 4-3(b) does show 3 more classes for a total of 7 but the total number of real methods is reduced from 12 to 7, while the instance variables are reduced from 14 to 7. Statistics sometimes lie, but in this case they indicate that we have saved ourselves some work, since the real body of work in writing a program is in writing the methods. We see a 42 percent reduction in this case.

There are more benefits from this technique that are not immediately apparent. The abstract classes **TShape**, **TQuad**, and **TLineShape** are well suited for reuse as superclasses for other shapes that may be added later in the life of the program. Since they are general classes, they can be reused in many other situations. This would not be possible with more specific classes like **TBox** and **TOval**.

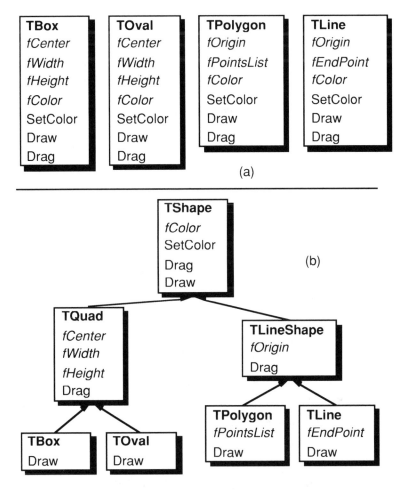

Figure 4-3.  Looking for commonality

## ▶ Assemble New Classes from Existing Ones

You will often find that you need objects that can share properties from more than one existing class of objects. As a whimsical example, consider the problem of designing a class to model the behavior of a seaplane. A seaplane has the properties of an airplane and also some of the properties of a boat. Is there a way that you could use existing plane and boat classes as a basis for solving your problem? As you might guess, there is more than one way to approach the problem. Figure 4-4 shows two solutions.

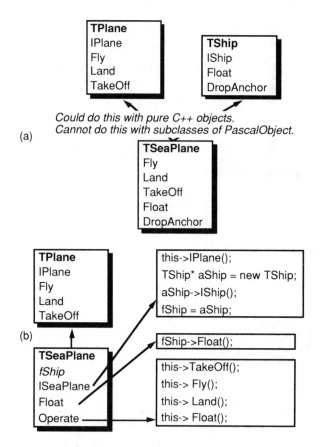

Figure 4-4. Composing a class from two other classes

Figure 4-4(a) illustrates a solution that can be used with some object-oriented languages — those that support a concept called *multiple inheritance*. Multiple inheritance allows you to design classes that inherit properties from more than one superclass, so a **TSeaPlane** class could be a subclass of **TPlane** and **TShip**. However, multiple inheritance has two drawbacks. First, supporting it complicates the design of a language. Second, using it when it is supported can turn a relatively simple inheritance tree into a very complex inheritance *lattice* that greatly complicates designing reusable classes.

Although MPW C++ supports multiple inheritance, MacApp's classes, since they are all written in Object Pascal, do not. Because most of the sample programs we will create in this book sub-class MacApp classes, we do not use multiple inheritance. If you build a MacApp application that includes any new classes of your own (i.e., those that do not sub-class an existing MacApp class), you may use multiple inheritance as described in Figure 4-4. We show a very simple example of using multiple inheritance in the Benchmark sample described in Chapter 6.

But we do have another way to solve the seaplane and similar problems. An example is the solution diagrammed in Figure 4-4(b).

| | |
|---|---|
| **By the Way ▶** | Many object programmers program happily for years without multiple inheritance; others feel that it is a necessity. It is supported in C++, many object-oriented extensions to LISP, and can be used in Smalltalk-80. Incidentally, one of the problems with multiple inheritance is that a subclass can have two superclasses, each of which has a variable or method with the same name. This conflict can lead to complicated rules to avoid conflicting properties. |

Notice in Figure 4-4(b) that you could design **TSeaPlane** to be a subclass of **TPlane** to get the desired ability to Fly, Land, and TakeOff. However, if you also want to be able to use the ability that **TShip** objects have to Float and DropAnchor, you can add this by adding a variable that references a **TShip** object. Consider the **ISeaPlane** initialization code shown in the figure.

| | |
|---|---|
| **By the Way ▶** | You may wonder if there is a good way to decide whether to create a new class by sub-classing or through referencing as shown in Figure 4-4(b). We have found that if you think in terms of the relationship between the new class you are creating and the class to which it is related, you can usually decide fairly easily. Use the *is-a* versus *has-a* test. If the new object *is-a* case of the class from which it is derived, then you should sub-class. If the new object *has-a* component that is an instance of the class from which it is derived, then you should use referencing. In our example, a seaplane *is a* plane but it *has a* ship (in the form of the two landing pontoons). So we sub-class the plane class and attach a reference to the ship class. |

To initialize the inherited **TPlane** behavior, you can call the **IPlane** initialization method first. Then you can create an instance of class **TShip**, and initialize that with the **IShip** method. The third step is to save a reference to that ship object in the *fShip* variable of your seaplane object.

Now consider operating the seaplane with the **Operate** method. To TakeOff, Fly, or Land, the seaplane need only call its own methods (inherited from its superclass, **TPlane**). To produce shiplike behavior, the **Float** and **DropAnchor** methods can be called through the auxiliary ship that was created in the **ISeaPlane** method. This produces the desired behavior, although a bit more indirectly than by using multiple inheritance.

## ▶ Moon Landing Simulator Example

The strategy of designing classes that contain references to other useful objects is used in many situations that would never call for multiple inheritance. You will see a concrete example of this as we design a very simple simulator for a moon landing mission.

Have you ever had the desire to write a flight simulator program? It seems to be a common fantasy for programmers, but we are usually deterred by the apparent complexity of the task and so we never create it. In the following pages we'll outline some possible designs for a very simple flight simulator in the hopes that you will try it and carry it further. One secret to success is to start modestly, so we will not try to design a full-color, three-dimensional, real-time simulator for an F16 or Lear jet. Instead, we'll start with the more modest problem sketched in Figure 4-5.

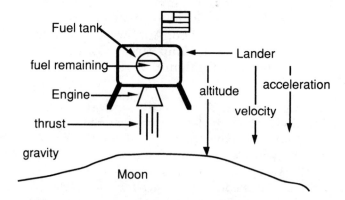

Figure 4-5. The moon lander problem

## ▶ Design Goal

Your assignment: Write a program that simulates an Apollo moon landing mission. The user of the program will have to land the vehicle within a specified elapsed time, using a given amount of fuel. The user must land at a low speed to avoid damage. To keep things simple, we'll constrain the problem to one dimension, altitude, and not let our lander move sideways. We'll also assume that the lander has only one engine and one fuel tank.

▶ Strategy

This type of simulation is best designed from the bottom up. Modeling the physical behavior of the lander should be completed before you worry about adding a user interface. You may have been encouraged to design other programs starting with the user interface, but that unnecessarily constrains your thinking in this type of problem. Think of a user interface as something optional that can plugged in between the user and the physical model. Many different models could be used, from a simple display of numbers to represent speed and altitude to a realistic, full-color display of the genuine Apollo instrument panel. In any case the underlying behavior of the lander will not change, so it is best to focus on that first.

In this exercise assume that you will get greedy — as soon as you get this simple simulation running successfully, you will want to add more features and complications. This parallels the real world: As soon as your program starts selling, the marketing department wants you to add six more features (and you only have a few days to do it). Once you accept the likelihood that you will have to add features in the future, you have a good incentive to design flexible classes that are easy to reuse and modify. Furthermore, as soon as you finish a project, you will probably be handed another problem to solve. You will find many long-term benefits from designing classes that might be reusable in other simulations in the future.

▶ First Try at a Moon Lander Design

Examine the diagram in Figure 4-5. The simplest design might have only one class, large and cumbersome like the one shown in the class diagram in Figure 4-6.

This class contains all the variables listed in the diagram in Figure 4-5 and contains reasonable message names for the desired types of behavior. Are we done? We could be, but this design has some basic flaws:

1. The class is too large and complex, which makes it harder to write the methods. As a general principle, smaller classes, ones with only a few methods, are generally easier to handle because they are less confusing.

2. The class is too specific. More abstract, general classes are easier to reuse in other situations.

3. The class is "hard-wired" to the original problem specification and will be difficult to modify if you wish to add features such as multiple engines and fuel tanks.

| MoonLanderSimulation |
|---|
| *elapsedTime* |
| *altitude* |
| *velocity* |
| *acceleration* |
| *mass* |
| *gravity* |
| *thrust* |
| *fuelRemaining* |
| StartMission |
| CalculateTime |
| CalculateThrust |
| CalculateAltitude |
| CalculateVelocity |
| FuelRemaining? |

Figure 4-6. A possible class design for the moon landing simulation

▶ Improving the Design

To improve the design, you might start by applying some of the principles we outlined earlier in the chapter. For instance, you can assemble new classes from existing ones (see Figure 4-4). The question of which pieces to use can often be answered by using the real world as a model for your design. Imagine that you were assembling an actual moon lander. You would probably not try to build the lander from a solid block of aluminum. You would buy an engine from one supplier and a fuel tank from another and then assemble the lander by bolting the pieces together. Our first design in Figure 4-6 is the equivalent of a lander made from a single block of aluminum.

The real world model suggests that we should have **Lander**, **Engine**, and **FuelTank** as classes. Is that obvious? Not at first, but another one of our strategies from earlier in the chapter can help you. Imagine a photograph of the situation. Now label the parts and then identify the nouns. We have effectively done this in Figure 4-5. The nouns describing concrete objects include Lander, Engine, FuelTank, and Moon. As a good guess, we can try these as class names. These ideas contribute to a better class design shown in Figure 4-7. (Note that the Mission object described in Figure 4-5 is not an object you could see if you photographed the lunar lander. This is characteristic of simulations, which must exist as part of a larger world. The **Mission** class is in essence the object that drives, or controls, the simulation. Simulations would virtually always include such an object even though it would not be explicitly present in a photograph of the process you are simulating.)

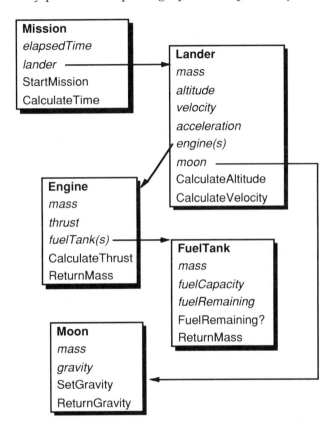

Figure 4-7. A better class design for the simulation

## ▶ An Even Better Design

Even a good design often offers opportunities for further improvement. Consider the design technique of looking for commonality illustrated in Figure 4-3. Can we find any common variables or methods among the classes shown in Figure 4-7? One obvious one is that many of the classes have the physical property of mass in common. We might add an abstract superclass called **Thing** to provide that property. We might also *factor* (that is, break into component parts) the **Mission** class by creating a separate, potentially reusable class called **Timer** to keep track of the elapsed time. These changes result in the design shown in Figure 4-8.

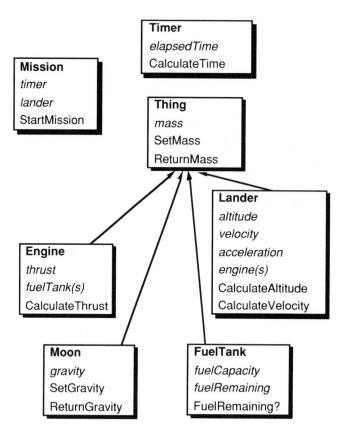

Figure 4-8. An even better class design

Do we now have the optimum design? Undoubtedly not, but it may be good enough so you can now start writing the methods and see how the design works in practice. Almost all object-oriented designs evolve as the code is written. This experimental approach is effective because object programming allows you to evolve a design without wasting much of your previous work.

Do not feel that your first design has to be perfect. The best approach is to relax and sketch a few designs using class diagrams. Then begin to write the methods, which will usually point the way toward a better design. In many cases, you will actually finish a first version of the program before worrying too much about writing reusable code. Then you can go back and redesign to produce more reusable classes and rewrite the code as necessary. In the long term, it is a good investment to do this.

## ▶ Summary

In this chapter, we have looked at one of the most important issues in object programming, namely how to design a program in an object-oriented way. We have seen that you can take one of two approaches: using a human-speech description of a problem and then classifying the object design in terms of nouns and verbs, or using a photographic model and identifying visible objects in the scene as objects in the program. We have looked at the iterative nature of design by examining a small example design for a lunar lander simulation.

Chapter 5 teaches you to set up your Macintosh system to make it possible and efficient to work with MacApp in C++ under the Macintosh Programmer's Workshop (MPW) . You can then use this system to develop code to test your design.

# ▶ Getting Started in MacApp

In Part Two, we will concentrate on the first stages of becoming acquainted with and beginning to use MacApp. This part consists of eight chapters.

▶ Chapter 5 describes one major programming environment in which MacApp can be used: Apple's Macintosh Programmer's Workshop (MPW) C++. It explains how to set up your MPW environment and how to build MacApp programs.

▶ Chapter 6 is an introduction to the C++ programming language. It assumes you know at least a little about C itself and focuses on the extensions to that language that make C++ suited to object programming and MacApp development. It also introduces basic ideas in Object Pascal, which you need to understand because all of MacApp's source code is written in Object Pascal.

▶ Chapter 7 describes the main classes in the MacApp class library. It points out why mastering the contents of this library is the most important aspect of learning MacApp and briefly describes the most important classes in the class library, helping you to focus your learning on those libraries where most of the work is done.

▶ Chapter 8 continues the discussion of Chapter 7 by describing the default behavior of the main MacApp classes. It specifies the common routines that you must write to support typical behavior in your program.

▶ Chapter 9 presents the simplest MacApp program you can create. It describes the basic techniques involved in creating, saving, editing, compiling, linking, and running a MacApp program.

▶ Chapter 10 outlines the classes and methods you will need to use when you are ready to enhance a simple program by adding a Macintosh user interface. It helps you to focus on design trade-offs and implementation decisions as well as on user interface design rules.

▶ Chapter 11 describes a number of tools you will find useful as you begin your work as a MacApp programmer. It talks about how to use these tools to create and manage resources as well as to debug your code.

▶ Chapter 12 ends Part 2 by providing a potpourri of object and MacApp programming tips and hints that will make your code easier to write, use, and maintain, as well as run more efficiently.

# 5 ▶ Setting Up MacApp with the Macintosh Programmer's Workshop

In this chapter you will learn how to use the Macintosh Programmer's Workshop (MPW) to compile MacApp programs, and you will learn about some of the tools and capabilities provided by the very powerful and complete MPW system.

## ▶ The MPW Philosophy

MPW is a unique development system developed by Apple that has its feet firmly planted in two worlds. Part of its character is rooted in the UNIX philosophy. MPW contains a command language that allows you to type text commands into a window and execute them. These commands allow you to

- perform sophisticated text editing
- perform Finder functions like duplicating and deleting files
- write scripts (also known as batch files or command files) to automate complex operations
- run a make file to compile and build your application automatically

On the other hand, it supports windows, menus, dialogs, and the other user-friendly features that made the Macintosh famous. In fact, you can combine the dual personality of MPW by creating custom menu items that can cause complex scripts to execute.

The MPW development system is complex by necessity. It lets you write code using Assembler, Pascal, C, C++, and other languages and then mix object code from all these into a single application. The MPW compilers can handle the large MacApp libraries and produces excellent code. The price you must pay to use MPW includes learning to use the command structure and tools and investing in the required hardware. The benefit is that you can use MacApp and Object Pascal or C++ to greatly enhance your software development productivity.

## ▶ What You Need to Get Started

### ▶ Software

Before you can use MacApp with MPW, you need to have the following:

- the MPW Shell and associated tools, version 3.1 or later
- the MPW Object Pascal compiler (unless you buy MacApp on CD, in which case it has been pre-compiled to satisfy most configuration needs)
- the MPW C compiler, version 3.1 or later
- MPW C++, version 3.1B1 or later
- MacApp itself, version 2.0 or later

All of these are available from APDA, the Apple Programmer's and Developer's Association.

### ▶ Recommended Hardware

MPW can be used with great difficulty on a small Macintosh, but the practical minimum requires at least the following:

- 4 MB of RAM, with 5-8 MB preferred to use MultiFinder
- a fast hard disk with at least 20 MB of free space
- a fast processor to reduce compile times

What do we mean by a fast processor? To let you judge, a very small MacApp program will need at least eight minutes to compile on a 68000-based Macintosh Plus or SE, but this is reduced to about two minutes on a 68020-based Macintosh II and under a minute on the newer 68030-based systems.

# ▶ Preparing the Hard Disk

Figure 5-1 shows a reasonable way to organize your hard disk to use MPW and MacApp. The folder containing MPW and its associated files is usually at the root level. The MacApp folder is also at the root level. Do the folder names matter? The ones inside the MPW and MacApp folders do because they are used as part of various path names by the compiler, linker, and other tools that are used to build your application. You can only change some of these folder names if you change appropriate path names in the startup files we will discuss shortly.

## ▶ The MPW Folder

The MPW folder contains a number of files and folders; the most important ones are shown in Figure 5-1. These include the following:

### MPW Shell

This is the main application, consisting of a multiple-window text editor and a command interpreter.

### Startup

This file contains MPW commands that execute as soon as the MPW Shell is launched. This file's main job is to define a number of shell variables to represent path names to many of the folders used in building your application. There are a number of other startup files executed after Startup, including UserStartup and UserStartup•MacApp. Since these files are dependent on the details of your version of MPW and the details have been changing every few months, you should read the documentation for further information about which files you will need.

### Interfaces

This folder contains other folders which contain interface library files for the Pascal compiler, C compiler, Assembler, and Rez resource compiler. You will generally have no reason to modify any of the files in this folder. You will, however, often have to reference various files in the #include statements in your C++ source code.

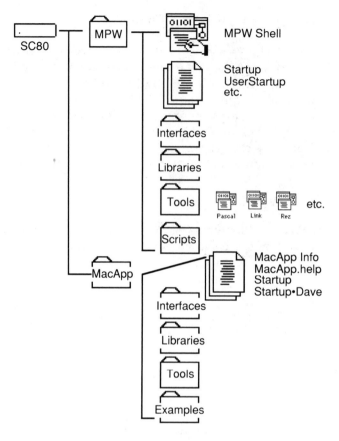

Figure 5-1. The MPW and MacApp folders

### Libraries

This folder contains object files needed by the Linker. These files will have the .o suffix to indicate that they are output files from the Assembler or one of the compilers.

### Tools

This folder contains miniprograms that can be executed only from the MPW shell. These items are called MPW tools and include the Assembler, Pascal, and C compilers; Linker; Rez resource compiler; and many more. You can write your own tools in any MPW language; in fact, we will write a simple one using C++ in the next chapter.

## Scripts

This folder contains a wide variety of useful command files. These are files written in the MPW command language to automate tasks that must be done fairly often. They are the equivalent of MS-DOS batch files, UNIX shell scripts, or various job control languages. MPW includes a complete command language that uses shell variables, if tests, do loops, pipes, filters, and so forth. Since you do not have to use these to use MacApp, we will not describe their language in this book. We do strongly recommend Joel West's book on using MPW, listed in the bibliography. There are other files and folders in the MPW folder with which you will gradually become familiar as you use this rich development system, but you will not have to know about them to get started.

## ▶ The MacApp Folder

The MacApp folder contains a similar set of files and folders; the most important ones are shown in Figure 5-1. These include the following:

## Startup

This file is executed by a command in the UserStartup•MacApp file, which you should be sure to place in the MPW folder. This startup file sets a number of additional path names used in building programs with MacApp.

## Startup•yourName

This file is executed from a command in Startup and is intended to allow you to customize the MPW environment. You will use this file to rename MPW commands, to define custom menus, to define new shell variables, and so forth.

An example is shown in Listing 5-1, which results in the Directory, Build, and Special menus shown in Figure 5-2.

Listing 5-1. The Startup•Dave file

```
1: # Create the Directory menu
2: DirectoryMenu `(Files -d -i ∂
3:         "{MPW}"  ∂
4:         "{CIncludes}"  ∂
5:         "{MacApp}" ∂
6:         "{MACIncludes}"  ∂
```

```
7:          "{MacApp}CPlusExamples:"≈ ∂
8:          || Set Status 0) ≥ Dev:Null` ∂
9:          `Directory`
10:
11: # Create the Build Menu
12: BuildMenu
13: AddMenu Build '(-' ''
14: AddMenu Build 'Build debug…/=' ∂
15:     'Begin; ∂
16:     Set NewProgram "`Request "Program Name? ∂
17:         (debug)" -d "{Program}" || Echo '""'`"; ∂
18:     Exit If "{NewProgram}" == ""; ∂
19:     Set Program "{NewProgram}"; ∂
20:     Open "{Worksheet}"; ∂
21:     Echo; Echo; ∂
22:     MABuild "{Program}" -Debug; ∂
23:     End >> "{Worksheet}" ≥≥ Dev:StdOut'
24:
25: # Create the Special menu
26: AddMenu  Special 'Recipes/1'      'Open "{MPW}Recipes"'
27: AddMenu  Special 'REZipes/2'      'Open "{MPW}REZipes"'
28: AddMenu  Special 'Make Recipes/3' 'Open "{MPW}Recipes.MAMake"'
29: AddMenu  Special 'ViewEdit/4'     '"{boot}ViewEdit"'
30: AddMenu  Special 'ResEdit/5'      '"{boot}ResEdit"'
31: AddMenu  Special 'Switch/\'       'Open "{target}"'
```

---

**By the Way** ▶ | Throughout this book, you will notice that program listings like the one shown in Listing 5-1 are numbered at the left margin. These numbers will not appear on the screen of your development system and are not a part of the programs. They are simply added here as a convenience so that we can provide you with more understandable explanations of what is going on in the programs.

---

Lines 2-10 of the listing show how to create a Directory menu that can access many of the folders in which you often will want to look for header files, sample code, etc. Notice that the Directory menu shown in Figure 5-2 always begins with the "Show Directory" and "Set Directory…" items. These can be used instead of typing the MPW Directory command to show or change the default folder.

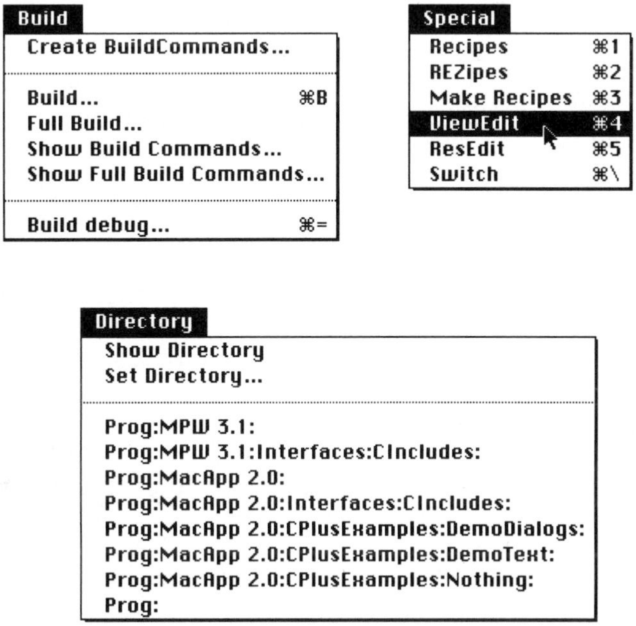

```
┌─────────────────────────────────┐      ┌───────────────────────────┐
│ Build                           │      │ Special                  │
├─────────────────────────────────┤      ├───────────────────────────┤
│ Create BuildCommands...         │      │ Recipes          ⌘1      │
│                                 │      │ REZipes          ⌘2      │
│ Build...                    ⌘B  │      │ Make Recipes     ⌘3      │
│ Full Build...                   │      │ ViewEdit         ⌘4      │
│ Show Build Commands...          │      │ ResEdit          ⌘5      │
│ Show Full Build Commands...     │      │ Switch           ⌘\      │
│                                 │      └───────────────────────────┘
│ Build debug...              ⌘=  │
└─────────────────────────────────┘
```

```
┌────────────────────────────────────────────┐
│ Directory                                  │
├────────────────────────────────────────────┤
│ Show Directory                             │
│ Set Directory...                           │
│                                            │
│ Prog:MPW 3.1:                              │
│ Prog:MPW 3.1:Interfaces:CIncludes:         │
│ Prog:MacApp 2.0:                           │
│ Prog:MacApp 2.0:Interfaces:CIncludes:      │
│ Prog:MacApp 2.0:CPlusExamples:DemoDialogs: │
│ Prog:MacApp 2.0:CPlusExamples:DemoText:    │
│ Prog:MacApp 2.0:CPlusExamples:Nothing:     │
│ Prog:                                      │
└────────────────────────────────────────────┘
```

Figure 5-2. Custom MPW menus created by the Startup•Dave file

**By the Way ▶**

If you have UNIX experience, you will find MPW similar to UNIX, but the syntax is different. The commands for changing the directory can be compared with the table below:

| Operation | MPW | UNIX |
|---|---|---|
| Show current directory | Directory | pwd |
| Change directory | Directory **path** | cd **path** |
| Path name separator | : | / |

Lines 12-23 of Listing 5-1 create the Build menu, which we will discuss later in the chapter. Lines 26-31 create the Special menu, which allows us to easily access our custom Recipes files, and utility applications such as ViewEdit and ResEdit. Recipes files are simply MPW text files that you can create to keep commonly used code fragments, such as typical versions of common MacApp methods. You should create your own Recipes files as necessary, so that you do not have to keep looking in other programs to see how to do certain jobs. These are discussed in more detail in Chapter 11.

Notice in all these uses of AddMenu that you first give the menu name, then the item name (in single quotes with / denoting a command key equivalent), followed by the MPW command to be executed when the menu item is selected (again in single quotes). We have included a typical Startup file on the samples disk.

### Interfaces

This folder contains other folders. Two particularly important ones are: the PInterfaces folder, which contains MacApp's Pascal interface files and the CIncludes folder, which holds the C++ header file for MacApp.

Before you can use any class defined in Object Pascal from C++, you must first translate the interface file into a C++ header file. Apple has done this for MacApp, but you may have to do it for other Object Pascal libraries. We provide MPW scripts to automate this process on the disk that accompanies this book.

### Libraries

This folder contains many other files and folders, including the compiled object files for MacApp.

### Tools

This contains the MABuild tool that you will use to build a program with MacApp. The Object Pascal source code for MABuild is included, so you can see how it works and modify it if necessary.

### Examples

This folder contains other folders, which hold the sample programs included with MacApp. These samples illustrate how to write a wide variety of programs using MacApp and represent a significant part of the MacApp documentation. These samples include:

- Calc — a rather complex sample spreadsheet program. It includes an example of how to use a splash screen as an opening dialog box.
- Cards — a program that keeps part of each document's data in RAM, while caching other parts to disk.

- DemoDialogs — a program with many different types of modal and modeless dialogs.

- DemoText — a text-editing example that creates documents with mixed fonts, sizes, styles, and colors. This program uses hierarchical menus on machines that support that feature.

- DrawShapes — a fairly complex drawing sample similar to Mac-Draw. This program uses Color QuickDraw on machines with the correct ROM.

- Nothing — a very simple example that does very little, merely providing a skeletal template for a MacApp program.

## ▶ Using MPW

As we said, the MPW shell is both a text editor and a command interpreter. To write your source code, you treat it as a normal programmer's text editor, pressing the Return key whenever you want to type on the next line. On the other hand, you can also use any window — including your C++ source files — as a place to type and execute MPW commands. In this case, you must use a special keystroke to tell MPW that you want to execute a command. This is done by pressing the Enter key rather than the Return key. You must indicate the command to be executed by clicking the cursor anywhere on the line containing the command, provided the command is the only text on that line. If the command is embedded in other text, then you should select the command with the mouse before pressing Enter.

For example, typing the word "files" on a separate line and then pressing Enter will cause MPW to display a list of all the files and folders in the current directory (or folder). Executing the "directory" command will display the path name of the current directory.

By the way, you can execute MPW commands with the mouse by clicking in the top-left area of the front window, in what is known as the Status Panel. This is equivalent to pressing the Enter key, in that the currently selected line of text will be executed as an MPW command. You can see an example of the status panel at the bottom of the upper-left window in Figure 6-1 in the next chapter. The panel displays the currently executing command or in this case the phrase "MPW Shell" since no command is being executed.

▶ Getting Help

Help

MPW has two different help systems, one with a UNIX flavor and one that is more like Macintosh. For a simple reminder of the options that can be used with an MPW command, all you need to do is type the word help, followed by the name of the command. For example, to see the options for the files command, type "help files" and press Enter. The result is shown in Listing 5-2.

Listing 5-2. Using the MPW Help command

```
 1: Files          # list files and directories
 2: Files [option...] [name...]  > fileList
 3:   -c creator # list only files with this creator
 4:   -d         # list only directories
 5:   -f         # list full pathnames
 6:   -i         # treat all arguments as files
 7:   -l         # long format (type, creator, size, dates, etc.)
 8:   -m columns # n column format, where n = columns
 9:   -n         # don't print header in long or extended format
10:   -o         # omit directory headers
11:   -q         # don't quote filenames with special characters
12:   -r         # recursively list subdirectories
13:   -s         # suppress the listing of directories
14:   -t type    # list only files of this type
15:   -x format  # extended format with format specifying fields
16:
17:   Note: The following characters can specify the format
18:      a Flag attributes
19:      b Logical size, in bytes, of the data fork
20:      r Logical size, in bytes, of the resource fork
21:      c Creator of File ("Fldr" for folders)
22:      d Creation date
23:      k Physical size in kilobytes of both forks
24:      m Modification date
25:      t Type
26:      o Owner (only for folders on a file server)
27:      g Group (only for folders on a file server)
28:      p Privileges (only for folders on a file server)
```

You can execute the help command alone to get a list of help categories, which yields the display shown in Listing 5-3.

Listing 5-3.  MPW Help summary

```
 1: MPW 3.0 Help Summaries
 2:
 3:    Help summaries are available for each of the MPW commands.
 4:    To see the list of commands enter "Help Commands". In
 5:    addition, brief descriptions of Expressions, Patterns,
 6:    Selections, Characters, Shortcuts, Variables, and Projector
 7:    are also included.
 8:    To see Help summaries, Enter a command such as
 9:
10:    Help commandName # information about commandName
11:    Help Commands    # a list of commands
12:    Help Expressions # summary of expressions
13:    Help Patterns    # summary of patterns (reg. expressions)
14:    Help Selections  # summary of selections
15:    Help Characters  # summary of MPW Shell special characters
16:    Help Shortcuts   # summary of MPW Shell shortcuts
17:    Help Variables   # summary of standard MPW shell variables
18:    Help Projector # summary of Projector, a project/source
            control system
```

In addition to the general MPW help files, there are two special help file provided for MacApp and C++. You can access these as shown in Listing 5-4. To get MacApp help, type "Help MacApp" and press Enter, as shown on line 1. You should place the insertion point on the command shown on line 4, and press Enter again to get MacApp help. You can use lines 6 and 10 in a similar way to get C++ help. By the way, MPW defaults to not being case-sensitive, so you do not need to capitalize these commands.

Listing 5-4. Getting help for MacApp and C++

```
 1: Help MacApp
 2: MacApp          # The application framework
 3: # Execute following command to get Help information for MacApp®
 4:                             Help -f "{MacApp}"MacApp.Help
 5:
 6: Help CPlus
 7: CPlus           # script to compile C++ source
 8: CPlus    # script to compile C++ source
 9: # Execute following command to get Help Information for CPlus
10:                             Help -f "{MPW}"CPlus.Help CPlus
```

Commando

If this help is not enough, you can use an elaborate set of on-line help dialogs known collectively as Commando. Commando dialogs allow you to execute a command by filling in the blanks for each of the command's options. You may prefer it for commands with many complex options. You can access a general Commando dialog by adding the ellipsis character (...), which is generated by typing Option-semicolon at the end of the command you wish to execute.

An example of Commando used with the files command is shown in Figure 5-3. You generate the dialog by typing "files", then the Option-semicolon key combination, and then the Enter key. Clicking the mouse on the (default) Files button will execute the command line displayed in the Commando window.

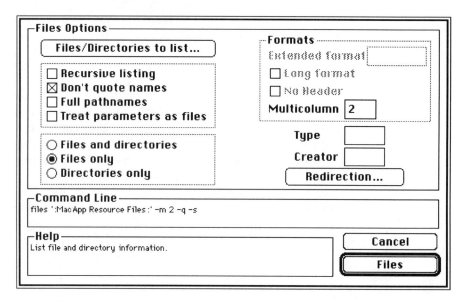

Figure 5-3. Using Commando for help in using the files command

## ▶ The Mark Menu

If you intend to write even a moderate-sized program, you may have to write at least thirty methods. In a larger program, you may easily write hundreds of methods. In any case, your source code files will become large and you will want help in navigating through them. MPW provides a way to mark various locations in the file and then to jump to those markers by making a menu selection. You can mark any text selection with the Mark... option from MPW's Mark menu shown in Figure 5-4.

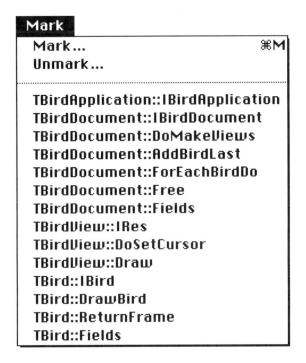

**Mark**

| Mark... | ⌘M |
| Unmark... | |

TBirdApplication::IBirdApplication
TBirdDocument::IBirdDocument
TBirdDocument::DoMakeViews
TBirdDocument::AddBirdLast
TBirdDocument::ForEachBirdDo
TBirdDocument::Free
TBirdDocument::Fields
TBirdView::IRes
TBirdView::DoSetCursor
TBirdView::Draw
TBird::IBird
TBird::DrawBird
TBird::ReturnFrame
TBird::Fields

Figure 5-4. The MPW Mark menu

### ▶ Pascal's Separately Compiled Units

MacApp is written using a number of separately compiled modules called Units. For this reason, we'll explain Units even though you will not create them in C++. The Unit structure was first defined by the UCSD Pascal P-System developed in the late 1970s and was adopted by Apple for the Apple II. It has been carried forward to both the Lisa and the Macintosh and is now a standard feature of all Pascal compilers for the Macintosh. The structure of a Unit is shown in Figure 5-5. A program written without Units is shown on the left; the same program rewritten with Units is on the right.

A Unit has these components:

• UNIT — The file begins with the Pascal keyword UNIT, instead of the keyword PROGRAM. This tells the compiler that this is only part of a program, rather than a complete one.

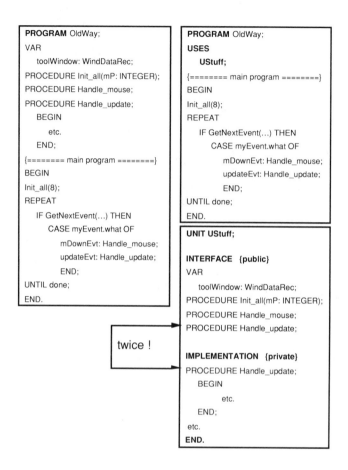

Figure 5-5. A program written without, and then with, separately compiled Units

- INTERFACE — You will define the name and parameter list for each message following this keyword, but you will not actually write the methods. The Interface represents the public description of your Unit. By public, we mean that the routines (and constants, variables, types, and so forth) defined in the Interface can be used by any other part of your program or any other program that uses this Unit. The C++ analogue to an interface file is the ".h" header file, which you will see used extensively starting in Chapter 6.

- USES — This is followed by a list of other Units that contain definitions needed by this program or Unit. The USES keyword therefore appears in the main program file, shown in the example in Figure 5-5.

• IMPLEMENTATION — This represents the private part of your code; the details are hidden from other parts of your program. You will write the actual code for your methods in the implementation section. Notice the duplication: The procedure name is defined in both the interface and the implementation. Pascal requires the parameter list only in the interface, but you should also show it in the implementation, since it makes it easier to understand. The C++ analogue to an implementation file is the ".cp" file which contains the implementation of the functions. You will see how to use these in the next chapter.

| By the Way ▶ | You may have noticed that Pascal keywords are shown in uppercase. That is only for readability; Pascal is not case-sensitive. There are certain four-letter codes that are case sensitive in Macintosh programming, such as resource types and file types. We will identify those as they appear. For the most part, both MPW and Pascal will accept a correctly spelled word whether you type it uppercase or lowercase. C++, like C, is case-sensitive, so type your code very carefully. |

## ▶ Creating Resources

Macintosh applications are primarily a collection of individual resources, each identified by a case-sensitive four-letter code and an integer which together are called the resource ID. Typical resources include:

• CODE — created from your source code by the compiler and linker
• CURS — custom cursors
• STR# — a list of strings
• WIND — a template for creating windows
• PICT — QuickDraw pictures
• view — a MacApp-specific resource that describes a window and its contents
• cmnu — a MacApp-specific resource that describes a menu title and its items

As you can see in Figure 5-6, there are a number of tools used to create these resources. A description of the tools follows.

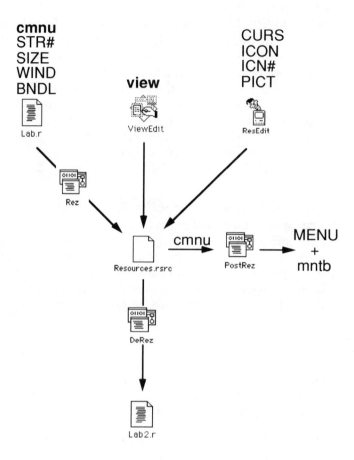

Figure 5-6. Creating resources with ViewEdit, ResEdit, Rez, DeRez, and PostRez

Rez

Rez is MPW's resource compiler that converts a text description of a resource into its compiled, binary format. You will see the Rez format for 'WIND', 'view', 'cmnu', and other resource types in later chapters. You will generally use Rez for text-oriented resources such as strings and menus. Standard file naming conventions for resource files append the .r suffix to text files used as inputs to Rez and the .rsrc suffix to files containing compiled resources.

### ViewEdit

ViewEdit is a MacApp tool for visual layout of your window contents. This allows the creation of very complex windows and dialogs. These windows can include buttons, check boxes, text, scroll bars, and other user interface components. We will describe the use of this tool in Chapter 14, "View Resources."

### ResEdit

ResEdit is Apple's tool for creating and editing all resources (except 'cmnu' and 'view' types). You will generally use ResEdit to create graphic resources such cursors, icons, and simple alerts. You can also use this powerful, flexible tool for copying and pasting resources between applications, as you often may do with PICT resources.

**By the Way ▶** Because ResEdit can modify applications, you can do great damage if you are not careful with it. This does not mean that you should not use it, but make sure you understand what you are doing. ResEdit's documentation is included as part of MPW. We will not use it in this book, so we will not describe its use further.

### DeRez

This resource decompiler does the opposite job from that done by Rez. It can process any file containing resources, including a finished application, and produce a text file description of those resources. You will occasionally need this tool to solve special problems or to document resources, but it will not be a part of the normal development process.

### PostRez

This resource processor is used only for MacApp programming. It is executed automatically by the MABuild tool that builds MacApp programs. Its main function is to convert MacApp's special 'cmnu' resources into normal 'MENU' resources (used by the Toolbox routines) plus a 'mntb' resource that contains the menu command numbers for each menu item. This menu table resource is used by MacApp methods that handle menu selection. You probably won't ever have to use these tables directly or even be concerned with them.

## ▶ Installing MacApp

Follow these steps to install MacApp on your hard disk.

1. Install the MacApp files. Currently you must do this manually, but we expect that installation scripts will automate this process in the future.

2. Choose a program to be built. A good test case would be the Nothing sample provided with MacApp. You must set MPW's default directory to the directory containing the source files before you can build the application. To do this for the Nothing sample, use the MPW Directory menu to select the directory containing the C++ version of the Nothing sample. Or you could type the following command in the Worksheet window:

```
Directory "{MacApp}"CPlusExamples:Nothing
```

3. Execute "MABuild Nothing" or use the Build menu shown in Figure 5-7. Figure 5-7 shows the Build menu item and resulting dialog box that you typically will use to compile any application. After you enter your application's name and click OK (or press Return or Enter), the MABuild tool will execute to build your program. The MABuild tool then displays the progress information in the Worksheet window, as shown in Listing 5-5.

4. Place the cursor on line thirteen of the progress information display and press Enter to launch the application. Note that the compiled application is stored in the ".Non-Debug Files" folder inside the source code folder.

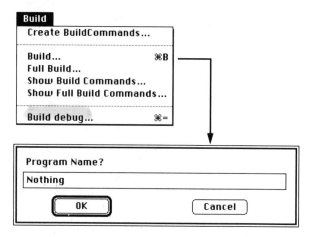

Figure 5-7. Building the Nothing sample program using the Build menu

Listing 5-5. Output of the MA Build process

```
 1:   MABuildTool - v. 2.0 Release 3/22/90
           Start: 11:47:11 PM 4/21/90
 2:
 3:   Copyright Apple Computer, Inc. 1986-1990
 4:   All Rights Reserved.
 5:
 6:   Target Folder: "Prog:MacApp 2.0:CPlusExamples:Nothing:.Non-
           Debug Files:"
 7:   AutoMaking:    Nothing
 8:   Compiling:     Nothing.cp
 9:   Linking:       Nothing
10:   AutoRezzing:   Default.r
11:   PostRezzing:   Nothing
12:   "Prog:MacApp 2.0:CPlusExamples:Nothing:.Non-Debug Files:
           Nothing"  # <- Execute to run your application
13:   Completion time for MABuild is Saturday, April 21, 1990 11:49
           :40 PM
```

## ▶ Debug and Non-debug Versions of MacApp

You normally build a MacApp program one of two ways: with debugging code or without. The MacApp debugging code actually represents a major portion of MacApp and is an important reason to use MacApp, since it makes finding bugs relatively easy. Therefore, you will generally write your program and test it with the debugging code included.

The Build menu shown in Figure 5-7 has two items that you can use to build your application. The standard item is "Build...", which builds a non-debug version of the program. The last item, "Build debug...", is used to build a version with the debugging code included. This last item is not found in the standard Build menu, but was added by lines 14-23 of Listing 5-1. Remember to add these lines to your Startup• file if you want this menu item.

If you prefer to create your program using text commands, you can use one of the following commands to create non-debug or debug versions:

```
MABuild Nothing
MABuild Nothing -debug
```

Either way, the assumption is that you are creating an application named Nothing, with a source file named Nothing.cp. The next section explores the file naming convention further.

There are two drawbacks associated with MacApp's debugging code. One is that your application becomes 150 to 200 KB larger, so a 100 KB program may grow to 270 KB. The other problem is that the debugging code is called frequently during program execution, slowing the program down quite a bit. For example, the debugging routines execute at the beginning and end of every method, which in some cases can make your program run ten times more slowly.

You will generally build your program with debugging code included during the development process, as you add features and remove bugs. You would build a non-debug version whenever you need to test size and performance, or need to demonstrate the program to your boss or a customer.

| By the Way ▶ | If you would prefer to have MABuild default to build debugging versions of your program, add the line |
| --- | --- |

```
-debug ∂
```

to the MABuildDefaults variable in the Startup file (in the MacApp folder). The "∂" character is produced by typing "option d", which must be followed by a carriage return as the next character.

## ▶ Five Magic Files

The MABuild tool is a fairly complicated program that takes the name of the application to be built as a parameter. It then looks for certain files that are named after the application. For example, if you wanted to make an application called Lab, MABuild would look for the following file names to use in the build process.

### MLab.cp

MLab.cp contains the main() function. You can write your whole program in this one file, as you will see with the simple example described in Chapter 9. However, it is usually not practical to place a large program in one file, so this file normally contains just enough code to get the program started. The real work is then done in the separate files ULab.h and ULab.cp.

### ULab.h

This separate file is not required, but it is almost always used. It contains the class definitions and function prototypes.

### ULab.cp

This file contains the actual code for the methods described in ULab.h — your real programming takes place here. This is the implementation section.

### Lab.r

This file contains the text description of your resources and is processed by the Rez resource compiler to produce the resources that support the user interface. If you do not provide this file, MABuild will use a file named Default.r. This default file contains definitions for normal Apple, File, and Edit menus, and for other resources that can be used to build very simple programs. You will generally need to create your own .r file for nontrivial applications.

### Lab.MAmake

This file is used by MPW's Make tool to help determine which files will be used in the build process. MABuild actually uses a number of make files supplied by Apple to manage most of the process, and they suffice in many cases. However, any time you create more files than these five, you must write this additional make file to tell MABuild how to handle these extra files. Examples of extra files are:

- files containing special resources created by ResEdit or ViewEdit
- extra C++ files containing special class libraries
- special library files for rarely used Toolbox routines

You will see that about half of the samples used in this book do not use this extra make file. The other samples contain small make files that will be described when they occur.

**By the Way** ▶ If you have used MPW without using MacApp, you are familiar with make files that have the .make extension. It is important that you use the .MAmake extension for your MacApp programs. If you do not use this extension, the wrong build scripts will be executed.

## ▶ Summary

In this chapter, you have learned all the steps involved in setting up your Macintosh system with MPW to use MacApp. You have also learned some of the basic steps involved in the use of MacApp, including how to get help in the environment.

Chapter 6 will look at MPW C++ and at the Object Pascal language in which MacApp is written.

# 6 ▶ The Languages: Object Pascal and C++

As we have said in previous chapters, a good object-oriented development system requires three components:

- an object-oriented language
- a rich set of tools to write, manage, and debug your code
- an extensive library of classes that are already written, tested, and documented.

MacApp is, of course, the large class library. The tools typically consist of such things as MPW with its editor and other elements, Mouser the Browser, ViewEdit, and other components that we will discuss in later chapters, particularly Chapter 11.

In this chapter, we will focus on the two major languages that you can use to write your MacApp program: Object Pascal and C++.

---

**By the Way ▶**

We make the assumption in this chapter that you already know the basics of programming in C. If you do not, you might want to read one of the many books on the C programming language for background information. If you do not have a good background in C, but would like to dive in anyway, please do. We have tried to avoid writing complex code or using obscure language features; as always, code clarity and maintainability are a major goal.

## ▶ A Bit of History

Apple realized in the early 1980s that developing software for window-based graphical user interfaces was highly complex. Since many of the Apple programmers had had experience using object-oriented systems such as Smalltalk, they understood the advantages of providing developers with a library of reusable classes that could easily support a complex user interface. However, before a library such as MacApp could be written, Apple needed an object-oriented language that supported classes, messages, and overriding. Since Pascal is a popular and well-known language, they decided to extend the Pascal language to support the features needed in MacApp. That initial effort resulted in what is called Object Pascal, and all the versions of the MacApp class library have been written in that language.

In 1989, Apple took pity on the C programmers of the world and released an implementation of C++ that could also use the MacApp classes. You can therefore write your application entirely in C++, using and subclassing classes defined in Object Pascal. Although all the MacApp samples described in this book are written in C++, we will start by first describing Object Pascal. "But wait," you may cry, "I don't like Pascal. Why should I care about it?" The main reason to become familiar with Object Pascal is that you often will want to examine the MacApp source code provided by Apple, and those sources will only make sense if you develop at least a reading familiarity with the language in which they are written.

We will therefore start with a brief look at Object Pascal, and then examine C++ in some detail. Why start with Pascal? Because it is much simpler than C++, and we want this introduction to be as gentle as possible. The majority of this chapter will be about C++, so bear with us for what may start out looking like a side trip. It will be brief.

## ▶ Object Pascal

In 1983, an Apple Computer team led by Larry Tesler developed Clascal, the first object-oriented Pascal. This was used to develop software for the Lisa computer. In 1984, Tesler collaborated with Niklaus Wirth to develop the next generation, called Object Pascal. There are now three compilers that support Object Pascal. Apple's implementation is part of the Macintosh Programmer's Workshop (MPW), while other versions are available from TML Systems and Symantec. Both MPW and Symantec's THINK Pascal 3.0 fully support MacApp 2.0.

One of Apple's Object Pascal design goals was simplicity, so relatively few things were added to the language. Pascal programmers have generally found it easy to learn the new syntax and keywords, even though the language allows you to do real object-oriented programming. In the next section you will see how a tiny Object Pascal program is written.

## ▶ The "Money" Accounting Program

Most of the world's computing involves data processing, which usually means one form or another of accounting. So we'll start off with an accounting example. (Most programmers who do not have to write accounting software find it dreadfully dull. Frankly, we agree, but we hope you'll find the object programming approach makes even accounting fun.)

Imagine that you must write a very simple program to keep track of a number of customers. For each customer your program must store two pieces of data: the customer's name (in an *fName* variable) and the customer's city (in an *fCity* variable). You will also need a **PrintAddress** method for printing invoices for each customer. As business improves, you must also support a category of foreign customers for which you also have to store the customer's country in an *fCountry* variable. The structure for such a program, which we will call the "Money" sample is shown in the class diagram in Figure 6-1.

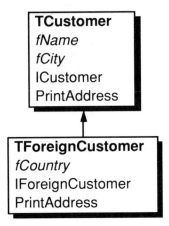

Figure 6-1. The class diagram for the Money sample

In the class diagram, you see two classes defined, with the class names shown in bold. The instance variables for the **TCustomer** class are shown in italics as *fName* and *fCity*, while the messages that can be sent are shown in normal type as ICustomer and PrintAddress. The subclass **TForeignCustomer** inherits the two instance variables and adds *fCountry* as a third. It defines a new initialization method, **IForeignCustomer**. It also overrides the **PrintAddress** method that it would have otherwise inherited from the **TCustomer** superclass.

Important ▶

At this point, we should mention some of the naming conventions used throughout both the MacApp source code and all the samples in this book. These include:

• Class names begin with an uppercase T (since Object Pascal classes are always defined in a **TYPE** statement, and since classes are a Template for building objects). Apple also uses this convention for classes defined in C++.

• Instance variable names always begin with lowercase f, since they are analogous to fields of a Pascal record or C struct.

• Initialization methods always use the name of the class with the uppercase T replaced with uppercase I.

• All variable names begin with a lowercase letter, while function names begin with an uppercase letter.

• Global variable names should begin with lowercase g (for example, *gCustomer*).

• Constants should begin with lowercase k, or in special cases, lowercase c (that is, kWindowID).

▶ MPW Tools

For each sample in this chapter, we will implement the programs as MPW Tools. A Tool is special mini-program that runs only inside the MPW Shell. MPW tools can use the console I/O of the Shell windows, so you do not need to create a real user interface for your program. This approach would be a terrible way to create end-user applications, but it works well for programmer utilities, or as a way to test a class or an algorithm. Because the samples do not define their own windows and menus, we will not need to use MacApp just yet. We will save that for later chapters, after you learn more about the C++ language and the MacApp development environment.

▶ The Money.p file

The code for the Money sample is written in a single file called Money.p, which is shown in Listing 6-1.

Listing 6-1. The Money sample in Object Pascal

```
 1: PROGRAM Money;
 2:
 3: USES
 4:    Memtypes, ObjIntf;
 5:
 6: {==== classes =================================================}
 7: TYPE
 8:    TCustomer = OBJECT
 9:        fName:  Str255;
10:        fCity:  Str255;
11:        PROCEDURE TCustomer.ICustomer(name, city: Str255);
12:        PROCEDURE TCustomer.PrintAddress;
13:        END;
14:
15:    TForeignCustomer = OBJECT(TCustomer)
16:        fCountry:   Str255;
17:        PROCEDURE TForeignCustomer.IForeignCustomer(
18:                               name, city, country: Str255);
19:        PROCEDURE TForeignCustomer.PrintAddress; OVERRIDE;
20:        END;
21:
22: {==== methods =================================================}
23: PROCEDURE TCustomer.ICustomer(name, city: Str255);
24: BEGIN
25:    SELF.fName := name;     {SELF. is optional}
26:    fCity := city;
27: END;
28:
29: {-----------------------------------------------------------}
30: PROCEDURE TCustomer.PrintAddress;
31: BEGIN
32:    WriteLn;                {for neatness}
33:    WriteLn(fName);
34:    WriteLn(fCity);
35: END;
36:
37: {===========================================================}
```

```
38: PROCEDURE TForeignCustomer.IForeignCustom (name, city,
                                                country: Str255);
39: BEGIN
40:    SELF.ICustomer(name, city);
41:    fCountry := country;
42: END;
43:
44: {-------------------------------------------------------------}
45: PROCEDURE TForeignCustomer.PrintAddress; OVERRIDE;
46: BEGIN
47:    INHERITED PrintAddress;
48:    WriteLn(fCountry);
49: END;
50:
51: { === global variables ======================================}
52: VAR
53:    gCustomer:           TCustomer;
54:    gForeignCustomer:    TForeignCustomer;
55:
56: {=== main program ==========================================}
57: BEGIN
58:    NEW(gCustomer);
59:    gCustomer.ICustomer('Mr. Smith', 'San Jose');
60:    gCustomer.PrintAddress;
61:
62:    NEW(gForeignCustomer);
63:    gForeignCustomer.IForeignCustomer('Mr. Nakajima', 'Tokyo',
                                         'Japan');
64:    gForeignCustomer.PrintAddress;
65: END.
```

This file is structured as follows:

The Pascal keyword PROGRAM on line 1 indicates that this is a complete program, rather than a separately compiled Unit.

The USES statements on lines 3 and 4 are analogous to statements that include header files in a C program. The USES statement tells the Pascal compiler to process the separately compiled Units, MemTypes.p, and ObjIntf.p, which contain definitions for various types, variables, procedures, and functions referenced later in our code. These files are provided with MPW Pascal in the PInterfaces folder. The classes of objects are defined on lines 7-20, and their associated methods are implemented on lines 23-49. Global variables are allocated on lines 52-54, while the main program is shown on lines 57-65. We will now examine this code in detail, starting with the class definitions as TYPE declarations.

## ▶ Defining a Class

The **TCustomer** class is defined on lines 8-13. The definition uses the keyword OBJECT, which is analogous to the keyword RECORD used to define data structures in non-object Pascal. It is important to remember that **TCustomer** is not an object, but merely a template for creating objects. The instance variables are defined with their types on lines 9 and 10, and the messages are listed last, on lines 11 and 12. Notice that each message is defined by the name of the class, followed by a period, followed by the name of the procedure or function and its parameter list. You can then see these lines repeated when the methods are implemented on lines 23-35.

---

**By the Way ▶**

When writing the actual method code, you must include the class name, such as in the **TCustomer.ICustomer** method on line 23. The class name is redundant in the class definition itself, so line 11 could actually be written as

```
PROCEDURE ICustomer(name, city: Str255);
```

We generally include the class name, however, since it allows you to write the method by copying the name from the class definition.

---

**By the Way ▶**

In Pascal, a procedure is a subroutine that carries out some operation but does not return a result. A Pascal function carries out some operation but always returns a result. In C, all routines are functions, although you can choose to ignore the result of a function call if you wish.

---

## ▶ Defining a Subclass

The **TForeignCustomer** class is defined on lines 15-20. It is described as a subclass of an existing class by placing the superclass name, **TCustomer**, in parentheses after the Object Pascal keyword OBJECT, as shown on line 15. (Notice on line 8 that **TCustomer** is defined with no superclass.) Each instance of **TForeignCustomer** will have storage for a total of three instance variables: *fName* and *fCity* inherited from the superclass, and *fCountry* defined in the subclass. Foreign customer objects can respond to a total of three messages: ICustomer, inherited from the superclass, and IForeignCustomer and PrintAddress defined in the subclass.

## ▶ Overriding a Method

Note that the version of **PrintAddress** defined in the class **TForeign-Customer** is an override of the version from the **TCustomer** class, so we must use the Object Pascal keyword OVERRIDE on line 19. This word, which has no equivalent in C++, is required to prevent you from accidentally overriding a method in a superclass. **PrintAddress** is our first example of a *polymorphic method* — one which is defined in more than one class in the hierarchy. By having two versions, we can send the same PrintAddress message to any customer object, and it will respond by executing the appropriate method.

## ▶ Creating Objects

When we describe C++ later in this chapter, you will see that you can define variables that directly represent objects, or you can define variables to be pointers or handles to objects. Object Pascal is not as flexible. Variables can only reference objects rather than being the objects themselves. In fact all Pascal objects must be created as relocatable blocks on the heap, accessed by a *handle* (an indirect address, which is a pointer to a pointer). Therefore, when you see line 53 defining a global variable, *gCustomer*, of type **TCustomer**, do not be deceived. The variable *gCustomer* only represents the indirect address of a potential object, that is, one that has not yet been created. This type of variable is called an *object-reference variable*, but you may nevertheless often think of it as a customer object.

| By the Way ▶ | The Application Heap is a part of random-access memory where most of your program is stored. It is divided into variable-size blocks that contain specific items.

Some data structures are created on the heap as nonrelocatable blocks. Typical examples are window records, bit images, and serial port buffers. Nonrelocatable blocks cannot be moved by the Macintosh system's built-in Memory Manager routines. This feature sometimes makes it easier to use them, but has the potential disadvantage of fragmenting memory. Nonrelocatable blocks are accessed through pointer variables.

Most data structures are created as relocatable blocks. Each resource is stored in its own relocatable block on the heap; the Apple menu is in one relocatable block, the File menu is in another, and your main program's CODE resource is in a third. Relocatable blocks may be moved from one address to another by the Memory Manager routines in the Toolbox. They must therefore be accessed indirectly through handles. To allow optimum use of memory, all Pascal objects are allocated as relocatable blocks on the heap.

To create an actual object, we use the Pascal NEW procedure shown on line 58. This creates a relocatable block in memory with enough room to store the *fName* and *fCity* instance variables defined for the class **TCustomer**. At this point, the variable *gCustomer* is set to be a reference (a handle) to that block. Similarly, a reference to a foreign customer object is defined on line 54, with the object itself created on line 62.

## ▶ Sending a Message

The designers of Object Pascal decided to send messages by borrowing the dot syntax used to access a field of a record. Therefore, we can send the ICustomer message to the gCustomer object as shown on line 59. In general, the message syntax is:

```
aReceiver.Message(parameters);
```

**Warning ▶**

If you have written Macintosh programs before, the syntax for sending a message may seem wrong. Since Pascal objects must be referenced through a handle, you might guess that the syntax would be the following:

```
aReceiver^^.Message(parameters); {wrong!}
```

The code above is incorrect. The fact that objects are referenced through handles is a compiler implementation detail, rather than being part of the language specification. For this reason, you must write your code as if your variables directly referenced the object. You must keep in the back of your mind, however, that this is not true, since there are occasional circumstances where you can get into trouble with dereferenced handles. We will point these out as they occur.

**By the Way ▶**

This same dot syntax is used when accessing a variable of an object, so you might see code as follows:

```
gCustomer.fName := 'Mrs. Smith';
```

> You will rarely see us write code that directly accesses the variables of another object, however, since an object's variables are best treated as private. We will usually only access an object's variables from within methods of that object, as is described below.

Messages can only be sent to real objects — those created with NEW (someObject). That means that you may not send a message to a class, so you have the following situation:

```
NEW(aCustomer);            {OK}
aCustomer.PrintAddress;    {OK}
TCustomer.PrintAddress;    {Wrong!}
```

## ▶ Initialization Methods and SELF

The **ICustomer** method shown on lines 23-27 initializes the two instance variables for the class. This simple code introduces another important Object Pascal keyword, SELF. SELF is a special pseudovariable defined only in the context of a method. It contains a reference to the object that received the message. Therefore, when the ICustomer message is sent to *gCustomer* on line 59, the value of *gCustomer* is passed as an implicit parameter to the **ICustomer** method shown on lines 23-27. This SELF reference allows a method to access the variables of the object for which it was called, as is done on line 25. In fact, if you directly access an instance variable inside a method, as shown on line 26, the compiler assumes that you are accessing one of your own, and compiles it as if the SELF keyword had been typed. In other words, SELF is optional. We generally do not use it when referring to instance variables within methods.

The **IForeignCustomer** initialization method presents our first example of code reuse, as shown on lines 38-42. This method must initialize the three instance variables, *fName*, *fCity*, and *fCountry*. We define the method to take the required three parameters on line 38. The obvious temptation would be to copy the code from the **ICustomer** method and paste it into the **IForeignCustomer** procedure, but the better way is shown on line 40. Here we reuse the code from our superclass by calling the **ICustomer** method inherited from the superclass. We again use the pseudovariable SELF, but it is now used to call one of our own methods, that is, to send ourselves a message. It is best to supply the SELF keyword when sending messages, since it reminds the person reading the code that you are calling a method defined for that class, not an ordinary procedure or function.

| Important ▶ | The general rule for writing initialization methods is to call the initialization method of the superclass to initialize any variables inherited from the superclass. You will see this rule followed in all the samples in this book. This generally makes your code more compact. More importantly, it makes your program more maintainable because you do not have two copies of the same piece of code to update as your program evolves. |
| --- | --- |

## ▶ Reusing Overridden Code

We will finally examine the **PrintAddress** methods defined in each class. The method for the **TCustomer** class is defined on lines 30-35 to simply use the Pascal WriteLn statement as an output mechanism. The results are then displayed in the MPW worksheet window. The more interesting case is the overridden version of **PrintAddress** shown on lines 45-49. We again want to reuse the code from the superclass, so you might be tempted to write the following:

```
PROCEDURE TForeignCustomer.PrintAddress; OVERRIDE;
BEGIN
   SELF.PrintAddress;   {Wrong! Do not do this!}
   WriteLn(fCountry);
END;
```

Can you see what unpleasant thing would happen with this code? The call to SELF.PrintAddress would be recursive. The routine would call itself over and over until you used up all of memory, leading to the dreaded ID 28 bomb when the heap collides with the stack. Fortunately, the Object Pascal keyword INHERITED has been provided as a way to avoid this problem, as shown on line 47 of Listing 6-1. INHERITED allows you to reuse code from inside a method that you have overridden. This permits you to override a method in a subclass, but still use the behavior from the superclass's version of that method. The two keywords, SELF and INHERITED, provide the foundation for code reuse in Object Pascal.

## ▶ The Main Program

In this program, as in all MacApp programs, the main program is very simple; most of your work will involve designing the classes and writing the methods. All we do in this main program is create two objects, initialize them, and put them to work printing invoices. This points to a major feature of programming with objects: If the classes are already written, then programming becomes very easy. That's because the messages of a well-designed class hide its data structures and the algorithms used in the methods as well. All you see as the client (user) of a class is a high-level message interface.

▶ The Make File

If you would like to experiment with the Money program using MPW, you must also have a "make" file to control the compile and link process. The Money.make file that we used is shown in Listing 6-2. We will explain the details of make files like these later in the book.

Listing 6-2. The Money.make file

```
 1: # ============================================
 2: AppName = Money
 3:
 4: LinkOptions = -w  ∂
 5:               -t 'MPST'  ∂
 6:               -c 'MPS '  ∂
 7:               -opt on
 8:
 9: PascalOptions = -h
10:
11: # ============================================
12: {AppName} ƒ {AppName}.make {AppName}.p.o
13:     Link   {LinkOptions} ∂
14:           {AppName}.p.o ∂
15:           "{Libraries}"Interface.o ∂
16:           "{Libraries}"ObjLib.o ∂
17:           "{Libraries}"Runtime.o ∂
18:           "{Libraries}"ToolLibs.o ∂
19:           "{PLibraries}"PasLib.o ∂
20:           -o {AppName}
21:
22: # ============================================
23: {AppName}.p.o ƒ {AppName}.p
24:     Pascal {PascalOptions}  {AppName}.p
```

▶ **Object Pascal Review**

This simple Money program illustrates the main features of Object Pascal. These include

- Define classes in a TYPE declaration using the keyword OBJECT.
- Put the superclass name in parentheses.
- Use the keyword OVERRIDE to indicate that you are overriding a method in a subclass.
- Variables that reference objects are actually handles to objects.
- Objects are created with the NEW procedure.
- Messages are sent with the dot separator.
- SELF is defined in any method to be the reference to the object that received the message.

With this knowledge, you should be able to read and understand the Object Pascal sample programs, and eventually, even the MacApp source code. You will also be able to contrast the simple features of Object Pascal with the more elaborate C++ language features that we will study and use for all the other programs in this book.

▶ **The C++ Language**

C++ was developed by Bjarne Stroustrup of AT&T Bell Laboratories in the early 1980s and released by AT&T initially in 1985. In mid-1989 AT&T released version 2.0, and Apple followed immediately with their beta-test version running under MPW. By early 1990, Apple had C++ and MacApp working well together as part of MPW 3.1.

C++ is a superset of ordinary C. Apple's current implementation uses a version of the AT&T "CFront" preprocessor that produces C code, which is then compiled by the MPW C compiler.

▶ Language Overview

To experienced C programmers, C++ may seem to be merely a better C language, one that provides a superset of the ANSI C features that began to be popular in the early 1980s. From our point of view, C++ is much more than just a better C — it is a language that supports object-oriented programming. The C++ design philosophy differs from that of Object Pascal. Object Pascal was designed to be simple to learn and provides just enough new features to support programming with objects. C++ is a much richer and more complex language, one that most programmers find much harder to master. The C++ philosophy is that if you will take the time to learn the details of the language, you will be able to optimize the size and performance of your program in many ways that you could not do with Object Pascal.

We have found that you can learn the basic techniques for object programming in C++ in a few days, but you will typically spend at least a few weeks becoming familiar with all the subtle techniques of program optimization. In this chapter, we'll introduce the basics in enough detail so that you can write good MacApp programs. To delve further into the mysteries of the language, you should read Dan Weston's book on C++ programming, listed in the bibliography.

## ▶ New Features (Not Specifically Object-Oriented)

There are many useful new features in C++ that do not involve supporting programming with objects. They are simply improvements to the C programming language. We will nevertheless use many of these in our MacApp programs, since they make the code easier to read and write. We list the new features and then illustrate using many of them in the sample programs later in this chapter.

### Single-line Comments Using //

The double-slash defines all text from the double-slash to the end of the line as a comment. It is easier to type and read than /* and */, which are used in standard C to bracket comments. The older style comments can still be used, but we will almost never use them in our samples. Consider the code fragment below:

```
FunctionA(b, c, d);    /* this is an old-style comment */
FunctionE(f, g);       // don't need to end the comment
```

### Function Prototyping and Strict Type Checking

Function prototyping allows you to define argument lists and the expected function result rigorously for each function. This ANSI C feature allows the compiler to check every usage of each function to ensure it is being called correctly. This will catch the kind of errors that used to sneak by old C compilers (unless you ran the Lint utility), but would often cause nasty run-time errors. This strict type checking requires that C programmers now be as careful as Pascal programmers have had to be for years.

A function prototype must specify the types of each argument and the function result. You can optionally include the argument names. The prototype is generally defined in a header file, with the actual function defined in a separate implementation file, as you will see later in the chapter. Both of the following prototypes are legal, since the compiler ignores the argument names:

```
float Calculate(short loopMax, float aNumber);
float Calculate(short, float);          // types only
```

### Default Function Arguments

You can define an argument list with default values for some of the parameters. When you call that function, you may either fill in the parameters, or leave out the last one or more of them and cause the default values to be used. Consider the following function prototype.

```
float Calculate(short loopMax, float aNumber = 0.0);
```

This function might normally be called with two arguments, but if only one short is passed, the second float argument will be set to the default value, as in the following code fragment:

```
anAnswer = Calculate(5, 3.14);   // aNumber = 3.14
myAnswer = Calculate(5);         // aNumber = 0.0
aMistake = Calculate( , 3.14)    // incorrect!
```

Notice that you can only use default arguments for the latter arguments; you cannot skip early ones by leaving a blank or a comma as a placeholder.

## ▶ Overloaded Function Names

In previous sections, we have talked about *overriding* a function in a subclass. This means writing a new version of an existing function, but keeping the argument list unchanged. By *overloading* a function, you can provide another version of it with a different argument list. This allows you great flexibility, but it does have a disadvantage. If you write too many versions of the same function, you can make your code harder for others to read and understand and therefore harder to maintain. For example, these two declarations create two separate and distinct **Calculate** methods:

```
float Calculate(short loopMax, float aNumber);
float Calculate(float aNumber);  // set loopMax = 10
```

## Inline Functions Instead of Macros

Instead of #define statements, you can specify the implementation of a function using the keyword inline, and instruct the compiler to substitute your block of code whenever you call that function. This can make your program run faster, but in certain circumstances it can also make the final program larger, so this technique must be used with care. An example of a macro and an equivalent inline function is shown below:

```
#define circumference(radius)    2*pi*radius
inline float circumference(float radius) {return 2*pi*radius;}
```

The inline function has the advantage of having typed arguments and a typed function result. The macro (using #define) is not typed so you could pass it an invalid argument, or use it where it returns the incorrect type, and the compiler could not catch the errors.

Warning ▶

A major problem facing programmers new to object programming is the tendency to optimize too soon. In fact, the C++ language tends to encourage this because it provides many ways to performance tune your code.

The technique that we recommend is to write your code initially to be as modular, maintainable, flexible, and reusable as you can. Then run the program and use the performance analysis tools in MPW to find the areas where your code can benefit from optimization and modify them.

Do not try to guess where the performance bottlenecks will occur as you write the code. This leads to premature and usually incorrect optimization, often at the expense of reusability and maintainability.

## Type void

A function that returns no value should be declared to return type void, as follows:

```
void Beeper(short ticks);
```

A function that takes no arguments can optionally be defined in the function prototype as having void as the argument, as follows:

```
float ReturnTaxRate(void);
```

A pointer to any data type can be defined to be of type void* when dealing with a pointer to something with a type that can vary. For example, you might declare vp as a pointer that can point to anything with the following code:

```
void *vp;
```

## Constant Declarations

Instead of declaring a constant with a #define, it is better to use the const keyword as shown. This insures that the compiler will type-check any use of the constant. With the const definition, the compiler will check that any reference to kMaxNumber uses a short type:

```
#define kMaxNumber 10            // no type checking
const short kMaxNumber = 10;   // safer and better
```

## Variables Declarable Anywhere

C++ allows you to declare a variable almost anywhere in the code you like. This permits you to do such things as declare a variable in the line of code where it is first used. The following code fragment illustrates defining *theSum* and *index* variables as they are needed:

```
float Calculate(short loopMax, float aNumber)
{
float theSum = aNumber;
for (short index = 0; index <= loopMax; index++){
  theSum = theSum + index;
  }
return theSum;
}
```

## ▶ Defining a Class

A new class of objects can be defined using either the keyword struct or class, as shown in Listing 6-3. We'll use the normal object programming terminology in describing this code, with the equivalent C++ terminology in parenthesis. We discussed the reasons for using our terminology at the beginning of Chapter 3.

Listing 6-3: Defining new classes of objects

```
 1: //==============================================================
 2: struct  TCustomer{
 3: private:
 4:      char     fName[256];
 5:      char     fCity[256];
 6: protected:
 7:      short    fCustomerNumber;
 8: public:
 9:      TCustomer(const char *name, const char *city);
10:      virtual void PrintAddress();
11: };
12:
13: //==============================================================
14: class  TForeignCustomer: public TCustomer {
15: private:
16:      char     fCountry[256];
17: public:
18:      TForeignCustomer(const char *name, const char *city,
19:                                         const char *country);
20:      virtual void PrintAddress();    // override
21: };
```

Interesting parts of this listing include:

Line 2: The keyword struct is used to define the class **TCustomer** with variables *fName* and *fCity,* and methods **ICustomer** and **PrintAddress**. The keyword struct can still be used to define a traditional C data structure.

Line 3: The keyword private indicates that the variables (data members) can only be accessed by the methods (member functions) of this class, but not by methods of a subclass (derived class), or by methods unrelated to this class. You can also declare some or all of your methods to be private.

Line 6: The keyword protected indicates that the variable *fCustomerNumber* can be directly read or set by methods of this class or any of its subclasses.

Line 8: The keyword public indicates that the ICustomer and PrintAd-dress messages can be sent to instances of this class from any part of your code. If you were to declare a method to be private, then it could only be called from other methods of this class. If you want all members of a struct to be public, you do not even need to use the keyword, since a struct defaults to public.

**By the Way ▶**

This ability to fine tune your program's data abstraction to be either private, protected, or public is one of the best features of C++.

By comparison, Object Pascal's variables and methods are all public. This means that the compiler will not stop you from writing code in which methods from one class directly access the variables of objects belonging to a different class. Tinkering with another object's varia-bles will generally lead to code that is hard to maintain, as we shall discuss in later chapters. For now, let's just say that private variables are safer to use than public ones.

To compare with another popular object language, Smalltalk uses protected variables, but the methods are always public. This pro-vides reasonable protection, but it is not as flexible as C++.

Symantec's THINK C 4.0 compiler's Object C language has only pub-lic variables and methods, just like Object Pascal.

Line 9: A function with the same name as the class is called a *construc-tor function*. A constructor is an initialization method called automati-cally whenever an instance of this class is created, as we shall see in the later samples. Note that a constructor cannot be virtual, and is not al-lowed to return a function result (not even void). Note the use of *const* for each string pointer. This tells the compiler that the constructor func-tion is not allowed to modify the strings that are passed as arguments — they are read-only.

**By the Way ▶**

You can also define a cleanup method called a *destructor function*, which is always named with the tilde symbol (~) followed by the class name, for example, **~TCustomer**. We will not use destructors in this book, since they offer no particular advantages when using MacApp.

Line 10: The keyword virtual indicates that this method can be overridden in a subclass. This leads to the fact that only virtual functions are polymorphic. Such methods are stored in a method lookup table (vtable, or virtual table) where they can be found at run-time. We generally recommend that you declare your methods to be virtual, because you never know when a client may want to override a method. Object Pascal makes life simpler, since the default is virtual. The keyword void means that the method does not return a function result.

Line 11: Note that the struct definition ends with a semicolon.

Line 14: The keyword class is used to define the **TForeignCustomer** class as a subclass (derived class) of **TCustomer** (the base class). The keyword public before the superclass name means that any public members of **TCustomer** will remain public to the users of the subclass. We will always use this form of public inheritance in our samples. The only difference between using the keyword class on line 14 and the keyword struct on line 2 is that a class definition defaults to private members, while the members of a struct default to public. Since we will be using private variables, we'll use the keyword class in all our class definitions that follow.

Line 18: This defines the constructor for the class **TForeignCustomer**. This constructor must be written to pass parameters to the **TCustomer** constructor defined on line 9.

Line 20: This indicates that we override the **PrintAddress** method defined in the superclass, **TCustomer**. Notice that, unlike Object Pascal, there is no OVERRIDE keyword. It is therefore possible to accidentally override a method in a subclass without being warned by the compiler. Be aware of what you are inheriting.

## ▶ Constructor Methods

As an example of writing C++ methods, consider the two constructor functions shown in Listing 6-4. The **TCustomer** function takes the customer's name and city as arguments as shown on line 2, while the **TForeignCustomer** function must be called with the arguments name, city, and country, as shown on lines 9-11.

The unusual syntax shown on line 12 indicates that the constructor of the superclass, **TCustomer**, will be called by the **TForeignCustomer** constructor, with name and city passed as arguments. This means that creating an instance of **TForeignCustomer** will cause its constructor to be called, which then invokes the **TCustomer** constructor. The result is that all three variables will be properly initialized.

Listing 6-4. Two constructors

```
 1: // ==============================================================
 2: TCustomer::TCustomer(const char *name, const char *city)
 3: {
 4:     strcpy(fName, name);
 5:     strcpy(fCity, city);
 6: }
 7:
 8: // ==============================================================
 9: TForeignCustomer::TForeignCustomer(const char *name,
10:                                    const char *city,
11:                                    const char *country)
12:                                  : TCustomer(name, city)
13: {
14:     strcpy(fCountry, country);
15: }
```

It is common, by the way, to have overloaded constructors, so that a single class may have many constructors with different argument lists.

## ▶ Creating Objects

There are two basic ways to create objects and send messages in C++. The simplest way is to create an object that is directly referenced by a variable. With a named object (known as a *static* or *automatic object*, you must use the dot operator to send a message, just as you would do with Object Pascal. This leads to the following code fragment:

```
TCustomer aCustomer ("Mrs. Smith", "New Orleans");
aCustomer.PrintAddress();
```

Notice that the arguments to the constructor are passed in parentheses after the variable name.

*Dynamically allocated* objects are normally defined to be referenced by a pointer, as follows. In this case, the object must be allocated with the "new" function, and a pointer operator is used to send a message.

```
TCustomer* aCustomer = new TCustomer("Mrs. Smith", "New Orleans");
```

With pointer-based objects, the arguments to the constructor are passed to the constructor itself. The constructor is also the class name.

You would most often use direct allocation of named objects to represent new data types like strings or complex numbers. We will use dynamic allocation for all the objects in our MacApp sample programs, since they will represent objects that model our problem area or objects that support the user interface. In these cases, we usually do not know how many objects we will need until the program is running.

## ▶ C++ Sample Programs

The easiest way to see how to write a program with C++ is to study a working program. We will describe three C++ samples in this chapter, using each one to illustrate certain features of the language.

In each case, we will implement the programs as MPW Tools. The first C++ tool we will study is called "TinyBenchmark."

## ▶ The TinyBenchmark Program

TinyBenchmark tests the speed of the function call mechanism by calling a trivially simple function many times. In fact, on a Macintosh II with a 16 MHz 68020 processor, it turned out to be necessary to call the function at least hundreds of thousands of times for it to take long enough to measure accurately. Later in this chapter, we will extend the program to measure the additional time necessary to send a message to an object (that is, to perform method lookup).

## ▶ Program Structure

The class diagram for TinyBenchmark is shown in Figure 6-2.

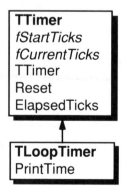

Figure 6-2. Class diagram for the TinyBenchmark program

The program uses only two classes: **TTimer** and **TLoopTimer**.

## The TTimer Class

**TTimer** is a utility class that implements a simple stopwatch behavior, working in units known as ticks (1/60 second) rather than in seconds. Since it can be used whenever you need to do timing, it represents the kind of reusable building block that should be kept in an easily accessible library for use in other programs.

*fStartTicks* and *fCurrentTicks* are instance variables used during timing.

The **TTimer** method is the constructor function for the **TTimer** class. The class name is always used for the constructor name. The constructor gets called automatically whenever an instance of **TTimer** is created. It initializes the instance variables of the timer object.

**Reset** is a method that resets the timer back to zero.

**ElapsedTicks** simply returns the time that has elapsed since the timer was last reset.

## The TLoopTimer Class

**TLoopTimer** is a very specialized subclass of **TTimer** that has a single method, **PrintTime**, for calculating and displaying the number of microseconds (millionths of a second) that it takes to call an ordinary function. This method displays its output in an MPW Shell text editing window.

## ▶ Program Files

The program itself consists of only two files. The TinyBenchmark.cp file contains all the C++ code, including the class definitions, the methods, the global variable allocations, and the main program. The TinyBenchmark.make file is used by the MPW Make tool to compile and link the code. The structure of this program's C++ file is shown in Figure 6-3. The TinyBenchmark.cp file is shown in Listing 6-5.

| By the Way ▶ | The generally accepted file name conventions for suffixes are |
|---|---|
| | .cp          C++ source file |
| | .cp.o        compiled object code from a C++ source file |
| | .c and .c.o  ordinary C code |
| | .a and .a.o  assembler code |
| | .p and .p.o  Pascal (or Object Pascal) code |
| | .r           text file description of resources |
| | .rsrc        compiled resources |

```
#include statements
       other headers needed by compiler

class definitions
       TTimer
       TLoopTimer

method implementations
       TTimer
       Reset
       etc.

global variables

ordinary function definitions
       TestJSR

main()
{
   ...
}
```

Figure 6-3. Structure of the TinyBenchmark.cp file

(Remember that the line numbers appearing in the program listing were added just for this book. You will not see these — and do not want them — in an MPW text editing window.)

Listing 6-5. The TinyBenchmark.cp file

```
1: // Copyright 1990 © David A. Wilson. All Rights Reserved.
2:
3: #ifndef __EVENTS__
4:     #include <Events.h>          // for TickCount toolbox call
5: #endif
6:
7: #ifndef __STREAM__
8:     #include <stream.h>          // for cout, cin
9: #endif
10:
11: //=============== class definitions =========================
12: class TTimer {
13: private:
14:     long    fStartTicks;
15:     long    fCurrentTicks;
16: public:
17:     TTimer(void);
```

```
18:     virtual void Reset(void);
19:     virtual long ElapsedTicks(void);
20: };
21:
22: //-----------------------------------------------------------
23: class TLoopTimer : public TTimer {
24: public:
25:     virtual void DisplayTime(long loops);
26: };
27:
28: //================== methods ====================================
29: TTimer::TTimer(void)
30: {
31:     this->Reset();
32: }
33:
34: // ----------------------------------------------------------
35: void
36: TTimer::Reset(void)
37: {
38:     fStartTicks = TickCount();
39:     fCurrentTicks = fStartTicks;
40: }
41:
42: // ----------------------------------------------------------
43: long
44: TTimer::ElapsedTicks(void)
45: {
46:     fCurrentTicks = TickCount();
47:     return (fCurrentTicks - fStartTicks);
48: }
49:
50: //===============================================================
51: void
52: TLoopTimer::DisplayTime(long loops)
53: {
54:     long ticks = this->ElapsedTicks();
55:     cout << "\nLoops = " << loops << "\n";
56:     cout << "Ticks = " << ticks << "\n";
57:     double microsecPerLoop = (ticks / 60.0) * 1e6 / loops;
58:     cout << "μsec/Loop = " << microsecPerLoop << "\n\n";
59: }
60:
61: //========== globals ===========================================
62: TLoopTimer  gLoopTimer;
63: short       gShort;
64: long        gLoopMax = 1000000;
65:
```

```
66: //========== test function ======================================
67: void
68: TestJSR(void)
69: {
70:     gShort = 1;
71: }
72:
73: //========== main program ======================================
74: void main()
75: {
76:     gLoopTimer.Reset();
77:     for (long index = 0; index < gLoopMax; index++) {
78:         gShort = 1;
79:         }
80:     gLoopTimer.DisplayTime(gLoopMax);
81:
82:     gLoopTimer.Reset();
83:     for (index = 0; index < gLoopMax; index++) {
84:         TestJSR();
85:         }
86:     gLoopTimer.DisplayTime(gLoopMax);
87: }
```

### The C++ Code

Line 1 contains the obligatory copyright notice, which uses C++'s double-slash syntax to comment out the line.

Lines 3-9 include other header files needed during the compilation process. The brackets around the file names on lines 4 and 8 tell the compiler to search for these files in the folders where standard libraries are kept. If you refer to one of your own header files, you should include the file name in double quotes to tell the compiler to start searching in your own source code directory.

The conditional #ifndef directives on lines 3 and 7 are there to prevent a header from being included more than once. This could otherwise occur if one of the header files included another header that you were also including. Each header file defines its own variable, which means that the Events.h file will begin with the following lines of code:

```
#ifndef __EVENTS__
#define __EVENTS__
```

Lines 12-20 define the **TTimer** class, which has no superclass.

*fStartTicks* and *fCurrentTicks* are defined as private instance variables of type long on lines 14 and 15. The private keyword on line 13 is not required, since the default is private because of the class keyword on line 12. It is a good idea to include this keyword as a reminder of the privacy, however.

**TTimer** is a constructor defined on line 17 that takes no arguments (void), and cannot return any function result, not even void. Constructors can be defined with arguments, but they can never return a result.

The **TTimer** constructor function is shown on lines 29-32. This method simply sends itself the **Reset**() message, that is, it calls another method of its own class using the pseudovariable "this". The variable "this" is always a pointer to the object that received the message, so you must use the -> notation to send the message.

**Important ▶** You are not required to type "this->" before calling one of your own methods from inside another method, but we recommend that you include it to improve code readability. If you leave it out when you call a method from another method of the same class, the compiler will effectively insert it, so your code will still work. The problem is that the code will look as if you are calling an ordinary function, so someone (perhaps you) maintaining the code months later will not know where to look to find the function. We recommend strongly that you use "this->" notation for all your messages.

**By the Way ▶** The reference to the object that received the message is called *this* in C++, but it is called *self* in Object Pascal, Smalltalk, and Objective-C.

**Reset** is a virtual method to reset the timer back to zero. It is defined on line 18 to return nothing (void) as a function result. It is not required that this be a virtual function, but it is generally a good idea, since this allows clients to override it in a subclass. The **Reset** method is shown on lines 35-40 of the listing. It merely sets the *fStartTicks* and *fCurrentTicks* instance variables to the value of the computer's internal timer using the TickCount Toolbox routine.

We must warn you that calling a virtual function from a constructor does not always do what you would expect. The function called will always be the one defined for the class of the constructor. In this example, **TTimer::Reset**() will always be called on line 31, even if **Reset**() had been overridden in a subclass. In case you care, this is because the vtable pointer will not refer to a subclass's vtable until the subclass's constructor starts executing.

| By the Way ▶ | The Macintosh has two system clocks. The tick count timer measures the ticks (each approximately 1/60 of a second) that have elapsed since the computer was last powered up. It is not a terribly accurate clock. If you need an accurate time measurement, you should use the clock used by the Control Panel and the Alarm Clock Desk Accessory. You can access this accurate date and time with Toolbox calls such as the GetTime procedure described in the Operating System Utilities chapter of *Inside Macintosh, Volume 2*. In special cases, you can also do very accurate timing using the Time Manager routines described in *Inside Macintosh, Volume 4*. |
|---|---|

**ElapsedTicks** is defined on line 19 to be another virtual function. This method returns the number of ticks since the timer object was last reset, as shown on lines 43-48.

The **TTimer** class is simple to define and the methods are easy to write. Instances of this class are general-purpose timers, but this program needed a more specialized timer, so we defined the **TLoopTimer** subclass on lines 23-26. Line 23 shows that **TTimer** is the superclass, with the public keyword on line 23 ensuring that any public members of the superclass remain public to the users of the subclass. (If the word public is omitted here, the public methods inherited from **TTimer** could still be called from the methods of the **TLoopTimer** subclass.) You will almost always use this public keyword when referring to the superclass.

The **DisplayTime** method is defined on line 25 to take one argument, loops, which is the number of loops that were executed in the test code. The method itself is shown on lines 51-59, and probably looks unintelligible if you have not yet worked with the C++ IOStream classes. Let's examine cout and iostreams, the routines C++ provides as object-oriented substitutes for the normal C functions printf and scanf.

On line 8, we included the standard C++ header file stream.h. This library file includes another library file, iostream.h, that defines a number of stream classes you will find useful for console input and output. These are just what we need for our simple MPW tool. We could use traditional scanf and printf functions, but since this is a book about programming with C++, we might as well use some goodies from this library.

The identifier *cout* is predefined in the headers as an instance of an output stream class. This class defines the two-character symbol << as an operator that takes a string as an argument, and writes it on the output stream to the console. In other words, the following code shows two different ways to do the same thing (\n is, of course, the newline character):

```
printf("Structs are fun\n");        /* using C */
cout << "Objects are fun\n";        // using C++
```

Calls to *cout* can be cascaded as follows:

```
printf("Structs are fun%s", " using C\n");
cout << "Objects are fun" << " using C++\n";
```

The **DisplayTime** method on lines 51-59 of Listing 6-5 makes extensive use of the *cout* stream to display the results of a test in an MPW window. A typical output looks like this:

```
Loops = 1000000
Ticks = 267
µsec/Loop = 4.45
```

Now let's make sense of this by examining the rest of the program to see how these timer methods are actually used.

## Global Variables

The global variables are defined on lines 62-64.

*gLoopTimer* is allocated on line 62 as the program's only object, an instance of the class **TLoopTimer**. This allocation sets aside enough room in global variable space for each of the object's instance variables (two 32-bit long integers), plus a 32-bit pointer to the "vtable" (the virtual table which is used for method lookup at run-time). When this program executes and the gLoopTimer object is allocated, its constructor is automatically called to initialize it.

*gShort* is allocated on line 63 to be a 16-bit integer, which we will use to carry out our test operations.

*gLoopMax* is a long integer initialized to 1,000,000, and represents the number of times we will run our test loops.

## ▶ The Main Program

The main program's job is to use an instance of **TLoopTimer** to test how long it takes to call a function. The function to be called is the simple TestJSR function defined on lines 67-71. We use the letters JSR in the name to reflect the fact that the **J**ump**S**ub**R**outine machine instruction is used for ordinary function calls.

A given test consists of three parts. First, we reset the timer by sending the ResetTimer message to our gLoopTimer object, as shown on lines 76 and 82. Next, we carry out some operation, such as setting *gShort* equal to 1, either directly on line 78 or indirectly through the TestJSR function call on line 84. Finally, we calculate and display the result by sending the DisplayTime message to the gLoopTimer object on lines 80 and 86. Notice one of C++'s nice features on line 77, where the counter for the loop index is declared to be a long integer where it is first needed. This variable, *index*, is then used for the rest of the main program.

| By the Way ▶ | If a variable is declared inside the scope of a block, then it is only defined in that block. |
| --- | --- |

Notice the syntax for sending a message to our timer object:

```
gLoopTimer.Reset();
```

Since the **gLoopTimer** object was created directly as a variable, we can send the Reset() message using the dot operator, just as if we were accessing a field of a struct. We will more often refer to objects using pointers to them, in which case we will send the message using the arrow (->) operator, as we saw on line 31 of Listing 6-5. We will discuss these options in detail in the next section.

## ▶ Building the Program

If you have a C++ compiler and a Macintosh sitting in front of you, you might want to try this program yourself. In that case, you also need a "make" file. The TinyBenchmark.make file that we used is shown in Listing 6-6.

| By the Way ▶ | The easy way to try all the samples in this book is to have purchased the version of the book that includes the disk. If you have that disk, you will find it contains all the code for these samples, ready to use. If you did not buy the disk with the book, you can order it separately using the coupon in the back of the book. If you prefer to type the code, please type carefully since C++ is case-sensitive. |
| --- | --- |

Listing 6-6. The TinyBenchmark.make file

```
1: # Copyright 1990 © David A. Wilson. All Rights Reserved.
2:
3: # ===== define variables ===============================
4: AppName = TinyBenchmark
5:
6: CPlusOptions =  -mf
7:
8: LinkOptions =  -mf ∂
```

```
 9:                    -w  ∂
10:                    -c 'MPS ' ∂
11:                    -t 'MPST'
12:
13:
14: ObjectFiles = "{AppName}".cp.o
15:
16: # ===== link the tool ====================================
17: "{AppName}" ƒ "{AppName}".make  {ObjectFiles}
18:     Link {LinkOptions}  ∂
19:         "{Libraries}"Stubs.o ∂
20:         "{CLibraries}"CRuntime.o ∂
21:         {ObjectFiles} ∂
22:         "{Libraries}"Interface.o ∂
23:         "{CLibraries}"StdCLib.o ∂
24:         "{CLibraries}"CSANELib.o ∂
25:         "{CLibraries}"Math.o ∂
26:         "{CLibraries}"CInterface.o ∂
27:         "{CLibraries}"CPlusLib.o ∂
28:         "{Libraries}"ToolLibs.o ∂
29:         "{Libraries}"ObjLib.o  ∂
30:         -o "{AppName}"
31:
32: # ===== compile the modules ============================
33: {AppName}.cp.o  ƒ  {AppName}.make  "{AppName}".cp
34:     CPlus {CPlusOptions}  "{AppName}".cp
```

MPW make files are quite strange. Their purpose is to describe dependencies between your various program files, so that the MPW Make tool can decide which files to reprocess when you make a change to any of your source files. Make files have their own programming language and syntax. We will describe a few of the features of our make file.

Lines 1, 3, 16, and 32 begin with the comment delimiter, #. This comments to the end of the line.

You can define a string as a local variable by assigning something to the string, as shown on lines 4, 6, 8, and 14. To use one of these variables, it must be enclosed in curly braces. For example, we define the variable *AppName* to be equal to TinyBenchmark on line 4, and then use it as {AppName} on line 14. To be more precise, we used it as "{AppName}". The double quotes are needed in cases where the variable represents a file name or path name that might contain spaces.

The -mf C++ compiler option on line 6 means we want to use Multi-Finder temporary memory during the compile step. This allows us to allocate only 1.5 MB for the MPW shell, and still have enough memory to compile large C++ programs, provided the computer has at least 4 MB of RAM available for the combination of MPW and MultiFinder.

| Warning ▶ | We do not recommend using C++ and MacApp with less than 4 MB of RAM, and suggest that you will be happier with 5 to 8 MB. Virtual memory under System 7.0 can provide part of this, but you will probably still want at least 4 MB of real memory. |
|---|---|

Lines 8-11 show the definition of the *LinkOptions* variable. The strange "∂" character (Option-d) is the key to this definition. It is a special MPW quotation mark character that hides the next character (the carriage return) from the Make tool. This means that Make thinks that all of the link options are on one line, which is necessary since a carriage return terminates the execution of a command in an MPW file. The -w option on line 9 tells the linker to suppress non-fatal linker warnings. The -c option on line 10 sets the program's creator name to 'MPS', the creator used by all MPW files. The -t option on line 11 sets the file type to be 'MPST', the type used by all MPW tools.

Lines 17 and 33 are dependency lines that use the *f* (Option-f) character. Lines 17-30 mean that the application "depends on" the make file and the object files that are output by the compiler. If any of those files have changed since the last build, then a new version of the program must be created by linking together all the object and library files.

Lines 33 and 34 mean that the object file produced by the compiler depends on the make file and the C++ source file. If either of these change, then we must recompile the source file by calling the CPlus script, which in turns calls the CFront tool, which then calls the C compiler.

After you have created the source code file and the make file, you can build the tool by choosing the Build… item from MPW's Build menu, and filling in the resulting dialog with the program name, TinyBenchmark. This is shown in Figure 6-4. After the build process is finished, execute the tool by placing the cursor on the line with the program name and pressing Enter.

## ▶ The Results

The results of running this TinyBenchmark MPW Tool on a Macintosh II (16 MHz 68020 processor) are shown below:

```
Loops = 1000000
Ticks = 121
μsec/Loop = 2.01667

Loops = 1000000
Ticks = 268
μsec/Loop = 4.46667
```

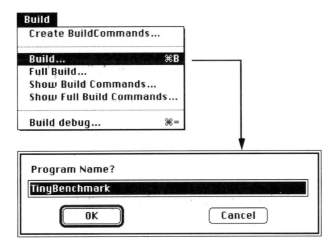

Figure 6-4. Building the program

What do these results mean? It means that the extra overhead due to a function call is the difference between the two final numbers, that is, about 2.5 microseconds. Is that important? Not in most cases. For example, consider a hypothetical, ordinary non-object-oriented program that might require 100 function calls to respond to the user clicking the mouse down in the menu bar. If you used subroutines, as opposed to coding everything inline, the user would face an extra delay of 250 microseconds, which is 0.00025 seconds. Most of us can wait that long without becoming bored.

On the other hand, if you were to carry out a complex math calculation involving the same computation 1,000,000 times, then the function call overhead would amount to an extra 2.5 seconds. This could be a problem in some circumstances.

Since we all take the overhead of function calls for granted, perhaps you are wondering why we even bothered to measure them. Apart from the fact that this showed a simple way to build an MPW tool, we did it mainly as a way to sneak up on a question that we hear from many programmers. As they evaluate whether to switch from procedural to object programming, they sometimes become concerned about performance and ask, "What is the overhead due to dynamic binding, when the program must look up methods at run-time?" We will use a somewhat more elaborate version of our benchmark program in the next section to measure that overhead. We will also use this new benchmark program to learn more about C++ and the wide variety of objects available.

## ▶ Benchmark, a More Elaborate Program

This second benchmark program uses the same **TTimer** class, but uses a more elaborate **TLoopTimer** subclass to do more extensive tests. The Benchmark tool creates objects of various kinds, and then tests the speed of method lookup by sending a message to one of these objects.

### ▶ Program Structure

The class diagram for the program is shown in Figure 6-5.

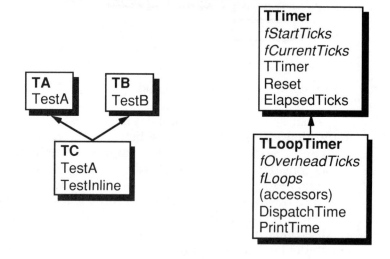

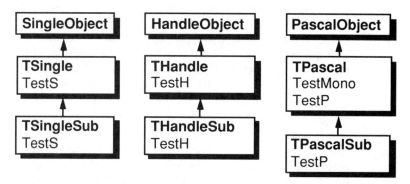

Figure 6-5. The class diagram for the Benchmark program

## ▶ Static and Dynamic Allocation of Objects

**TA** and **TB** are C++ version 2.0 base classes, each with no superclass. C++ objects can be allocated *directly* or *dynamically*. Direct allocation means that you can access the object directly by its variable name. If defined by a global variable, these are called static objects. If defined locally to a function, they are called automatic objects. Dynamic allocation means that the object is allocated on the heap (that is, in free store). If you create a C++ object dynamically, it is created as a nonrelocatable block accessed through a pointer. The following code shows how each kind of object can be allocated, and then sent a message:

```
TA anObject;        // direct allocation as a variable
anObject.TestA();  // send message

TA *anObjectPtr = new TA;    // dynamic allocation on the heap
anotherObject->TestA();      // send message
```

Notice that dynamic objects must be allocated with the **new** function. Note also that static or automatic objects are sent a message with the "." operator, analogous to accessing a field of a struct, while dynamic objects use the "->" operator to dereference the pointer to the object before sending the message. We will discuss allocating objects in more detail later in this chapter.

**By the Way ▶** Object Pascal objects are always allocated dynamically; in C++, you have a choice. Why does C++ offer this choice? For the same reason that C++ has many more features than Object Pascal: to allow you to optimize your code size and/or performance. As you will see, dynamically allocated objects can have more performance overhead. On the other hand, dynamically allocated objects generally allow more efficient use of memory because you have explicit control over when objects are created and deleted.

**TC** is a class that uses multiple-inheritance to inherit methods from both classes **TA** and **TB**. It overrides the **TestA** method inherited from superclass **TA**. It also has a special **TestInline** method for high-performance method lookup using the inline capabilities of C++. We will describe this usage in detail below.

**SingleObject**, **HandleObject**, and **PascalObject** are special base classes that represent Apple-only extensions to C++. They allow better performance in certain cases, and they allow your C++ programs to access classes defined in Object Pascal (that is, the MacApp class library). You will not find these classes in non-Apple versions of C++.

**SingleObject** represents the kind of objects defined in C++ version 1.2 from AT&T. Subclasses of **SingleObject** provide somewhat better performance than normal C++ classes, but you cannot use multiple-inheritance with them. **TSingle** and **TSingleSub** are subclasses defined in our Benchmark program to test this special base class. Instances of these classes can be allocated directly or as pointer-based dynamic objects on the heap, using the same code we saw for normal C++ objects.

**HandleObject** is a class whose objects must be allocated dynamically, as relocatable blocks on the heap accessed by a handle (which you will recall is a pointer to a pointer). Subclasses of **HandleObject** cannot use multiple-inheritance, but they do allow more efficient use of Macintosh memory than subclasses of **SingleObject**. **THandle** and **THandleSub** are subclasses we define in our Benchmark program to test **HandleObject** behavior.

| By the Way ▶ | On operating systems with demand-paged virtual memory, such as Apple's A/UX implementation of UNIX, you have a very large logical address space. You therefore do not have to worry about fragmenting memory, even with thousands of pointer-based objects. However, the Macintosh O/S, using Finder or MultiFinder (even with System 7.0), gives your application a fixed, relatively small physical address space — typically in the range of 384 KB to a few megabytes. In this smaller world, heap fragmentation can waste valuable memory, so relocatable handle-based objects are often the best choice. |
| --- | --- |

**PascalObject** is the last special class added by Apple. As the name implies, it behaves like a class defined in Object Pascal, with exactly the same kind of relocatable, handle-based objects and the same kind of method lookup tables. Just as in Object Pascal, multiple-inheritance is not allowed. **PascalObject** provides a base class in C++ from which the MacApp class **TObject** can be derived. With this nice technique, you can access all the classes defined in MacApp, since they are all subclasses of **TObject**. In the Benchmark program, we test the behavior of these kinds of classes with the **TPascal** and **TPascalSub** classes.

The following code shows how instances of **HandleObject** or **PascalObject** object can be allocated, and then sent a message:

```
THandle *aHandle;   // really a handle
aHandle->TestH();   // send message

TPascal *aPascalHdl; // really a handle
aPascalHdl->TestP(); // send message
```

| Important ▶ | We must write our code as if Pascal objects were pointer-based, even though they are actually handle-based. The C compiler does an extra dereference behind the scenes. Do you care about this extra dereference? Normally you will not. The only thing to keep in mind is that handle-based objects are often moved by the Macintosh's Memory Manager routines, so you have to be careful about using instance variables in situations where the associated object may be moved. We will show examples of where you have to be careful as we examine real MacApp programs in later chapters. |
|---|---|

## ▶ Defining the Test Class

Although the class diagram looks complicated, almost all of the classes are trivially simple. In fact, the complete program fits into these three very small files:

- Classes.h — the header file that defines all 9 classes (about 95 lines of code).
- Classes.cp — the implementation of the 14 methods (150 lines of code).
- Benchmark.cp — the main program that creates and uses the objects (125 lines of code).

| Important ▶ | It is generally a good idea to divide even small programs into multiple files. A common approach is to place all the class definitions in a header file, and the method implementations in a corresponding ".cp" file. You can then write your main program in its own ".cp" file. The main program usually creates, initializes, and uses one or more instances of these classes to perform some useful task.

As your program grows in size, you may even find it best to place each class definition in its own header file, and each class's methods in a separate .cp file. This makes it harder to write the make file, but it simplifies version control using a source code management system such as MPW's Projector. |
|---|---|

Since the classes in this program are very small, we defined all of them in the single header file "Classes.h". The part of this file that defines the classes we wish to test is shown in Listing 6-7.

Listing 6-7. Definitions for the classes to be tested

```
 1: //==============================================================
 2: class  TA {
 3: public:
 4:     virtual void TestA(void);
 5: };
 6:
 7: //==============================================================
 8: class  TB {
 9: public:
10:     virtual void TestB(void);
11: };
12:
13: //==============================================================
14: class  TC : public TA, public TB {
15: public:
16:     virtual void TestA(void);                    // override
17:     void TestInline(void)        {gShort = 1;}   // inline
18: };
19:
20: //==============================================================
21: class  TSingle : public SingleObject{
22: public:
23:     virtual void TestS(void);
24: };
25:
26: //==============================================================
27: class  TSingleSub : public TSingle{
28: public:
29:     virtual void TestS(void);               // override
30: };
31:
32: //==============================================================
33: class  THandle : public HandleObject{
34: public:
35:     virtual void TestH(void);
36: };
37:
38: //==============================================================
39: class  THandleSub : public THandle{
40: public:
41:     virtual void TestH(void);               // override
42: };
43:
44: //==============================================================
45: class  TPascal: public PascalObject {
46: public:
```

```
47:     pascal void TestMono(void);
48:     virtual pascal void TestP(void);
49: };
50:
51: //=============================================================
52: class  TPascalSub: public TPascal {
53: public:
54:     virtual pascal void TestP(void);          // override
55: };
```

**TA** is a class defined on lines 2-5 to have one method, **TestA**. The **TestA** function takes no arguments, returns no function result, and is designated as virtual so that we can override it in a subclass. We will look at the code for this method shortly. Remember that each class definition is terminated by a semicolon, as shown on line 5.

**TB** is a similar class defined on lines 8-11.

**TC** is a class demonstrating multiple inheritance, as shown on line 14, where it inherits the **TestA** method from class **TA** and the **TestB** method from class **TB**.

## Inline Methods

One interesting aspect of class **TC** is the **TestInline** method defined and implemented on line 17. As its name implies, it is defined inline, meaning that the code for the body of the method is shown in curly brackets right after the method definition. This code may (at the compiler's option) be directly substituted in place by the compiler whenever you call this function, as if it were a macro substitution using #define. The inline definition is better than a macro, however, for two reasons. First, type checking is performed to insure that an inline function is called with the correct arguments. Second, the function is bound to the class just like any other method.

An advantage to using inline functions is that they remove the overhead for a function call. A good use of inline functions is for accessing instance variables, for example. Inline functions are not useful if the function is very complicated. One reason is the compiler will not substitute complicated functions inline (the compiler always has the option of ignoring your suggestion to make a function inline). Another reason is that the object code for the inline function is duplicated each time it is called, which expands the overall code size.

In addition, if you declare a virtual function inline, the compiler will usually not be able to substitute the text at compile time because it must defer polymorphic method lookup until run time. For this reason, we don'at recommend using virtual inline functions.

| Warning ▶ | Non-virual inline functions provide speed at the expense of code reusability. Use non-virual inline functions only when you are absolutely sure that you need every microsecond of performance, and you are sure that no one will ever want to override the method in a subclass. |

**TSingle** is defined as a subclass of Apple's **SingleObject** class on lines 21-24. A subclass, **TSingleSub**, is defined on lines 27-30. Notice that we override the **TestS** method of class **TSingle** (line 23) in the subclass **TSingleSub** (line 29). In Object Pascal, you would have to use the keyword OVERRIDE in the subclass method, but there is no corresponding keyword in C++. To override a method, you simply define another version of it.

| Warning ▶ | The lack of an OVERRIDE keyword can lead to subtle bugs, because the CFront preprocessor cannot warn you if you accidentally override a method from a superclass. It is important to know about all the methods you inherit from your superclasses before you define new methods in a subclass. The best way to know what you inherit is to use a code browser such as MacApp's Mouser. We will describe Mouser in Chapter 11. |

**THandle** is defined on line 33 to be a subclass of Apple's **HandleObject** class. It is followed by the definition for the class **THandleSub**.

**TPascal** is defined to be a subclass of Apple's **PascalObject** class on line 45. As we mentioned, **PascalObject** is particularly important because it is the hook that allows C++ programmers to use, and subclass from, the great MacApp class library. Notice that we have defined two methods for the class **TPascal**. We override the **TestP** method in the class **TPascalSub**, while the **TestMono** method is not overridden. This latter method is known as a monomorphic method, because it is never overridden. This has an effect on method lookup for Pascal objects, as we shall see below.

### ▶ The Test Methods

Before we examine the timer classes, let's look at the implementation of the methods for the classes we will test. Each test method is essentially the same, with two typical ones shown in Listing 6-8.

Listing 6-8. Typical test methods

```
1: // ===============================================================
2: void
3: TC::TestA(void)              // override
4: {
5:     gShort = 1;
6: }
7:
8: // ===============================================================
9: void
10: TSingle::TestS(void)
11: {
12:     gShort = 1;
13: }
14:
```

Notice on lines 3 and 10 that we must precede the function name with the class name followed by the "::" scope-resolution operator. Without **TC::** preceding the function name, the compiler would think you were writing an ordinary function rather than a method (also known as a member function). The global variable *gShort* was defined in the header file to be of type short, that is, a 16-bit integer. Assigning the integer 1 to this variable is the only work that our test methods do, as shown on lines 5 and 12.

Notice on lines 6 and 13 that the methods are not terminated by a semicolon. Another detail to remember is that we list the function result preceding the method name on lines 2 and 9. We do not, however, use the keyword virtual that we used in the class definitions for these methods.

Now that you have seen the simple test classes, we can examine the timer classes that do the real work, allowing us to measure the speed of the program.

## ▶ The Timer Classes

We described the **TTimer** class in the previous discussion of the Tiny-Benchmark program. In this sample, we again subclass it to provide methods that are specific to the needs of this more elaborate set of tests. The new version of the subclass **TLoopTimer** is defined in Listing 6-9.

Listing 6-9. The TLoopTimer class definition

```
 1: class TLoopTimer : public TTimer {
 2: private:
 3:     long    fOverheadTicks;    // for loop without message send
 4:     long    fLoops;            // number of loops
 5:     virtual double DispatchTime(long messageTicks);
 6: public:
 7:     virtual void SetOverhead(long loopTime);
 8:     virtual long GetOverhead(void);
 9:     virtual void SetLoops(long loops);
10:     virtual long GetLoops(void);
11:     virtual void PrintTime(char* labelPtr);
12: };
```

**TLoopTimer** is defined as a subclass of **TTimer** on line 1.

On Line 3, we define an instance variable called *fOverheadTicks*. It stores the results of a measurement that results from making ordinary function calls; that is, calls that are not bound to an object. This overhead will be subtracted from the results of making virtual method calls to determine the extra time required when sending messages. The **GetOverhead** and **SetOverhead** accessing functions to read or modify this variable are defined on lines 7 and 8.

**Important ▶**

Your code will be more maintainable if an object's variables are not read or modified by any other object. In other words, you should keep the variables private, and only access them by sending the object a message. By using so-called *accessing methods* or *accessors* to isolate the rest of your program from the details of your variables, you are free to modify the name or type of an instance variable without breaking other parts of your program.

On line 4, we define *fLoops*, with its accessing methods **SetLoops** and **GetLoops** defined on lines 9 and 10. The *fLoops* variable simply stores the number of times in our test loop that we sent a message to an object.

We define the method **PrintTime** on line 11. It will be called after a timing test has been run. This method performs some calculations using the instance variables defined for this class, and displays the result in an MPW text window. It uses the private method **DispatchTime** defined on line 5. This method is defined to be private since it should not be used by clients of this class. It is intended to be used only by the **PrintTime** method.

## ▶ TLoopTimer Methods

The **TLoopTimer** subclass in this program is similar to the version used with the TinyBenchmark program described earlier in the chapter. It has four accessing methods to insure hiding of its instance variables, and two methods for performing calculations and displaying the results. These are shown in Listing 6-10.

Listing 6-10. TLoopTimer Methods

```
 1: // ===========================================================
 2: void
 3: TLoopTimer::SetOverhead(long loopTime)
 4: {
 5:     fOverheadTicks = loopTime;
 6: }
 7:
 8: // -----------------------------------------------------------
 9: long
10: TLoopTimer::GetOverhead(void)
11: {
12:     return (fOverheadTicks);
13: }
14:
15: // -----------------------------------------------------------
16: void
17: TLoopTimer::SetLoops(long loops)
18: {
19:     fLoops = loops;
20: }
21:
22: // -----------------------------------------------------------
23: long
24: TLoopTimer::GetLoops(void)
25: {
26:     return (fLoops);
27: }
28:
29: // -----------------------------------------------------------
30: double
31: TLoopTimer::DispatchTime(long messageTicks)
32: {
33:     long netTicks = messageTicks - this->GetOverhead();
34:     double microSeconds = (netTicks / 60.0) * 1.0e6;
35:     return ( microSeconds / this->GetLoops() );
```

```
36: }
37:
38: // ------------------------------------------------------------
39: void
40: TLoopTimer::PrintTime(char* labelPtr)
41: {
42:     long totalTicks = this->ElapsedTicks();
43:     double netPerLoop = this->DispatchTime(totalTicks);
44:     double netPerFuntionCall = netPerLoop / 2.0;
45:     cout << form("%s%.1f\tµsec\n",
46:                 labelPtr,
47:                 netPerFuntionCall)
48:                 << flush;
49: }
```

The accessing methods **SetOverhead**, **GetOverhead**, **SetLoops**, and **GetLoops** are typical one-line methods shown in lines 1-27.

The *fLoops* instance variable is simply a convenient place to store the number of times each test loop is executed. The *fOverhead* variable stores the number of ticks that it takes to perform the calculation directly, i.e., without using any function call.

The **PrintTime** method is called to make the calculation and display the result. The method is shown on lines 39-49. It measures how long the loop took on line 42, translates this to the net time per function call using a call to **DispatchTime** on line 43, and displays the result on lines 45-49. We divide the result by 2 on line 44 because each loop will perform two test calculations for subtle reasons having to do with the **PascalObject** tests described below.

The use of the *cout* stream is a bit more complicated than we used in the last program. On line 45, we use the form function defined in the Stream.h header to format the output text and numbers. The formatting uses *%s* for a string and *%.1f* for a floating point number with one digit to the right of the decimal. These strings are similar to the formatting strings used in printf. The word "flush" on line 48 flushes the output buffer so the text appears immediately in the MPW window.

▶ Testing With a Main Program

The main program, Benchmark.cp, is shown in Listing 6-11. It is a more elaborate version of the TinyBenchmark program, with tests for many different combinations of function calls.

## Listing 6-11. The Benchmark.cp program

```
 1: #ifndef __Classes__
 2:     #include "Classes.h"
 3: #endif
 4:
 5: // ===========================================================
 6: TLoopTimer  gLoopTimer;
 7: long        gLoopMax;
 8:
 9: // ===========================================================
10: void
11: TestJSR(void)
12: {
13:     gShort = 1;
14: }
15:
16: // ================== main program ===========================
17: void main()
18: {
19:     cout << "Type loops; press enter\n";
20:     cin >> gLoopMax;
21:
22:     //-------------------------------------------------------
23:     gLoopTimer.Reset();
24:     for (long index = 0; index < gLoopMax; index++) {
25:         gShort = 1;
26:         gShort = 1;
27:         }
28:     long ticks = gLoopTimer.ElapsedTicks();
29:     cout << "direct ticks = " << ticks << "\n\n" << flush;
30:     gLoopTimer.SetOverhead(ticks);
31:     gLoopTimer.SetLoops(gLoopMax);
32:
33:     //-------------------------------------------------------
34:     TC aCObject;                      // static allocation
35:     gLoopTimer.Reset();
36:     for (index = 0; index < gLoopMax; index++) {
37:         aCObject.TestInline();
38:         aCObject.TestInline();
39:         }
40:     gLoopTimer.PrintTime("Inline\t\t\t");
41:
42:     //-------------------------------------------------------
```

```
43:     gLoopTimer.Reset();
44:     for (index = 0; index < gLoopMax; index++) {
45:         TestJSR();
46:         TestJSR();
47:         }
48:     gLoopTimer.PrintTime("JSR\t\t\t\t");
49:
50:     //----------------------------------------------------------
51:     TC bCObject;                       // static allocation
52:     gLoopTimer.Reset();
53:     for (index = 0; index < gLoopMax; index++) {
54:         bCObject.TestA();
55:         bCObject.TestB();
56:         }
57:     gLoopTimer.PrintTime("TC\t\t\t\t");
58:
59:     //----------------------------------------------------------
60:     TSingle aSingle;                   // static allocation
61:     gLoopTimer.Reset();
62:     for (index = 0; index < gLoopMax; index++) {
63:         aSingle.TestS();
64:         aSingle.TestS();
65:         }
66:     gLoopTimer.PrintTime("TSingle\t\t\t");
67:
68:     //----------------------------------------------------------
69:     TSingle  *aSinglePtr = new TSingle;    // pointer-based
70:     gLoopTimer.Reset();
71:     for (index = 0; index < gLoopMax; index++) {
72:         aSinglePtr->TestS();
73:         aSinglePtr->TestS();
74:         }
75:     gLoopTimer.PrintTime("TSinglePtr\t\t");
76:
77:     //----------------------------------------------------------
78:     THandle  *aHandle = new THandle;        // handle-based
79:     gLoopTimer.Reset();
80:     for (index = 0; index < gLoopMax; index++) {
81:         aHandle->TestH();
82:         aHandle->TestH();
83:         }
84:     gLoopTimer.PrintTime("THandle\t\t\t");
85:
86:     //----------------------------------------------------------
87:     TC *aCPtr = new TC;                     // pointer-based
88:     gLoopTimer.Reset();
```

```
 89:       for (index = 0; index < gLoopMax; index++) {
 90:           aCPtr->TestA();
 91:           aCPtr->TestB();
 92:           }
 93:       gLoopTimer.PrintTime("TCPtr\t\t\t");
 94:
 95:       //------------------------------------------------------------
 96:       TPascal *cPascal = new TPascal;          // handle-based
 97:       gLoopTimer.Reset();
 98:       for (index = 0; index < gLoopMax; index++) {
 99:           cPascal->TestMono();
100:           cPascal->TestMono();
101:           }
102:       gLoopTimer.PrintTime("TPascal(mono)\t");
103:
104:       //------------------------------------------------------------
105:       TPascalSub  *aPascalSub = new TPascalSub;   // handle-based
106:       gLoopTimer.Reset();
107:       for (index = 0; index < gLoopMax; index++) {
108:           aPascalSub->TestP();
109:           aPascalSub->TestP();
110:           }
111:       gLoopTimer.PrintTime("TPascal(same)\t");
112:
113:       //------------------------------------------------------------
114:       TPascal     *bPascal = new TPascal;          // handle-based
115:       TPascalSub *bPascalSub = new TPascalSub;   // handle-based
116:       gLoopTimer.Reset();
117:       for (index = 0; index < gLoopMax; index++) {
118:           bPascal->TestP();
119:           bPascalSub->TestP();
120:           }
121:       gLoopTimer.PrintTime("TPascal\t\t\t");
122: }
```

Some of the more interesting added features include those discussed in the next few paragraphs.

**Input with *cin*.** We have been using *cout* to display data to the user. The input stream object, *cin*, is used on line 20 to get a number from the user. This is similar to the use of the common C function scanf.

**The baseline test** is carried out with the direct calculations of lines 25 and 26. The time required to execute these two assignment statements is computed on line 28, displayed on line 29, and saved for reference in the timer object on line 30. The number of loops executed is saved on line 31.

**Inline method** calls are tested with the code on lines 34-40. An instance of the class **TC** is directly allocated on line 34, and sent the Test-Inline message on lines 37 and 38. Inline methods result in a direct code substitution at compile time, so this code should be equivalent to that in lines 25 and 26.

**Normal** function calls are tested on lines 43-48.

**Directly allocated C++** objects are sent messages on lines 51-57, with tests on pointer-based normal C++ objects shown on lines 69-75. These are the kind of objects available in any implementation of C++ based on AT&T version 2.0.

**An automatic instance of TSingle** is tested on lines 60-66, with a pointer-based version tested on lines 69-75. These are the types of objects originally defined in CFront version 1.2. They cannot make use of multiple inheritance, and consequently use a simpler method lookup mechanism. Apple has extended CFront 2.0 to support these older-style objects by adding the base class **SingleObject**.

We tested instances of other Apple extensions to C++ in the other parts of the program.

**Handle-based** objects are tested on lines 78-84. Remember that these look like pointer-based objects in the code.

Objects based on the Apple class **PascalObject** are tested three different ways, since the Object Pascal method lookup mechanism has several ways to optimize the performance.

Sending messages to instances of two different **PascalObject** subclasses is shown on lines 113-121. A similar test is shown on lines 105-111, but here the messages are sent to instances of the same class. Would you expect the results to change? It turns out that performance improves, because of a run-time optimization performed by the Object Pascal method dispatch mechanism. When a message is sent to an object, the address of the method is cached. If the same message is sent again, the method lookup time is reduced by using the address in the cache.

One final test for the use of monomorphic methods is shown on lines 96-102. The **TestMono** method is not overridden in a subclass, which means that the function call can be treated as a subroutine call, rather than using the normal method lookup mechanism. This optimization is performed by the MPW Linker provided the "-opt on" option is added to the link options in the make file.

## ▶ Building the Program

The complete make file is shown in Listing 6-12. The changes to the previous make file include the linker optimization option on line 12, the additional file to link with on line 14, and the additional compile dependencies on lines 33-37.

Listing 6-12. The Benchmark.make file

```
 1: # Copyright 1990 © David A. Wilson. All Rights Reserved.
 2:
 3: # ===== define variables ========================================
 4: AppName = Benchmark
 5:
 6: CPlusOptions =  -mf
 7:
 8: LinkOptions =  -w  ∂
 9:                -c 'MPS '  ∂
10:                -t 'MPST'  ∂
11:                -mf  ∂
12:                -opt on
13:
14: OBJECTS = "{AppName}".cp.o   Classes.cp.o
15:
16: # ===== link the tool ========================================
17: "{AppName}" ƒƒ "{AppName}".make  {OBJECTS}
18:    Link {LinkOptions}  ∂
19:        "{Libraries}"Stubs.o ∂
20:        "{CLibraries}"CRuntime.o ∂
21:        {OBJECTS} ∂
22:        "{Libraries}"Interface.o ∂
23:        "{CLibraries}"StdCLib.o ∂
24:        "{CLibraries}"CSANELib.o ∂
25:        "{CLibraries}"Math.o ∂
26:        "{CLibraries}"CInterface.o ∂
27:        "{CLibraries}"CPlusLib.o ∂
28:        "{Libraries}"ToolLibs.o ∂
29:        "{Libraries}"ObjLib.o  ∂
30:        -o "{AppName}"
31:
32: # ===== compile the modules ==============================
33: {AppName}.cp.o  ƒ {AppName}.make  "{AppName}".cp Classes.h
34:     CPlus {CPlusOptions}  "{AppName}".cp
35:
36: Classes.cp.o  ƒ "{AppName}".make  Classes.cp Classes.h
37:     CPlus {CPlusOptions}  Classes.cp
```

▶ Test Results

The results of a typical test of the Benchmark sample on a Macintosh II are shown below:

```
Type loops; press enter
2000000
direct ticks = 242
```

| | | | | | |
|---|---|---|---|---|---|
| Inline | 0.0 | μsec | THandle | 4.7 | μsec |
| JSR | 2.5 | μsec | TCPtr | 5.8 | μsec |
| TC | 2.9 | μsec | TPascal(mono) | 3.4 | μsec |
| TSingle | 2.9 | μsec | TPascal(same) | 11.4 | μsec |
| TSinglePtr | 5.3 | μsec | TPascal | 18.3 | μsec |

A typical test on a Macintosh Plus yielded performance that was usually about four times slower. Here are a few observations about the meaning of these results:

- Inline functions have no overhead; they are faster than ordinary function calls and any type of method dispatching. They should be used judiciously, however, since virtual (polymorphic) functions are not substituted inline for dynamically allocated objects.

- Performance usually is better for directly allocated objects than for pointer- or handle-based ones. This is true because the compiler will usually optimize these method calls into ordinary function calls, since the class of the object is known at compile time. The most common case of using pointer-based C++ version 2 objects provides relatively slow method lookup, in addition to having the potential for causing heap fragmentation.

- C++ method dispatching is generally faster than that of Object Pascal, but under optimum conditions, Object Pascal is quite competitive. Object Pascal method calls and method dispatch tables take up less space, however.

Benchmark was written as an excuse to show you the choices you have for creating objects and sending messages to them. Please do not worry about performance issues, and start writing bad code to save a few microseconds. Even in the worst cases, you would have to send thousands of messages before the user could even perceive a delay. You can usually get excellent performance through good program and algorithm design, and still write maintainable, reusable code.

## ▶ Back to Accounting

We started this long chapter with a simple "accounting" program called Money, written in Object Pascal. We used this program to introduce the basic syntax for defining classes and subclasses, creating objects, and sending messages. We then developed a simple C++ program, Tiny-Benchmark, that showed how to accomplish similar tasks in C++. We followed this with the more elaborate Benchmark program designed to show you the syntax for multiple inheritance, and how to use the interesting Apple-only classes like **HandleObject** and **PascalObject**. These programs illustrate many of the important features of the language, but there are some things we have not yet described.

### ▶ What We Still Have to Do

For example, we haven't shown you how to call a method that you have overridden. We also haven't shown a real example of an overloaded function. Most importantly, our samples so far have not shown how to use two of the most common techniques of object programming:

- using objects that collaborate with each other
- using polymorphism to enhance code maintainability

We will cover these techniques in a new, slightly fancier version of the Money program, this time written in C++.

### ▶ The New, Improved Money Program

Imagine that our accounting program has been translated from Object Pascal into C++, so that we have the classes **TCustomer** and **TForeign-Customer** to represent the people with whom we do business. Let us further imagine that we want to extend the program to model a simple order entry system in which a customer calls in to place an order for a certain quantity of our product. For simplicity, we'll assume we only make one product, and that a customer only places one order. After the customer places an order, we want to print an invoice that contains the address of the customer and the amount they owe us.

The design for such a program could use a **TOrder** class that is specialized to represent the details of a given customer order. Each order object would then need to be associated with the customer object that placed the order. In this case, we could view the **TOrder** class as a collaborator of the **TCustomer** class. When it is time to print the invoice, we can have the customer object's methods print the address, while the collaborating order object's methods compute the amount the customer owes us. Furthermore, we need some way to keep track of our customers, especially if we have more than a few. One way to handle this is to define a **TDataBase** class that can manage a collection of customer objects. This is the program design we will use, which leads to the class diagram shown in Figure 6-6.

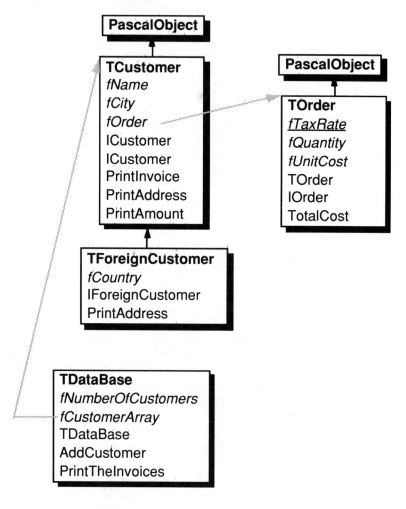

Figure 6-6. Class diagram for the C++ version of Money

The **TCustomer** class is defined to be a subclass of **PascalObject**, and has **TForeignCustomer** as its subclass. We will also define the **TOrder** class to be a subclass of **PascalObject**. We use Pascal objects so that we can describe some of the features available to this type of object. These are important because all of the classes defined in the MacApp library are indirect subclasses of **PascalObject**. Since we are not required to use only Pascal objects, we choose **TDataBase** be a normal C++ version 2.0 class, with no superclass. Before we look at the actual code, we should become familiar with the basic design of these classes, as shown in the class diagram.

The **TOrder** class keeps track of the information about a particular order in its *fQuantity* and *fUnitCost* variables. It also uses *fTaxRate*, a static variable that is shared among all order objects, to compute the total tax on the order. This result is, of course, returned by the **TotalCost** method. The only other methods are the constructor, **TOrder**, and the equivalent initialization method, **IOrder**. We include both of these so you can see two different ways to initialize the object. In a real program, you would be likely to use one or the other, but not both. In MacApp programs, we will use initialization methods, as we will discuss in later chapters.

The **TCustomer** class has the expected *fName* and *fCity* instance variables, but adds a third variable, *fOrder* that will hold a pointer to its collaborating order object. It is extremely common for one object to keep a pointer to another object. Why would that be valuable? For the simple reason that you cannot send a message to another object unless you have a reference to it. A customer object will keep a pointer to the order object so it can send it a message asking for the total cost of the order.

A number of messages were added to the **TCustomer** class since our original design, including:

We had one **ICustomer** method in the Object Pascal sample, but we have two versions in the C++ sample. By using an overloaded function, we can see two different ways to initialize the customer's variables.

**PlaceOrder** tells the customer object which order object to query for information about the current order.

**PrintInvoice** prints the customer's address and amount owed, plus a cute little border (it is not necessary that the border be cute — yours may differ).

**PrintAmount**, a method used by **PrintInvoice**, prints the amount owed.

| By the Way ▶ | Using instance variables to hold pointers to other objects allows us to design the program with distributed responsibilities: the **Customer** object processes information about the customer, while details of the last order are managed in a separate class. This is a common design technique that allows us to define two relatively small, specialized classes, rather than one larger class. This divide-and-conquer technique generally makes it easier to write and debug the methods. It also makes it more likely that some of your code can be reused in future projects. This and other design strategies are discussed in Chapters 4 and 21. |
|---|---|

We purposely kept the **TDataBase** class simple for this example. It merely keeps a fixed-size array of references to customer objects in the variable *fCustomerArray*. It has a simple constructor method (**TDataBase**), a method to add another customer to the data base (**AddCustomer**), and an iterator method (**PrintTheInvoices**) that will tell each customer in the data base to print its own invoice.

If this doesn't sound terribly impressive, wait until you see the special capability of this class to handle a mixed collection of customers. The power of polymorphism allows this class to deal with a mixed list of domestic and foreign customers with no special handling or switch statements. In fact, if you choose to define other subclasses of **TCustomer**, the **TDataBase** class can also handle those, with no changes whatsoever. We will explain this in detail below.

## ▶ Using Multiple Source Files

This program also provides an opportunity to show you how to handle a program composed of multiple source files. We defined the order class and its methods in one pair of files, the customer classes in another pair, and the database class in a third. This structure allows better version control, and keeps the source files from becoming too large. However, it requires that you carefully structure the make file with the correct dependencies, a process we will describe later in the chapter. Multiple files also require the use of #include statements to keep the compiler happy, and careful use of #define statements to minimize recompile times after modifications are made to a file. The relationships among the seven source files used in the Money sample are shown in Figure 6-7.

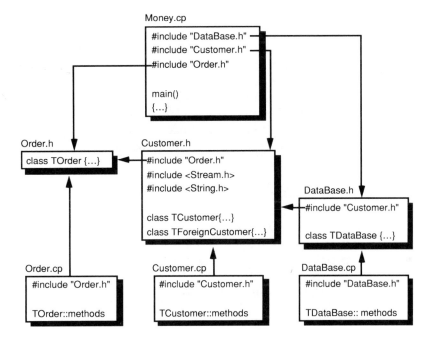

Figure 6-7. The Money program's seven source files

The source files are as follows (the files with the .cp suffix are the ones that are actually compiled):

- Money.cp — the main program. It includes references to the three header files that define the classes we use.
- Order.h — the header file that defines the class **TOrder**.
- Order.cp — the methods for the class **TOrder**. This file includes a reference to the Order.h header file.
- Customer.h — the header file for the **TCustomer** and **TForeignCustomer** classes. Notice that this file includes references to other header files needed by the class definition and method implementation.
- Customer.cp — the methods for the customer classes.
- DataBase.h and DataBase.cp — the files for the **TDataBase** class.

| By the Way ▶ | A careful study of Figure 6-7 reveals that the main program has more #include statements than necessary. All you really need to include is a reference to the DataBase.h header file, since that file references Customer.h which in turn references Order.h. We nevertheless recommend using the redundant #include statements, since they make it easier for the reader of the Money.cp file to know where to look for the appropriate class definitions. The header files will not be included more than once because of the use of conditional includes with #ifndef, as shown below. |
|---|---|

## ▶ The Main Program

The easiest way to understand the programming details of this sample is to see how instances of these classes are created and used in the main program. That file, Money.cp, is shown in Listing 6-13.

Listing 6-13. The main Money.cp file

```
 1: #ifndef __DataBase__
 2:     #include "DataBase.h"    // class TDataBase
 3: #endif
 4:
 5: #ifndef __Customer__
 6:     #include "Customer.h"    // class TCustomer, TForeignCustomer
 7: #endif
 8:
 9: #ifndef __Order__
10:     #include "Order.h"       // class TOrder
11: #endif
12:
13:
14: // ============================================================
15:     TDataBase    gDataBase;        // static allocation of object
16:     TCustomer    *gCustomer;       // pointer-based object
17:     TOrder       *gOrder;          // pointer-based object
18:
19: // ================== main program ============================
20: void main()
21: {
22:     gOrder = new TOrder(0);                // unit cost
23:     gOrder->IOrder(24.99, 4);              // unit cost, quantity
24:     gCustomer = new TCustomer;
25:     gCustomer->ICustomer("Mrs. Smith", "Cupertino");
26:     gCustomer->PlaceOrder(gOrder);
27:     gDataBase.AddCustomer(gCustomer);
```

```
28:
29:     gOrder = new TOrder(4.25, 2);        // unit cost, quantity
30:     gCustomer = new TCustomer;
31:     gCustomer->ICustomer("Mr. Jones", "New York", gOrder);
32:     gDataBase.AddCustomer(gCustomer);
33:
34:     gOrder = new TOrder(79.99);          // unit cost; quan = 1
35:     TForeignCustomer* aForeignCustomer = new TForeignCustomer;
36:     aForeignCustomer->IForeignCustomer(
37:                         "Mr. Nakajima", "Tokyo", "Japan")
38:     aForeignCustomer->PlaceOrder(gOrder);
39:     gDataBase.AddCustomer(aForeignCustomer);
40:
41:     gDataBase.PrintTheInvoices();
42: }
```

Lines 1-11 reference the header files that define our classes, with the #ifndef statements used to insure that no header file is included more than once.

Line 15 allocates a global instance of **TDataBase**. This static allocation means that **gDataBase** is the object, rather than being a pointer to the object. When this allocation occurs at the beginning of program execution, the **TDataBase** constructor method will be called automatically.

Lines 16 and 17 define pointers we will use to reference customer and order objects. Can you guess why these were not allocated directly? The reason is that the customer and order classes are subclasses of **Pascal-Object**, so we must define them as pointer-based (although they are actually handle-based), and allocate them with the "new" operator.

An order object is created and initialized on line 22, using the **TOrder** constructor method, passing zero as the unit cost of the order. Notice that if the constructor method takes arguments, you pass them in parentheses, just as with any other function. In case you would prefer not to define a constructor, you can initialize an object by sending it an initialization message (see line 23).

A customer object is created and initialized on lines 24 and 25.

| By the Way ▶ | Although you can use constructors in MacApp programs, we will not use them in our MacApp samples later in the book. Since the MacApp classes themselves are written in Object Pascal, those classes cannot use constructors. There is consequently no advantage in our using them when we subclass the MacApp classes.

Our technique when writing MacApp programs will be to create objects with the "new" operator, and then initialize them by sending them an explicit initialization message. This works well in all circumstances. |

| Warning ▶ | There is something missing between line 24, where we create the object, and line 25, where we send it a message. Our code makes the assumption that nothing can go wrong. What could happen, of course, is that allocation of the object could fail because we are out of memory. We really should check for that every time an object is allocated with the new operator. We will do this in all of our MacApp programs, and you should do it in any programs that you write that are for any purpose other than a quick test or rapid prototype. |
| --- | --- |

We associate the order with the ordering customer using the **Place-Order** message on line 26, and then the customer is added to the database with the **AddCustomer** message on line 27.

## Using Default Arguments

Another order and customer are created on lines 29-32, but the code is subtly different. If you compare lines 22 and 29, you will notice that the constructor can be passed either one argument or two. That is because it is defined with a default second argument. If you do not pass a number for the quantity ordered, it will default to one unit. We will examine the code for this shortly.

## Using Overloaded Functions

You can see another difference by comparing lines 25 and 31. These use two different versions of the **ICustomer** message, each with a different argument list. This is an example of using function overloading. You can call whichever version you like, and the compiler will choose the correct one based on the number and type of arguments that you pass. If you want to use overloaded functions with a subclass of PascalObject, then those functions must be non-virtual.

Lines 34-39 show another order and customer being created and used. The only difference is that we create an instance of the subclass **TForeignCustomer** instead of **TCustomer**. This new customer can still be added to the database, however.

Finally, the code on line 41 carries out the important task of printing the invoices for each customer. This code is maintainable because there is nothing in this main program that tells us how the customers are stored in the database, and nothing that tells us how invoices are printed. We can nevertheless write a program that uses these classes to do real work. The implementation details are hidden within the private instance variables, and in the implementations of the methods.

## ▶ Program Results

Before we look at those implementation details, we can look at the result of compiling and running the program, shown in the following simple text display.

```
$$$$$$$$$$$$$$$$$$$$$$$$$
Mrs. Smith
Cupertino
You owe us: $106.96
$$$$$$$$$$$$$$$$$$$$$$$$$

$$$$$$$$$$$$$$$$$$$$$$$$$
Mr. Jones
New York
You owe us: $9.10
$$$$$$$$$$$$$$$$$$$$$$$$$

$$$$$$$$$$$$$$$$$$$$$$$$$
Mr. Nakajima
Tokyo
Japan
You owe us: $85.59
$$$$$$$$$$$$$$$$$$$$$$$$$
```

## ▶ Details of the TOrder class

The **TOrder** class definition is in the file Order.h, as shown in Listing 6-14.

Listing 6-14. The Order.h file defines the **TOrder** class

```
 1: #ifndef __Order__          // only process this file once
 2:     #define __Order__
 3:
 4: //=============================================================
 5: class TOrder: public PascalObject {
 6: private:
 7:     static  float    fTaxRate;
 8:             short    fQuantity;
 9:             float    fUnitCost;
10: public:
11:     TOrder(float unitCost, short quan = 1);     // constructor
12:     virtual void IOrder(float unitCost, short quan = 1);
13:     virtual float TotalCost();
14: };
15:
```

```
16: //================================================================
17: #endif    __Order__
```

The preprocessor statements on lines 1, 2, and 17 enable you to prevent the definitions in this file from being processed more than once during a compile. To do this, you must be sure to conditionally include this file as shown below:

```
#ifndef __Order__
   #include "Order.h"
#endif
```

We use this construct, for example, in the main program on lines 9-11. Line 7 defines a static variable that will be shared among all instances of **TOrder**. We will describe this code in detail in the next section. Line 11 defines the constructor **TOrder** with two arguments. By defining the second parameter to have a default value of 1, you will not have to pass the second value if you are happy with the default. This technique can reduce the typing that you need to do, but could make your code more confusing to read, so use it with care.

The corresponding methods for the TOrder class are defined in the Order.cp file, are shown in Listing 6-15.

Listing 6-15. The Order.cp file has the TOrder methods

```
 1: #ifndef __Order__
 2:    #include "Order.h"          // class definitions
 3: #endif
 4:
 5: // ============================================================
 6: float TOrder::fTaxRate = 0.07;  // static variable
 7:
 8: // ============================================================
 9: TOrder::TOrder(float unitCost, short quan)
10: {
11:     fQuantity = quan;
12:     fUnitCost = unitCost;
13: }
14:
15: // ------------------------------------------------------------
16: void
17: TOrder::IOrder(float unitCost, short quan)
18: {
19:     fQuantity = quan;
```

```
20:      fUnitCost = unitCost;
21: }
22:
23: // ----------------------------------------------------------
24: float
25: TOrder::TotalCost()
26: {
27:      return fQuantity * fUnitCost * (1.0 + fTaxRate);
28: }
```

### Allocating a Static Variable

The only unusual code is shown on line 6, where we allocate and initialize the static variable, *fTaxRate*, defined for the class **TOrder**. Although this variable was defined to be private, you must nevertheless allocate storage for it this way. Notice the use of the class name and the "::" scope-resolution operator to tell the compiler which static variable we are allocating. Why do we need to allocate storage for a static variable explicitly? Because it is not associated with any particular instance of the class; therefore, no object has storage allocated for it. We must warn you that after you allocate a static variable this way, it reverts back to being private. Thereafter, it can only be accessed by the methods of the **TOrder** class (as we do, for example, on line 27).

## ▶ Details of the Customer Classes

The **TCustomer** and **TForeignCustomer** classes are defined in the Customer.h file shown in Listing 6-16.

Listing 6-16. The Customer.h file defines the **TCustomer** class

```
1: #ifndef __Customer__          // only process this file once
2:     #define __Customer__
3:
4: #ifndef __STREAM__
5:     #include <Stream.h>        // for cout
6: #endif
7:
8: #ifndef __STRING__
9:     #include <String.h>        // for strcpy
10: #endif
11:
12: #ifndef __Order__
```

```
13:      #include "Order.h"            // for class TOrder
14: #endif
15:
16: //===========================================================
17: class  TCustomer: public PascalObject {
18: private:
19:      char     fName[256];
20:      char     fCity[256];
21:      TOrder   *fOrder;
22: public:
23:      void ICustomer(const char *name, const char *city);
24:      void ICustomer(const char *name, const char *city,
25:                                TOrder* theOrder);   // overload
26:      virtual void PlaceOrder(TOrder *anOrder);
27:      virtual void PrintAddress();
28:      virtual void PrintAmount();
29:      virtual void PrintInvoice();
30: };
31:
32: //===========================================================
33: class TForeignCustomer: public TCustomer{
34: private:
35:      char     fCountry[256];
36: public:
37:      virtual void IForeignCustomer(const char *name, const char
                                                           *city,
38:                                const char *country);
39:      virtual void PrintAddress();                // override
40: };
41:
42: //===========================================================
43: #endif  __Customer__
```

Other necessary header files are referenced on lines 4-14. We must include Order.h since the **TCustomer** class has an instance variable of type **TOrder**. We include String.h and Stream.h because some of the methods use functions from those libraries (specifically strcpy and cout).

| Warning ▶ | You must type identifiers such as __STREAM__ exactly as shown in the #ifndef macros. C++ is case-sensitive, and any error in typing these identifiers would cause the #ifndef test to fail. This would cause the header file to be included more than once. In some cases, this will lead to compiler errors, while in other cases the compiler would merely take longer than necessary to process the headers.<br><br>The only way to know how to spell the identifiers correctly is to look in each header file's #define statement. Examples of these files include line 2 of Listings 6-14 and 6-16. For the C++ support file headers, such as Stream.h, look in the "CIncludes" folder, which is in the "Interfaces" folder, inside your "MPW" folder. |
|---|---|

### Function Overloading

Lines 23 and 24 show two versions of the **ICustomer** message. The second version takes a pointer to an order object as an argument, so that you can initialize all of the customer's instance variables at once. If you use the simpler version that only takes name and city as arguments, then you must explicitly send the **PlaceOrder** message to associate an order with a customer. Why have two versions? In this example, we added them only to show you how to handle them. There are cases, however, when it actually makes your code simpler to have the flexibility to pass different sets of arguments.

The code for these two methods is shown on lines 5-23 of Listing 6-17, which describes the Customer.cp file.

Listing 6-17. The Customer.cp file has the **TCustomer** methods

```
1: #ifndef __Customer__
2:     #include "Customer.h"            // class definitions
3: #endif
4:
5: // =============================================================
6: void
7: TCustomer::ICustomer(const char *name,
8:                      const char *city)
9: {
10:     strcpy(fName, name);
11:     strcpy(fCity, city);
12:     fOrder = NULL;      // no object yet
13: }
```

```
14:
15: // ----------------------------------------------------------
16: void
17: TCustomer::ICustomer(const char *name,
18:                            const char *city,
19:                            TOrder* theOrder)
20: {
21:     this->ICustomer(name, city);
22:     fOrder = theOrder;
23: }
24:
25: // ----------------------------------------------------------
26: void
27: TCustomer::PlaceOrder(TOrder *anOrder)
28: {
29:     fOrder = anOrder;    // reference to another object
30: }
31:
32:
33: // ----------------------------------------------------------
34: void
35: TCustomer::PrintAddress()
36: {
37:     cout << this->fName << "\n";
38:     cout << fCity << "\n";
39: }
40:
41: // ----------------------------------------------------------
42: void
43: TCustomer::PrintAmount()
44: {
45:     float    amount;
46:
47:     amount = fOrder->TotalCost();
48:     cout << form("%s%.2f", "You owe us: $", amount)
             << "\n";
49: }
50:
51: // ----------------------------------------------------------
52: void
53: TCustomer::PrintInvoice()
54: {
55:     cout << "\n$$$$$$$$$$$$$$$$$$$$$$$$$$\n";
56:     this->PrintAddress();
57:     this->PrintAmount();
58:     cout << "$$$$$$$$$$$$$$$$$$$$$$$$$$\n" << flush;
```

```
59: }
60:
61: // ==============================================================
62: void
63: TForeignCustomer::IForeignCustomer(const char *name,
64:                                    const char *city,
65:                                    const char *country)
66: {
67:     this->ICustomer(name, city);
68:     strcpy(fCountry, country);
69: }
70:
71: // --------------------------------------------------------------
72: void
73: TForeignCustomer::PrintAddress()          //override
74: {
75:     inherited::PrintAddress();
76:     cout << fCountry << "\n";
77: }
```

## ▶ Overriding a Method

Line 39 of Listing 6-16 defines a **PrintAddress** function that is an override of the **PrintAddress** function defined on line 27. The method for **TCustomer::PrintAddress** is shown on lines 34-39 of Listing 6-17, while the overridden method is shown on lines 72-77. The most important line of code is line 75.

The "inherited" keyword performs the same function as in Object Pascal; it tells the compiler to call the **PrintAddress** method from the superclass of **TForeignCustomer**. You must be careful, however, to use this syntax only for subclasses of **PascalObject**. Standard C++ does not define this keyword; it is an Apple-only extension. To reuse code from a method you have overridden, you will normally explicitly use the class name, as follows:

```
TCustomer::PrintAddress();
```

This syntax would also have worked in our example, but we prefer to use "inherited" when possible, since it adapts automatically to changes in the class hierarchy.

▶    Printing an Invoice Using Method Lookup

The **TCustomer::PrintInvoice** method shown on lines 52-59 of Listing
6-17 illustrates some of the power of object programming. Consider executing the following line of code:

```
gCustomer->PrintInvoice();
```

To see what will happen, we must now think like a compiler. When
the customer object receives the message, method execution begins on
line 55, where we print a border. On line 56, we must perform method
lookup, based on the class of "this". Since we sent the message to an instance of class **TCustomer**, "this" is a pointer to a customer object. We
must therefore find **TCustomer::PrintAddress**, so we go to line 35 and
continue execution. When we return to line 57, we again use "this" to
perform method lookup, and jump to the **TCustomer::PrintAmount**
method. Finally, we print another border and we are done.

In this thought experiment, all of the methods that executed belonged
to the **TCustomer** class. Imagine that we wrote these methods in January, 1991. Now imagine that we added the **TForeignCustomer** subclass
in February 1991, and overrode the method **PrintAddress** as shown in
the Money sample. What happens when we send the same message to
an instance of the subclass, as shown in the following line of code?

```
gForeignCustomer->PrintInvoice();
```

If you send the **PrintInvoice** message to an instance of **TForeignCustomer**, the method lookup process will first look for a **TForeignCustomer::PrintInvoice** method. Since there is none, execution will begin at
the **TCustomer::PrintInvoice** method, just as before. We print the border on line 55, but on line 56 we encounter "this", which is now a
pointer to an instance of **TForeignCustomer**. The method lookup process therefore transfers control to the **TForeignCustomer::PrintAddress**
method beginning on line 73. The inherited keyword on line 75 calls
**TCustomer::PrintAddress**, after which execution continues on line 76.
We then return to line 57, where the "this" keyword still refers to an instance of **TForeignCustomer**. We look for a **TForeignCustomer::PrintAmount** method, and do not find one. We therefore use the
**TCustomer::PrintAmount** method, just as before.

Did you follow all that? If so, you can now answer the question as to
what changes we had to make to the **TCustomer** methods to adapt to
the **TForeignCustomer** subclass. The answer is none! This is really
quite remarkable. In printing the invoice for a foreign customer object,
we were able to reuse all of the code from the **TCustomer** class written
one month earlier. Through the magic of method lookup, the old code

dynamically adjusted to call the new **PrintAddress** method when necessary, while the rest of the time calling the older methods. We hope you are as impressed as we are.

## ▶ Details of the DataBase Class

The last section gave an example of using polymorphism (multiple versions of the **PrintAddress** method) and method lookup to reuse code efficiently. The class **TDataBase** makes use of method lookup for one of its simple but powerful methods. The database class also depends on special type checking that is used with objects in C++.

The simple **TDataBase** class is defined in the DataBase.h header file shown in Listing 6-18.

Listing 6-18. The DataBase.h file defines the **TDataBase** class

```
 1: #ifndef __DataBase__          // only process this file once
 2:     #define __DataBase__
 3:
 4: #ifndef __Customer__          // for class TCustomer
 5:     #include "Customer.h"
 6: #endif
 7:
 8: // ============================================================
 9: const short kMaxNumber = 10;
10:
11: // ============================================================
12: class TDataBase {
13: private:
14:     short       fNumber;
15:     TCustomer   *fCustomerArray[kMaxNumber];
16: public:
17:     TDataBase();
18:     virtual void AddCustomer(TCustomer *aCustomer);
19:     virtual void PrintTheInvoices();
20: };
21:
22: // ============================================================
23: #endif __DataBase__
```

The *fCustomerArray* variable on line 15 is defined as an array of 10 pointers to customer objects. The *fNumber* variable on line 14 keeps track of how many customers are in the database, that is, how many slots in the array are filled. In a real accounting program, we would not use a fixed-size array, but it was the simplest thing to use here.

By the Way ▶ MacApp provides a number of collection classes that could be used in this situation, including the **TList** class that we will describe in detail in Chapter 17.

## ▶ Type Checking for Objects

Notice that the array is defined to hold pointers to instances of the class **TCustomer**. Also notice that we defined the **AddCustomer** message to take a pointer to an instance of **TCustomer** as an argument. This is the way in which we will add customers to the database. This looks fine, unless you consider the code in the main program, on line 39 of Listing 6-13. There we passed a reference to a foreign customer as the argument to the **AddCustomer** method and the compiler did not complain.

The rule for type checking in C++ (and, incidentally, for Object Pascal) is as follows: If the compiler expects a reference or pointer to a certain class, it will accept a reference or pointer to a subclass. If we define a method to expect an instance of **TCustomer**, it will accept an instance of **TForeignCustomer**.

The methods for the database class are found in the DataBase.cp file shown in Listing 6-19.

Listing 6-19. The DataBase.cp file with the **TDataBase** methods

```
 1: #ifndef __DataBase__
 2:     #include "DataBase.h"              // class definitions
 3: #endif
 4:
 5: // ================================================================
 6: TDataBase::TDataBase()
 7: {
 8:     fNumber = 0;
 9: }
10:
11: // ----------------------------------------------------------------
12: void
13: TDataBase::AddCustomer(TCustomer *aCustomer)
14: {
15:     fCustomerArray[fNumber++] = aCustomer;
16: }
17:
18: // ----------------------------------------------------------------
19: void
20: TDataBase::PrintTheInvoices()
21: {
22:     for (short index = 0; index < fNumber; index++)
23:         fCustomerArray[index]->PrintInvoice();
24: }
```

The most interesting code is the use of polymorphism and dynamic binding in the *for* loop on lines 22-23 of the **PrintTheInvoices** method. This loop sends the PrintInvoice message to every object in the database. If the object is a customer, the **TCustomer::PrintInvoice** method will be called, but if the object is a foreign customer, the **TForeignCustomer::PrintInvoice** method will be called. We get this behavior without needing switch statements, since we instead have the power of dynamic binding.

The nice thing about this code is that it could be used, unchanged, if we decided to define other subclasses of **TCustomer** or **TForeignCustomer**. If we were to add a class **TFrenchCustomer**, the database would happily accommodate it.

A final comment about the **PrintTheInvoices** method. When the DataBase.cp file is compiled, the compiler cannot determine what objects will be stored in the database, so it cannot determine which **PrintInvoice** methods will be called. This code requires the dynamic binding (method lookup) mechanism. Without this capability, we could not write the program this way, which means we could not write it this way in traditional C or Pascal.

## ▶ Reusability and Maintainability

The Money sample shows that subclassing is a powerful technique for customizing your program, a technique that allows you to continue to reuse code as you add new features. Polymorphism and dynamic binding allow you to write code that can be used unchanged as new features are added.

## ▶ Building the Program

The last piece of the puzzle is the Money.make file shown in Listing 6-20.

Listing 6-20. The Money.make file

```
1: # ================================================================
2: AppName = Money
3:
4: CPlusOptions =  -mf
5:
6: LinkOptions =  -w  ∂
7:                -c 'MPS '  ∂
8:                -t 'MPST'  ∂
```

```
 9:                     -mf  ∂
10:                     -opt on
11:
12: OBJECTS = "{AppName}".cp.o  Order.cp.o  Customer.cp.o  DataBase.
              cp.o
13:
14: # ================================================================
15: "{AppName}" ƒ "{AppName}".make  {OBJECTS}
16:     Link {LinkOptions} ∂
17:         "{Libraries}"Stubs.o ∂
18:         "{CLibraries}"CRuntime.o ∂
19:         {OBJECTS} ∂
20:         "{Libraries}"Interface.o ∂
21:         "{CLibraries}"StdCLib.o ∂
22:         "{CLibraries}"CSANELib.o ∂
23:         "{CLibraries}"Math.o ∂
24:         "{CLibraries}"CInterface.o ∂
25:         "{CLibraries}"CPlusLib.o ∂
26:         "{Libraries}"ObjLib.o ∂
27:         "{Libraries}"ToolLibs.o ∂
28:         -o "{AppName}"
29:
30: # ================================================================
31: {AppName}.cp.o ƒ "{AppName}".cp  Order.h  Customer.h  DataBase.h
32:     CPlus  {CPlusOptions}  "{AppName}".cp
33:
34: DataBase.cp.o ƒ DataBase.cp  DataBase.h  Customer.h
35:     CPlus  {CPlusOptions}  DataBase.cp
36:
37: Customer.cp.o ƒ Customer.cp  Customer.h  Order.h
38:     CPlus  {CPlusOptions}  Customer.cp
39:
40: Order.cp.o ƒ Order.cp  Order.h
41:     CPlus  {CPlusOptions}  Order.cp
```

With this file in the same folder as your source code, you can build and test the Money sample using MPW's Build menu, just as we have done before.

## ▶ What Kind of Objects Get Created?

Earlier in this chapter, we described an Object Pascal sample program that used the class **TCustomer** and its subclass **TForeignCustomer**, as described by the class diagram in Figure 6-1. As a final discussion of polymorphism, consider the following C++ code fragment:

```
1: TCustomer aCustomer;
2: aCustomer.PrintAddress();
3: TCustomer aCustomerPtr = new TForeignCustomer;
4: aCustomerPtr->PrintAddress();
```

What kinds of objects get created? Line 1 clearly allocates aCustomer as an instance of class **TCustomer**. When this code is compiled, there is really no need for method lookup on line 2, so a smart C++ compiler will generate a direct function call to **TCustomer::PrintAddress**. In this case of directly allocating an object, the overhead of method lookup may be avoided even for virtual functions, although the C++ language specification does not guarantee that this opitmization will happen.

We know that aCustomer is an instance of **TCustomer**, but what about the aCustomerPtr variable on line 3? Does it point to an instance of **TCustomer** or **TForeignCustomer**? In fact, line 3 actually creates an instance of class **TForeignCustomer**. Let's see why.

If you were a C++ compiler (it's just a dream — do not get your hopes up), here is how you would parse line 3. The left side of the expression tells you that aCustomerPtr will be a pointer to an instance of class **TCustomer** — *or to one of its subclasses!* As we will see in the next section, type checking for objects is relaxed over that for normal types. Therefore C++ will happily allow a pointer to an instance of a class to actually point to an instance of a subclass. Since the left side merely allocates a 32-bit address, you do not yet know what class it references.

The right side of the expression creates an instance of class **TForeign-Customer**. How can you tell? Because that is the name of the class that follows the *new* operator. Will the compiler optimize the code in line 4 to a direct function call? Not if **PrintAddress** is defined as a virtual function. When dealing with pointers to objects, the compiler knows that the type that the pointer was declared to be can be deceiving, so it waits until runtime to see what type of object was really created on the heap. Ordinary method lookup at runtime will then lead to the **TForeignCus-tomer::PrintAddress** method being called.

| Important ▶ | The class name that follows the *new* operator determines the actual class of a dynamically-allocated object, no matter what type its pointer is defined to be. |
| --- | --- |

## ▶ C++ Review

Some of the many features of C++ include

- Define classes using the keyword class.
- Variables and methods (members) can be defined to be private, protected, or public. Private members can only be accessed from methods of that class.
- Variables can represent an object directly, or be a pointer or a handle to the object.
- Pointer or handle-based objects are created with the new operator.
- Messages to directly allocated objects are sent using dot notation, while messages to pointer or handle-based objects use the arrow operator.
- "this" is defined in any method to be a pointer to the object that received the message.

## ▶ Summary

In this chapter, we have dissected one Object Pascal program (Money), and three C++ programs (TinyBenchmark, Benchmark, and Money). You have seen programs that define classes and subclasses, create and initialize objects, and send them messages. You have seen the syntax for defining constructor methods, for overloading methods, for overriding methods, and for reusing code that has been overridden. We have described how to manage multiple source code files, and how to make use of polymorphism.

We could not cover all the features of C++ in this chapter, but we have described the features necessary to understand the MacApp programs that we will be studying in later chapters. Of course, you cannot write a MacApp program without becoming familiar with the rich MacApp class library, which brings us to Chapter 7.

# 7 ▶ The MacApp Class Library

MacApp is a large library of classes that you will use, and modify through subclassing, to create your program. This requires becoming familiar with the overall function and behavior of the major classes, which are the subject of this chapter. Furthermore, you will need to become familiar with the most important methods in great detail, knowing exactly when they are called by MacApp and what to do when you override them. That will be discussed in the next chapter. In this chapter, we'll describe important variables and methods in general terms, so that you can get a feeling for the overall properties without getting bogged down in the details.

## ▶ Why Do We Need MacApp?

MPW C++, even without the MacApp class libraries, allows you to write the modular, reusable, maintainable code that is promised by the object programming techniques that we have been describing. What does MacApp bring to the party? To answer that, consider the process of writing a program without it. When you write an application for the Macintosh, you have to support the standard Macintosh user interface, which features menus and windows, and which is driven by events such as mouse clicks and keystrokes. In fact, you might start with a checklist of desired, and often required, features including

- handling events and the main event loop
- displaying graphics and text on the screen

- displaying complex dialogs
- handling simple text editing
- supporting resizable, draggable windows with scroll bars
- storing data in memory and on disk
- handling Undo
- supporting the Clipboard
- printing

Without MacApp, a good object programmer would first write a large collection of classes to provide these features. You would have methods to handle the main event loop, manipulate windows, handle update events, print things, respond to menu items, and so forth. Since every normal application needs to do these things, it would be terribly wasteful for each of us to have to invent classes to support exactly the same things. Therefore, the MacApp programming team at Apple has done this for us with MacApp.

MacApp provides elaborate classes to provide the behavior that is common to all normal Macintosh applications. Many of the important classes are shown in the hierarchy in Figure 7-1; the classes that we will discuss in detail are filled with gray. In this chapter, we'll describe the major functions of each class and describe the properties in terms of important variables and methods. In later chapters, you will learn about these classes in detail and see how the methods are used — and overridden — in typical programs.

There are about seventy-five classes provided with MacApp, but you will not have to work directly with most of them in a typical application. There are certain classes that you will have to become quite familiar with and that you will usually subclass. These include

- **TObject** — provides useful methods that are inherited by all other classes.
- **TEvtHandler** — superclass of all classes that handle events.
- **TApplication** — handles the main event loop and runs the program.
- **TDocument** — manages user data storage in memory and on disk.
- **TView** — displays information in windows and to the printer.
- **TList** — manages collections of other objects.
- **TCommand** — supports Undo for user operations and supports mouse tracking when the user must draw and manipulate visual items.

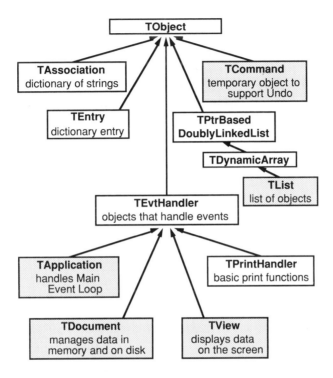

Figure 7-1. The top of the MacApp class hierarchy

There are many other classes, primarily specialized views, that you will come to know and love; we will discuss them later in the chapter.

Some of the MacApp classes are quite complicated. For example, the **TWindow** class has twenty-two instance variables defined directly, with fourteen more inherited from its superclass, **TView**. It also has thirty-eight direct methods and inherits many more from its superclass. In fact, MacApp provides over twelve hundred methods, which is clearly a good news/bad news situation. The good news is that you will not have to write these twelve hundred methods yourself in the course of creating a MacApp program. The bad news is that you have to learn how find and use the most important MacApp methods among the documentation for all of them. Providing you with that information will be the task of much of the rest of this book.

Remember that you need not understand how all twelve hundred methods work to use MacApp; you certainly need to know the details of only about twenty of these methods to write a simple application using MacApp. We will now describe some of the major classes.

## ▶ TObject: Everyone's Ancestor

All the MacApp classes shown in Figure 7-1 are subclasses of **TObject** — the ultimate abstract superclass. **TObject** does not have enough interesting behavior ever to be useful by itself, hence the term abstract (that is, you will never create an instance of **TObject**). It is nevertheless very useful, because it provides valuable methods that are inherited by all of its subclasses. Because of this, you should always define your new classes to be either a subclass of **TObject** or of one of its subclasses, even though C++ does not require a class to have a superclass.

The behavior of an object is determined by its variables and its methods. You should think of the variables as private to that object and usually of interest only to the programmer who has to write methods for that class. The messages of course are important to anyone who needs to use that class.

### ▶ Variables

**TObject** has no instance variables. This means that making one of your classes a subclass of **TObject** should cause no concern, because there are no inherited variables to add excess baggage to your subclass.

### ▶ Methods Often Used by Your Application

**Clone** copies the object and its variables exactly; it is used rarely but is extremely valuable at times.

### ▶ Methods Often Overridden in Your Application

**Fields** shows fields in the Debug and Inspector windows; it is usually overridden.
**Free** throws away the object and related data structures; it is often overridden.

## ▶ TEvtHandler: Handling Menu Items, Mouse Clicks, and Typing

This is another abstract class, so you will never make an instance of **TEvtHandler**. However, you will depend heavily on classes that inherit properties from this class. These subclasses include most of the classes upon which you will build your program, including **TApplication,**

**TDocument**, **TView**, and **TStdPrintHandler**. MacApp defines each of these to be a subclass of **TEvtHandler** so they can each inherit the useful variables and methods described in the following sections.

▶ Variables

*fIdleFreq* is the minimum time interval, in ticks (1/60 second), between times that the object's **DoIdle** method should be called by MacApp. This method enables you to implement background processing under MultiFinder or to carry out some repeated operation such as blinking a block cursor in a communications program.

*fNextHandler* refers to the next event handler object in a linked list called the target chain. MacApp normally manages this list for you. For example, in a text editing program with an active text view, MacApp will normally set the *fNextHandler* variables for each object such that the target chain begins with your view, and then goes to your document and application objects (with stops along the way for other minor event handlers). MacApp will then send certain messages to all objects in this chain. These messages include the DoIdle message, the DoKey-Command message if the user types a key, or the DoMenuCommand message if the user chooses a menu item. MacApp keeps a global variable called *gTarget* that points to the beginning of the target chain. We'll discuss the target chain in more detail in later chapters.

▶ Methods Often Used

**DoCreateViews** creates views from view resources designed in View-Edit. We'll describe these in Chapter 14.

▶ Methods Often Overridden

**DoIdle** operations are to be carried out when there is no event pending.

▶ **TApplication: Running the Main Event Loop**

You will always subclass **TApplication** and each program will have one, and only one, instance of that subclass. You will only use one application object because only one is needed to run the main event loop; Macintosh programs always have only one main event loop.

| By the Way ▶ | All Macintosh applications are driven by events. Events include user actions such as clicking the mouse button or typing a key on the keyboard. Other events are generated by the operating system, including window update events that signal your program to redraw the contents of a window, and window activate events that signal your program to change a window's appearance if it is brought to the front or placed behind another window. |
|---|---|
| | Macintosh applications are structured to idle in a program loop called the main event loop, waiting for events to be processed and then responding to each event as it happens. As a result, the user is in command, rather than being a servant to the program — which often happened with programs written for earlier computer systems. |

The application object is responsible for running the main event loop, which means it gets information about each event from the operating system, analyzes it, and sends messages to other objects to carry out appropriate actions. This means that the application object handles many common menu items and mouse clicks. It also must create document objects on demand (this is because document objects are often created when the only existing object is your application object). This will be discussed in more detail later in the chapter.

## ▶ Instance Variables

There are only a few variables defined directly in **TApplication**, but the following global variables are managed by the application class. For the sake of modularity, many of these could have been defined as instance variables of **TApplication**, but they were instead defined to be global to enhance the performance and convenience in accessing them. You will see these global variables occasionally used in the sample programs.

### Some Global Variables

| | |
|---|---|
| *gApplication* | reference the one application object |
| *gConfiguration* | record holding data about system being used (see below) |
| *gFinderPrinting* | Finder launching application just to print? |
| *gInBackground* | application is currently in background? |
| *gPrinting* | currently printing? |
| *gTarget* | first event handler to try for menus, and so on |
| *gZeroRect* | 16-bit rectangle of (0, 0, 0, 0) |
| *gZeroVPt* | 32-bit point of (0, 0) |
| *gZeroVRect* | 32-bit rectangle of (0, 0, 0, 0) |

The Configuration Record

The global variable *gConfiguration* is particularly interesting because it is a struct that contains information about the machine on which your application is currently running. It includes obviously useful Boolean fields like

    hasColorQD
    hasDesktopBus
    hasSCSI
    hasROM128K
    hasHFS
    hasHierarchicalMenus
    hasScriptManager
    hasStyleTextEdit
    hasSoundManager
    hasWaitNextEvent

MacApp uses these fields to determine, for example, whether to open a color window or a monochrome window whenever a window is created. This is necessary because some Macintosh models don't have the color QuickDraw extensions in their ROMS. An example of their use might look like this:

```
if (gConfiguration.hasColorQD)
   RGBForeColor(&anRGBColor);       // color QD
else
   ForeColor(redColor);            // "classic" QD
```

▶ Methods Always Used

**IApplication** initializes the menu bar and global variables.
**Run** runs the whole program.

▶ Methods Often Overridden

**DoIdle** governs idle actions not dependent on a single window or document.
**DoMakeDocument** creates a document object.
**DoMenuCommand** handles nonstandard items for the application.
**DoSetupMenus** enables and checkmarks those items.

These methods will be discussed in detail in the various programs that you will build in later chapters.

▶ **TDocument: Storing Information**

The **TDocument** class is responsible for storing user data in memory and for reading and writing document files to disk. You will make a subclass of **TDocument** for each type of document that you need on disk. (No **TDocument** subclass is needed if you are not storing information on disk.) In a simple text editing program, you might have only one class of documents, while a complicated spreadsheet program might need four or five subclasses of **TDocument**. Examples of programs with multiple document types are given in Chapter 10.

| By the Way ▶ | **Macintosh Disk Files** |
|---|---|

**Macintosh Disk Files**

All files stored on disk using the normal Macintosh operating system are tracked in the disk directory. The directory stores a number of pieces of information about each file, including

- file name
- creation date and time
- last modification date and time
- four-character code called the file type
- four-character code called the creator name, or signature
- information about the data fork
- information about the resource fork

The two most common types of files stored on your disk are applications and documents. Applications contain executable code and always have the file type 'APPL'. Documents are usually created by an application to store data. For example, the MPW Shell text editor creates documents of type 'TEXT', and graphics programs often create documents of type 'PICT'. Your program may use a custom document format, in which case you will use a unique file type — perhaps 'XYZ4'. All unique file types must be registered with Apple's Developer Services to avoid conflicts.

There are two parts to a disk file: the data fork and the resource fork. The data fork represents a normal random access data file, like one you would see on almost any computer. The resource fork holds resources that may include 'MENU', 'WIND', 'CODE', and many other structured types of information. The resource fork is unique to the Macintosh file system.

Document objects have other jobs besides managing data. In particular, they usually create the views and windows that display the data stored in the document. While the document is busy creating views, it may also create instances of **TStdPrintHandler** to print the views.

## ▶ Instance Variables

Most of these variables are managed by existing routines, so you won't have to worry about them. The few you might care about are underlined in the following list. All of the underlined variables are initialized with arguments passed to the **IDocument** method, as we shall see in later chapters. Instance variables include

| | |
|---|---|
| *fWindowList* | windows belonging to document |
| *fViewList* | views belonging to document |
| *fChangeCount* | changes since last Save |
| *fSavePrintInfo* | save Print info in data fork of disk file? |
| *fTitle* | file name |
| *fFileType* | file type |
| *fCreator* | creator ID |
| *fVolRefNum* | volume refNum |
| *fSaveExists* | disk file already exists on disk? |
| *fUsesDataFork* | store data in data fork? |
| *fUsesRsrcFork* | store resources in resource fork? |
| *fDataOpen* | data fork open all the time? |
| *fRsrcOpen* | resource fork open all the time? |

## ▶ Method Always Used

**IDocument** initializes variables.

## ▶ Methods Usually Overridden

**Free** frees windows, views, SELF, plus data stored in document.
**FreeData** frees data in document for Revert… menu item.
**DoMakeWindows** creates windows for views.
**DoMakeViews** creates views, print handlers (and windows if use view resource templates).
**DoMenuCommand** handles menu items specific to your document.
**DoNeedDiskSpace** calculates bytes needed for file.

**DoRead** reads from opened file.

**DoSetupMenus** enables and checkmarks menu items specific to this document.

**DoWrite** writes to opened file.

## ▶ TView: Displaying Information on the Screen

Macintosh programmers must be concerned with the user interface, which includes displaying data on the screen and providing ways for the user to interact with the display. The MacApp class responsible for both displaying information and responding to most user input is **TView**. Views display data in windows and send it to the printing graf-Port during printing. Views also handle mouse clicks in a view, usually handle typing of characters, and often handle menu items that involve manipulating data shown in a view.

| By the Way ▶ | All drawing on a Macintosh computer takes place in a graphics port, usually referred to as a *grafPort*. A grafPort is a complete drawing environment containing all the data QuickDraw and Color QuickDraw need to create and manipulate graphic images. Each window contains one grafPort. |
|---|---|

| By the Way ▶ | Since a basic principle of the Macintosh is WYSIWYG (What You See Is What You Get), you normally print by executing the same Quick-Draw graphics instructions to the printer device as you do the screen. MacApp supports this by calling the same view method (**Draw**) for printing as it does for screen display. |
|---|---|

Notice that **TView** is shown in Figure 7-1 to be a subclass of **TEvtHandler**. **TView** has many subclasses that are shown in Figures 7-2 through 7-4. Since the view classes include windows, scroll bars, and even push buttons, you can see that everything on the screen except menus and some alerts and dialogs are specialized kinds of views. We'll discuss many of these specialized views in later chapters. For example, we'll use the **TTEView** class to create a text editor in Chapter 15. We'll use many of the dialog-like items in Chapters 14 and 20.

An important property of a view is that it can be installed as the subview of another view. This means that a window (which is a type of view) will have one or more subviews inside it. In this way, you can easily assemble arbitrarily complicated windows. For example, Figure 7-6 shows a window with a number of subviews, including four TIcons, two TScrollBars, and one TSScrollBar. We'll describe MacApp's subview/superview architecture in detail in Chapters 13 and 14.

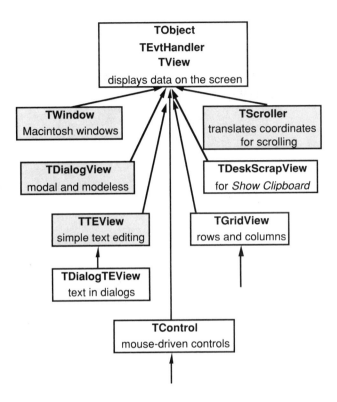

Figure 7-2. Some of the View classes

## ▶ Instance Variables

We'll describe these in more detail in Chapter 13, but here is a brief description of the variables:

| | |
|---|---|
| *fSuperView* | the superview (container view) of this view |
| *fSubViews* | a list of subviews of this view (NULL if none) |
| *fDocument* | the document that stores the data this view displays |
| *fLocation* | the top left corner relative to the superview |
| *fSize* | the width and height of this view |
| *fSizeDeterminer* | how the view width and height is determined |
| *fHLDesired* | current highlight state for window (see Chapter 8) |
| *fIdentifier* | four-character code used to identify subviews (see Chapter 14) |
| *fShown* | should view be drawn? |
| *fViewEnabled* | will view accept mouse clicks? |
| *fPrintHandler* | object that handles printing |

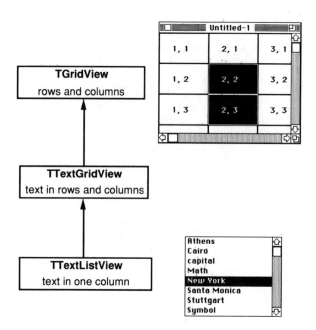

Figure 7-3. The **GridView** classes that handle one-and two-dimensional lists

## ▶ Methods Often Used

Only a few typical ones are listed. These and others are described in Chapters 8 and 13.

**Adorn** draws a border around the view.
**FindSubView** returns a reference to a view.
**ForceRedraw** forces the whole view to be redrawn.
**InvalidRect** forces part of the view to be redrawn.
**IView** initializes the variables when creating views by procedure.

## ▶ Methods Usually Overridden

Again, only a few are mentioned here. More detail will be given in later chapters.

**DoHighlightSelection** highlights selected items in the view.
**DoKeyCommand** responds to a keystroke.
**DoMenuCommand** responds to a menu item being chosen.

**DoMouseCommand** responds to a mouse click in the view.

**DoSetupMenus** enables and checkmarks menu items specific to this view.

**Draw** draws the view to the screen or printer.

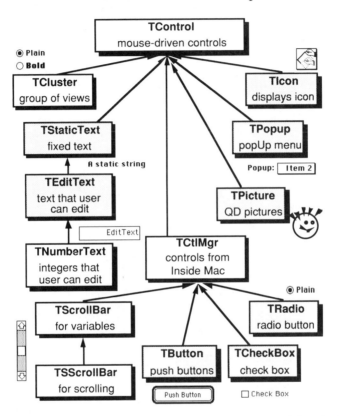

Figure 7-4. Mouse-operated subclasses of TControl

## ▶ Methods Sometimes Overridden

**DoChoice** determines the selected control in a dialog window.

**DoIdle** is called when no events are pending.

**DoSetCursor** changes cursor shape as it moves over view.

**IRes** initializes view made from a 'view' resource.

## ▶ TWindows

If you were to guess which things on the Macintosh screen were represented by objects, you would probably start with windows. The MacApp class responsible for window behavior is, logically enough, called **TWindow**. **TWindow** is a subclass of **TView**, which you might not guess. This merely means that an instance of **TWindow** inherits all the variables and methods defined for **TView**, so that a window is considered a view with extra features and behavior. Actually, you will not have to know very much about the **TWindow** class, since its default behavior is generally satisfactory. You will therefore rarely subclass it or even call window methods directly. Therefore, we will not describe any methods below, but we will mention a few of the variables.

| By the Way ▶ | If you have written software for the Macintosh using traditional techniques, you know that activating, dragging, zooming, and resizing windows does not happen automatically. In fact, much of your initial code in a Macintosh program involves managing windows. MacApp programs remove that burden because **TWindow** objects already know how to respond to messages to move, resize, zoom, and so forth. Furthermore, **TApplication** has event handling methods that send these messages to the window object as needed. Therefore, you can typically ignore the window handling totally and worry only about managing the views contained in the window. |
|---|---|

### ▶ Instance Variables

Some interesting **TWindow** instance variables are listed below. Most of these can be set in ViewEdit when you define your windows.

| | |
|---|---|
| *fWMgrWindow* | pointer to the Toolbox window record |
| *fResizeLimits* | minimum and maximum window size |
| *fTarget* | make referenced view object *gTarget* when window activated; important with ViewEdit (see Chapter 14) |
| *fTargetID* | four-character identifier for the target view |
| *fDoFirstClick* | activate window and handle mouse click on first click |
| *fHorzCentered* | center window on screen when created |
| *fVertCentered* | center window on screen when created |
| *fStaggered* | offset document windows as opened |
| *fForceOnScreen* | move on screen if last position was at edge of larger screen |

## ▶ Scrolling

One of the less intuitive classes is **TScroller**, which is responsible for scrolling your view when it is larger than the window. Consider the typical case of a large view, with part of it visible in the window, as shown in Figure 7-5. The scroller's job is to manage the scrollbars (which are instances of another view class, **TSScrollBar**) and to move the view relative to the window. (Of course, according to Albert Einstein, it is just as valid to say that the window moves relative to the view, but you get the idea.)

Scrollers usually work in conjunction with scrollbars, but not always. For example, the hand tool in the original MacPaint program permitted scrolling without scrollbars.

You might have noticed that MacApp provides two different classes of scrollbars. One class is the **TSScrollBar** class already mentioned which teams with scroller objects to manage scrolling a view in a window. However, if you want to use a scrollbar to adjust the value of a variable, such as the speech rate and pitch in the speech synthesis program shown in Figure 7-6, you would use an instance of **TScrollBar**.

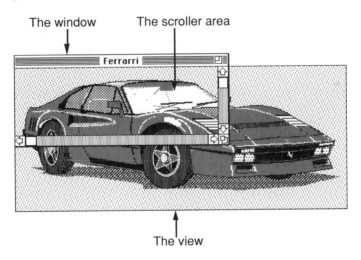

Figure 7-5. A window within a larger view

We do not elaborate on the classes **TSScrollBar** and **TScrollBar** because you will rarely modify or even directly instantiate these classes in your MacApp applications. **TSScrollBar**'s default behavior is generally acceptable without modification and **TScrollBar** is used only in the rare application that uses the scrollbar to control the value of a variable or a display.

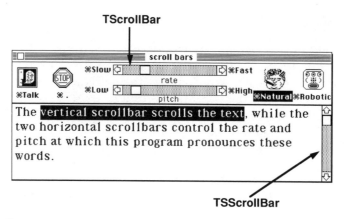

Figure 7-6. TScrollBar and TSScrollBar

## ▶ Dialogs

MacApp includes special dialog support using the MacApp view classes instead of using the Toolbox's Dialog Manager routines that are used by all other applications. Why not use the Dialog Manager? Because it is not flexible enough. For example, the Dialog Manager requires that all controls in a dialog window have text displayed in the same font, size, and style. MacApp does not limit you in this way. MacApp also allows any dialog to be in a resizable, scrollable window — something else that is not supported by normal dialogs. A third advantage is that you can use the same techniques to build dialogs you might use for any other window.

## ▶ View Review

As you have seen in Figures 7-2 through 7-4, MacApp provides about twenty-five view classes. You should become familiar with the ones in the following list, and use them whenever possible. Otherwise, you may find yourself reinventing the wheel by recreating a class that already exists. Remember, as an object programmer, your job is to reuse as much existing code as possible and do as little work as possible. Life does not have to be hard.

| Class | Typical use |
| --- | --- |
| **TView** | abstract superclass |
| **TWindow** | normal or dialog window |
| **TScroller** | provide scrolling in window |
| **TTEView** | large editable text block |
| **TDeskScrapView** | display TEXT or PICT on Clipboard |
| **TDialogView** | enclosing superview for dialog items |
| **TGridView** | tabular, spreadsheet-like display |
| **TTextGridView** | table of text items |
| **TTextListView** | list of text items (like a Standard File dialog) |
| **TControl** | mouse-operated views — rarely instantiated |
| **TCluster** | group of views — often with radio buttons |
| **TStaticText** | display fixed string in dialog |
| **TEditText** | fill-in-the-blank dialog item |
| **TNumberText** | fill-in-the-number dialog item |
| **TPicture** | display color or black-and-white QuickDraw picture |
| **TPopup** | popup menu |
| **TIcon** | display color or black-and-white icon |
| **TCtlMgr** | controls defined in *Inside Macintosh* (abstract class) |
| **TScrollBar** | volume, pitch, or speed control |
| **TSScrollBar** | for normal scrolling with TScroller |
| **TButton** | normal push button |
| **TCheckBox** | normal check box |
| **TRadio** | normal radio button |

# ▶ TList: Keeping Track of a Collection of Objects

We have introduced classes that have obvious importance like **TApplication**, **TDocument**, and **TView**. We now come to a class that does not sound very impressive: **TList**. All a list object does is manage a list of other objects. To be specific, a list really holds the object reference variables, so only objects can be in the list — not strings or numbers or records. As a data structure, a list behaves like a dynamic array, in that you start with an empty list and add objects as needed. What makes object programming special is that objects are not just data structures — they also include methods. The methods for **TList** elevate it from being a dumb data structure to an intelligent one. These include methods to access an object by an index into the list, methods to add and delete objects, and some really nifty methods to carry out a given operation on every object in the list. There is even a **TSortedList** subclass of **TList**, when you need to keep objects in a certain order.

You should not have to deal with the instance variables of **TList**, so we do not discuss them. You also will rarely have to subclass **TList**, so there are no methods that you commonly override. There are quite a few that you will use, including the following.

## ▶ Methods Often Used

**IList** initializes empty list.
**At** returns object at certain index.
**AtPut** replaces the object at a certain index.
**Delete** deletes an object from the list.
**Each** calls a function for each item in the list.
**First** returns first object in list.
**FirstThat** returns first object that satisfies some test.
**FreeAll** frees all objects in list but not list itself.
**FreeList** frees all objects in list and list itself.
**GetSize** returns the number of objects in list.
**InsertFirst** inserts object at beginning of list.
**InsertLast** inserts object at end of list.
**Last** returns last object in list.
**LastThat** returns last object that satisfies some test.
**SetEltType** defines class of object contained in the list, for debugging.

## ▶ TCommand: Supporting Undo

Command objects are temporary objects that carry out user requests — while storing information about the previous state so the user can Undo the operation if required. You will generally use many different subclasses of **TCommand** — one for each type of user action that you want to be undoable. These include

• typing characters
• mouse operations, such as drawing, dragging, and selecting
• menu items, such as Rotate and Delete

Command objects should be used when the user action will change data important enough to be stored in the document file on disk. They are also used when you must track mouse movement while the button is pressed. For example, you generally will not use a command object for something as simple as the user selecting a different tool in a palette of drawing tools. When the user clicks in the palette, you will just change the selection. On the other hand, if the user draws a new shape with that tool, you would want to use a command object to do the drawing, so that the user can choose Undo from the Edit menu to undo that drawing operation. You will, in fact, use command objects for tracking mouse operations, even when you do not need to support Undo. Scrolling with the "hand" in a paint program would be an example of this.

Three standard methods are used to create command objects. Menu command objects are created by your **DoMenuCommand** methods. Mouse command objects are created by your **DoMouseCommand** methods. Typing command objects are created by your **DoKeyCommand** methods. These methods are originally defined in the **TEvtHandler** class, but are usually overridden in your application, document, and view classes.

## ▶ Instance Variables

The following is a partial list of instance variables.

| | |
|---|---|
| *fCmdDone* | is command in done or undone state? |
| *fCanUndo* | can the user undo this operation? (normally TRUE) |
| *fCausesChange* | does performing the command change the data in the document? |
| *fView* | view in which MacApp tracks the mouse |
| *fConstrainsMouse* | should MacApp call TrackConstrain? (see below) |
| *fScroller* | the scroller used for autoscrolling |

## ▶ Methods Always Used

**ICommand** — remember to call this to initialize variables.

## ▶ Methods Often Overridden

**DoIt** carries out the command object's action.
**UndoIt** is called when user chooses Undo from the Edit menu to undo the action.
**RedoIt** is called when user chooses Redo from the Edit menu to redo the action.
**TrackMouse** is called while mouse is being dragged.
**TrackConstrain** constrains mouse dragging.
**TrackFeedback** provides user feedback during dragging.

Command objects will be covered in detail in Chapters 18 and 19. You will come to know and love them.

## ▶ Summary

In this chapter, we have looked at the top-level architecture of the MacApp class library. Along the way we have looked at the makeup of each major class, including its important methods and instance variables. Throughout the rest of the book we will make intensive use of these libraries and, in so doing, gain even greater insight into their operation and use.

Chapter 8 concludes our general overview of MacApp and its environment by describing the default behavior that is exhibited by key elements of the MacApp class library.

# 8 ▶ MacApp Default Behavior

This chapter examines several key MacApp classes, describing their default behavior, that is, what they provide in terms of behavior that you can use without modification. Knowing this default behavior is important because if you know what these classes and their methods do without any intervention on your part, you will know which need modification for a particular application and how to approach these changes. In this chapter, you'll see quite a bit about how MacApp works behind the scenes — what's inside the black box. You do not have to know all the details, but it helps to remove some of the mystery.

## ▶ Supporting the User Interface

Classes such as **TApplication, TDocument,** and **TView** are provided as part of MacApp. The MacApp developers looked at what applications should do in normal operation and wrote most of the methods needed to provide that behavior. For example, Apple's Human Interface Guidelines tell us that the user should be able to click in the title bar of a window and drag to move the window on the screen. The methods provided with MacApp will do this. If the user chooses Open... from the file menu, the user expects to see the Standard File Package's SFGetFile dialog appear. The MacApp methods will do this for you, so that you do not even have to know that there is such a thing as the Standard File Package.

| By the Way ▶ | The Standard File Package is a set of Toolbox routines that provide user-friendly access to the files on disk. The package of routines provides Open and Save file dialogs by calling Toolbox routines such as SFGetFile and SFPutFile that are described in Volume I of *Inside Macintosh*. |
| --- | --- |

## ▶ Making Your Program Different

You might ask, what does MacApp *not* do? The answer lies in the tens or hundreds of things that make your program different from someone else's. For example, MacApp knows enough to open a file on disk when the user requests Open... from the File menu. MacApp then calls that document's **DoRead** method to read data from the disk file. Clearly, the MacApp programmers could not anticipate what data or resources might be stored in your file, so you have to provide a new version of **DoRead**. You do that, of course, by creating a new subclass of **TDocument**, and then overriding the **DoRead** method. Your new version must be able to read in the appropriate data and resources.

What else might be unique to your program? The text and graphics contents of your windows are obvious examples. Since every program is different, the only default behavior provided by MacApp is to call each view's **Draw** method when the window contents need to be updated. What would you guess TView's generic **Draw** method does? Looking in the Object Pascal source code to MacApp, we find:

```
PROCEDURE  TView.Draw(area:  Rect);
BEGIN
END;
```

As you can see, you must override the default **Draw** method if you want your program to display anything in its views. In fact, you typically must override at least fifteen methods in the course of creating a relatively simple application. We'll discuss these methods in this chapter. Remember that the only place you can override a method is in a subclass of the class that contains the original method. Therefore, when we talk about overriding the **TView::Draw** method, we are implying that you will have created a subclass of **TView** and defined that new **Draw** method in your new class. When you see us mention the word override, you should also think of the word subclass.

# ▶ How Much Code Will You Have to Write?

Overriding MacApp's methods is the way you distinguish your application from an empty, generic one. To give you an idea of how much work this represents, note the number of lines of code listed for various applications:

| Text editor sample programs | Lines of C++ | |
|---|---|---|
| Text: Simple MacApp | 220 | |
| DemoText: Fancy MacApp | 1,000 | |
| MiniEdit: Simple non-MacApp | 2,200 | (actually Pascal) |

As you can see, writing the very simple editor called Text (described in Chapters 15 and 16) means that you must write about two hundred lines of C++ code. This program is very easy to write and yet it supports multiple documents, Undo, Cut, Copy, Paste, and multiple-page printing. To write a fancy text editor such as the DemoText sample (provided with MacApp) requires about five times as much code. This program allows each character that you type to be in a different font, size, style, and color.

For comparison, the simple MiniEdit text editor written without MacApp is larger than either of the two MacApp samples, but provides much less functionality, for example, no Undo and no printing. Even the DemoText program, at one thousand lines of code, represents less than 2 percent of the total code in MacApp itself. Still, you will have to write hundreds or thousands of lines of source code to customize the MacApp classes as needed for your unique application. To give you an idea of what you are getting into, consider the following table which shows the approximate code size for some larger applications written in MacApp.

Table 8-1. Some typical MacApp sizes

| Program | Description | Lines of code |
|---|---|---|
| DrawShapes | Fancy draw sample — in color | 3,400 |
| ExampleDraw | Draw sample in Chapters 21-25 | 6,300 |
| FalseImage | Geophysical data display — in color | 9,600 |
| PictDetective | Commercial pict analysis tool | 10,300 |
| Jonathan CAD | Commercial CAD — in color | 65,000 |
| Author/Editor | Commercial word processor | 70,000 |
| MacApp 2.0 | The source code itself | 57,000 |

## ▶ Which Methods to Override

At this point, you know that you will have to subclass some of the MacApp classes and override some of the methods, but which ones? During the rest of this chapter, we'll introduce the most important methods called by MacApp in response to normal user actions. Your job in each case is to examine MacApp's default behavior and see if that is what you need for your program. If so, you can leave that method unchanged. If you need to change the behavior, then you must override that method. The situations listed below are ones that commonly require you to override existing methods. We'll briefly mention the situations first and then describe which methods you need to override.

## ▶ Launching the Application

The user has three different ways to start your application from the Finder. The most obvious way is to launch the application by double-clicking on it, in which case the user probably expects the program to create a new document named Untitled-1. Another way is for the user to select one or more documents from the Finder and then launch those. In this case the program should open and display those documents. The final way is for the user to select one or more documents and choose Print from the Finder's File menu. In this case, the application should be launched and should print each document without displaying any windows and then return to the Finder.

The class **TApplication** provides the **HandleFinderRequest** method to manage all three of these cases. You generally will not need to change this method. You will, however, need to override some of the methods called by **HandleFinderRequest** to insure that MacApp creates the types of documents, views, and windows that you need for your application.

Note that because we use 'view' resources in the sample applications in this book, we can use **DoMakeViews** to create not only the views but the windows in which they reside; we do not usually write a **DoMakeWindows** method. If you choose to use ViewEdit as your approach to view creation (as explained in Chapters 13 and 14), you will therefore avoid the necessity of writing a **DoMakeWindows** method in your program.

In the following sections, we'll show pseudo-code to explain how **HandleFinderRequest** calls these important routines that you must write. The methods you need to write are shown in bold. Remember that program execution always begins at the first line of your main program. (The pseudo-code has a Pascal feel because, after all, MacApp was written in Pascal.)

## ▶ Application Launched from Finder

The following is the pseudo-code for the framework of an application that is to be launched from the Finder.

```
Main Program
    gYourApplication->Run
        SELF.HandleFinderRequest
            SELF.OpenNew
                aDoc := SELF.DoMakeDocument   {function}
                aDoc.DoInitialState
                aDoc.DoMakeViews
                aDoc.DoMakeWindows
                aDoc.ShowWindows
        SELF.MainEventLoop
```

## ▶ Document Opened from Finder

The following is the pseudo-code for the framework of an application that is to be launched from the Finder by the user double-clicking on a document's icon.

```
Main Program
    gYourApplication->Run
        SELF.HandleFinderRequest
            SELF.OpenOld
                aDoc := SELF.DoMakeDocument
                aDoc.ReadFromFile
                    FSOpen          {Toolbox call: open data fork}
                    SELF.DoRead     {read the data from disk}
                    FSClose         {Toolbox call: close data fork}
                aDoc.DoMakeViews
                aDoc.DoMakeWindows
                aDoc.ShowWindows    {make windows visible}
        SELF.MainEventLoop          {for the rest of the time}
```

## ▶ Document Printed from Finder

The following is the pseudo-code for a document that is to be printed from the Finder by the user selecting the document's icon and then choosing Print from the File menu.

```
Main Program
    gYourApplication->Run
        SELF.HandleFinderRequest
            SELF.PrintDocument
                aDoc := SELF.DoMakeDocument
```

```
aDoc.DoRead
aDoc.DoMakeViews
aDoc.fPrintHandler.Print
        eachView.Draw(pageArea)
```

## ▶ Opening an Existing File

A Macintosh program should respond to the Open… menu item by first displaying the open file dialog box that allows the user to choose a file. The program must then open an existing file, read in the data, close the file, and finally display some representation of those data in one or more windows. In other words, the program must do most of what we just described if the user double-clicks on a document from the Finder. The only difference is that the standard file dialog must first be displayed. Therefore the pseudo-code shown next is very similar to what you saw already, with the addition of the **ChooseDocument** method being called before the **OpenOld** method.

```
gApplication.DoMenuCommand
    SELF.ChooseDocument
        SFGetFile
    SELF.OpenOld
        aDoc := SELF.DoMakeDocument
        aDoc.ReadFromFile
        FSOpen
        SELF.DoRead
        FSClose
        aDoc.DoMakeViews
        aDoc.DoMakeWindows
```

## ▶ Saving a File to Disk

Choosing Save from the File menu causes the **TDocument.Save** method to execute. This calls two methods that you must write: **DoNeedDiskSpace** and **DoWrite**. In **DoNeedDiskSpace**, you should compute how many bytes your file will require on disk. The **Save** method will then verify that there is room for your new version of the file, after which it will open the file, call your **DoWrite** method, and then close the file and flush the disk cache. The following piece of pseudo-code shows how MacApp handles the Save menu item. The methods that you must write are shown in bold.

```
aDocument.DoMenuCommand
    SELF.Save
        SELF.DoNeedDiskSpace
```

```
FSOpen
SELF.DoWrite
FSClose
FlushVol
```

You may be wondering if the **DoNeedDiskSpace** method is important. Let's consider a text editing program in which the user has typed
10,500 characters into the document window. When the user asks to Save
the file, the **Save** method will call **DoNeedDiskSpace**, which should return the number 10,500. MacApp will then see if that much space is free
on the disk. If it is, the **DoWrite** method will be called to save the characters. If not, the user will see the alert shown in Figure 8-1 if enough space
can be reclaimed by deleting the existing version of the file.

Otherwise, the user will see the alert shown in Figure 8-2.

Figure 8-1. Error message when the disk is almost full

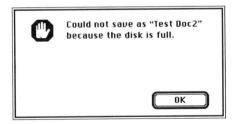

Figure 8-2. Error message when the disk is full

If you do not provide a **DoNeedDiskSpace** method, then the user will
not be presented the choice of deleting the existing version, since
MacApp will always conclude that there is room on the disk. This may
eventually lead to failure of your **DoWrite** method when it runs out of
disk space, which will then cause the alert shown in Figure 8-2 to appear.

| By the Way ▶ | You can choose whether to store data in the data fork or store resources in the resource fork of your file. Generally, user data are stored in the data fork; this is required for any file that must be simultaneously accessed by multiple users over a network. The resource fork would most often be used to store the state of the document. This state might include the print record and the final window and scrollbar positions. You will write to either or both forks in the **DoWrite** method. |
| --- | --- |

## ▶ Handling Window Events

The Macintosh Toolbox provides two main types of events specifically for windows: update events and activate events. Update events occur whenever all or part of a window's contents must be redrawn. In this case, the application's **HandleUpdateEvent** method will (eventually) call two methods for each view that needs updating: **Draw** and **DoHighlightSelection**. As shown in Figure 8-3, **Draw**'s job is to draw the view, while **DoHighlightSelection** is called to highlight the view's selection. As you can see, the names are well chosen.

If a rear window is brought forward or the front window is placed behind other windows, then the Toolbox generates an activate event. Apple's Human Interface Guidelines say that highlighting should be turned on when a window is activated (brought to the front), while the highlighting should be dimmed or turned off when a window is deactivated. MacApp will send each view in the window the DoHighlightSelection message in that case to adjust the highlighting accordingly.

### ▶ Update Event

This pseudo-code shows how MacApp handles Update events.

```
gApplication.HandleUpdateEvent
    aWindow.Update (in TView)
        BeginUpdate
        aView.DrawContents
            SELF.Focus
            SELF.Draw
            SELF.DoHighlightSelection
            SELF.EachSubView(DrawSubView)
        EndUpdate
```

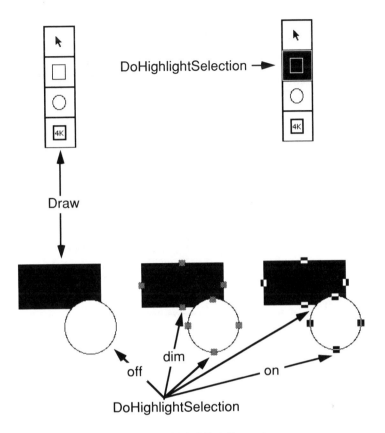

Figure 8-3. Drawing and highlighting views

Windows that have been brought to the front must have their appearance changed so that they look active; windows that have been placed in the back must be made inactive. The methods that follow are called when a window has been activated or deactivated. Parameters are passed by MacApp to your **DoHighlightSelection** method so you will know whether the view's highlighting should be set to on, dim, or off.

## ▶ Activate Event

gApplication.HandleActivateEvent
   aWindow.Activate
      aView.**DoHighlightSelection**

| By the Way ▶ | Dim highlighting is a relatively new addition to Apple's Human Interface Guidelines. Something that is highlighted in high contrast in an active window would be highlighted at lower contrast when that window is deactivated, as shown in the lower half of Figure 8-3. Dim highlighting provides better feedback to the user about the state of inactive windows than if the highlighting is turned off completely. We will show one example of how to do this in Chapter 19. |
|---|---|

## ▶ The Ubiquitous Draw Method

The **Draw** method we mentioned would obviously be important if all it did was draw the view whenever your window was covered and then uncovered. However, Draw is even more important because it is used during scrolling and printing. The Draw message includes an argument that describes the area to be drawn, which you can use to optimize performance. Your view's **Draw** method is called in these cases.

| When | Area passed by MacApp |
|---|---|
| Update events | Rect enclosing Update region |
| Scrolling | Area exposed by scroll |
| Printing | Area of each page, in sequence |

Some of the view building blocks provided with MacApp have **Draw** methods already, including **TTEView, TPicture, TIcon, TScrollBar,** and many others used to create elaborate dialog windows. In many other cases, you will want to write your own **Draw** method to display custom graphics and text. You will see examples of these custom views in later chapters.

## ▶ Handling Menus

This section discusses menu handling operation in MacApp.

## ▶ Enabling Menu Items

If you have written software for the Macintosh, you know that you must include in your program some logic to insure that menu items are enabled and disabled at the correct times. MacApp reduces your burden by disabling all menu items (except those in the Apple menu) each time an event occurs. All you need to do is enable the appropriate items at the right times. MacApp calls your **DoSetupMenus** method to do that. In this method, you should enable any items that are meaningful and checkmark any items that need it.

By the Way ▶ MacApp will not enable or disable items in the Apple menu, since that menu is generally managed by MultiFinder. In this one case, you should therefore be sure to enable the correct items when you define them in your resource file. For other menus, it will not matter what you do in the resource definition.

## ▶ Command Menus and Command Numbers

In traditional Macintosh programs, Toolbox routines enable or check-mark a menu item. These Toolbox routines unfortunately require you to refer to each menu item by its menu number and position in that menu. This technique is not flexible enough to allow you to rearrange your menu items freely, so MacApp includes an extension to the regular menu type known as 'cmnu', for command menus. These menus have a constant known as the command number associated with each item. All you need to do to handle a menu is know its command number.

This means, for example, that if the Help item in a menu had a command number of 1000, you could enable it with the following line of code:

```
Enable(1000, true);
```

## ▶ Multiple Menu Methods

We implied that you may have more than one **DoSetupMenus** method in your program. That is because the responsibility for the various menu items is distributed throughout your application, document, and view classes. In fact, any subclass of **TEvtHandler** can control a menu item. Figure 8-4 shows some of the typical menu items and their handlers.

## ▶ The Target Chain

As you might guess, having many objects that can handle menus leads to a problem: How does MacApp know which objects should be sent the DoSetupMenus message? In fact, it doesn't. Instead, MacApp keeps a linked list of event handlers called the *target chain*. Each of the handlers in the event chain will be sent the DoSetupMenus message. MacApp keeps the head of the chain in a global variable called *gTarget*, so that it can call *gTarget*.**DoSetupMenus** whenever the menus need to be setup. MacApp manages setting *gTarget* to the correct handler under normal circumstances, so you generally will not have to worry about it.

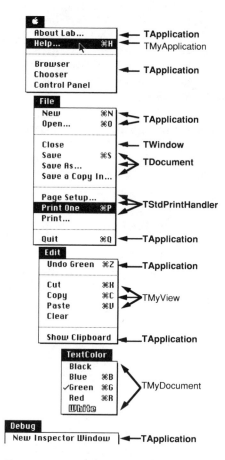

Figure 8-4. Typical menu items and their handlers

## ▶ User Chooses a Menu Item

When the user chooses any enabled menu item, MacApp's **TApplication.MenuEvent** method will call *gTarget*.**DoMenuCommand**, passing the command number of the selected item as a parameter. That method will handle that item if it can. Otherwise it calls the **DoMenuCommand** method in its superclass to give other handlers in the target chain a chance to react. MacApp's many **DoMenuCommand** methods will handle most of the Apple, File, and Edit menu items. You will have to write **DoMenuCommand** methods for any items you add to the program.

▶ Command Objects

Your **DoMenuCommand** method should return a command object as a function result if the requested operation changes the data stored in the document. If the function result is a command object (that is, not NULL), then the **TApplication.PerformCommand** method will send the Command object the message DoIt. You will need to define a subclass of TCommand and implement methods such as **DoIt**, **UndoIt**, and **RedoIt** to support undoable commands.

## ▶ Handling Mouse Clicks

Mouse clicks are easier for MacApp to handle than menu items, since MacApp can use the location of mouse click to determine which view should handle it. The pseudo-code for handling a mouseDown event follows.

```
gApplication.HandleMouseDown
  CASE
  inMenuBar: SELF.SetupTheMenus
      SELF.MenuEvent
  OTHERWISE: aWindow.HandleMouseDown
      inGrow: SELF.ResizeByUser
      inDrag: SELF.MoveByUser
      inGoAway: SELF.GoAwayByUser
      inZoom: SELF.ZoomByUser
      inContent: INHERITED HandleMouseDown
              theSubView.DoMouseCommand
```

Notice that most cases are handled by MacApp methods for **TApplication** and **TWindow**, but you must handle a mouse click in one of your views. The way you handle it is to override the view method **DoMouseCommand**, which is a function that must return a command object. If your mouse click handling should lead to an operation that the user might want to Undo, you should create a command object and return it as a function result in **DoMouseCommand**. Otherwise, you can carry out some operation directly and then return NULL, or *gNoChanges* (a dummy command object that tells MacApp not to support Undo for that operation).

If your **DoMenuCommand** method returns a command object, MacApp goes into a loop waiting for the user to release the mouse button. While the user holds the mouse down, MacApp repeatedly sends the command object these three messages: TrackMouse, TrackFeedback, and TrackConstrain. You must implement these methods in your subclass of **TCommand** to fully support mouse tracking. We will give specific examples of using mouse-driven command objects in Chapter 19.

## ▶ User Falls Asleep

Should your program do anything when there is no user input? In many cases, the answer is no, but if you need to process information in the background or even blink a text insertion point, then you may have to put your program to work when the user is not working. You can do this with the **DoIdle** method. **DoIdle** gets called when there are no other events pending, so that you can do work during idle times when your application is active. If you set the canBackground bit in your 'SIZE' resource, your **DoIdle** methods will also be called when your application is in the background. (See Listing 11-3 in Chapter 11 for a sample 'SIZE' resource.)

Any subclass of **TEvtHandler** can have a **DoIdle** method. The rate at which it will be called depends on the *fIdleFreq* variable of each object. *fIdleFreq* should be set to the minimum number of ticks (a tick is 1/60 second) which must elapse between calls to **DoIdle**.

For example, if you want your application to get idle time once per second, then you might use the following code:

```
void
TMyApplication::IMyApplication()
{
   this->IApplication(kDocType);
   fIdleFreq = 60;
}
```

## ▶ Summary

You will generally write the following methods to handle these typical situations:

Launching your application

Main Program  ==> aMyApplication
aDocument := **DoMakeDocument**
aDocument.**DoMakeViews**  ==> aMyView, aPaletteView
aDocument.**DoMakeWindows**  ==> aScroller, aWindow

Enabling menu items

gTarget.**DoSetupMenus**
many other **DoSetupMenus**

User chooses any menu item

gTarget.**DoMenuCommand**
many other **DoMenuCommand** ==> aMenuCmdObject
aMenuCmdObject.**DoIt**

User chooses Open...

aDocument.**DoRead**

User chooses Save

aDocument.**DoNeedDiskSpace**
aDocument.**DoWrite**

User clicks mouse in yourView

aMyView.**DoMouseCommand** ==> aMouseCmdObject
aMouseCmdObject.**TrackMouse**
aMouseCmdObject.**TrackConstrain**
aMouseCmdObject.**TrackFeedback**
aMouseCmdObject.**DoIt**

Window activate event

aMyView.**DoHighlightSelection**

Window update event

aMyView.**DoHighlightSelection**
aMyView.**Draw**

User falls asleep

gTarget.**DoIdle**
other **DoIdle**

In later chapters, you will see how these methods are typically written. However, in the next chapter we will study a program that is so simple, none of these methods is needed. You will find it to be a very gentle introduction to MacApp. We will get to more elaborate programs later in the book.

# 9 ▶ Simple: The Simplest MacApp Program

In previous chapters we have described how MacApp works, but we have not studied a MacApp program in detail. In this chapter, we'll examine a very simple MacApp program — one that is perhaps as simple as a MacApp program can ever be. This program is therefore named Simple. When you study the C++ source code, you will see why. Most MacApp programs use an application object and one or more document and view objects. This example uses an application object but does not open any documents or views. The program can only do two useful things: open desk accessories and show the contents of the Clipboard (if it contains either text or a picture). Figure 9-1 shows the Simple program.

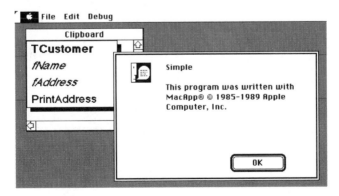

Figure 9-1. Simple, the simplest MacApp program

195

By the Way ▶ The Desk Scrap is the place in the Application Heap where the operating system stores what the user last cut or copied. To the user, this is the Clipboard. In some programs, you may choose to use some part of memory other than the Desk Scrap for this storage. This area is then called a *private scrap*. We'll discuss Clipboard support in detail in Chapter 25.

Our program can do other things, although they are not very useful. The menus work, so that you can select About Simple… from the Apple menu, which displays a simple alert box. The Close menu item also works to close a Desk Accessory or the Clipboard window. Figure 9-2 shows the class diagram for Simple.

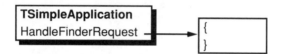

Figure 9-2. Simple's class diagram

The class diagram is, of course, quite modest. We must define **TSimpleApplication** as a subclass of **TApplication**, since an application object is required for all MacApp programs. This object is responsible for running the main event loop, as we discussed in Chapter 7. The only method we need to write is **HandleFinderRequest** in order to override the standard version, which normally opens documents, views, and windows. This program does not define any documents, views, or windows, so we disable **HandleFinderRequest** by overriding it with a method that does absolutely nothing. Note that you usually override a MacApp method to add functionality, while in this case we are removing functionality.

Figure 9-3 depicts the two source files you must write to make a program like this one. There is one C++ source file named MSimple.cp, where the M stands for Main and contains the main program. The resources used in the program are described in the file Simple.r. The .cp file will be processed by the CFront pre-processor and the C compiler as well as the MPW linker to produce CODE resources, while the .r file will be compiled by Rez into menu, alert, and other resources.

**Main Program**
Define the classes
Write the methods
Declare the variables
Run the program

MSimple.cp

**Resource description file**
ALRT
cmnu
SIZE
etc.

Simple.r

Figure 9-3. Simple's two files

**By the Way ▶**

As we mentioned in Chapter 6, the .cp suffix means it contains C++ source code. An .a suffix is used for assembly language files, and a .c suffix is used for ordinary C source code. Pascal source files have a .p suffix.

After any of these files is compiled, an .o suffix is added to indicate that it is machine language object code. This means that the compiler output file might be named MSimple.cp.o. By the way, object code is a traditional term that has nothing to do with object-oriented programming.

## ▶ MSimple.cp, the C++ Source Code

Listing 9-1 shows the C++ code for this tiny program. The line numbers are not shown by MPW, but have been added to these listings so we can reference them more easily.

Listing 9-1. MSimple.cp, the C++ source code

```
1: #ifndef __UMacApp__
2:    #include <UMacApp.h>
3: #endif
4:
5: const OSType kDocFileType =  '????';   / don't care - no files
6:
```

```
 7: /======== define classes ====================================
 8:   class TSimpleApplication : public TApplication {
 9:         virtual pascal void HandleFinderRequest();
10: };
11:
12: //====== implement methods ===============================
13: pascal void
14: TSimpleApplication::HandleFinderRequest()
15: {
16:   //don't create any documents or views
17: }
18:
19:
20: //=========== global variables ===========================
21: TSimpleApplication *gSimpleApplication;    // 32-bit reference
22:
23:
24: //========= main program =================================
25: void main()
26: {
27:     InitUMacApp(8);
28:     gSimpleApplication = new TSimpleApplication;
29:     FailNIL(gSimpleApplication);
30:     gSimpleApplication->IApplication(kDocFileType);
31:     gSimpleApplication->Run();
32: }
```

As you read from the top, notice the following features:

Line 2: # include <UMacApp.h> — This statement means that the header file, UMacApp.h, contains interfaces to the needed MacApp classes.

Line 5: kDocFileType — This constant is the file type for the type of document file to be read in from disk when the program is launched. In our case, there are no documents, so this constant can be set to anything.

Line 8-10: **TSimpleApplication** — This is the class of application object to be used. It is a subclass of MacApp's standard class, **TApplication**.

Lines 13-17: **HandleFinderRequest** — This method normally opens documents, views, and windows at program launch time. In this program, we have no documents, so our new version of this method is defined to do absolutely nothing. (Normally, you wouldn't override this method.) Note how easy it is to debug this method.

Another way to prevent documents from being opened at launch time is to set **TApplication**'s instance variable *fLaunchWithNewDocument* to false. This would be used if you still wanted **HandleFinderRequest** to be able to open documents selected by the user from the Finder.

Line 21: gSimpleApplication — This global variable represents the reference (a 32-bit handle) to the application object. This object's methods run the main event loop. You will absolutely always have one, and only one, application object in each MacApp program.

Line 25: The main program — When a Macintosh application is launched, execution begins here, at the first line of the main program. This main program has been simplified a bit from what you will see in later examples, but it is correct and will work perfectly for Simple.

Line 27: InitUMacApp(8) — This function initializes the Toolbox and MacApp. It also allocates 8 blocks of 64 Master Pointers, so that the program can use up to 512 handles without requiring more allocation of Master Pointers. Each object that you create will use at least one handle, as will each resource that is brought into memory. Each window will use at least five handles, so they get used up in a hurry.

Line 28: gSimpleApplication = new TSimpleApplication — This statement creates the application object on the heap, with gSimpleApplication as the reference to it.

Line 29: FailNIL(gSimpleApplication) — This line checks gSimpleApplication to see if it is a valid handle or if it is nil (or NULL). How could it be nil? It will be set to nil by the new statement if there is not enough room in memory to allocate the object on the heap. In other words, Fail-NIL is there to handle out-of-memory conditions. It is a standard MacApp error handling routine (a global procedure, not a method) that must be called after every use of new or other routines that allocate new data structures on the heap. It does nothing if gSimpleApplication is not nil (i.e., was allocated), but triggers MacApp's error handling if gSimpleApplication is nil. In this case, the error-handling routine will display the alert shown in Figure 9-4, terminate the program, and return to the Finder. By the way, for testing purposes you can cause this message to appear by changing line 24 to read:

```
FailNIL(nil);
```

| By the Way ▶ | It is purely a matter of taste as to whether you choose to use nil or NULL. Just be careful to capitalize correctly. |

Line 30: gSimpleApplication ->IApplication — This line sends the initialization message IApplication to the application object. In this program, we have no extra initialization to perform, so we can merely use the initialization method we inherit from the superclass, **TApplication**. This method initializes a large number of global variables managed by the application object and displays the menus in the menu bar.

| By the Way ▶ | C++ allows you to initialize an object one of two ways. You can explicitly send an initialization message as we did here, or you can define a constructor method that is called automatically after the object is created. In this book, we use explicit initialization methods, because we are usually subclassing from classes defined in MacApp. None of the original MacApp classes could be defined with constructors, since Object Pascal does not support them.

We also find separate initialization methods easier to maintain, since the C++ syntax for how a subclass constructor calls the constructor of its superclass is somewhat hard to understand. |

Figure 9-4. The error message when there is not enough memory to start the program

| By the Way ▶ | One guiding principle of modern software engineering is to minimize global variables, since they provide a mechanism for coupling various parts of your application together in undesirable ways. Many of MacApp's more than fifty globals could have been defined as instance variables of the class **TApplication**, and they probably will be in future versions of MacApp. In MacApp version 2.0, they have been left as globals. Some of these were described in Chapter 7. |

Line 31: gSimpleApplication->Run — The **Run** method runs the application. It first calls **HandleFinderRequest**, which we wrote to do nothing in this example. It then calls the **MainEventLoop** method, which runs the main event loop. This method continues to execute for the life of your program, terminating when the user selects Quit from the File menu.

## ▶ Simple.r, the Resources

Any Macintosh application consists of compiled code in CODE resources and many different user interface components in other resources. All resources have a four-character resource type. If you were to examine most applications with Apple's ResEdit resource editor, you would see resources such as:

- MENU — menus
- ALRT — the window templates for Alerts, which are a special form of dialog used for messages that require only a simple yes-or-no type of response
- DLOG — the window template for more complicated modal and modeless dialogs
- DITL — a Dialog ITem List that describes the items in an alert or dialog window
- SIZE — information used by MultiFinder to allocate memory and background processing time for your application

These .r files are formatted for MPW's Rez resource compiler, which uses a syntax very much like the C programming language. Like C, Rez uses special symbols, some of which are presented in the following paragraphs.

The symbol # indicates a preprocessor directive. This means that the text file is processed before the resources are compiled. For example, the line

```
#define cHelp  1001
```

causes Rez to search the file for all places where you use the word cHelp and substitute the number 1001. You could use this same statement in your C++ code, but it is better to use:

```
short CHelp = 1001;
```

This allows C++ to do type-checking on your use of cHelp.

Notice in the Rez format that a line that begins with # does not have a semicolon at the end, since it is not an executable line.

The symbols { and } designate the beginning and end of a block exactly as they do in C. Comments are marked in C++, with a double slash. You can also use traditional C comments, bracketed by /* and */.

▶ The Include Statements

The Simple.r file is shown in Listing 9-2.

Listing 9-2. The Simple.r file

```
1: #ifndef __TYPES.R__
2:    #include "Types.r"    // SIZE, WIND, STR , MBAR etc.
3: #endif
4:
5: #ifndef __SYSTYPES.R__
6:    #include "SysTypes.r"    // needed for version resource
7: #endif
8:
9: #ifndef __MacAppTypes__
10:    #include "MacAppTypes.r"      // cmnu, etc.
11: #endif
12:
13: #ifndef __ViewTypes__
14:    #include "ViewTypes.r"        // view resources
15: #endif
16:
17: #if qDebug
18:    include "Debug.rsrc";         // always include
19: #endif
20:
21: include "MacApp.rsrc";                      // always include
22:
23: include $$Shell("ObjApp")"Simple" 'CODE';  // always include
24:
25: // ==============================================================
26: include "Defaults.rsrc" 'SIZE' (-1); // 534, 246; 384, 96 KB
27: include "Defaults.rsrc" 'ALRT' (phAboutApp); // About... window
28: include "Defaults.rsrc" 'DITL' (phAboutApp); // About... contents
29: include "Defaults.rsrc" 'STR#' (kDefaultCredits);  // credits
30: include "Defaults.rsrc" 'vers' (1);        // application version
31: include "Defaults.rsrc" 'vers' (2);        // overall package
32: include "Defaults.rsrc" 'cmnu' (mApple);  // default Apple menu
33: include "Defaults.rsrc" 'cmnu' (mEdit);   // default Edit menu
34:
35: // ==============================================================
36: resource 'cmnu' (2) {
37:    2,
38:    textMenuProc,
39:    0x7FFFFBBB,
```

```
40:    enabled,
41:    "File",
42:    {
43:        "Close", noIcon, noKey, noMark, plain, cClose;
44:        "-", noIcon, noKey, noMark, plain, nocommand;
45:        "Quit", noIcon, "Q", noMark, plain, cQuit;
46:    }
47: };
48:
49: resource 'MBAR' (kMBarDisplayed,
50: #if qNames
51: "Simple",
52: #endif
53:    purgeable) {
54:    {mApple; 2; mEdit;}
55: };
56:
57: // ============================================================
58: resource 'seg!' (256,
59: #if qNames
60: "Simple",
61: #endif
62:    purgeable) {
63:    {
64:        "GNonRes";
65:    }
66: };
```

Lines 1-15: #ifndef, etc. — These lines begin every MacApp .r file. They include resource type declarations needed by Rez to compile the rest of this file. The #include statement tells Rez to include a text file before compiling the resources.

Lines 17-19: #if qDebug, etc. — This group of lines is always used to tell Rez to include all the resources needed by the MacApp debugging code, if you are compiling the sample with debugging code included. The include statement, not preceded by #, tells Rez to copy all the compiled resources from this file to your final application.

Line 21: include "MacApp.rsrc" — This line tells Rez to include a set of resources used by all MacApp programs.

Line 23: include "Simple" 'CODE' — This line includes the 'CODE' resources from the existing version of the application. These are created by the compile and link steps. Notice the tricky way that Rez files can use the MPW shell variable {ObjApp} which is the path name to the object code produced by the compiler.

▶ The cmnu Command Menus

Menus in MacApp are described with resources of type 'cmnu'. You must define one 'cmnu' resource for each menu that appears in the menu bar. If you are an experienced Macintosh programmer, you are probably wondering what a 'cmnu' is. It is a special MacApp resource that is an extension of the normal 'MENU' resource. A 'cmnu' is defined just like a 'MENU', with the addition of a unique command number for each item. This number is used in the C++ code to identify the menu item. For example, when the user chooses a menu item, MacApp will send you the DoMenuCommand message, passing the item's command number as a parameter. You will then determine what action to carry out based on the command number. This allows you to rearrange menu items without changing your code. The command numbers for standard menu items such as New, Open..., Close, Quit, Show Clipboard, and others, are predefined in MacApp and are handled by MacApp's versions of DoMenuCommand. You must arrange to handle your own unique items, as you will see in later chapters.

| By the Way ▶ | Resource types are case sensitive. Therefore, a resource of type 'MENU' is not the same as the type 'menu'. Be sure to use the resource types exactly as listed. The reason the case matters is that resource types are defined by four characters, so that numbers, letters, spaces, and even non-ASCII characters can be used in a resource type. |
|---|---|

Listing 9-2 also shows the part of the Simple.r file that describes the menus. In this example, the Apple menu is in 'cmnu' number 1, followed by the File and Edit menus in resources 2 and 3. The resulting menus are shown in Figure 9-5. We'll examine the File menu as a typical example.

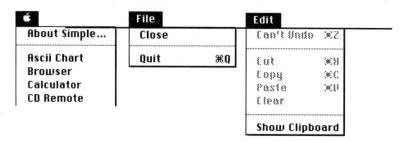

Figure 9-5. The menus in the Simple program

Each of the *include* statements in lines 26-33 adds a standard resource to your application. These resources are contained in a file called Defaults.rsrc provided with MacApp. You can examine the original definition of these resources in the Defaults.r file found in the Libraries folder inside the MacApp folder.

Line 26: This includes the default 'SIZE' resource, which contains information used by MultiFinder to control your application. The default resource tells MultiFinder that your application prefers a 534 KB memory partition when compiled in the normal debugging case, but will work with a minimum of 246 KB. In the optimized, non-debug case, the preferred allocation is 384 KB, while the minimum size is only 96 KB. These will work well for all our small samples; in a larger application, or for one that opens large data files, you will have to provide your own 'SIZE' resource, as described in Listing 11-30.

Lines 27-28: These define the default Alert number 201 that MacApp displays when the user chooses About Simple... from the Apple menu. This is shown in Figure 9-6.

Figure 9-6. The default About Simple... alert

Line 29: This very optional line includes a list of strings that the MacApp code will display in sequence in Alert 201. The default list includes the names of MacApp's developers. You could substitute the names of your friends and relatives by providing your own string list resource.

Lines 30-31: These provide version resources that are displayed by the Finder when the user selects your application and chooses Get Info... from the File menu.

Lines 32-33: These provide the standard Apple and Edit menus, as shown in Figure 9-5.

By the Way ▶

As a program gets more complex, there are obviously times when the default resources are not sufficient. Then you must write your own versions of these. You can see examples of real ones in the Calc example (in Pascal) that comes with MacApp, and the ExampleDraw sample on the disk that accompanies this book.

Line 36: resource 'cmnu' (2) { — The keyword *resource* tells Rez that you are defining a specific resource, as opposed to the keyword *type* that you could use to define the format for a new type of resource. The four characters, which must be in single quotes, identify the resource type. Be sure to enter cmnu in lowercase letters. The number in parentheses is the resource ID. The curly bracket begins the resource data for this menu.

By the Way ▶

In MacApp 2.0, MacApp menu resource IDs must be assigned numbers in the range from 1 to 63, with popup menu resources numbered from 64 on up. In the future, Apple plans to renumber the menu resources starting at 128 to be consistent with Apple's general guidelines for numbering resources. The Apple guidelines state that an application's resource IDs should always be greater than 127. Here are the recommended ranges:

- -32768 to -1: used by the operating system and Desk Accessories
- 0 to 127: shared resources in the System file that can be used by applications
- 128-999: reserved for MacApp
- 1000 to 32767: available for your applications resources

Line 37: 2 — This is menu ID number 2. You should always make the menu ID be the same as the resource ID.

Line 38: textMenuProc — This constant indicates that these will be normal text menus. Other constants would indicate that you were using custom menus, which are beyond the scope of this book. They would be used for graphical menus, for example.

Line 39: 0x7FFFFBBB — This hexadecimal number determines which menu times are initially enabled. If you were to convert this to a binary number, the least-significant bit controls the first item in the menu (0 = disabled, 1 = enabled), while the next bit controls the second item, and so forth. Before you worry about this, we must mention that MacApp controls which items are to be enabled in the Pascal code — for all menus except the Apple menu. Specifically, MacApp will use these enable flags to determine which items are enabled in the Apple menu, but ignore the flags on all other menus. You can therefore supply any arbitrary value for this number in all except Apple menu cases.

Line 40: enabled — This is the correct constant for all menus, since it initially enables the menu title in the menu bar for each menu.

Line 41: "File" — This is the menu title. It must be enclosed in double quotes, since it is a string variable.

Line 43: "Close", etc. — This line describes the first item in the file menu. The command number cClose is defined in the file MacApp-Types.r shipped as part of MacApp. This item will be handled by the MacApp code.

Line 44: "-" — This is translated by the Mac's ROM Toolbox routines into a dotted line drawn all the way across the menu rectangle. It is used to isolate menu items visually and spatially. The command number *nocommand* is used for menu items that cannot be chosen by the user. Dividing lines like this are the most common example of such passive items.

Line 45: "Quit" etc. — MacApp also handles this item.

Lines 49-55: resource 'MBAR' — This resource is defined solely to contain the menu IDs that will be displayed in the menu bar when the program is launched.

The 'seg!' resource in lines 58-66 is used by MacApp to determine which code segments are loaded into memory in situations when your program is making maximum use of memory. MacApp will then keep a code reserve to make room for these code segments, so that the program can never run out of memory while loading a code segment. In this program, we used the MacApp debugger to determine that we must always be able to load the GNonRes code segment. The details of this code reserve and the technique to determine the 'seg!' resource are described in Curt Bianchi's excellent article on "Memory Management with MacApp" in *Dr. Dobb's Macintosh Journal*, Fall 1989.

## ▶ Using a Separate Module

All the C++ source code in Simple is included in the main program's file, MSimple.cp, as shown in Listing 9-1. However, a real program you write will have more features than this tiny example, so that you will have to define more classes and methods. For example, the Calc sample program shipped with MacApp has 21 classes and 173 methods. For efficiency reasons, it is better not to squeeze all this into a single file. Therefore, a typical MacApp program uses at least three files, as shown in Figure 9-7.

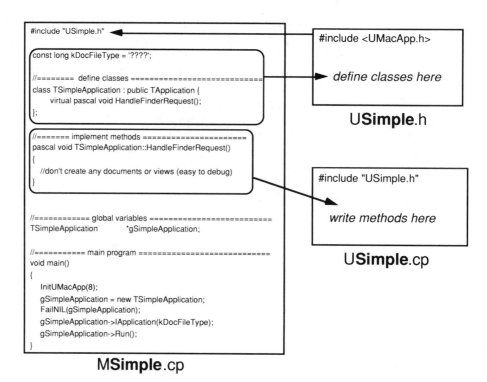

**Figure 9-7.** Breaking the code into the usual three Pascal source files

The standard set of three files includes

- MSimple.cp — the main program file differs little from one application to the next. In the main program, you typically allocate an application object, initialize it, and send it the Run message. The standard main program is a bit more complex than the one shown in this example, although this one works fine for our purposes. We'll show one in Chapter 13 that is a bit more complex and more typical.

- USimple.h — the header file in which you will place the definitions for your classes. Notice that the main program then references this file in its #include statement. Any constants, variables, and types defined in the header file are available for use in any file that includes this file.

- USimple.cp — this include file contains the methods for all the new classes. The information in this file is private and should not be accessed by other files. This allows you to define constants, variables, types, and even functions that can be used by any of your methods, but will be hidden from the rest of your code.

## ▶  Summary

In this chapter we have built and examined the simplest possible MacApp program. This has given us an opportunity to examine C++ and MacApp programming methods and approaches in a practical situation. Future examples will be more complex and, therefore, more functional, than the Simple example of this chapter.

Chapter 10 describes the process by which you can design a real application — that is, one that uses the full capabilities of MacApp. This is a continuation of the design process we began in Chapter 4.

# 10 ▶ Object Design: Adding the User Interface

Chapter 9 demonstrated a simple MacApp program, one that required no user interface decisions. In this chapter we'll look at the design process for more complex programs that add the user interface.

Apple's Human Interface Guidelines describe principles for designing software that is both powerful and easy to use. If you are an experienced user of Macintosh software, you have probably learned most of these rules by using good applications. As a programmer, you probably have also read the official guidelines, which clarify the rules and make it easier to design your program's user interface.

## ▶ Details, Details

The personal computer trade press often describes the Macintosh user interface as consisting of menus, windows, a mouse, and a trash can for deleting files. That is a great oversimplification. A good user interface does more than that; it also

- Provides consistency.
- Provides a metaphor that guides users in how to use the software.
- Pays attention to detail. (It is said that Jean-Louis Gassée, former president of Apple Products, has been heard to say that "God is in the details." Whether or not he actually said it, experience has shown that fanatical attention to detail characterizes the best Macintosh programmers and the best Macintosh software.)

After you have become familiar with the guidelines and principles, you are ready to deal with the user interface specification, which involves answering three questions:

1. On what kind of data will your program operate? This question may be easy to answer on a broad scale, because you may know that the program will be a word processor, or a computer-aided-design application, or a front-end to your company's mainframe database. The question gets more complicated when you have to deal with specifics such as what file formats the program needs to be able to read and write. You will often have to deal with issues of large data files, so that you may have some on remote machines, some on a local hard disk, and some in memory. We will not try to address all these possibilities in this chapter, but we will provide a framework for you to use on your own.

2. What will your program look like on the screen? This is related to the next question about how the user will interact with the program. You need to decide what windows you will display and what should appear in each window. MacApp offers excellent support for as many complicated windows and menus as you would like. It is up to you to put yourself in the user's place and not make things any more complicated than necessary.

3. How will you let the user interact with the program? You need to decide which commands the user can select from menus and which ones will be mouse and/or keyboard operated. You need to decide which commands are undoable and what kind of Clipboard support to provide. MacApp will help with all of these things, but in most cases you will have to write additional code to support these features.

The following nine-step plan presents the decisions you might face as you elaborate on these three issues. In this chapter we'll provide some advice on making those decisions in terms of the classes provided by MacApp. We believe you'll see that the MacApp classes provide an excellent framework for supporting the Macintosh user interface.

| Step | MacApp Class |
|------|--------------|
| 1. Choose data to be stored | **TDocument** |
| 2. Choose views to be displayed | **TView** |
|     Text | **TTEView** |
|     Graphics | **TIcon, TPicture** |
|     Grids | **TGridView** |
|     Other views | **TTextListView**, etc. |
| 3. Decide which views are scrollable | **TScroller** |
| 4. Decide which views are printable | **TStdPrintHandler** |
| 5. Arrange views in windows | **TWindow** |
| 6. Design modal dialogs | **TDialogView, TButton**, etc. |
| 7. Design modeless dialogs | **TDialogView** |
| 8. Choose operations to be undoable | **TCommand** |
|     Menu commands | |
|     Mouse commands | |
|     Key commands | |
| 9. Plan Clipboard support | **TDeskScrapView** |

## ▶ Storing Data in Documents

In many ways, documents are the most important part of a typical application, because documents store data and computers are data-processing machines. First, decide what type of document files your program will need to read and write to disk. You will generally use a subclass of **TDocument** for every different file format that you need to handle. If you are lucky, you will need to handle only one document type, but many programs require more. Some specific examples are shown in Table 10-1, and their icons are shown in Figure 10-1.

Table 10-1. Document types for various applications

| Program | Primary type | Other types |
|---------|-------------|-------------|
| MacWrite | WORD | TEXT |
| MacDraw II | DRWG | PICT, STAT |
| Excel 1.5 | XLBN(Excel 1.0) | TEXT(WKS) |
| " | XLBN(Normal) | TEXT(SYLK) |
| " | | TEXT(WK1) |
| " | | TEXT(Text) |

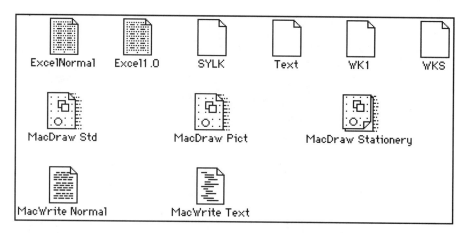

Figure 10-1. Finder icons for programs that support multiple document types

To elaborate on this table and the associated Finder icons, consider MacWrite, a popular word processor for the Macintosh. Its main file type is 'WORD', which has been defined to store a complicated combination of text and formatting information in the data and resource forks of the file. For compatibility with other, simpler text editors, MacWrite can also read and write files of type 'TEXT', which contain simple ASCII characters in the data fork.

In a case like MacWrite, you could define a **TTextDocument** class, which could hold onto the unformatted ASCII text, and a **TFormatted-Document** subclass that could store the formatting information. Each document class would implement the **DoRead** and **DoWrite** methods for handling the appropriate disk files.

Another option would be to define classes that each read and write a particular file type. Then you could create an instance of the appropriate class, based on the file type. Your document's **DoRead** and **Do-Write** methods would call methods of the file-handling object to perform the actual read or write.

| By the Way ▶ | Notice that Figure 10-1 shows that different document types have different Finder icons. To provide this feature, you would also need to define *bundle* information for each type of document file that your program created. See *Inside Macintosh*, Volume II for more information. Look at the resources defined for the Calc sample program provided with MacApp for an example. |

Table 10-1 also shows the multiple file formats that are used by two other popular programs, MacDraw II and Microsoft Excel.

The class diagram for a simple document class is shown in Figure 10-2; only the methods you would be likely to have to write are shown. The underlined methods are new — not overrides of standard methods.

```
┌────────────────────────┐
│ TMyDocument            │
│ fMyData                │
│ IMyDocument            │
│ DoMakeViews            │
│ DoSetupMenus           │
│ DoMenuCommand          │
│ DoNeedDiskSpace        │
│ DoRead                 │
│ DoWrite                │
│ SetData                │
│ GetData                │
└────────────────────────┘
```

Figure 10-2. Typical document class diagram

## ▶ Views

The next step is to decide how your graphics, text, spreadsheet data, palettes, rulers, and so forth, should look on the screen. In Figure 10-3, you can see some of the views that might be needed in an outlining application such as Symantec's More.

At this point you can design your views. You don't need to be concerned yet about how they are to be arranged in windows; you will do that step later. In fact, MacApp does such a good job of handling windows that it usually does not matter whether you place all your views in one window or place each view in its own window. The amount of work you will do is about the same in either case.

The indented outline view on the left of Figure 10-3 might remind you of a simple text editor, so you might define a **TOutlineView** as a subclass of MacApp's text building block **TTEView**. The palette of tools represents a mouse-operated view that could be defined as a subclass of MacApp's **TGridView** class. The graphic view of your outline might be defined as a **TTreeView**. This could be a subclass of the generic class **TView**, since there is no view provided with MacApp that seems close to this tree display in appearance.

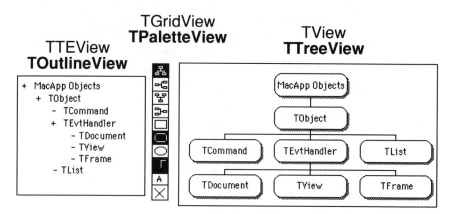

Figure 10-3. Three views that might be used in one program

An important point about this example is that both the outline view and the tree view represent different views of the same data. Where are those data stored? In the document. The virtue in this model is that user interaction can take place as follows:

1. User operates on either view.
2. New data are sent to the document.
3. Update events are forced for both views.
4. The **Draw** methods for each view are therefore called.
5. Each view queries the document to decide what to draw.

With this mechanism, you can allow the user to interact with either view of the data, but you need to keep only one copy of the data. Both views always stay synchronized with it.

After choosing the view classes, you could begin to choose variables and methods. A beginning class diagram for these views is shown in Figure 10-4. Notice that we define DoMenuCommand messages for both the outline view and the tree view. That assumes that there are menu items that apply to only one of the views but not the other. If your menu commands applied to both views, you could handle them in the document and you would not need these methods in each view.

We also define variables in both **TOutlineView** and **TTreeView** to refer to the document, so the views can query the document for the data to be drawn. Furthermore, we defined variables in **TPaletteView** that refer to the other views. In this way, we can send messages to the outline and tree views regarding the state of the palette.

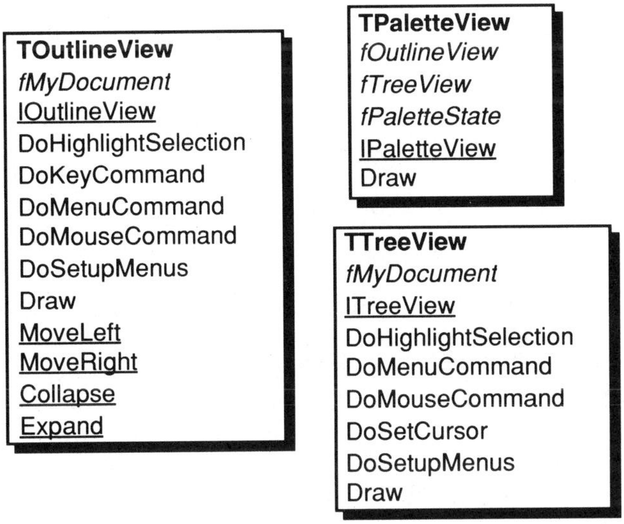

**TOutlineView**
*fMyDocument*
IOutlineView
DoHighlightSelection
DoKeyCommand
DoMenuCommand
DoMouseCommand
DoSetupMenus
Draw
MoveLeft
MoveRight
Collapse
Expand

**TPaletteView**
*fOutlineView*
*fTreeView*
*fPaletteState*
IPaletteView
Draw

**TTreeView**
*fMyDocument*
ITreeView
DoHighlightSelection
DoMenuCommand
DoMouseCommand
DoSetCursor
DoSetupMenus
Draw

Figure 10-4. Class diagram for views of an outline processor

## ▶ Scrollable Views

Remember that views can be any size from small rectangles a few pixels on a side to very large views — conceivably as large as four billion pixels on a side. (To be specific, the width and the height are specified by 32-bit long integers.)

What sizes would you expect for the three views shown in Figure 10-3? The outline view would typically be one printed page wide, but potentially many pages long. That means that it could be much larger than a window, so it would probably be installed as a subview of a scroller object which has scrollbars to move the view relative to the window. The scroller object will usually be an instance of class **TScroller**. You will only need to subclass **TScroller** if you want to modify MacApp's normal scrolling behavior, which is rare. We will describe nested views and scrollers in detail in Chapters 13 and 14.

The palette view is usually a relatively small fixed size, so you will not need a scroller for that. The tree view may be many pages wide and tall, so you would again install this view as a subview of a scroller.

## ▶ Printing

Most Macintosh programmers hate to write routines to handle printing because they require complex, subtle code that is prone to errors and crashing. For that reason few hobbyists even attempt to get printing to work, and many professionals have never done it well. Will you support printing in your MacApp program? Of course you will, because it is so easy. All you really have to do to make a view printable is to create an instance of class **TStdPrintHandler** and initialize it correctly. The **TStd-PrintHandler** class has methods to support multiple-page printing using any standard print driver that appears in the Chooser Desk Accessory.

The standard printing methods support simple, multiple-page printing, but do not give you special page breaks, headers, footers, and the like. MacApp provides methods to support these features; you will have to override these methods to change the behavior. Some of these methods actually belong to the **TView** class, so your view subclasses can be customized to provide special print behavior. In the particular case of adding headers, footers, and page numbers, you will override **TStdPrintHandler::AdornPage**.

## ▶ Windows

You will have to make a number of design decisions regarding your windows. First, you must decide how to arrange your views in windows. As we mentioned, it does not matter to MacApp if you choose to put all your views in one window or distribute them in multiple windows. In either case, you will create window objects that are instances of **TWindow**, which is a class with methods to handle normal window behavior. You must also decide on such mundane, but important, matters as whether or not to include a close box, zoom box, and resize icon for resizing each window. Since **TWindow** provides the standard Macintosh window behavior, it is rarely overridden.

### ▶ Simple Windows

A simple window is one that is filled with only one view. They are so common that MacApp provides the **NewSimpleWindow** utility function to create them. **NewSimpleWindow** creates and initializes a window object — and a scroller object with associated scrollbars if you want them. It also installs your view in the window, as shown in Figure 10-5.

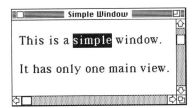

A simple window

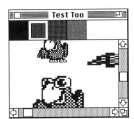

A palette window

Figure 10-5. A simple window and a palette window

By the Way ▶    Most of the behavior provided by MacApp is embedded in the methods that are part of MacApp's class definitions. However, there are
many situations — such as creating a new window object with
**NewSimpleWindow** — for which it was much easier for Apple to
define a normal Pascal procedure or function to do the job.

Other common examples of this include the **FailNIL** and **FailOSErr**
error handling routines, which must be called from many different
parts of your program. Since the behavior they support is used in
methods that belong to a wide variety of classes, the error handling
routines are not defined as part of any class. They are simply global
procedures.

## ▶ Palette Windows

A palette window is one with two views: a main view that fills most of
the window and a fixed-size view on the top or left that usually contains a
palette of tool icons. The lower window in Figure 10-5 is an example of a
palette window. MacApp provides the **NewPaletteWindow** utility function to make palette windows easy to create. You can also define such a
window using view resources, and then create it with the NewTemplate-
Window function. This technique will be described in Chapter 14.

## ▶ Dialogs

In traditional Macintosh software, there are three types of special windows associated with the Dialog Manager: (1) alerts for informing the user of special conditions such as errors, (2) modal dialogs for allowing a dialogue with the user that must be completed before normal program operation can resume, and (3) modeless dialogs that allow user input but behave like normal windows. When the MacApp team was developing the MacApp 2.0 architecture, they realized that the Dialog Manager Toolbox routines were severely limiting programmers' flexibility, so they made the brave decision to invent a better version of the Dialog Manager using high-level MacApp methods. The result is that modal and modeless dialogs are now special cases of normal windows in MacApp, but the Toolbox's alert mechanism still is used for presenting simple modal displays to the user.

### ▶ Alerts

You are expected to provide at least one alert when using MacApp: the alert box that is displayed by MacApp when the user chooses "About this program...," the first item on the Apple menu. By default, MacApp will display ALRT 201 and its associated dialog item list, DITL 201, both of which you can provide, or use the default ones mentioned in Chapter 9.

| By the Way ▶ | If you wish to provide a more interactive "About this program..." dialog than can be displayed using a simple alert box, you can easily modify the behavior of MacApp to provide that. Handling your own menu items is described in Chapter 18; dialog handling is described in Chapter 20. |
|---|---|

### ▶ Modal Dialogs

Decide which modal dialogs you need and then sketch each dialog on a piece of paper. This may lead to dialogs such as the one shown in Figure 10-6, taken from the DemoDialogs sample program shipped with MacApp. This was based on the layout of the MPW Format dialog box. From that sketch, you should be able to identify each element, as shown in the figure. For each of these elements you can use an instance of one of the classes provided for dialog support in MacApp, shown in parentheses in Figure 10-6. Each of these classes is actually a subclass of **TView**, so you will be assembling your dialog boxes from a large set of views — usually installed as a subview of the **TDialogView** class provided by MacApp.

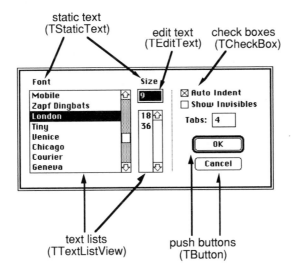

Figure 10-6. A modal dialog composed of many MacApp view objects

## ▶ Modeless Dialogs

The design process for modeless dialogs is essentially the same as for modal dialogs. The difference is that modal dialogs must be dismissed by clicking on the OK or Cancel button, while modeless dialogs do not need to be dismissed before continuing. You will usually define a modeless view that is a subclass of **TDialogView** for each modeless dialog in your program.

## ▶ Modeless Versus Modal

Apple's Human Interface Guidelines state that we should avoid a mode that "restricts the user's freedom of action." We agree and encourage you to choose modeless dialogs rather than modal ones when you have a choice.

Users find dialogs easier to use when they can place the dialog in the background and still see the settings they have chosen, rather than having to dismiss the dialog first. For example, if your user is changing text settings with the dialog shown in Figure 10-6, it is convenient to keep the dialog on the screen to try different font settings or to see which current settings are in effect. (In fact, the dialog shown in Figure 10-6, taken directly from MPW 3.0, would be better designed as a modeless dialog. It would be more usable and more closely follow Apple's guideline.)

## ▶ Undo

You may remember that we described printing as something that intimidates many Macintosh programmers. Well, printing is usually considered easy when compared to providing Undo for user operations such as typing, choosing menu items, or handling mouse clicks. Should your program support the Undo item on the Edit menu? Of course it should. If you are not sure about Undo, then ask the user who has selected all of the text in his or her resume in order to change the font, but accidentally pressed Delete and erased it all. Or ask the user who wanted to use the spilled paint bucket tool in MacPaint to fill in a shape, but accidentally covered the whole screen with black paint. In most cases, users will hate your program if it does not support Undo.

When should Undo be provided? Certainly not in all cases, since users do not expect to be able to undo printing, saving to disk, scrolling, or selecting a tool in a palette of tools. The rule for providing Undo is generally taken to be:

| Important ▶ | You should provide Undo for user operations that change any data that you care enough about to save to disk. These would include drawing shapes, typing, deleting customer records, or changing the page header on a word processing document. For more information, refer to *Apple's Human Interface Guidelines*, published by Addison-Wesley. |
| --- | --- |

Now that you have been pressured to support Undo, you may be hoping that MacApp will make it easy. In most cases you are in luck, because MacApp does contain considerable support for command objects that support Undo.

## ▶ Command Objects

Command objects are temporary objects that carry out user actions and remember what the user did so that those actions can be undone when requested by the user. You will have to design subclasses of the MacApp **TCommand** class to provide this functionality. MacApp expects command objects to be created in certain cases and calls the methods of these command objects to perform the desired tasks. The standard user actions supported by MacApp are shown in Table 10-2, along with the methods that MacApp calls in response.

Table 10-2. Methods that create command objects

| User action | Method called by MacApp |
| --- | --- |
| Press mouse | DoMouseCommand |
| Press key | DoKeyCommand |
| Choose menu item | DoMenuCommand |

To support Undo, you should provide these methods as part of your event handling classes, which usually means your Application, Document, and/or View subclasses. Each of the methods shown in Table 10-2 returns a command object to carry out the desired user action.

For each operation that will support Undo you should define the command object as a subclass of **TCommand**. These are three examples:

- **TSketcher** for drawing
- **TColorCmd** for color menu
- **TTypingCmd** for typing

For each of your command object classes, you will have to write methods to carry out the desired actions, undo them, and then redo them once they have been undone.

## ▶ Clipboard: Cut, Copy, and Paste

The Macintosh computer succeeded in the business world (probably) because of the Clipboard more than any other feature. Macintosh initially made its way into many businesses because of its desktop publishing capability. (It was usually encouraged by those forward-thinking people who recognized the potential of the machine in many other ways.) What does desktop publishing have to do with the Clipboard? Everything. The concept first succeeded because users could integrate text created on word-processing programs with pictures created in graphics programs using the Clipboard's support for Cut and Paste.

If your software is going to be popular with end users, you should support Cut and Paste of both text and graphics if at all possible. What does Clipboard support entail? It includes supporting many of the menu items in the typical Edit menu shown in Figure 10-7.

Cut, Copy, Paste, Clear, and Select All are usually supported by your view classes; MacApp provides automatic support for the Show Clipboard item whenever possible. To know when that is possible, we must investigate how the Macintosh handles the Clipboard.

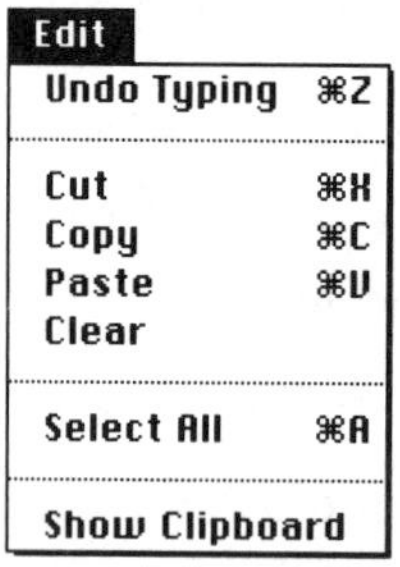

Figure 10-7. A typical Edit menu

▶ The Desk Scrap

When the user performs the cut or copy operation, a copy of the se-lected data is placed in a memory location called the *scrap*. Users never know about this scrap directly, of course. They think of this simply as the Clipboard. The Macintosh operating system supports a special scrap called the Desk Scrap, and the ROM provides a number of Tool-box calls for this.

▶ Multiple Scrap Formats

The Desk Scrap can only hold the last item that the user cut or copied, but it can hold copies of that item in different formats, as you can see in Figure 10-8. You might need multiple scrap formats to save complex in-formation on the scrap that only your program knows how to use; a sim-pler version of those same data should be provided for most other pro-grams to use.

For example, MacWrite uses a scrap format (of scrap type MWRT) that requires saving the ASCII text and some relatively complicated data structures that contain the font, size, and style information. MacWrite needs this complex format to enable a paste operation inside MacWrite to carry along the formatting information. On the other hand, most pro-grams do not support using the MWRT scrap format, so MacWrite also places the simple ASCII characters on the scrap as type 'TEXT'. When an-other program performs the paste operation, it will check to see if the scrap contains 'TEXT' information and use it if it does.

You must decide what scrap formats are needed by your program and support those; you should also support the two common scrap for-mats, TEXT and PICT, if possible and appropriate.

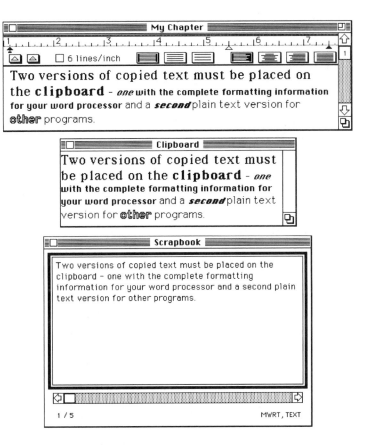

Figure 10-8.  Multiple scrap formats are commonly used

▶ Private Scraps

The Desk Scrap can only hold the last item that the user cut or copied. You may wish to provide more sophisticated support than that provided by Apple's standard scrap. An example of richer support is provided by the MindWrite word-processing program, which has what is known as an accumulating scrap, as shown in Figure 10-9. MindWrite adds each copied item to the data already on the scrap, and the user can select one or more items in the Clipboard window to be pasted. Although an accumulating scrap can eventually use up quite a bit of memory, it allows the user great flexibility. You will have to decide if your application warrants the effort required to provide this enhancement. (MacApp defaults to support only the standard scrap.)

Figure 10-9.  A Clipboard that accumulates copied information

## ▶ MacApp Clipboard Support

MacApp will help you by providing the Clipboard window as an instance of class **TWindow** and a view of the Clipboard as an instance of class **TDeskScrapView**. These work well within their limitations, which are:

- only the Desk Scrap contents are displayed
- only scrap contents of type TEXT or PICT will be displayed

If you need other scrap types or private scrap locations, you will need to help MacApp by overriding certain methods to add this functionality. Clipboard support will be described in more detail in later chapters.

## ▶ Summary

This chapter has presented a nine-step approach to designing and incorporating a full user interface on a MacApp program.

Chapter 11 describes some of the useful tools available to you as you design and build MacApp programs.

# 11 ▶ Tools for MacApp Programmers

A good object-oriented development system is composed of three closely coupled pieces: (1) the language, (2) the class library, and (3) the program development tools that allow you to use the language and the library efficiently. In previous chapters, we discussed the language and class library. In this chapter, we will describe some of the tools that you can use to write applications with MacApp and show how they fit into the program development process.

The languages that we are using for our examples are Object Pascal and C++. The rich library of reusable classes is called MacApp. But what are the tools? There are tools for each of these functions:

- managing resources for user interface design
- creating and managing source code
- debugging your code

In this chapter, you will see how to use some of these tools; others will be described in later chapters. In developing a program for the Macintosh you generally need to think about two things at once, because you must develop your software along two parallel tracks: (1) creating resources to describe various parts of the user interface, and (2) writing program code that uses these resources while the program is running. Let's consider resource creation first.

## ▶ Managing Resources

Figure 11-1 illustrates the process of creating resources using the three most popular tools for MacApp programmers: Rez, ViewEdit, and Res-Edit. (MPW also provides the DeRez and PostRez tools that will be described later.)

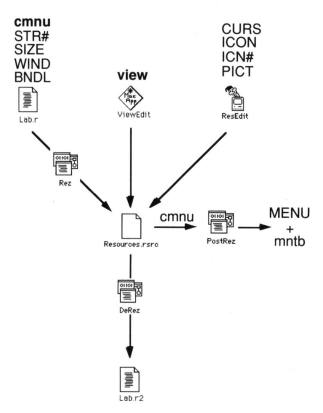

Figure 11-1. Tools for creating and editing resources

You will generally use all three of these in developing a typical program. For example, you will use the ViewEdit application (shipped with MacApp) to lay out the windows and the views contained in each window. In addition, you will usually use Apple's ResEdit utility program to create other graphic resources, such as icons, cursors, and pictures imported from the Scrapbook. Finally, you will describe string-based resources, such as menus, error messages, and string lists, using the special resource programming language of MPW's Rez resource compiler tool.

▶ ViewEdit

ViewEdit is generally used to describe view resources for each window and the associated views it contains. The resulting resources are stored in a file typically called views.rsrc, where the suffix indicates the resources are already in the binary format used by the Macintosh Toolbox. A typical screen from an early version of ViewEdit is shown in Figure 11-2. We will describe ViewEdit and view resources in more detail in Chapter 14.

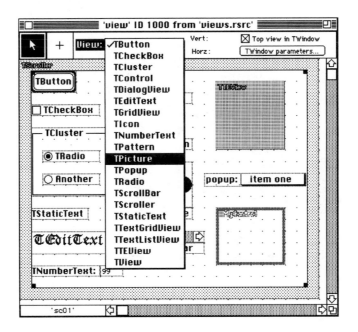

Figure 11-2. An early version of ViewEdit

▶ ResEdit

ResEdit is best suited to creating, editing, copying, and pasting graphic-based resources such as PICT, CURS, and ICON. If, for example, your program needed a 32-by-32 pixel stop sign image, you could draw an ICON resource in ResEdit, as shown in Figure 11-3. For further details on using ResEdit, you should consult the user's manual that comes with MPW or any other MacApp development system.

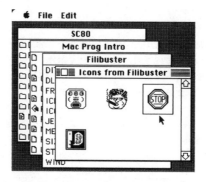

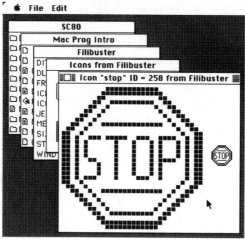

Figure 11-3. Using ResEdit to create an ICON resource

## ▶ Rez

Resources composed of strings of characters are best created by typing a description of them into a text file and then processing that text file with a resource compiler such as Rez. Rez is part of the MPW development system and represents a dramatic improvement over RMaker, which was the early resource compiler used by Macintosh programmers as far back as 1984.

Rez is particularly important because it serves two functions. Besides being able to compile a text description of resources such as menus and strings, Rez can include compiled resources from other files to build the final, completed application, as we described in Chapter 9. Consider the code fragment in Listing 11-1 taken from a typical .r file.

Listing 11-1. Including other resources

```
#if qDebug
    include "Debug.rsrc";
#endif
include "MacApp.rsrc";
include "views.rsrc";
include "Icon.rsrc";
include "Simple" 'CODE';
```

The include statements mean that the new version of the application will contain all the resources in the first four .rsrc files but only the CODE resources from the previous version of the application. The CODE resources are, of course, produced by the compile and link steps. In this way, Rez can be used to assemble a new version of the application from a number of separate resource files, created with ViewEdit, ResEdit, and/or Rez.

## ▶ DeRez

Figure 11-1 also shows the use of another MPW tool called DeRez, which is a resource decompiler. This is used most often for providing written documentation on the resources that you have created with utilities such as ViewEdit and ResEdit. DeRez takes any file containing resources as input and produces a text file description of those resources. For example, to derez the file produced by ViewEdit, you would execute the following MPW command:

```
DeRez "views.rsrc" "{MARIncludes}ViewTypes.r" > views.r
```

The meaning is as follows:

| | |
|---|---|
| DeRez | The name of the MPW tool |
| "views.rsrc" | The file containing the compiled resources |
| {MARIncludes} | An MPW shell variable path name to a Folder |
| ViewTypes.r | A MacApp file that describes the text format for views |
| > | Output redirection — from the Worksheet to a file |
| views.r | The new text file to which the text is redirected |

## ▶ PostRez

There is one more resource tool shown in Figure 11-1, called PostRez. This tool is used only with MacApp, because only MacApp programs use the special 'cmnu' resource described in Chapter 9. These command number menus are easy for programmers to use, since you only need to worry about the command number for each item rather than the menu and item numbers. The problem is that the Macintosh Toolbox routines do not understand command numbers — the Toolbox knows how to deal only with 'MENU' resources. Therefore, PostRez is executed by the MABuild tool each time new resources are created for your application, to convert your 'cmnu' resources into ordinary 'MENU' resources. PostRez also creates a lookup table to be used by MacApp at runtime to determine the command number when the user chooses a menu item. You will not have to use PostRez directly, so you don't need to know how it works. This explanation is provided just to satisfy the typical programmer's curiosity.

| By the Way ▶ | The Toolbox... the ROM... the operating system... system software... what do these phrases mean? Usually, they mean the same thing: the low-level calls upon which Macintosh programs depend. In the original 128K Macintosh introduced in 1984, programmers generally talked about the ROM calls when describing these routines, since the vast majority of them were burned into the 64 K ROM in each computer. These routines included the QuickDraw graphics libraries, the Window Manager library, the low-level operating system calls, and others. |
|---|---|

However, some of the functionality also resides in disk files such as the typically huge System file, which contains patches to the ROM routines, libraries of other useful routines called Packages, and many shared resources used by applications on that disk. The result is that many of the ROM routines are not in the ROM, so they are usually now called Toolbox routines or merely system software. Whatever you choose to call them, MacApp is based on them and uses these Toolbox calls to move windows, operate scrollbars, process events, print, and so forth.

## ▶ Creating and Managing Source Code

Resources usually play a major role in your user interface, but you are likely to spend much more time writing and debugging your source code than on resource definition. MPW provides a multiple-window text editor in which you can enter your source code or examine the MacApp source code provided by Apple. However, our experience with other object-oriented development systems such as Smalltalk-80 or Smalltalk/V has shown that it would be preferable to have a source code management system organized around the hierarchy of available classes of objects. Such tools are called code browsers, or just browsers.

## ▶ Browsers

Currently two browsers are available for use with MacApp. The most powerful one is an application shipped with MacApp called Mouser (pronounced to rhyme with browser), shown in Figure 11-4.

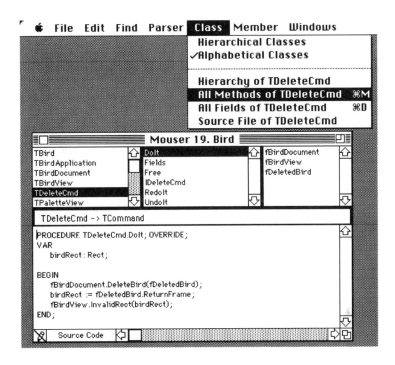

Figure 11-4. The Mouser code browser

Mouser displays a list of class names in the top left view, and displays method and variable names for the selected class in the next two views. The large view on the bottom displays the text of any selected method. You can actually use Mouser as a substitute for the MPW text editor and modify the method code directly.

In the 1.0D7 version of Mouser shipped with MacApp 2.0, you can modify the code in a method, but you cannot add new classes or methods. That is promised in later versions of Mouser.

Furthermore, it allows many types of searching and cross-referencing through both your code and the original MacApp source code. For example, you can find all methods that send the message DoIt to any object, or flatten the hierarchy and see all the methods inherited from your superclasses in one scrollable list. You should spend time learning to use your current version of Mouser, as it will make it much easier to navigate through the large class library you are using and customizing. Mouser, by the way, is written in MacApp, as is the ViewEdit tool mentioned previously. It can handle source code in Object Pascal or C++.

Another useful, but less powerful, browser is the Browser Desk Accessory sold by the MacApp Developers Association. It is a read-only browser without Mouser's searching and cross-reference capabilities, but by being a Desk Accessory, it is often more convenient to use. We use both tools at various times. It can be used only with Object Pascal source code, however, such as the MacApp source code.

## ▶ Recipes Files

Whether you use an ordinary text editor or a sophisticated data base access system with a browser front end, you still need to decide what code to write for each method. One helpful way to do this is to keep files full of typical code fragments available. These recipe files contain the complete code for typical versions of most of the common MacApp methods. They are particularly valuable for MacApp programming, since almost every program that you write will have similar versions of standard MacApp methods such as **DoMakeDocument**, **DoMake-Views**, **DoMenuCommand**, **DoRead**, **DoHighlightSelection**, and so forth. Similarly, practically every program will have a Rez .r file with definitions for resources such as 'SIZE', 'cmnu', 'ALRT', and 'DITL'.

Two typical recipes follow. The custom menu that we use in MPW to open the Recipes files is shown in Figure 11-5. These standard text files can be organized into the following:

- Recipes — C++ code fragments
- REZipes — resource descriptions for Rez
- MakeRecipes — a typical MPW Make file

A typical C++ recipe looks like Listing 11-2.

Listing 11-2. Typical C++ Recipe

```
1: //================================================================
2: #pragma segment AOpen
3: Pascal void TBirdDocument::IBirdDocument()
4: {
5:     this->IDocument (kFileType, kSignature, kUsesDataFork,
6:         !kUsesRsrcFork, !kDataOpen, !kRsrcOpen);
7:     fSavePrintInfo = true;
8: }
```

Figure 11-5. Our Special menu

Here is how you might use such a Recipe:

1. Copy the code fragment from your Recipe file. Be sure to include the #pragma statement, so that this method is placed in the correct code segment. This allows MacApp to optimize the memory management of your code segments.
2. Paste it into your implementation file (the .cp file).
3. Change the class name to your document class.
4. Copy the function declaration.
5. Paste this into the header file (the .h file).
6. Return to the implementation and modify the body of the method as needed.

A typical Rez resource recipe looks like Listing 11-3.

Listing 11-3. Typical Rez Recipe

```
 1: resource 'SIZE' (-1) {
 2:     saveScreen,                 // used by Switcher
 3:     acceptSuspendResumeEvents,  // always for MacApp
 4:     enableOptionSwitch,         // used by Switcher
 5:     canBackground,              // or cannotBackground
 6:     MultiFinderAware,           // always for MacApp
 7:     backgroundAndForeground,    // or onlyBackground
 8:     dontGetFrontClicks,         // or getFrontClicks
 9:     ignoreChildDiedEvents,      // use for apps
10:     is32BitCompatible,          // always for MacApp
11:     reserved, reserved, reserved, reserved,
12:     reserved, reserved, reserved,
```

```
13: #if qDebug
14:    500 * 1024,              // preferred with debugging
15:    400 * 1024               // minimum with debugging
16: #else
17:    400 * 1024,              // preferred without debugging
18:    300 * 1024               // minimum without debugging
19: #endif
20: };
```

## ▶ Debugging

Have you ever written a program that worked perfectly the first time? No? Well, neither has anyone else we know, so you will probably get to know the MacApp debugger quite well before you ship your first award-winning application. There are a number of different approaches and tools for debugging an application in MacApp.

One common way is to use a low-level debugger such as Apple's MacsBug or ICOM Simulation's TMON. A related approach is to use higher-level debuggers such as Jasik Designs' Debugger or MPW's SADE. In these cases, the debugger is a separate program, operating on a normal version of your application. A problem with this approach is that bugs in your program can often crash the program and even wipe out the debugger in the process. Another drawback is that it is often hard to solve many types of problems without using time-tested techniques such as printf statements that you embed in your application. A third problem with using traditional debuggers has to do with the method lookup process. Since many of your procedures and functions are accessed dynamically, through run-time lookup tables, most debuggers have trouble showing you where your code is as you single-step or trace code execution.

For these reasons, the MacApp programmers have provided very strong debugging support right in the MacApp source code. This debugging code is conditionally compiled. You can choose whether or not it should be included in your application. If you build your application in MPW by executing 'MABuild Sample -debug', then the debugging code is included. This will typically add 150 KBytes or more to the size of the application, so you can see that massive amounts of debugging support are included. If you build your program by executing MABuild Sample, then the debugging code will not be included.

## ▶ The MacApp Debugger

The debugging support that is part of MacApp includes the following:

- A special Debug menu
- A special Debug Transcript window
- The capability to set multiple breakpoints and to single step on method calls
- Various ways to examine an object's variables
- Support for optimizing memory management and usage
- Error checking and trapping to warn you of problems without crashing the program

There are a number of different ways to use any debugger. Of course, one use is to trap fatal errors. When serious bugs are encountered, normal program execution will stop, and you will then drop into the MacApp debugger (instead of dropping into MacsBug, for example). In this case, you can use the MacApp debugger to help you analyze the problem by examining the recent history of method calls, inspecting your objects' variables, and so forth. We will describe this process in more detail shortly.

The debugger is also valuable in many cases that do not involve fatal errors. For example, you can set a breakpoint at any method call and then single-step or trace through succeeding method calls to watch your program execute in slow motion. This technique is often used to analyze the cause of nonfatal errors, or even just to learn how MacApp performs a given operation. Furthermore, you can examine the Applications Heap and the execution stack to determine the memory requirements of your program. You will see some of these operations carried out in the next few pages.

**By the Way ▶**

Apple's MacApp programming team loves to add features to the debugger, so we can safely predict that there will be new goodies available every few months. Therefore, after you read the description that follows, be sure to check the latest documentation for new features that might have been added.

## ▶ The Debug Menu

The Debug menu and Debug window are both shown in Figure 11-6. Some of the functions of the Debug menu are shown in Figure 11-7.

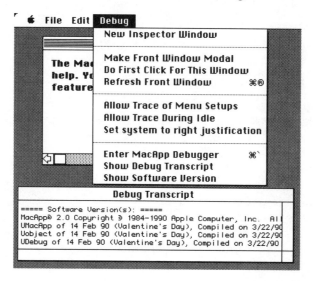

Figure 11-6. MacApp's Debug menu and Debug Transcript window

We'll describe the use of the Inspector and Debugger windows shortly. First, we should mention a few items of special interest in the menu. These include:

- Make Front Window Modal — This converts a modeless window into a modal one (or vice versa). Use this to compare the feel of a dialog box in the two cases, or to use debugger windows with a modal window.

- Do First Click For This Window — This choice means that a mouse click in this window, when it is inactive, will activate the window and also pass the mouse click to the appropriate view to be handled by the **DoMouseCommand** method. The Finder behaves this way, but most application windows do not. This option toggles the *fDoFirstClick* variable in the **TWindow** object.

- Refresh Front Window — This forces an update event for the front window, so that each view's **Draw** and **DoHighlightSelection** methods get called. Use this to test your **Draw** methods.

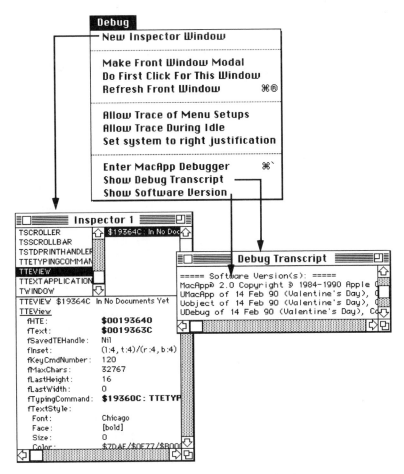

Figure 11-7. The Debug menu and its windows

## ▶ Inspector Windows

The first item in the menu will open special windows called Inspector windows, shown in more detail in Figure 11-8. An Inspector's job is to display the instance variables of any object in your program. A particularly nice feature of these Inspectors is that they can be used while the program continues to execute and some of the data they display is dynamically updated as your code executes.

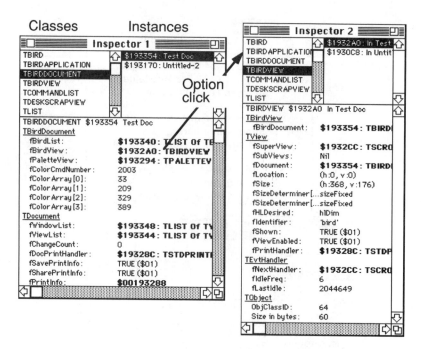

Figure 11-8. Inspector windows displaying instance variables

Consider the Inspector 1 window shown on the left side of Figure 11-8. Its upper-left view displays a list of all classes for which objects currently exist in memory. By selecting the **TBirdDocument** class in that view, you can see all the current instances of the class in the upper-right view. By selecting one of those actual objects, you can examine all of its instance variables in the lower view. The top line of this lower view shows the class name (TBIRDDOCUMENT), the hexadecimal handle to the object ($193354), and the document name (Test Doc). Below it are the current values for the instance variables defined for this class. Below them are the instance variables inherited from the superclasses.

Notice how nicely these values are formatted, with Boolean variables shown as TRUE or FALSE, integers shown in decimal rather than hex, strings shown as strings, and so on. That is the good news. The bad news is that you must help out the debugging code in order to get this useful display by writing a **Fields** method for each class that you define in your program. This method must give MacApp information about each instance variable defined for the class. MacApp calls these **Fields** methods to display this information in the Inspector windows.

## ▶ The Fields Method

A typical **Fields** method format may look strange to you. The example that follows shows the special *b* constants that you must use to identify the type of each instance variable. It deserves a bit of explanation. First, keep in mind that this method is called by MacApp when you inspect an object in an Inspector window or in the MacApp debugger. Therefore, it is MacApp's job to write the **DoToField** procedure that is passed in as a parameter to the **Fields** method. You do not have to know what the **DoToField** procedure does, but you should use it as follows: First, write the class name as a string, followed by NULL, followed by the constant bClass that tells MacApp that this line displays the class name in the Inspector, as shown in Listing 11-4. Then list an instance variable on each succeeding line (giving the name in double quotes), the address of the instance variable using the @ operator, and a constant for the type of variable. (See lines 7–10.) The current set of constants is listed in Table 11-1.

Listing 11-4. Typical Fields method

```
 1: pascal void
 2: TTextDocument::Fields(pascal void (*DoToField)(StringPtr
    fieldName,
 3:                        Ptr fieldAddr, short fieldType,
 4:                        void *DoToField_StaticLink),
 5:                        void *DoToField_StaticLink)
 6: {
 7:     (*DoToField)("\pTTextDocument", NULL, bClass, DoTo
    Field_StaticLink);
 8:     (*DoToField)("\pfTextHdl", (Ptr)&fTextHdl, bHandle,
 9:                                 DoToField_StaticLink);
10:     (*DoToField)("\pfTEView",(Ptr)&fTEView, bObject,
11:                                 DoToField_StaticLink);
12:     inherited::Fields(DoToField, DoToField_StaticLink);
13: }
```

Table 11-1.  Fields method constants

| *Constant* | *Meaning* |
| --- | --- |
| bInteger | 16-bit integer (base 10) |
| bHexInteger | 16-bit integer ($hexadecimal) |
| bLongInt | 32-bit long integer (base 10) |
| bHexLongInt | 32-bit long integer ($hex) |
| bString | Pascal string |
| bBoolean | TRUE or FALSE |
| bChar | single character |
| bPointer | address ($hex) |
| bHandle | indirect address ($hex) |
| bPoint | QuickDraw point (h:, v:) |
| bRect | QuickDraw rectangle (t:, l:, b: , r:) |
| bObject | reference to an object ($hex) |
| bByte | 8-bit value |
| bCmdNumber | Command number used in menu items |
| bClass | class name |
| bOSType | four character code for file types |
| bWindowPtr | pointer to Toolbox Window Record |
| bControlHandle | handle to Toolbox Control Record |
| bTEHandle | handle to Toolbox TextEdit Record |
| bLowByte | low 8 bits of a word |
| bHighByte | high 8 bits of a word |
| bPattern | QuickDraw pattern |
| bFixed | fixed point number |
| bReal | single precision floating-point number |
| bRgnHandle | handle to QuickDraw Region Record |
| bRGBColor | Color QuickDraw color specification |
| bTitle | string |
| bGrafPtr | pointer to QuickDraw GrafPort Record |
| bStyle | Toolbox Text style specification |
| bVCoordinate | 32-bit long integer coordinate |
| bVPoint | pair of VCoordinates (VPoint) |
| bVRect | four VCoordinates (VRect) |
| bFontName | Toolbox font name |
| bStringHandle | handle to Str255 |
| bCntlAdornment | adornment spec for a TControl |
| bSingle | single precision floating point number |
| bDouble | double precision floating point number |
| bExtended | extended precision floating point number |
| bIDType | view identifier |
| bResType | resource type |
| bSizeDeterminer | view size determiner (enum) |
| bHLState | highlight state of view (enum) |

By the way, you can open as many Inspector windows as you wish using the Debug menu. You can also open new ones by Option clicking on any variable in the lower view that references another object. For example, Figure 11-8 shows that holding the Option key while clicking the mouse on the *fBirdView* variable in Inspector 1 will open Inspector 2 which displays the variables inside that view object.

The Inspector shows special information under the **TObject** heading. You can see the Class ID, which is shown to be 60 for **TBirdView**. For Pascal objects, the class ID is stored in the first two bytes of each object — before the first variable. It is used as part of the method lookup process. You will rarely use the class ID in your programming, but we will mention a possible use for it in Chapter 22. The Inspector also shows the size in bytes of each object in the heap, in case you are concerned about memory use. Note that Figure 11-8 shows that each view object uses 56 bytes.

These Inspectors are extremely easy to use and can often display problems that would be very difficult to recognize using traditional debugging techniques. As one example, consider a program where the user creates **TCustomer** objects every time a new order is received by phone. You would be able to count each of the instances of **TCustomer** in the Inspector and see if the program was handling it correctly when reading a file from disk or handling Undo. A typical cause of a bug is forgetting to **Free** a customer object when it is no longer needed — you will be able to see this happen using the Inspector.

## ▶ The Debug Transcript Window

By default, the Debug window will not be visible, but you can make it appear using the Show Debug Transcript item on the menu, as shown in Figure 11-7. This menu item causes the window to appear but will not stop the execution of your program. If you want to stop the program and enter the debugger, you should use the Command-` (Command-backquote) keystroke combination, or choose the Enter MacApp Debugger menu item. (Of course, your program will also stop in the debugger when particularly bad code is encountered.)

There are two major uses for the Debug Transcript window: You can see the results of printf statements in this window, and you can interact with the MacApp debugger. Consider the method in Listing 11-5.

Listing 11-5. Writing to the Debug window

```
 1: #include <StdIO.h>    // for printf
 2:
 3: pascal void
 4: TSimpleApplication::ISimpleApplication()
 5: {
 6:     Point    aPoint;
 7:     Rect     aRect;
 8:
 9:     this->IApplication(kDocFileType);
10:     SetPt (&aPoint, 5, 12);
11:     SetRect (&aRect, 25, 50, 100, 246);
12: #if qDebug
13:     ProgramBreak ("\pShow this string in Debug Window");
14:     ProgramReport("\pShow in Debug Window, break if true",true);
15:     printf ("This is a number %d\n", 12345);
16:     WriteBoolean (true); printf ("\n");
17:     WrLblBoolean ("\pThe variable is", true); printf ("\n");
18:     WrLblPtr ("\pThe app is at", (long) this); printf ("\n");
19:     WrLblPt ("The point is", aPoint); printf ("\n");
20:     WrLblRect ("\pThe rectangle is", &aRect); printf ("\n");
21: #endif
22: }
```

This results in the Debug Transcript window display shown in Figure 11-9.

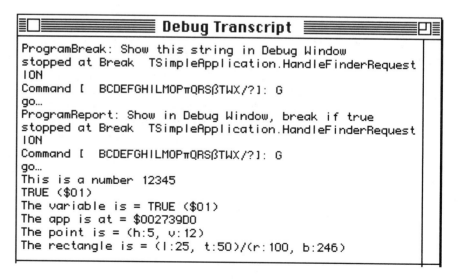

Figure 11-9. Write commands to the Debug window

Here are a few important points:

1. Be sure to include your debugging code between preprocessor conditional commands, so that it will not be included in your final shipping application. Line 12 of Listing 11-5 shows the use of the MacApp defined macro qDebug for this purpose. In the rare case where you would like it to be included, you should read the MacApp documentation on using the Transcript window.

2. You can use the normal printf function, by using #include <stdIO.h> in your file. MacApp also includes support for procedures such as

   - WriteBoolean, WrLblBoolean — for Boolean variables
   - WritePtr, WrLblPtr — for any pointer or handle address
   - WritePt, WrLblPt — for QuickDraw x-y coordinate pairs
   - WriteRect, WrLblRect — for QuickDraw rectangles
   - WriteVPt, WrLblVPt — for view coordinate pairs
   - WriteVRect, WrLblRect — for view coordinate rectangles
   - Others are defined in the header files UMacAppUtilities.h

   These routines format the output to make it easy to read, as shown in Figure 11-9, but, as you can see, they do not generate a carriage return. If you need one, you should add a printf ("\n") statement, like the one in the method we showed you.

3. You can include a breakpoint by calling the ProgramBreak function or a conditional breakpoint with the ProgramReport function, as shown in lines 13 and 14.

   Of course, the MacApp programmers are not going to let us have all the fun, so they make extensive use of these facilities in the thousands of lines of debugging code that are included in the MacApp source code. We will now describe how to use some of these features. If you have a Macintosh running a MacApp program that includes debugging code, you might run that program and work along with us.

## ▶ Entering the Debugger

The ways to enter the debugger include:

1. Compile a breakpoint into your code with the ProgramBreak or ProgramReport procedures.

2. Use the Enter MacApp Debugger menu item, or press Command-`. This will enter the debugger at a standard method.

3. Hold down the Shift, Option, and Command keys. This will drop you into the debugger of the next function boundary. However, the way described in step 2 above is preferred, since it enters the debugger at a well-defined location in the code.

4. Set one or more breakpoints from inside the debugger, and then run the program until you encounter one of these breakpoints.

5. Write bad code, so your program triggers the debugger's error checking routines. This will happen, for example, when you try to send a message to a nonexistent object, or when you try to use an object whose methods have been stripped by the Linker. This latter error is quite common, as you will see in Chapter 14's description of view resources.

6. Write really bad code, so that the Macintosh Operating System drops you into the debugger with errors such as ID 28: the heap and the stack have collided. If you get to the debugger this way, you may have damaged the heap and/or the stack enough so that the debugger will not be able to help you. However, in most cases, the debugger will prevent you from destroying everything and can then help you determine what went wrong.

## ▶ Debugger Commands

The debugger uses an old-fashioned command-line interface, so you must type the first letter of the desired command to execute it. You can use the mouse to manipulate the debug window, but not to choose a command. After entering the debugger, you can get a summary of commands by typing ?, which currently results in the display shown in Listing 11-6.

Listing 11-6. Summary of debugger commands

```
 1: ?/Help -- Display Help
 2: B -- Set a breakpoint
 3: C -- Clear a breakpoint
 4: D -- Display Memory
 5: E -- Enter Macsbug
 6: F -- Fields
 7: G -- Go
 8: H -- Heap & Stack...
 9: I -- Inspect
10: L -- Locals
11: M -- More
12: O -- Output Redirection
```

```
13: P -- Parameters
14: π (option-p) -- Performance Monitor...
15: Q -- Quit
16: R -- Recent PC history
17: S -- Stack Crawl
18: ß (option-s) -- Signal Failure(0, 0)
19: T -- Trace toggle
20: W -- Window...
21: X -- Toggle Flag...
22: Space -- Single step OVER deeper levels
23: Option-Space -- Single step INTO deeper levels
24: Cmd-BS/Cmd-CR, Arrows, Page keys -- Scroll
25: Cmd-` -- Break at normal entry
26: Cmd-Option-Shift -- Break at next procedure boundary
27: Cmd-Option-Control-Shift -- Break at next VBL (Danger Will
    Robinson!)
```

The ellipsis character (...) following certain descriptions indicates that they have subcommands. We discuss these debugger commands in the order you will most often use them rather than in the arbitrary alphabetical order in which they appear on the command line.

## B: Set Breakpoint

This command allows you to set a breakpoint upon entering and exiting any method. If a class name is entered, it will only break when that message is sent to an instance of that class. Multiple breakpoints can be set and later cleared with the C command. Breakpoints are useful for a number of reasons: You can determine if a certain message ever gets sent; stop before a crash occurs, so you can slowly step toward the problem; and stop at a method and examine the recent history to see how you got there. This last technique is commonly used to study how the MacApp methods work. For example, you can see what parts of MacApp called one of your own routines.

## Listing 11-7. Setting a breakpoint

```
1: Command [ BCDEFGHILMOPπQRSßTWX?]: B
2: Break at [Typename.ProcName or ProcName]?: TBirdView_Draw
3: Trace: OFF; Performance Monitor: OFF; Break[s] set at:
   TBIRDVIEW_DRAW
4: Last Broke at: Break TAPPLICATION.PERFORMCOMMAND Seg#: 25
   Self: $0019D7E8 is TBIRDAPPLICATION
```

| Warning ▶ | Breakpoints on C++ methods will not work with the MPW 3.1 C compiler. It should work with MPW 3.2 C and MPW 3.1 CFront, providing you use the '-trace on' option for CPlus. You can set this option in the Startup file in the MacApp folder, as one of the MA-Build Defaults. |
| --- | --- |

## G: Go

Use this command to continue execution of your program. This works after you encounter breakpoints or enter the debugger manually. This may not work if you have entered the debugger due to a serious code error, because many of these errors damage the contents of memory or the processor registers.

```
Command [ BCDEFGHILMOPπQRSTWX?]: G
go. . .
broke at Begin TBIRD3VIEW_DRAW Seg#: 26 Self:$0019DF58 is TBIRDVIEW
```

## C: Clear Breakpoint

Use this command to remove a breakpoint, so that your program will not stop there in the future. You can selectively clear breakpoints.

```
Command [ BCDEFGHILMOPπQRSTWX?]: C
Cleared the breakpoint.
Trace: OFF; Performance Monitor: OFF; No Break set.
Last Broke at: Begin TBIRD3VIEW.DRAW Seg#: 26 Self: 0019DF58 is
TBIRDVIEW
```

## R: Recent History

This command is extremely useful because it can show you what happened before your code ran into trouble. The reason it works is that the MacApp debugging code continually monitors and logs all method calls. This feature is always available, showing you the last fifty or so calls that occurred. The most recent call is shown last, in an indented display to show the nesting of subroutines. The display uses codes as follows:

> ">" means entering a routine (lines 7, 10, and so on)
> "<" means leaving a routine (lines 2, 3, and so on)
> "=" means a method call to SELF (lines 3, 6, and so on)
> "|" shows nested subroutine level routine with no class name means
> ordinary procedure (line 4)

Listing 11-8. Displaying the recent history

```
 1: Command [ BCDEFGHILMOPπQRSßTWX?]: R
 2: <TVIEW.ISFOCUSED
 3: | | | | | | | | | | | | | | | <=.VIEWTOQDRECT
 4: | | | | | | | | | | | | | | | <VISIBLERECT
 5: | | | | | | | | | | | | | | | <TVIEW.GETVISIBLERECT
 6: | | | | | | | | | | | | | | | =.DRAW
 7: | | | | | | | | | | | | | | | >=.COUNTSUBVIEWS
 8: | | | | | | | | | | | | | | | | TLIST.GETSIZE
 9: | | | | | | | | | | | | | | | <TVIEW.COUNTSUBVIEWS
10: | | | | | | | | | | | | | | | >MAKENEWRGN
11: | | | | | | | | | | | | | | | | TFAILNIL
12: | | | | | | | | | | | | | | | <MAKENEWRGN
13: | | | | | | | | | | | | | | | >TVIEW.EACHSUBVIEW
14: | | | | | | | | | | | | | | | >TLIST.EACH
15: >DRAWSUBVIEW
16: | TVIEW.ISSHOWN
17: | =.GETFRAME
18: | >=.DRAWCONTENTS
19: | | >=.FOCUS
20: | | | =.ISFOCUSED
21: | | | >=.FOCUSONSUPERVIEW
22: | | | |>TSCROLLER.FOCUS
23: | | | | |>TVIEW.FOCUS
24: | | | | | | =.ISFOCUSED
25: | | | | | | >=.GETWINDOW
26: | | | | | | | TWINDOW.GETWINDOW
27: | | | | | | | <TVIEW.GETWINDOW
28: | | | | | | <=.FOCUS
29: | | | | | <TSCROLLER.FOCUS
30: | | | | <TVIEW.FOCUSONSUPERVIEW
31: | | | | >=.QDTOVIEWRECT
32: | | | | | =.ISFOCUSED
33: | | | | <=.QDTOVIEWRECT
34: | | | | =.GETFRAME
35: | | | | >=.VIEWTOQDRECT
36: | | | | | =.ISFOCUSED
37: | | | | <=.VIEWTOQDRECT
38: | | | | >=.CLIPFURTHERTO
39: | | | | | =.ISFOCUSED
40: | | | | <=.CLIPFURTHERTO
41: | | | <=.FOCUS
42: | | | >=.GETVISIBLERECT
43: | | | | =.GETEXTENT
44: | | | | >=.VIEWTOQDRECT
45: | | | | |=.ISFOCUSED
46: | | | | <=.VIEWTOQDRECT
47: | | | | VISIBLERECT
48: | | <TVIEW.GETVISIBLERECT
```

### S: Stack Crawl

This command is extremely valuable because it shows all of the routines that are currently executing — that is, the nested subroutine calls that represent the execution stack. Listing 11-9 shows the output of a typical stack crawl that is a full 18 levels deep.

### Listing 11-9. A stack crawl display

```
 1: Command [ BCDEFGHILMOPπQRSßTWX?]: S
 2:    9 $001F5696: TVIEW.DRAWCONTENTS Seg#: 25 Self: $0019D690 is
       TWINDOW
 3:    8 $001F567E: TVIEW.EACHSUBVIEW Seg#: 25 Self: $0019D690 is
       TWINDOW
 4:    7 $001F5610: TLIST.EACH Seg#: 22 Self: $0019D61C is TLIST
 5:    6 $001F55E0: DRAWSUBVIEW Seg#: 25
 6:    5 $001F5560: TVIEW.DRAWCONTENTS Seg#: 25 Self: $0019D624 is
       TSCROLLER
 7:    4 $001F5548: TVIEW.EACHSUBVIEW Seg#: 25 Self: $0019D624 is
       TSCROLLER
 8:    3 $001F54DA: TLIST.EACH Seg#: 22 Self: $0019D5F0 is TLIST
 9:    2 $001F54AA: DRAWSUBVIEW Seg#: 25
10:    1 $001F542E: TVIEW.DRAWCONTENTS Seg#: 25 Self: $0019D5F8 is
       TBIRDVIEW
11:    0 $001F540E: TBIRDVIEW_DRAW Seg#: 26 Self: $0019D5F8 is
       TBIRDVIEW
12: More... [M]:
13: Command [ BCDEFGHILMOPπQRSßTWX?]: M
14: 18 $001F58D4: BIRD Seg#: 1
15: 17 $001F58BE: TAPPLICATION.RUN Seg#: 22 Self: $0019D7E8 is
       TBIRDAPPLICATION
16: 16 $001F58B2: TAPPLICATION.MAINEVENTLOOP Seg#: 22 Self:
       $0019D7E8 is TBIRDAPPLICATION
17: 15 $001F582C: TAPPLICATION.POLLEVENT Seg#: 25 Self:
       $0019D7E8 is TBIRDAPPLICATION
18: 14 $001F577A: TAPPLICATION.HANDLEEVENT Seg#: 25 Self:
       $0019D7E8 is TBIRDAPPLICATION
19: 13 $001F575A: TAPPLICATION.DISPATCHEVENT Seg#: 25 Self:
       $0019D7E8 is TBIRDAPPLICATION
20: 12 $001F5742: TAPPLICATION.HANDLEUPDATEEVENT Seg#: 25 Self:
       $0019D7E8 is TBIRDAPPLICATION
21: 11 $001F572A: TVIEW.UPDATE Seg#: 25 Self: $0019D690 is TWINDOW
22: 10 $001F5716: TWINDOW.DRAWCONTENTS Seg#: 25 Self: $0019D690
       is TWINDOW
```

You would read this display as follows:

Line 1: Type S to display the stack levels.

Lines 2-11: This shows the last 10 levels, with each horizontal line giving information about that stack frame. The information shown on each horizontal line is detailed in Figure 11-10. For example line 11 shows that the last method entered (stack level 0) was the **Draw** method, implemented in the class **TBirdView**. The code for that method is found in code segment number 26, while the object that actually received the Draw message was an instance of **TBirdView** with a handle of $19D5F8. Remember that the object that received the message may be an instance of a subclass of the class for which the method is written, due to polymorphism. You can see this on line 10, where the instance of **TBirdView** is sent the DrawContents message, which is implemented in the class **TView**.

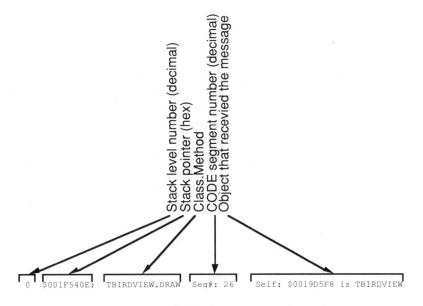

Figure 11-10. A line from the stack crawl

Line 12: More… tells you that there are more than 10 stack levels. By pressing M, you can see the rest of the levels displayed in lines 14-22.

Line 14: You would interpret this to mean that the application's main program began execution first, as you would expect. It then sent the **Run** message (line 15) to your application object, which called the **MainEventLoop** method (line 16), and so forth.

Notice that this program has at least 26 code segments, which is typical of a MacApp program.

By the Way ▶ The original Macintosh Operating System required that CODE resources be kept to no more than 32,767 bytes each. This means that a typical program with over 100 KBytes of code had to be broken into at least four code segments. However, efficient use of memory is easier to obtain by using a larger number of smaller code segments, as discussed in detail in Scott Knaster's excellent book *How to Write Macintosh Software*.

## I: Inspect

Inspect displays the same information that we saw in the Inspector windows above, except in a much less convenient format. You might wonder then why you would use this command. If your program has broken or crashed into the debugger, you cannot normally use the Inspector windows, so you would use this command instead.

By the Way ▶ At the risk of crashing the Macintosh, you can still try to use Inspector windows with a currently undocumented feature that can make your program come alive while stopped in the debugger. All you need do is hold down the Control key, and you can then use menus, windows, and so on. Remember, this may crash your program, so use this with care. The danger is that you may have entered the debugger while a handle is dereferenced and operating your program may move the heap object to which that dereferenced handle points. If your code later tries to use that address, you will be "in a heap o' trouble" — as the Memory Management Sheriff would say.

In the example shown in Listing 11-10, we are inspecting the object at stack level 0 (line 2), which happens to be an instance of **TBirdView**, with a handle of $0019D5F8. Notice that its document (line 4) has a hex handle of $0019D6C4. You can see how we inspect that document object on lines 8 and 9 using the handle rather than the decimal stack level. You can reference an object either way. Of course, we now come to the question of what you might do with the information displayed. The most common use for inspecting your objects is to try to determine why your program crashed. The most common single cause is uninitialized variables, so you should start by looking for those.

Listing 11-10. Inspecting objects in the debugger

```
 1: Command [ BCDEFGHILMOPπQRSßTWX?]: I
 2: Inspect what object [hex handle, or decimal stack level #]?: 0
 3: TBIRDVIEW $0019D5F8
 4: fSuperView=$0019D624 fSubViews=Nil fDocument=$0019D6C4
    fLocation=(h:0, v:0)
 5: fSize=(h:368, v:176) fSizeDeter[h]=sizeFixed fSizeDeter
    [v]=sizeFixed fHLDesired=4
 6: fIdentifier='bird' fShown=true ($01) fViewEnabled=true ($01)
    fPrintHandler=$0019D5E4
 7: fNextHandler=$0019D624 fIdleFreq = 0 fLastIdle=134487 ObjClass
    ID=60 Size in bytes=56
 8: Command [ BCDEFGHILMOPπQRSßTWX?]: I
 9: Inspect what object [hex handle, or decimal stack level #]?:
    19d6c4
10: TBIRDDOCUMENT $0019D6C4
11: fBirdView=$0019D5F8 fPaletteView=$0019D5EC fBirdList=$0019D6B0
    fColorCmdNumber=2001
12: fWindowList=$0019D6B8 fViewList=$0019D6B4 fChangeCount=0
    fDocPrintHandler=$0019D5E4
13: fSavePrintInfo=true ($01) fSharePrintInfo=true ($01)
    fPrintInfo=$0019D6AC fTitle=Test Doc
14: fFileType='varb' fCreator='varb' fVolRefNum=-32621 fModDate=
    -1585380552 fReopenAlert=true ($01)
15: fSaveExists=true ($01) fCommitOnSave=true ($01)
    fUsesDataFork=true ($01)
16: fUsesRsrcFork=false ($00) fDataOpen=false ($00)
    fRsrcOpen=false ($00) fDataPerm=1 fRsrcPerm=1
17: fDataRefnum=-32766 fRsrcRefNum=-32766 fSaveInPlace=2
    fNextHandler=$0019D7E8
18: fIdleFreq=2147483647 fLastIdle=0 ObjClassID=90 Size in bytes=
    86
```

## O: Output Redirect

The debugging window typically displays only the last hundred or so lines of debugging information, and you may want to see much more than that. If so, you should redirect the debugging output to a ordinary text file using this command. You can turn off the redirection by using the same O command and entering a blank file name. Output redirection is particularly valuable with the trace command described next.

```
Command [BCDEFGHILMOPπQRSTWX?]: O
Redirect to file?: trace.text
```

## T: Trace

The Trace command, followed by the Go command, causes your program to execute slowly, stopping to print debugging information at every method call as shown in Listing 11-11. This is particularly useful for sneaking up slowly on a place where you expect your program to crash. If it does, then you will have a trace of exactly what happened before the crash.

### Listing 11-11. Tracing program execution

```
 1: Command [ BCDEFGHILMOPπQRSßTWX?]: T
 2: Trace: ON; Performance Monitor: OFF; No Break set.
 3: Last Broke at: Begin TBIRDVIEW.DRAW Seg#: 26 Self: $0019D5F8 is
    TBIRDVIEW
 4: Command [ BCDEFGHILMOPπQRSßTWX?]: G
 5: go...
 6: Begin TVIEW.GETQDEXTENT Seg#: 25  Self: $0019D5F8 is TBIRDVIEW
 7: Begin TVIEW.VIEWTOQDPT Seg#: 25  Self: $0019D5F8 is TBIRDVIEW
 8: Begin TVIEW.ISFOCUSED Seg#: 25  Self: $0019D5F8 is TBIRDVIEW
 9: End  TVIEW.ISFOCUSED Seg#: 25  Self: $0019D5F8 is TBIRDVIEW
10: End  TVIEW.VIEWTOQDPT Seg#: 25  Self: $0019D5F8 is TBIRDVIEW
11: Begin TVIEW.VIEWTOQDPT Seg#: 25  Self: $0019D5F8 is TBIRDVIEW
12: Begin TVIEW.ISFOCUSED Seg#: 25  Self: $0019D5F8 is TBIRDVIEW
13: End  TVIEW.ISFOCUSED Seg#: 25  Self: $0019D5F8 is TBIRDVIEW
14: End  TVIEW.VIEWTOQDPT Seg#: 25  Self: $0019D5F8 is TBIRDVIEW
15: End  TVIEW.GETQDEXTENT Seg#: 25  Self: $0019D5F8 is TBIRDVIEW
16: Begin TBIRDDOCUMENT_FOREACHBIRDDO Seg#: 26  Self: $0019D6C4 is
    TBIRDDOCUMENT
17: Begin TLIST.EACH Seg#: 22  Self: $0019D6B0 is TLIST
18: Begin LOCAL Seg#: 26
19: Begin TBIRD_RETURNFRAME Seg#: 14  Self: $0019D6A8 is TBIRD
20: End  TBIRD_RETURNFRAME Seg#: 14  Self: $0019D6A8 is TBIRD
21: Begin TBIRD_DRAWBIRD Seg#: 26  Self: $0019D6A8 is TBIRD
22: Begin FAILNILRESOURCE Seg#: 1
23: End  FAILNILRESOURCE Seg#: 1
24: Begin TBIRD_RETURNFRAME Seg#: 14  Self: $0019D6A8 is TBIRD
25: End  TBIRD_RETURNFRAME Seg#: 14  Self: $0019D6A8 is TBIRD
26: End  TBIRD_DRAWBIRD Seg#: 26  Self: $0019D6A8 is TBIRD
27: End  LOCAL Seg#: 26
28: stopped at Begin LOCAL Seg#: 26
```

By the way, once you begin tracing, you will need to enter the debugger again to turn tracing off. You can enter the debugger with the Debug menu command or by holding down the Shift-Option-Command key combination. Then you can turn off tracing by again typing T.

## Space Bar: Single Step

If tracing happens too fast to allow you to observe its progress, you can single step through method calls by pressing the Space Bar; or you can trace slowly and continuously by holding down the Space Bar. You must, of course, be stopped in the debugger for this to work. Holding down the Option key while pressing the Space Bar steps into deeper levels. Without the Option key, you step over deeper levels, which progresses more quickly.

## H: Heap and Stack Commands

Typing H leads to another command line with the options shown in lines 3-10 of Listing 11-12. These commands will not be used too often in the process of chasing down bugs, but are usually used to study and optimize your memory management. Line 12 shows how to determine which code segments are currently in memory. This information is needed when creating the seg! resource that tells MacApp how much memory to allocate for your code segments. Lines 35 and 36 show how to determine memory and stack usage.

## Listing 11-12. Heap and Stack commands

```
 1: Command [  BCDEFGHILMOPπQRSßTWX/?]: H
 2: Heap/Stack Cmd [+BDIMRSß?]:
 3: + -- set breakpoint on procedure stack usage
 4: B -- set breakpoint on total stack usage
 5: D -- reset maximum stack depth
 6: I -- show heap/stack info
 7: M -- show heap/stack info AND MaxMem
 8: R -- show/set heap reserve
 9: S -- list LOADED segments
10: ß (option-S) -- list ALL segments
11:
12: Heap/Stack Cmd [+BDIMRSß?]: S
13: Total # segments = 32
14: • = resident, L = loaded
15: $0055484C Seg#:  1 • Main              9668 bytes
16: $0055480C Seg#:  2 L GNonRes          11860 bytes
17: $00554800 Seg#:  5 • GDebug           11448 bytes
18: $005547F8 Seg#:  7 • GFields          19660 bytes
19: $005547E4 Seg#: 12 • GInspector       18288 bytes
20: $005547E0 Seg#: 13 L GOpen            13412 bytes
21: $005547D8 Seg#: 15 L GSelCommand       7272 bytes
22: $005547CC Seg#: 18 • BBRes2            6148 bytes
23: $005547C8 Seg#: 19 • GWriteLn         16764 bytes
```

```
24: $005547C4  Seg#: 20 • GRes2                        19524 bytes
25: $005547C0  Seg#: 21 • GRes                         27444 bytes
26: $005547BC  Seg#: 22 • GDebugger                    29288 bytes
27: $005547B8  Seg#: 23 • GError                         684 bytes
28: $00554838  Seg#: 24 • MAMain                       16364 bytes
29: $005547B0  Seg#: 26 • GPerformanceTools             6048 bytes
30: $005547AC  Seg#: 27 • %_MethTables                  9794 bytes
31: $005547A8  Seg#: 28 • ARes                          1076 bytes
32:
33: Total loaded code = 224878
34:   Current temp space: locked = 224878, unlocked = 13852, total =
        238730
35: Command [  BCDEFGHILMOPπQRSßTWX/?]: H
36: Heap/Stack Cmd [+BDIMRSß?]: I
37: STACK
38:   Current total stack = 408        Maximum stack used = 4798
39:   Current procedure stack = 0       Available stack = 24584
40: RESERVES
41:   code = 261762 (OK) low space = 409(OK)  allocation flag:
        temporary
42: TEMP SPACE
43:   Current temp space: locked = 224878, unlocked = 13852, total =
        238730
44:   Needed reserve handle size = 23032
45: OTHER
46:   Max resource usage = 227138
47:   (permanent) FreeMem = 212928      Free master pointers = 291
48: Command [  BCDEFGHILMOPπQRSßTWX/?]: O
49: Redirect to file?:
```

## E: Enter Debugger

This command is used to enter a low-level debugger like MacsBug or TMON. You will not have to do this nearly as often as you would in ordinary Macintosh programming, but it is still useful. You might use it, for example, to look at the applications heap with a Heap Dump command or to set a breakpoint on a ToolBox call such as CopyBits. When you resume execution from a debugger like MacsBug, you will find yourself back in the MacApp debugger.

```
Command [  BCDEFGHILMOPπQRSßTWX/?]: E
```

### Q: Quit to Shell

This command is used after a serious crash. It returns you to the application from which you were launched (either the Finder or your development system). This is equivalent to executing the E command to enter a low-level debugger and then executing an ExitToShell command from that low-level debugger.

```
Command [  BCDEFGHILMOPπQRSßTWX/?]: Q
Exit to shell.  Are you sure [NY?]: Y
```

### Other Debugger Commands

There are a number of other debugger commands available but these are the ones you will use most often. If possible, you should experiment with a MacApp program, trying these various commands to see what happens. They are generally fun to try and you will learn quite a bit about how MacApp works by experimenting with breakpoints, tracing, and inspecting in the debugger.

## ▶ Debugging a Crash

If your program drops into the debugger, here are a few things to check.

First, read the first message printed in the debugger window. It will tell you why your program entered the debugger. For example, you may see something like *ProgramBreak: This method should be overridden.* When you encounter a program break, it means that either the MacApp code or your own code is warning you that you have done something wrong. Be sure to look at this warning, because it may tell you all you need to know.

Alternatively, it may say *Object that failed discipline = $F1F1F1.* This means that the MacApp error trapping code determined that you sent a message to something that was not a valid object. With this information and the information from a stack crawl, you can often determine exactly where the problem is. The principle is to look at the obvious clues before diving into any elaborate and complicated debugging sessions.

Second, look at what the screen status was when your program stopped. This can tell you what state the program was in when the problem occurred. For example, if the menu bar has not yet been installed, you know that the program crashed during the initialization of the main program. If the menus are up, but no window has appeared, then the problem may be in your **DoMakeViews** or **DoMakeWindows** methods. If the window appears, but it has no contents, the problem may be in your **Draw** method. Again, be sure to look at the obvious clues before starting any low-level debugging.

If you have no good clues yet, then a good strategy is to look at the recent history with R, do a stack crawl with S, and then inspect your documents and views with I. Be sure to look for variables that are not initialized, since that is a very common problem.

A special problem that occurs quite often involves the failure to return a command object from methods like **DoMenuCommand** or **DoMouseCommand**. These are functions that should return either a real command object, or the special global variable *gNoChanges* (or NULL). If you forget to return a command object, then MacApp will take whatever happens to be on the stack as the function result and try to send it a message. As an example, consider the case of a menu item that should display a Help dialog. You might have the code to display the Help dialog contained in your **DoMenuCommand** method, and it may work perfectly well to display the dialog. However, after the user closes the dialog, execution resumes in your **DoMenuCommand** method, which then exits without returning a valid command object. The program will then crash. Now that you are aware of this potential problem, you will probably never encounter it — but it's good to be prepared.

## ▶ Debugging conclusion

Bugs are unavoidable. The MacApp debugger will be of great help in trapping errors, and in helping you determine what went wrong. You will be glad that you took the time to become comfortable with using it.

## ▶ Summary

This chapter has described the use of tools that help you design your program, write it, and debug it. These tools include programs such as Rez and DeRez to manage resources, and a browser to manage source code. The MacApp debugging code is, of course, not a separate tool, but rather is part of every program that you write. Learning to fully use these tools will increase your productivity, and help you get the most benefit out of object programming with MacApp.

Chapter 12 is a collection of miscellaneous MacApp design and programming tips and techniques that will make your life as a MacApp programmer easier and your work more efficient.

# 12 ▶ Techniques and Mechanisms

This chapter is a collection of various techniques used by MacApp programmers, along with some behind-the-scenes explanations of how C++ works.

## ▶ Method Lookup: this and inherited

Method lookup is the mechanism by which your compiled code finds the correct method to execute when an object receives a message. C++ normally does this with vtables (virtual tables) that are automatically constructed by the compiler and Linker when your program is built. These tables are stored in certain CODE resources in the application heap when your program is launched. This is all done for you. In theory, you should not even care how the C++ compiler stores objects in memory or does method lookup, but in practice you will find it helpful to have a general understanding of the mechanisms. It helps in debugging at times, and it particularly helps in avoiding some nasty memory-management bugs regarding handles to relocatable objects, as we will see.

As you saw in earlier chapters, one of the great strengths of programming with objects is the ability to define subclasses that modify the behavior of an existing class. Consider, for example, that you want to write a graphics program structured like MacDraw, involving various shapes like boxes, ovals, and so forth. You might begin by defining a class **TBox**, as shown at the top of Figure 12-1.

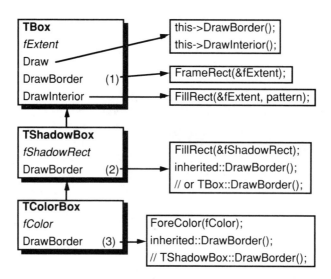

Figure 12-1. Subclassing to show the use of the "this" and inherited keywords

Note that its **Draw** method calls two other methods, **DrawBorder** and **DrawInterior**. For a simple box shape, these methods might be implemented using QuickDraw graphics calls (FrameRect and FillRect) as shown in the figure. Later you might decide to define a subclass of **TBox** called **TShadowBox** with a new **DrawBorder** method that provides a drop shadow of some sort, also shown in Figure 12-1. As the program grows and your customers buy machines with color displays, a third subclass, **TColorBox**, might then be added. You would now have defined three **DrawBorder** methods, two of which use the inherited keyword to reuse code from their superclasses. The original **Draw** method uses the "this" keyword to call the appropriate **DrawBorder** and **DrawInterior** methods.

---

**By the Way ▶** | Macintosh applications use the QuickDraw graphics library in the ROM to draw lines, boxes, ovals, polygons, and even text. In fact, other Toolbox routines call the QuickDraw routines to draw menus, window frames, scrollbars, dialog boxes, and so forth. Every pixel drawn anywhere on the screen is drawn using QuickDraw.

The questions now are: To what objects does "this" refer? and To which classes does "inherited" refer? Consider the code fragment in Listing 12-1.

Listing 12-1. Code that uses polymorphism

```
1: TBox *aBox = new TBox;
2: aBox->Draw();              // (1)
3: TShadowBox *aShadowBox = new TShadowBox;
4: aShadowBox->Draw();        // (2) (1)
5: TColorBox *aColorBox = new TColorBox;
6: aColorBox->Draw();         // (3) (2) (1)
```

When *aBox* receives the Draw message on line 2, the **Draw** method refers to "this". "this" is always a reference to the object that receives the message — in this case, *aBox*. Therefore, since *aBox* is an instance of class **TBox**, the **DrawBorder** method for **TBox** will be called.

When *aShadowBox* receives the Draw message on line 4, "this" refers to an instance of **TShadowBox**, so method lookup starts in the **TShadowBox** class, and its **DrawBorder** method will be used. Notice how this works. You might have written the **TBox::Draw** method first (say, in January), and the **TShadowBox::DrawBorder** method one month later (in February), but the method written in January will correctly call the method written one month later! This is very difficult to do without dynamic binding that looks up the correct method at runtime. We'll discuss how method lookup works in the next section.

"this" and "inherited" are two keywords that often lead to confusion, because they seem closely related. "this", as we have just seen, causes method lookup to begin at the class of the object that received the message. "inherited" is usually defined to mean "use the method of the superclass." However, it's not obvious exactly what that means. In our example, consider the aColorBox->Draw message on line 6. Since the receiver of the Draw message is an instance of **TColorBox**, that is the class where method lookup begins. **Draw** is not implemented there, so the method lookup continues to the **TShadowBox** class, and then to the **TBox** class, where **Draw** is finally found. The **Draw** method looks like this:

```
this -> DrawBorder();
this -> DrawInterior();
```

Since "this" is of class **TColorBox**, method lookup again starts there, and the **TColorBox::DrawBorder** method is called. Its code looks like this:

```
ForeColor(fColor);        // QD routine
inherited::DrawBorder(); // TShadowBox::DrawBorder();
```

inherited tells MacApp to use the method of the superclass, but which superclass? Should we use the superclass of "this" or the superclass of the class of the method we are executing? In this code fragment they are the same, so the question seems moot. But let's look at a situation that is just a little trickier. The **TShadowBox::DrawBorder** method looks like this:

```
FillRect(&fShadowRect);      // QD routine
inherited::DrawBorder();     //??::DrawBorder();
```

We have another use of inherited. If the rule were to use the superclass of the receiver, we would have a major problem, because this routine would then call itself. We do not want this method to call itself, but rather to call **TBox::DrawBorder**. Therefore, you can see that the rule is:

**Important ▶**

**"inherited" means use the method from the superclass of the method that contains the keyword "inherited."**

To summarize, "this" is dynamically determined (at runtime) to refer to the class of the object that receives the message. "inherited" is statically determined (at compile time) to refer to the superclass of the method containing the keyword. We'll discuss how dynamic method lookup is actually performed in the next section.

**By the Way ▶**

The "inherited" keyword requires some thought for you to be sure which method it will call. It is also only defined for methods in subclasses of **PascalObject**. You might well wonder why we prefer to use it. Consider the following two lines of code:

```
inherited::DrawBorder();//forPascalObject
TBox::DrawBorder();      // for any C++ class
```

Either way would work if you were writing the **TShadowBox::DrawBorder** method. The problem arises if you change the class hierarchy. What happens if you insert a new class in the hierarchy between **TBox** and **TShadowBox**? The inherited call will automatically adjust and call the method of **TShadowBox**'s immediate superclass. The explicit call to the **TBox** method will not adjust to the change, sometimes making your code less maintainable. We therefore recommend that you use the inherited keyword when using Pascal objects. Of course, sometimes it is useful to call a specific version of a method, which you can do by specifying the class name instead of inherited.

## ▶ How Are Objects Stored in Memory?

To see how objects exist on the heap and how their methods are found, we will examine some simple code fragments. Consider the class definitions in Listing 12-2, showing an abstract class **TShape**, and two concrete classes, **TCircle** and **TPolygon**:

Listing 12-2. Three graphics classes

```
1: class TShape: public TObject {
2:     private:
3:         short fColor;           // classic QD color
4:         short fPenSize;         // square pen
5:     public:
6:         virtual pascal void IShape(short color, short penSize);
7:         virtual pascal void DrawShape();
8:         virtual pascal void ChangeColor(short newColor);
9: };
10:
11: class TCircle: public TShape {
12:     private:
13:         float fRadius;
14:     public:
15:         virtual pascal void ICircle(short color,
16:                               short penSize, short diam);
17:         virtual pascal void DrawShape();    // override
18: };
19:
20: class TPolygon: public TShape {
21:     private:
22:         short fNumberSides;
23:     public:
24:         virtual pascal void IPolygon(short color,
25:                               short penSize, short sides);
26:         virtual pascal void DrawShape();    // override
27: };
```

Since class definitions are information used only by the compiler, these statements do not create any objects or allocate any memory. The code in Listing 12-3 does create objects, however. The heap diagram in Figure 12-2 shows the resulting objects in memory.

Listing 12-3. Creating circle and polygon objects

```
 1: void main()
 2: {
 3:     TCircle *aCircle = new TCircle;
 4:     FailNIL(aCircle);
 5:     aCircle->ICircle(redColor, 4, 13);
 6:
 7:     TPolygon *aPolygon = new TPolygon;
 8:     FailNIL(aPolygon);
 9:     aPolygon->IPolygon(greenColor, 1, 5);
10:
11:     aCircle->ChangeColor(yellowColor);
12:     aCircle->DrawShape();
13:     aPolygon->DrawShape();
14: }
```

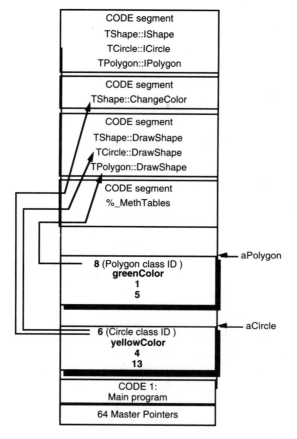

Figure 12-2. CODE resources and objects on the applications heap

Blocks of data on the heap are usually created starting at the bottom of the heap and growing upwards. The first (that is, the lowest) block on the heap is a block of 64 Master Pointers, followed by the main program (which is designated as CODE segment number 1 by most linkers). In addition to other data structures in the heap, Figure 12-2 shows that the call to new in line 3 of Listing 12-3 results in a relocatable block on the heap, accessed by *aCircle* as a handle.

**By the Way ▶**

Some blocks on the heap are created with the Toolbox call **NewPtr**, a function that returns the address of the beginning of the created block. This address is referred to as a pointer to the block. These nonrelocatable blocks can never move.

Most data on the heap are stored in relocatable blocks, created with the Toolbox call **NewHandle**. This function returns the indirect address of the block on the heap; the indirect address is called a handle. A handle is a pointer to a special Master Pointer which is created and managed by the Toolbox's memory management routines.

The new operator is used in MacApp programming to allocate relocatable objects on the heap when referring to Pascal objects, or nonrelocatable objects when referring to normal C++ classes.

The block does *not* contain the methods associated with *aCircle*, because that would be wasteful if more than one instance of **TCircle** were created. Each object does contain storage for its instance variables, however, because that is what distinguishes one instance of **TCircle** from another.

An easy way to think of it is that the variables in your class definition belong to each instance of the class (hence the name instance variables). Conversely, the methods belong to the class as a whole (since they are exactly the same for each instance).

**By the Way ▶**

We should mention that these would still be called *instance methods* because they result from messages that are sent to an instance of a class. In some object-oriented languages, like Smalltalk-80, you can also send messages to the class, so there are therefore also *class methods*. Calling a static method (member function) in C++ is somewhat like using a class method.

Note that the circle object contains storage for the variables we defined for the class **TCircle** and for any variables defined in a superclass of **TCircle**, the inherited variables. There is one additional piece of information stored in each object, and that is a 16-bit Class Identifier, which we rarely use. It is generated by the compiler/linker and is used in Object Pascal method lookup, which we'll discuss next. If we had not defined these classes as subclasses of **TObject** (and therefore of **Pascal-Object**), there would be one change. Instead of each object having a 16-bit Class Identifier, it would have a 32-bit pointer to the C++ vtable for that class. In any case, a reference to an object can be used by the compiled code to find the correct method.

▶ Method Lookup and Method Tables

Consider sending the ChangeColor message to the *aCircle* object shown in Figure 12-2. The compiler generates code that does the following:

1. Find the *aCircle* object in memory by dereferencing the *aCircle* handle.
2. Determine its class using the class identifier (arbitrarily shown to be 6 for all instances of **TCircle**).
3. Go to the CODE segments containing method tables and do a table lookup to find the address of the **ChangeColor** method for the class **TCircle**.
4. Execute that method.

The method lookup process for Pascal objects is actually a bit more complicated than that, but this is the general flow. Note that the table lookup that implements our dynamic binding ends up executing the **ChangeColor** method for **TShape**, since we never overrode that method in this example. However, when the DrawShape message is sent, we need the table lookup to determine which of the possible **DrawShape** methods should be used.

▶ Optimizing Performance

Dynamic binding through this table lookup is necessary to support the reusability of code provided by subclassing and overriding. Consider our current example. There are three **DrawShape** methods, so we need method lookup to find the correct one. Fortunately, there is only one **ChangeColor** method, so we should be able to skip the table lookup and jump directly to that subroutine.

The MPW linker allows that optimization for Object Pascal classes with the -opt option. The CFront preprocessor also performs optimization on code that does not use polymorphic methods. For further optimization, you can define methods inline as we discussed in Chapter 6.

## ▶ Cloning Versus Multiple References to an Object

Consider the code shown in Listing 12-4. Note that five pointers to **TCircle** objects are declared on line 3. What does that mean? Does it mean we have five circle objects in memory? Not necessarily. All it means (assuming **TCircle** derives from **PascalObject**) is that we have five handles (32-bit indirect addresses) available for our use. Whether or not they refer to circle objects depends on how we use them. Let's examine the code in sections to see what results.

Listing 12-4. Creating circle objects

```
 1: void main()
 2: {
 3:     TCircle    *aCircle, *bCircle, *cCircle, *dCircle, *eCircle;
 4:
 5:     aCircle = new TCircle;                  //make object
 6:     FailNIL(aCircle);                       //enough memory?
 7:     aCircle->ICircle(redColor, 4, 13);    //initialize
 8:
 9:     bCircle = new TCircle;
10:     FailNIL(bCircle);
11:     bCircle->ICircle(greenColor, 2, 67);
12:
13:     cCircle = aCircle;
14:
15:     dCircle = (TCircle *)aCircle->Clone();
             //Clone returns a TObject
16:     FailNIL(dCircle);
17:
18:     eCircle = new TCircle;
19:     FailNIL(eCircle);
20: }
```

Lines 5-7 create and initialize an instance of class **TCircle**, with *aCircle* as the variable that refers to it. We check to see if we have enough memory to create the object using the MacApp error handling routine, FailNIL. Be sure to always call FailNIL after allocating dynamic objects. We'll discuss this more in later chapters.

Lines 9-11 create and initialize another instance of **TCircle**, with *bCircle* as the variable that refers to it. However, things are about to get tricky.

Line 13 leaves two variables, *aCircle* and *cCircle*, which point to the same place in memory. We now have two references to the same object. Would you guess that this is a common situation? It turns out to be very common because any object that needs to send a message to our circle objects needs to have its address, so it would have a copy of the *aCircle* variable.

Line 15's slightly weird code creates a new object — referred to by the *dCircle* object reference variable — that is an exact copy (a clone) of the object referred to by the *aCircle* variable. You can see the new object in memory in Figure 12-3. The **Clone** method is provided in the **TObject** class, so it is available to all subclasses of **TObject**. Its only job is to make exact duplicates. Since the **Clone** function is defined to return a pointer to a **TObject**, we use *type casting* to tell the compiler that it is really returning a pointer to a **TCircle**.

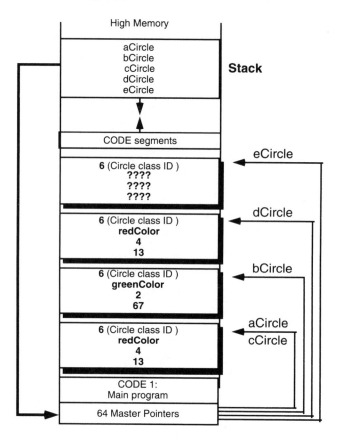

Figure 12-3. Five circle objects on the heap

**By the Way ▶**
Type casting in C, known as *type coercion* in Pascal, is used to keep the compiler from generating spurious error messages about type mismatch errors. Type casting does not change the actual machine code generated by the compiler.

Line 18 creates an object, referred to as *eCircle,* that is never initialized. This is legal, although potentially dangerous. In general, you will send each object an initialization message before using it to do any work.

## ▶ Using Variables

Before we begin to discuss initializing your variables, we should discuss what an object's variables are used for. There are at least three different categories of variables, including

- Variables that store data entered or needed by the end user of the application. These might be a ZIP code, a paragraph of text, or the size of a circle drawn on the screen. These data are often stored in, or referenced by, document objects and written to document files on disk.

- Variables that maintain the internal state of an object. For example, a circle might have an *fSelected* variable that is a Boolean. It will be set to true if the user clicks on it with the mouse, or false otherwise. Another example might be an *fSaved* variable that keeps track of whether or not the data in the file have been saved to disk. These variables are important to the operation of your program but are rarely saved as part of the document file on disk.

- Variables that hold references to other objects, so you can send them messages. If your moon lander object needs to send a message to your engine object to determine the current thrust, then the moon lander would have an *fEngine* variable that contains a handle to the associated engine object. Without maintaining this address, you can't send the message. These variables are particularly important; using an uninitialized variable as the receiver of a message will cause your program to crash spectacularly.

## ▶ Initializing Variables

Missing or incorrect initialization is a common source of bugs in object programming. We will cover this in some detail. The concept is simple: Before you use an object's variables, you must usually set them to reasonable values. Since we do not choose to use constructors in our MacApp samples, we will follow this rule: Define an initialization method for every class we create. Derive the variable name from the class name by replacing the T with an I. Consider the dog classes shown in the class diagram in Figure 12-4. The class **TDog** has an initialization method **IDog**, while the class **TBigDog** has an initialization method **IBigDog**. We'll explain why we do not override **IDog** in **TDog**'s subclasses shortly.

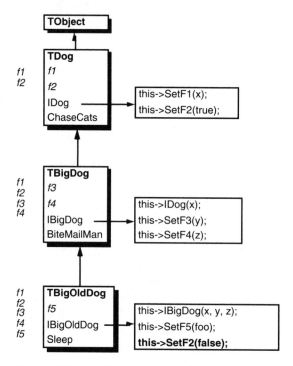

Figure 12-4. Initializing variables inherited from a superclass

Let's examine the initialization routines one at a time. **IDog** initializes the *f1* and *f2* variables defined in the **TDog** class. **IBigDog** directly initializes the *f3* and *f4* variables defined in its class, and calls **IDog**, the initialization method inherited from its direct superclass, to initialize the variables inherited from that superclass. Notice that **IDog** is a method for class **TBigDog** by inheritance, so we call that method using this->IDog rather than inherited::IDog. This initialization technique leads to another rule:

To initialize the variables in a class, first call the initialization method from the superclass to initialize any inherited variables and then initialize any variables defined in the subclass.

You can see how this rule is used in the **TBigOldDog::IBigOldDog** method to get variables *f1* through *f5* initialized. If this is so simple, why do novice object-oriented programmers make mistakes in this area? Most often, it is because they forget to call the initialization method from the superclass, and some of the unseen inherited variables do not get set to the right values.

For a more complicated and realistic example, study the class diagram and methods shown in Figure 12-5 and then mentally execute the **MakeTwoDogs** method in Listing 12-5.

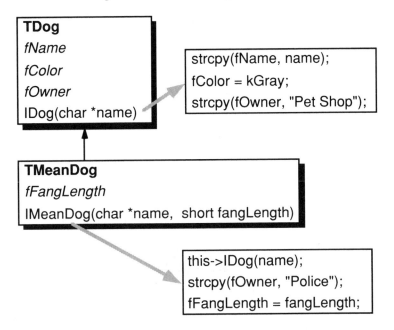

Figure 12-5. The class diagram and methods from a more elaborate initialization method

Listing 12-5. Initializing two different dog objects

```
1: void
2: TMyDocument::MakeTwoDogs(void)
3: {
4:     TDog *aDog = new TDog;
5:     aDog->IDog("Lassie");
6:     TMeanDog *aMeanDog = new TMeanDog;
7:     aMeanDog->IMeanDog("Fido", 4);
8: }
```

When this program executes, it results in the objects shown in Figure 12-6 being initialized on the heap.

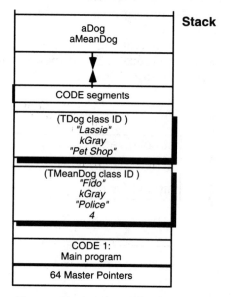

Figure 12-6. Initialized objects on the heap

Notice that the **IMeanDog** method has a different argument list than the **IDog** method. This is quite common, since a subclass often has extra variables to be initialized. This change in parameter lists is one reason why initialization methods have unique names for each class, rather than being an override of a superclass's initialization method. (This is true in Object Pascal, but in C++ we could use overloading.) Another reason involves optimizing your program. We pointed out earlier in this chapter that unique methods can be removed from the method lookup process and accessed as normal procedures and functions. Since your initialization methods will be unique, they can be optimized, making the program slightly smaller and faster.

## ▶ Variables that Reference Other Objects

As we have mentioned, many of your variables will be references to other objects. Although this is reasonable, it still is generally quite confusing at first, so an example is in order. Consider the Demo sample program shown at the top of Figure 12-7.

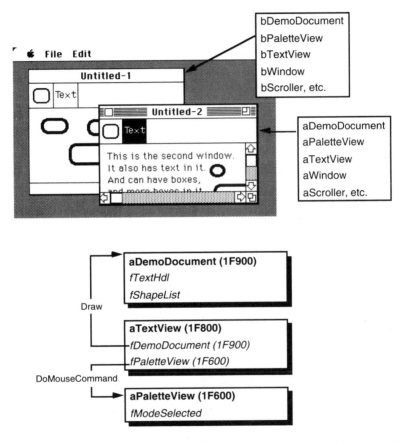

Figure 12-7. A typical application with groups of objects that work as teams

Each window in this sample program displays a tool palette on the top (in an instance of **TPaletteView**) and text and boxes entered by the user in the lower view, which is an instance of **TTextView**. Each window also has associated with it an instance of **TDemoDocument** that holds onto the data, and, of course, an instance of **TWindow** to hold onto the views. These objects work together, and consequently many of these objects need to send messages to others belonging to the same document.

Let's take a specific example. The document object associated with window Untitled-2 has two variables. They are

- *fTextHdl* — a handle to the raw text characters typed by the user. The document needs this so it can read and write disk files containing the text.
- *fShapeList* — a reference to the list object (an instance of **TList**) that holds onto a list of references to the individual boxes drawn by the user. The document needs this so it can read and write disk files containing the boxes. The text and graphics view (*aTextView*) will query the document to get this information so the boxes can draw themselves on the screen when necessary.

Note that the objects associated with window Untitled-1 do not generally need to send messages to the objects associated with window Untitled-2, so *aDemoDocument* does not keep a reference to *bDemoDocument*.

Now consider *aPaletteView*. It has only one variable, *fModeSelected*, which keeps track of whether the user has selected the text editing mode or the box-drawing mode of the palette.

Finally, consider *aTextView*. It needs

- *fDemoDocument* — a reference to the associated document, so it can send the document a message telling each of the shapes to draw themselves
- *fPaletteView* — a reference to the associated palette view, so that it can send a message to determine which mode the user has selected

An obvious question is: How does a person know which variables are needed when you design the program? The answer is that you often do not know until you begin to write the methods. During the implementation of your design, you often see the need for new variables so that messages can be sent to other objects. When the need arises, just go back to the class definition and add new variables as needed. But remember, you must then modify your initialization methods accordingly so those variables have correct values.

## ▶ MacApp's Variables

There are obviously hundreds of situations in the MacApp libraries when messages need to be sent to other objects. MacApp already has many variables that reference other objects. Some of these standard variables are shown in Figure 12-8. For example, each document keeps a list of all windows that display its data and each window keeps a reference to the document it belongs to. These variables are defined in the standard classes such as **TDocument, TWindow**, and **TView**. They are initialized as part of the code in **IDocument, IView**, and so on, so you can use them without worrying much about setting them up.

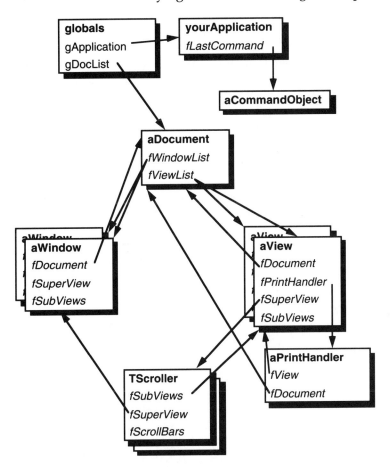

Figure 12-8. Some MacApp variables that reference other objects

For example, when you initialize a view that is a subclass of **TView**, your view's initialization method should remember to call the **IView** method, if you are creating views by procedure. We will see an example of that in the VProc sample described in Chapter 13.

A typical use of the IView method would be:

```
this->IView( itsDoc,      //  document that created view
             NULL         //  superview
             &gZeroVPt,   //  topLeft; here (0,0) as VPoint
             &itsSize,    //  width, height as VPoint
             sizeFixed,   //  width
             sizeFixed);  //  height
```

In some cases, you may use views that are not associated with a document, such as a floating palette view, or a view of a fixed picture that might be stored as a 'PICT' resource. In that case, merely pass NULL or Nil as the reference to the document. NULL is often used when an initialization method requires a reference to a nonexistent object.

## ▶ Display Lists

It is common in many object-oriented languages to keep dynamic lists of objects to be displayed. These lists are usually kept in your document object. They often contain mixed items belonging to an abstract superclass, so that a structured graphics program like MacDraw might keep a mixed list of shapes, some of which might be boxes and others ovals. We'll show you how to write a program that does this in Chapter 17.

Each item in the list is an object that stores data about itself. Each item usually has the capability of carrying out operations such as drawing itself or writing itself to disk. Examples of applications that might use display lists are shown in Table 12-1.

Table 12-1.  Applications that use display lists

| Application | Object in list |
| --- | --- |
| Accounting | Customers (TCustomer) |
| CAD/CAM | Shapes (TBox, TOval, TPolygon) |
| Chess Game | Chess Pieces (TPawn, TKing) |
| Kennel Mgmt | Pets (TDog, TCat) |

▶ # Garbage Collection

One of the challenges faced by programmers is how to avoid running out of memory. You can probably think of hundreds of things in your program that will use RAM, including your CODE segments, menu resources, QuickDraw data structures, and so forth. With MacApp, you have the extra problem of finding room in the heap for tens or hundreds (or, very rarely, thousands) of objects. This means that you must be neat and make sure that either you or MacApp disposes of anything in memory that you no longer need. Disposing of unneeded things in the heap is known as garbage collection.

MacApp does quite a bit of garbage collection for us. In particular, when the user clicks on a window's close box with the mouse, MacApp will normally dispose of the window, along with the associated document and view objects. This is done by sending the **Free** message to each of these objects. A problem arises when one of these objects — usually your document object — contains references to other heap objects. Unless you are careful, your document object may be disposed of, leaving behind other "dead bodies" on the heap. In a graphics program, these may be QuickDraw pictures or off-screen bitmaps. In a text editing program, they may be blocks of ASCII characters.

The solution to this problem is easy: Provide a new version of the **Free** method that disposes of the objects or data structures that would otherwise clutter the heap. Consider the Demo example program shown in Figure 12-9.

The document object contains references to a block of information text with the *fTextHdl* variable and holds onto a list of Shape objects with the *fShapeList* variable. When the document is sent the **Free** message, you would want to free the text, each shape object, the list of shape objects, and then the document object itself. The **TDemoDocument::Free** method shown in Listing 12-6 will do that.

Listing 12-6. A document's free method

```
1: #pragma segment AClose
2: pascal void TDemoDocument::Free()
3: {
4:     DisposeIfHandle(fTextHdl);  // free text
5:     if (fShapeList != NULL)
6:         fShapeList->FreeList(); // free Shape objects & List
7:     inherited::Free();
8: }
```

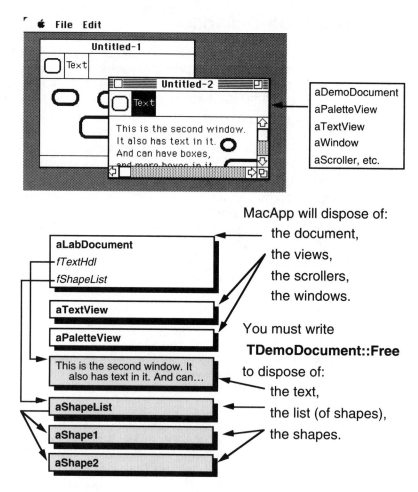

Figure 12-9. Disposing of blocks on the heap

MacApp's DisposeIfHandle utility routine is used on line 4 to free the text block if *fTextHandle* is not NULL. The rest of the garbage is disposed of with the **TList::FreeList** method shown on line 6, which frees each shape object in the list, and then frees the list itself.

## ▶ Summary

This chapter has presented a number of useful and interesting MacApp design and programming techniques that you could otherwise accumulate only by long experience in the MacApp environment.

Chapter 13 begins the process of exploring key MacApp class libraries in depth, starting with the use of various classes to display information to a user. In most cases we will show you how to use these classes in small MacApp programs.

# PART THREE

# ▶ Presenting Information to the User

In Part Three we will focus on the use of MacApp's classes and methods that play a role in displaying information to the user of your programs. This part contains five chapters.

▶ Chapter 13 describes and demonstrates the use of the basic display element in MacApp, the view. It explains the basic architecture of views and discusses how view classes work and what they contain. It provides a short sample program that you can use to create simple windows and views, and then describes how to support multiple-page printing of any view.

▶ Chapter 14 teaches you how to use MacApp's ViewEdit tool. This tool enables you to build complex windows and views without doing a significant amount of programming.

▶ Chapter 15 presents you with the information you need to create a window that will enable the user to edit text. It discusses the main code components that you'll need to create when you are ready to build a real application.

▶ Chapter 16 discusses the process of storing information in documents from a MacApp program. It explains how to use MacApp to read and write document files to disk. It then describes, in detail, how to write a simple multiple-window text editor that can read and write standard text files.

▶ Chapter 17 outlines the use of lists of objects in your MacApp programs. It describes a sample program that stores its data using lists of objects, and then uses those objects for screen display and disk file support.

# 13 ▶ Displaying Information in Views

The term *view* in MacApp has broader significance than you might realize at first glance. It also has a broader meaning than in other Macintosh applications or programming languages. From MacApp's perspective, nearly everything that gets displayed on the screen — with the major notable exception of menus — is a view. From the user's viewpoint, virtually all program input and output — again with the exception of menus — takes place through views. (Keyboard and other kinds of input are sometimes handled outside views, but these tend to be rare exceptions rather than the rule.)

This chapter

- explains basic view architecture: its properties, geometry, and spatial hierarchy
- reviews MacApp's view classes (including **TView**, **TWindow**, **TScroller**, **TGridView**, **TTEView**, and **TControl**)
- examines the relationships between views arranged in a hierarchy of superviews and subviews
- demonstrates how to create views by procedural methods

As a convention, when we describe methods associated with instances of each class, we will specifically point out where a method is one you should normally override. Any other methods mentioned are those you would normally use or call.

## ▶ Basic View Architecture

Views can respond to two different categories of messages: display messages and input-handling messages. They display information to the user by responding to such messages as Draw and DoHighlightSelection. They respond to user input related to their contents by responding to messages such as DoMenuCommand, DoMouseCommand, and DoKeyCommand.

Geometrically, each view has its own coordinate system, which means that its upper-left corner has a coordinate location of 0,0. Views can be placed inside other views, so there is a spatial subview/superview relationship, as shown in Figure 13-1.

Important ▶ | When you draw or place any information within a view, your drawing methods should always assume that the view's top-left corner is located at 0,0, even if the view is contained within another view.

In Figure 13-1, even though subview B's upper-left corner is at the location 50,50 when viewed from the perspective of superview A, drawing methods for subview B would operate on the assumption that its upper-left corner is located at 0,0. Remember that

- Each view has its own coordinate system.
- Each view may be installed in a superview.
- Each view may have a list of subviews installed in it.
- TopLeft is specified in superview coordinates.
- Size is specified by height and width.

### ▶ Scrolling a View

Figure 13-2 dissects a simple Macintosh window into its component parts: an instance of **TWindow**, an instance of **TScroller**, two instances of **TSScrollBar**, and the view of interest, arbitrarily called an instance of **TDogView**. Each of your application's windows will use a **TWindow** object, but you have a choice as to the use of scroller and scrollbar objects. The rule is that you should make the view of interest (e.g., a **TDogView**) a subview of a **TScroller** if the view can be larger than the part of the window in which it will be displayed. In other words, if you want the user to be able to scroll to see various parts of a view, then use an instance of **TScroller** as the superview. In most programs, this means you will also use one or two instances of **TSScrollBar** to control the scrolling. However, in a program like Apple's original MacPaint, the user scrolled using a "hand" tool, and no scroll bars were used.

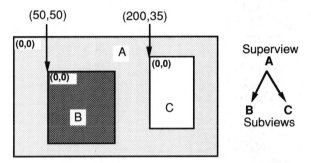

Figure 13-1. B and C as subviews of A; A as superview of B and C

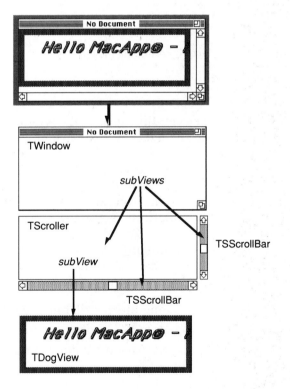

Figure 13-2. A simple window and its subviews

▶ View Clipping

In Figures 13-2 and 13-3, note that the scroller and the two scrollbars are subviews of the window, while the dog view is a subview of the scroller. There is a natural tendency to assume that the scrollbars would be subviews of the scroller, but they are not — they are merely objects that work as a team with the scroller. There is, in fact, an important rule that insures that the scroll bars cannot be subviews of the scroller:

| Important ▶ | Drawing of any subview is clipped to the borders of its superview. |
|---|---|

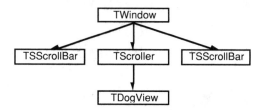

Figure 13-3. Superview/subview relationships

▶ Controlling Scrollbars

Keep in mind that the scroller fills most of the window in a simple window, and it resizes with the window. This means that a scroller can be larger than the view it scrolls, or it can be smaller. If the user resizes the window to be larger than the view (as in Figure 13-2), then the scrollbars are made inactive, as shown in the top of Figure 13-2. On the other hand, if the window and scroller were made smaller than the dog view, then the scrollbars are automatically activated, so the user can scroll the view relative to the window. To allow programmers to create extremely large views, such as are often needed for large word processing documents, the coordinate system used in views uses 32-bit values. To support this coordinate system, MacApp defines three new data types:

- VCoordinate, which is a long integer (32 bits)
- VPoint, which consists of two VCoordinate values
- VRect, which consists of either two VPoint or four VCoordinate values

This differs from most of the Toolbox which uses the QuickDraw-supported 16-bit coordinate system.

## ▶ MacApp View Classes in Review

In Chapter 7 we took a look at all of the classes of MacApp. We noted that the class **TView** is a subclass of the class **TEvtHandler**. Some subclasses of **TView** are shown in Figure 13-4. We will take a close look at many of these classes in this and the next few chapters as we discuss how to design and build the user interface portion of a MacApp program.

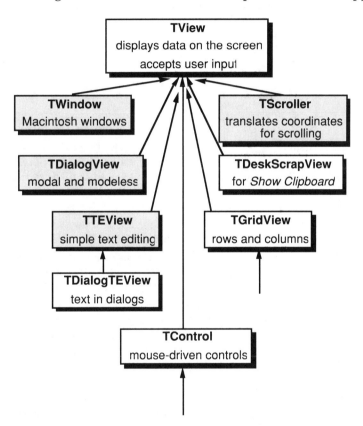

Figure 13-4. Subclasses of TView class

## ▶ The TView Class

**TView** is an abstract class that must be subclassed to create a usable view. This section describes the **TView** class in terms of some of the variables it contains and the messages it understands.

### TView Variables

**TView** defines a number of instance variables, the most important of which are shown in Table 13-1.

Table 13-1. TView variables

| Variable name | Description |
| --- | --- |
| fSuperView | Name of view containing this view; NULL if none. |
| fSubViews | List of views contained in this view; NULL if none. |
| fLocation | Upper-left corner location within superview, if any (32-bit coordinates). |
| fSize | Height and width of this view (32-bit coordinates). |
| fSizeDeterminer | Describes the minimum size of the view in terms of one of the enumerated types shown in Table 13-2. |
| fHLDesired | Defines the type of highlighting to be used to draw the current selection in the view, if any. Set to hlOn when the view is activated and to hlOff or hlDim when the view is deactivated. |
| fIdentifier | A four-character identifier. With this identifier's value, you can obtain a reference to the view by calling the **TView::FindSubView** method. |
| fShown | Determines whether the view is visible or not. Generally, this variable is not accessed directly; rather the **IsShown** and **Shown** methods are used to set or get its value. |
| fViewEnabled | Boolean value. If true, view responds to mouse clicks; if false, it does not. Generally, this variable is not accessed directly; rather the **ViewEnable** and **IsViewEnabled** methods are used to set or get its value. |
| fPrintHandler | Reference to the print handler associated with this hander; NULL if this is a nonprintable view. |

Table 13-2 shows the enumerated types that can be assigned to the variable *fSizeDeterminer*. (Note that the methods used to calculate the height of a view can be different from those used to calculate its width.)

Table 13-2. Legal enumerated types for variable *fSizeDeterminer*

| Value | Interpretation |
| --- | --- |
| sizeFixed | Height and/or width of view is constant as determined by your initialization routines. |
| sizeVariable | View determines its height and/or width by overriding the method **CalcMinSize**. |
| sizeSuperView | Height and/or width is same as superview so that any change in size of superview directly alters view's size. |
| sizeRelSuperView | Height and/or width is related directly to superview so that any change in size of superview directly alters view's size (not 100% of the size of the superview as with sizeSuper-View). For example, if the superview's size is increased by 125 pixels, this view's size will also be increased by 125 pixels. This choice is commonly used for scrollers such as the one shown in Figure 13-2. |
| sizePage | View is exactly the size of a page as defined by the view's print handler, as set by the user in the Page Setup dialog box. |
| sizeFillPages | Uses the **CalcMinSize** method to determine the view's minimum size, with the result rounded up to fill the last page. |

## TView Messages

An instance of class **TView** understands a total of more than seventy-five messages in addition to printing-related messages. Let's take a quick look at about two dozen of the more important ones. We'll focus on those that are most commonly used; the others are documented in the MacApp reference manuals.

*Coordinate Conversion Messages* Two coordinate conversion routines are significant. The functions QDToViewPt and ViewToQDPt both involve converting between points expressed in the view's coordinates and those expressed in QuickDraw coordinates. If the height and width of the view are both less than 30,000 (the value for global constant kMaxCoord), then no conversion is necessary. Otherwise, there is some difference between the two point expressions. Here are the interfaces to these routines:

```
virtual pascal void QDToViewPt(Point qdPoint, VPoint *viewPt);
virtual pascal Point ViewToQDPt(VPoint *viewPt);
```

*Subview Management Messages* There are four significant messages associated with the management of subviews in the class **TView**: AddSubView, RemoveSubView, EachSubView, and FindSubView. The purposes of the first two are self-evident from their names. The message

EachSubView takes a function name and parameters as an argument and applies it in turn to each subview in the view that receives the message. FindSubView is used to locate a particular view with a particular *fIdentifier* that is a subview (even indirectly) of the recipient of the message. Here are the interfaces for these four routines:

```
virtual pascal void AddSubView(TView *theSubview);
virtual pascal void RemoveSubView(TView *theSubview);
virtual pascal void EachSubView(pascal void (*DoToSubview)(TView
    *theSubview, void * DoToSubview_StaticLink), void
    *DoToSubview_StaticLink);
virtual pascal TView *FindSubView(ResType itsIdentifier);
```

*Size Messages* Managing the size of a view based on user actions and determining the current size of a view are supported by four messages known to the class **TView**: AdjustSize, CalcMinSize, GetExtent, and GetFrame. The first, AdjustSize, is called any time a change occurs that could affect the size of the view, notably when the data displayed in the view change. MacApp responds to the message by automatically sending the appropriate messages to the view if the size should be changed. The interface to this procedure looks like this:

```
virtual pascal void AdjustSize(void);
```

The method **CalcMinSize** returns the view's current size unless it is overridden. You often override **CalcMinSize** so it returns the minimum size the view is permitted to occupy. Its interface is

```
virtual pascal void CalcMinSize(VPoint *minSize);
```

To obtain the boundaries of the rectangle now occupied by a view, call the **GetExtent** method. It returns the upper-left and lower-right corners as points. Its interface looks like this:

```
virtual pascal void GetExtent(VRect *itsExtent);
```

The **GetExtent** method has a counterpart called **GetFrame** that also returns the view's rectangle, but expresses this rectangle in terms of the superview's coordinates. **GetFrame's** interface is

```
virtual pascal void GetFrame(VRect *itsFrame);
```

In Figure 13-1, for example, assume that subview B has a location of 50, 50 and a size of 150, 200. Sending it the message:

```
GetExtent (& itsExtent);
```

would assign the value 0, 0, 150, 200 to the variable *itsExtent*. But the message

```
GetFrame (& itsFrame);
```

would assign the value 50, 50, 200, 250 to the variable *itsFrame*.

*Focus Message* One of the most powerful and useful methods in MacApp's view-handling vocabulary is the **Focus** method. This method takes care of a number of highly complex tasks in a single, simple call. It is a function that returns a Boolean value: true if it succeeds, false if an error arises because, for example, the view is not installed in a window. Its interface is simple:

```
virtual pascal boolean Focus(void);
```

The **Focus** method performs three crucial operations, using the following QuickDraw routines:

1. **SetPort** — The window in which the view is installed is set to be the active grafPort, which means that QuickDraw instructions will apply to this window.
2. **SetOrigin** — The window's origin (i.e., its (0, 0) point) is set to be the top-left corner of the focused view. This insures that drawing will take place in the local coordinate system of your view, even if the view is offset from the normal origin of the window. This coordinate system shift also corrects for offsets due to scrolling your view or any of its superviews.
3. **SetClip** — This insures that drawing is clipped to the borders of your superview. Without this, your **Draw** method might write all over your scrollbars and adjacent views.

This wonderful **Focus** message is sent to your view by MacApp before it sends your view the **Draw** message in response to update events. This means that your view's **Draw** method does not have to care where in the window it is located, or what the scrollbar positions are. This feature alone makes Macintosh programming with MacApp much easier than it ever was before. If you ever find your view drawing in the wrong place in the window, you may not be focused.

A good rule is to never call **Draw** directly, but rather force update events by invalidating the view. MacApp can then focus your view before the **Draw** message is sent. If you do wish to call **Draw** directly for performance reasons, then be sure to focus first.

*Messages to Draw View Contents* Once a view has been set up for drawing by the **Focus** method, it can be sent a number of messages to draw its contents. The most significant of these methods are **Draw**, **DoHighlightSelection**, and **Adorn**.

The **Draw** method draws the view itself. You will often override the **Draw** method. Its interface looks like this:

```
virtual pascal void Draw(Rect *area);
```

The argument passed to the method is a rectangle (defined in Quick-Draw coordinates) that encloses the area that needs to be updated or printed. Using this rectangle, your Draw method can be optimized to only draw the part of the view that needs to be updated. This can make for fast screen updating.

Another drawing method that you will often override is **DoHighlightSelection**. It highlights any selection the view contains. Handling the selection in all the possible combinations of circumstances of the view's activation and deactivation can be terribly complex if you write a Macintosh program without using MacApp, but this method makes it practical to give the user the feeling of a rich interface that is intelligent about the way it handles text and other selected items. The interface to **DoHighlightSelection** looks like this:

```
virtual pascal void DoHighlightSelection
(HLState fromHL, HLState toHL);
```

The three states to which the two arguments can be set are hlOn, hlOff, and hlDim. A transition from any of these states to another requires special handling. For example, to change the selection in an active view, you could use:

```
DoHighlightSelection(hlOn, hlOff);  // turn off current selection
...                                 // change selection
DoHighlightSelection(hlOff, hlOn);  // turn on new selection
```

Figure 13-5 shows the differences among the three values of highlighting in a collection of two graphic objects. Notice that the selection description applies in this case to the handles defining the boundaries of the objects and not to the graphic shapes themselves. In the case of text, it is the shadowing of the highlighted text that is affected by the value of the arguments to the **DoHighlightSelection** method.

The **Adorn** method simply draws a frame around the view. The interface to the method is

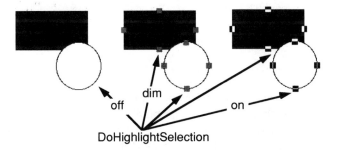

DoHighlightSelection

Figure 13-5. The three highlighting states

```
virtual pascal void Adorn (Rect *area, Point itsPenSize, unsigned
short itsAdornment);
```

The value of itsAdornment is set to define the way you want the view's border drawn. It can contain any of the values shown in Table 13-3.

Table 13-3. Adornment elements

| *Value* | *Meaning* |
| --- | --- |
| adnLineTop | Draw a line at the top of the extent. |
| adnLineLeft | Draw a line at the left of the extent. |
| adnLineBottom | Draw a line at the bottom edge of the extent. |
| adnLineRight | Draw a line on the right side of the extent. |
| adnOval | Draw an oval frame (with Toolbox call to FrameOval) around the extent. |
| adnRRect | Draw a round-cornered rectangle around the  extent (with a call to the Toolbox of (16,16) FrameRoundRect). |
| adnShadow | Draw drop shadows against framed selections. |

*Messages for Redrawing*  When the contents of a rectangle are no longer valid as displayed, Macintosh deals with it by redrawing the contents. It is up to the program to notify the Macintosh operating system's Toolbox routines when it is necessary. When a view is displaying data that is being changed, for example, your application must notify the Macintosh that some or all of the contents of your application's window are no longer valid. Two methods facilitate this process in MacApp. The **InvalidRect** method is passed a specific portion of your view and forces the Macintosh to redraw it. This method focuses the view, and then calls the Toolbox routine InvalRect. Its interface is

```
virtual pascal void InvalidRect(Rect *r);
```

To invalidate the entire view, you use the **ForceRedraw** method:

```
virtual pascal void ForceRedraw(void);
```

*Mouse Messages* The **DoMouseCommand** method is one you will override for each view that must be able to respond to a mouse click. If you don't override it, nothing will happen when the user clicks in your view because that is MacApp's default behavior (see Chapter 8). Here is the interface to the **DoMouseCommand** method:

```
virtual pascal struct TCommand *DoMouseCommand (Point *theMouse,
EventInfo *Info, Point *hysteresis);
```

If the mouse-click being dealt with is not undoable and need not be tracked while the mouse button is held down, then your call to **DoMouseCommand** should return the global *gNoChanges* (or NULL). But if the mouse-click is either undoable or requires tracking, then your method should create a command object. (We will have more to say about command objects in Chapter 18 when we discuss mouse interaction in greater detail. For the moment, just note that whether or not you create such an object is strictly a function of whether you need an object related to the mouse behavior so that you can communicate with it as needed. If the mouse-click is a one-time event, no such command object is needed.)

*Cursor Shape* You may want to customize the shape of the mouse pointer as it moves into your view or when it passes over certain parts of your view. Many Macintosh word processing programs, for example, alter the normal I-beam cursor to an italic shape when the cursor is placed over italic text. To accomplish this kind of customization, you will override the method **DoSetCursor**:

```
virtual pascal boolean DoSetCursor(Point localPoint, RgnHandle
cursorRgn);
```

## ▶ The TWindow Class

We will look briefly at the class **TWindow**, focusing on its important variables. Methods understood by this class are not discussed because they are seldom overridden, so you don't need to understand their operation. (We will never override a method of the class **TWindow** in any of our sample applications.) Table 13-4 summarizes the significant variables of the **TWindow** class.

Table 13-4.  Major variables of TWindow

| Variable | Description/notes |
|----------|-------------------|
| *fIsActive* | Indicates whether this window is active. |
| *fIsResizable* | Indicates whether the window includes a grow box. |
| *fIsClosable* | Indicates whether the window can be closed. If true, then the Close menu item is available when this window is active. If the window type includes a close box, this value is set to true. |
| *fIsModal* | If true, indicates that the window is modal (that is, that no other window can be activated while this window is active). If false, window is a normal modeless Macintosh window. |
| *fDoFirstClick* | Default is false, indicating this window does not respond to mouse clicks unless it is the front window. If set to true, this window will always respond to the first mouse click, even when it isn't the top window. (The operation of the Finder demonstrates this behavior.) |
| *fFreeOnClosing* | If true, this object is freed when the window is closed. Default value is false, indicating no automatic freeing of memory. |
| *fDisposeOnFree* | If true, then when the window object is sent the Free message, MacApp calls the Window Manager Toolbox routine DisposeWindow — on the window record. |
| *fClosesDocument* | If true, closing the window also closes its associated document. |
| *fOpenInitially* | If true, this window opens automatically when its associated document is opened. |
| *fAdapted* | If the window adapts to different screen sizes by calling **TWindow. AdaptToScreen**, this variable is true. Otherwise, it is false. |
| *fStaggered* | If true, this window was staggered by its custom **Stagger** method. This is the normal behavior you would choose for document windows. |
| *fForcedOnScreen* | If true, this window was forced onto the display even when its location would put it completely or partly off the display. |
| *fHorzCentered* | If set to true, the window is centered horizontally on the screen. |
| *fVertCentered* | If set to true, the window is centered vertically on the screen. |
| *fProcID* | The Window Proc ID that defines this window's type. |

▶ The TScroller Class

Scrollers differ from the other views in that they are invisible, but you must have an instance of the **TScroller** class if you want to scroll any other views in a window. Generally, a scroller is a subview of a window. A large view you wish to scroll will then be defined as a subview of the scroller. Figure 13-2 illustrates this. The **TScroller** class has a small number of variables associated with it. Some of these are summarized in Table 13-5.

Table 13-5. Important variables of TScroller

| Variable | Description/notes |
|----------|-------------------|
| fScrollLimit | Maximum horizontal and vertical location point that can be displayed in scroller. |
| fScrollUnit | Number of pixels change to be made in the view when the scroller receives a message indicating the user has pressed the mouse on a scrollbar's arrow. |
| fConstrain | If true, translation values of the scroller will be constrained to even multiples of *fScrollUnit* in the applicable direction. |

## The TGridView Classes

The **TGridView** class and its subclasses are shown in Figure 13-6. These classes are useful for building views of spreadsheets, tables of data, and lists of data on the screen. Notice that the class **TGridView** itself defines an array of rows and columns, and that as we travel down the class diagram in Figure 13-6, the functions of the class become more specialized. Note, too, that the class **TTextListView** is a grid view even though it has only one column. The MacApp library provides the abstract classes **TGridView**, **TTextGridView**, and **TTextListView**. You must always subclass these to override methods such as **DrawCell** and **GetItemText**, as shown in Figure 13-6.

▶ The TTEView Class

The **TTEView** class is part of the UTEView unit in MacApp. It is used to create text-editing windows that support full-styled text editing.

This **TTEView** class works extremely well in MacApp and seldom requires you to do any subclassing to make it usable in your applications.

A method you will have frequent need to call is **StuffText**. This method sets the text displayed in the view, overwriting the existing text and style information. Its interface looks like this:

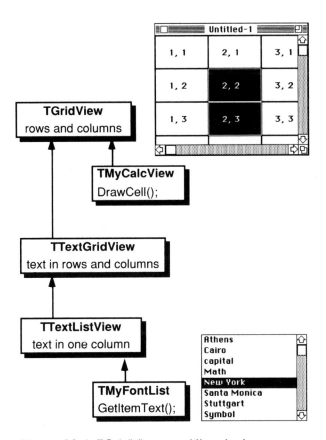

Figure 13-6. TGridView and its subclasses

```
virtual pascal void StuffText(Handle theText);
```

You will occasionally want to override the **DoMouseCommand** method to handle mouse clicks differently from the way instances of class **TTEView** normally deal with mouse clicks. The interface to this method looks like this:

```
virtual pascal TCommand *DoMouseCommand(Point *theMouse,
EventInfo *info, Point *hysteresis);
```

The **Draw** method in the class **TTEView** draws and prints the text. Normally, its behavior is exactly what you want but if you wish to define a special type of behavior, you can override it. Its interface looks like this:

```
virtual pascal void Draw(Rect *area);
```

In addition to these methods, there are three other methods that are used to create command objects in instances of **TTEView**. (Command objects support the Undo command. They are covered in greater detail in Chapter 18 when we discuss menu operations where such command objects are more commonly required.) A call to the **DoMakeTyping-Command** method, for example, creates an instance of the class **TTETypingCommand**; that instance is an object that supports undoing typing operations. Similarly, the **DoMakeEditCommand** method creates instances of the command object classes **TTECutCopyCommand** and **TTEPasteCommand**, and a call to **DoMakeStyleCommand** generates an instance of the command object class **TTEStyleCommand**. These routines are called by the normal methods of **TTEView**, and instances of these command objects are created. The result is that **TTEView** supports Undo for typing, Cut, Copy, and Paste automatically. All you need to do is create the view, and everything works. It is quite impressive.

### ▶ The TControl Classes

Among the more important classes in MacApp are the classes derived from the **TControl** class. Figure 13-7 gives some indication of the degree of complexity involved in this group of classes. We'll use many of these views in Chapters 14 and 20.

## ▶ Documents, Views, and Windows

The relationship among documents, views, and windows is important. In general, your MacApp program will follow a three-step process in creating a new view to display the contents of a document. It does it in this order:

1. It creates and initializes the document.
2. It creates and initializes the view that displays the document data.
3. It creates the window that holds the view.

After this, the Macintosh operating system generates an update event when the window is opened. This event results in a call to each view's **Draw** methods. The document's data then appears in the window.

More specifically, if a program is launched directly (without a document associated with it) or if the user chooses the New menu option, MacApp calls **TApplication.OpenNew**, which in turn calls the following methods in the order shown:

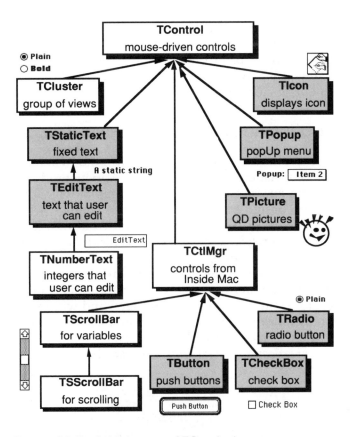

Figure 13-7. Subclasses of TControl

1. aDocument:=SELF.**DoMakeDocument**
2. aDocument.**DoMakeViews**
3. aDocument.**DoMakeWindows**

The process is almost identical for an existing document launched by the user from the Finder or from the menu with the Open option, except that between the second and third steps, MacApp calls the **Do-Read** method:

1. aDocument:=SELF.**DoMakeDocument**
2. aDocument.**DoRead**
3. aDocument.**DoMakeViews**
4. aDocument.**DoMakeWindows**

(The fourth step in this process is skipped if the user launches the document from the Finder with the Print option indicating he or she wishes only to print the document. In that case, the window for the document is never created. This approach complies with Apple's *Human Interface Guidelines*.)

## ▶ Creating Views and Windows Procedurally

There are two ways to create views and windows: by writing C++ functions that create them with MacApp methods and Toolbox calls, or by using an appropriate resource template, usually created using the MacApp design tool ViewEdit. In this chapter, we will concentrate on the procedural creation of views and windows. In Chapter 14, we will examine ViewEdit and related tools for defining complicated windows without programming.

Generally, it is easier and faster to use procedural definition to create very simple windows. We recommend the use of ViewEdit and other tools for creating more complex views and windows. In fact, many programmers use ViewEdit to design all their windows. If you use the procedural method, you will create views separately from windows; template creation methods will generate both views and windows in a single step.

| By the Way ▶ | The MacApp documentation refers to "procedural" view creation, since it involved using Pascal procedures. We will use C++ functions, of course, to do this, but we will still describe this as creating views by "procedure" to be consistent with history. |

You may also want to create views and windows in scattered places throughout your program as you need them. This is particularly useful when you are building views and windows that are not document-related. Figure 13-8 shows a typical painting program. We recommend that you create the main Untitled window and its associated views in the document's **DoMakeViews** and **DoMakeWindows** methods, using the techniques outlined at the beginning of this section. However, you would normally create the three floating palette views in your application's initialization routine, since they are not directly related to a specific document.

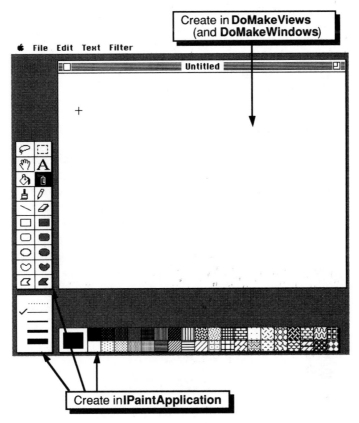

Figure 13-8. A typical painting program

## ▶ General Process

The general process for creating simple views and windows procedurally involves four steps:

1. Create the new view with the C++ new operator.
2. Use the MacApp utility procedure FailNIL to confirm that you have enough memory to create the object.
3. Call your initialization routine for the view.
4. Use the MacApp utility function NewSimpleWindow to create the window, the scroller, and scrollbars (if desired), and to place the view in the window.

Here is a code fragment that demonstrates these steps:

```
TView* aView = new TView;
FailNIL(aView);
aView -> IView(...);
TWindow* aWindow = NewSimpleWindow(...);
```

## ▶ A Small Example

Let's put all of what we've just learned together by building a small program called VProc that will produce the output shown in Figure 13-9.
This program will use functions to create the fixed-view window in the
figure. No documents are involved in the application, and the view is
created when the application is opened and initialized. Because of its
utter simplicity, this sample does not even need a **DoMakeViews**
method, so none is implemented. The class diagram for the VProc sample is shown in Figure 13-10.

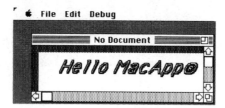

Figure 13-9. Output of VProc Program

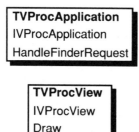

Figure 13-10. VProc class diagram

Listing 13-1 shows the main program for the VProc application.

Listing 13-1. The MVProc.cp main program

```
1: #ifndef __UVProc__
2:     #include "UVProc.h"
3: #endif
4:
5: TVProcApplication    *gVProcApplication;
6:
7: #pragma segment Main
8:
9: void main()
10: {
11:     InitToolBox();
12:     if (ValidateConfiguration(&gConfiguration)){
13:         InitUMacApp(8);
14:
15:         gVProcApplication = new TVProcApplication;
16:         FailNIL(gVProcApplication);
17:         gVProcApplication->IVProcApplication();
18:         gVProcApplication->Run();
19:     }
20:     else
21:         StdAlert(phUnsupportedConfiguration);
22: }
```

This Listing shows the standard format for a MacApp main program. Lines 1-3 include the header file that defines the **TVProcApplication** class. A reference to an instance of that class is defined on line 5, and the application object is created with the C++ new operator on line 15. We check to make sure there was enough memory on line 16 and initialize the object on line 17. On line 18, we send the Run message to the application and execute until the user quits the application.

Lines 11 initializes the Macintosh Toolbox routines and tests the hardware on which the program is running to set the gConfiguration struct accordingly. For example, on a Macintosh that supports Color QuickDraw, gConfiguration.hasColorQD would be set to true. Line 12 then checks gConfiguration against the flags set by MABuild when the application was created. Consider, for example, the case of creating a color graphics program that required the use of Color QuickDraw. You would build it with the following MPW command:

```
MABuild ColorPaint -needsColorQD
```

If the ValidateConfiguration test returned true, then the program would run normally. If it returned false, then execution would jump to line 21, which would display an alert to the user explaining that the program would not run on that machine.

Listing 13-2 shows the UVProc.h header files that define the classes. Notice that we override the **Draw** method in line 21. As we mentioned earlier in this chapter, this is necessary because TView's default **Draw** method does nothing.

Listing 13-2.  VProc class definitions

```
 1:    #ifndef __UVProc__
 2:    #define __UVProc__
 3:
 4:    #ifndef __UMacApp__
 5:        #include <UMacApp.h>
 6:    #endif
 7:
 8:    #ifndef __FONTS__
 9:        #include <Fonts.h>
10:    #endif
11:
12:    class TVProcApplication: public TApplication {
13:    public:
14:        virtual pascal void IVProcApplication();
15:        virtual pascal void HandleFinderRequest();   //override
16:    };
17:
18:    class TVProcView: public TView {
19:    public:
20:        virtual pascal void IVProcView();
21:        virtual pascal void Draw(Rect *area);        //override
22:    };
23:
24:    #endif __UVProc__
```

▶  Creating a Window with a View

The methods for the application and view classes are shown in Listing 13-3 from the file UVProc.cp. Since this simple program uses no documents, the single view and the window in which it lives is created when the application is initialized, in the **IVProcApplication** method. The interesting code is described after the listing.

## Listing 13-3.  Methods for the VProc sample

```
 1: #ifndef __UVProc__
 2:     #include "UVProc.h"
 3: #endif
 4:
 5: const long  kFileType   =   '????';
 6: const short kWindowID   =   1000;
 7:
 8: //============================================================
 9: #pragma segment AInit
10: pascal void
11: TVProcApplication::IVProcApplication()
12: {
13:     this->IApplication(kFileType);
14:
15:     TVProcView* aVProcView = new TVProcView;
16:     FailNIL(aVProcView);
17:     aVProcView->IVProcView();
18:
19:     TWindow* aWindow = NewSimpleWindow( kWindowID, //WIND resrce
20:                 kWantHScrollBar,    // or !kWantHScrollBar
21:                 kWantVScrollBar,    // or !kWantVScrollBar
22:                 NULL,               // document
23:                 aVProcView);        // main view
24:     aWindow->Open();        // normally done by the document
25: }
26:
27: //------------------------------------------------------------
28: #pragma segment ARes
29: pascal void
30: TVProcApplication::HandleFinderRequest()
31: { // so we don't open any documents
32: }
33:
34: //============================================================
35: #pragma segment AOpen
36: pascal void
37: TVProcView::IVProcView()
38: {
39:     VPoint  itsSize;
40:
41:     SetVPt(&itsSize, 300, 200); //  width, height
42:     this->IView(    NULL,       //  document that created view
43:                     NULL,       //  superview
44:                     &gZeroVPt, // topLeft; here = 0,0 as VPoint
```

```
45:                              &itsSize,   // width, height as a VPoint
46:                              sizeFixed, // width is fixed
47:                              sizeFixed);// height is fixed
48: }
49:
50:
51: //-------------------------------------------------------------
52: #pragma segment ARes
53:
54: pascal void
55: TVProcView::Draw(Rect*  /* area */)
56: {
57:     Rect    itsQDExtent;
58:     VPoint  textVLocation;
59:     Point   textQDLocation;
60:
61:     PenNormal();              //  in case someone else changed it
62:
63:     PenSize(10, 10);
64:     PenPat(qd.dkGray);
65:     this->GetQDExtent(&itsQDExtent);
66:     FrameRect(&itsQDExtent);
67:
68:     SetVPt(&textVLocation, 30, 45);                // left, top
69:     textQDLocation = this->ViewToQDPt(&textVLocation);
70:     MoveTo(textQDLocation.h, textQDLocation.v);
71:     TextFont(applFont);
72:     TextFace(italic + shadow);
73:     TextSize(24);
74:     DrawString("\pHello MacApp®");
75:
76:     PenNormal();
77: }
```

Lines 15-17 create and initialize an instance of **TVProcView**, with the same style we usually use to create an object.

Lines 41-47 show the details of initializing the view. First we define the view's width and height in 32-bit VCoordinates in lines 41 and 45, using the MacApp utility procedure **SetVPt**. Then we instruct the view to actually use that size by setting the horizontal and vertical sizeDeterminers to be *sizeFixed* in lines 46 and 47. We also pass NULL as references to the document (because we have none in this program) and to the superview (because this view is not yet installed in a window).

Lines 19-23 finally do create a window and install our view object in the window, using the MacApp utility function **NewSimpleWindow**. Line 19 passes a WIND resource ID described below to define the desired type of window. Lines 20 and 21 insure that our view will be installed as a subview of a scroller, and that the scroller will have associated scrollbars. Those two innocuous lines of code are all you need to provide your window with scrollbars that work to scroll your view and that resize correctly as the window is resized. If you have ever written code to operate scrollbars using only the Toolbox routines, you should by now be very impressed.

Line 24 makes the window visible by sending it the **Open** message. Windows are initially created to be invisible when using MacApp, so that MacApp can move and resize them before the user sees them. When windows are created by documents, the document methods open the window, but in this case, there is no document so we must do it ourselves.

## ▶ Drawing the View

The simple **Draw** method in lines 55-76 merely draws a rectangle around the view border, and then draws the string "Hello MacApp®" inside, as you can see in Figure 13-9.

Lines 61 and 76 call the QuickDraw routine **PenNormal** to set our grafPort to a known state before we begin drawing and after we finish. This is generally recommended.

Line 65 uses the view method **GetQDExtent** to return the rectangle enclosing our view, in 16-bit (QuickDraw) coordinates. A rectangle of that size is then drawn on the screen with the QuickDraw routine FrameRect in line 66. These two lines illustrate two important principles:

First, your code will be more readable and maintainable if you *always include the optional this->* when calling one of your own methods. Otherwise, there is no visible distinction between methods and ordinary functions. The other thing to note is that MacApp is primarily a set of classes defined to support the Macintosh User Interface. MacApp does not include classes to support specialized graphics, sound, databases, accounting, and other application-specific areas. Therefore, you will still use the Toolbox to draw graphics, play a digitized sound, read data from a file, and so forth. You can, and should, define your own custom classes for these jobs, but they are not part of the standard MacApp library.

## ▶ VProc's Resources

Listing 13-4 shows the VProc.r file describing the resources. We discussed almost all of these items in Chapter 9. The only addition is in lines 28-35. Here we define an ordinary 'WIND' resource, of the type Macintosh programmers have used since 1984. An ID of this window resource was passed to the MacApp function **NewSimpleWindow** described above.

Listing 13-4. The VProc.r resource file

```
 1: #ifndef __TYPES.R__
 2:    #include "Types.r"            // SIZE, WIND, STR  , MBAR etc.
 3: #endif
 4:
 5: #ifndef __SYSTYPES.R__
 6:    #include "SysTypes.r"         // needed for version resource
 7: #endif
 8:
 9: #ifndef __MacAppTypes__
10:    #include "MacAppTypes.r"      // cmnu, etc.
11: #endif
12:
13: #ifndef __ViewTypes__
14:    #include "ViewTypes.r"        // view resources
15: #endif
16:
17: #if qDebug
18:    include "Debug.rsrc";         // always include
19: #endif
20:
21: include "MacApp.rsrc";                          // always include
22:
23: include $$Shell("ObjApp")"VProc" 'CODE';   // from your app
24:
25: #define kWindowID 1000
26:
27: // ============================================================
28: resource 'WIND' (kWindowID, purgeable) {
29:    {50, 40, 250, 450},
30:    zoomDocProc,
31:    visible,
32:    noGoAway,
33:    0x0,
34:    "No Document"
35: };
```

```
36:
37: // =============== optional includes =========================
38: include "Defaults.rsrc" 'SIZE' (-1);      // 534, 246; 384, 96 KB
39: include "Defaults.rsrc" 'ALRT' (phAboutApp); // About... window
40: include "Defaults.rsrc" 'DITL' (phAboutApp); // About... contents
41: include "Defaults.rsrc" 'vers' (1);       // application version
42: include "Defaults.rsrc" 'vers' (2);       // overall package
43: include "Defaults.rsrc" 'cmnu' (mApple); // default Apple menu
44: include "Defaults.rsrc" 'cmnu' (mEdit);  // default Edit menu
45:
46: // ============================================================
47: resource 'cmnu' (2) {
48:    2,
49:    textMenuProc,
50:    0x7FFFFBBB,
51:    enabled,
52:    "File",
53:    {
54:       "Close", noIcon, noKey, noMark, plain, cClose;
55:       "-", noIcon, noKey, noMark, plain, nocommand;
56:       "Quit", noIcon, "Q", noMark, plain, cQuit
57:    }
58: };
59:
60: resource 'MBAR' (kMBarDisplayed,
61: #if qNames
62: "VProc",
63: #endif
64:    purgeable) {
65:    {mApple; 2; mEdit;}
66: };
```

## ▶ Making an Existing View Printable

We conclude our discussion of using MacApp to display information in views with a brief examination of what it would take to convert our VProc application into a printing view. The ease with which this kind of change can be made is one of the best arguments for using object programming techniques in general and MacApp specifically. You will be especially convinced if you have ever tried to tangle with the complex print routines of the Macintosh without the aid of MacApp's printing classes.

Adding just thirteen lines of code and four lines of resource file description will convert our nonprinting VProc program to a printable one.

Here are the steps necessary to add printing to the VProc sample.

1. Include a reference to UPrinting.h in your header file, since the MacApp printing routines are defined in the UPrinting.h header file:

```
#ifndef__Printing__
    #include <UPrinting.h>
#endif
```

2. Add the line InitUPrinting(); to the main program, after the call to InitUMacApp(8);.

3. Add the following line to the VProc.r file to include resources needed by the TStdPrintHandler methods:

```
include "Printing.rsrc";
```

4. Add the following items to the File menu defined in VProc.r:

```
"-", noIcon, noKey, noMark, plain, nocommand;
"Page Setup...", noIcon, noKey, noMark, plain, cPageSetup;
"Print One", noIcon, "P", noMark, plain, cPrintOne;
"Print...", noIcon, noKey, noMark, plain, cPrint;
```

5. Modify the **IVProcApplication** method as shown in Listing 13-5.

Listing 13-5. Adding the printing code

```
 1: pascal void
 2: TVProcApplication::IVProcApplication()
 3: {
 4:     this->IApplication(kFileType);
 5:
 6:     TVProcView* aVProcView = new TVProcView;
 7:     FailNIL(aVProcView);
 8:     aVProcView->IVProcView();
 9:
10:     TWindow* aWindow = NewSimpleWindow( kWindowID,// WIND resr
11:                                         kWantHScrollBar,
12:                                         kWantVScrollBar,
13:                                         NULL,      // document
14:                                         aVProcView); // main view
15:
16:     TStdPrintHandler* aStdHandler = new TStdPrintHandler;
17:     FailNIL(aStdHandler);
```

```
18:    aStdHandler->IStdPrintHandler (NULL,  // document
19:                        aVProcView,     // view
20:                        !kSquareDots,   // kSquareDots = bitMaps
21:                        kFixedSize,     // horiz page size fixed
22:                        kFixedSize);    // vert page size fixed
23:
24:    aWindow->Open();    // normally done by the document
25:    }
```

Line 16 declares a reference to an object of MacApp's **TStdPrintHandler** class, and lines 18-22 create and initialize that object. In line 18, you should pass a reference to the document that created the view, so in this case we pass NULL. Line 19 refers to the view to be printed. Line 20 sets the Apple ImageWriter printer's Page Setup dialog to default to Not Tall Adjusted. Set this parameter to *kSquareDots* if your view contains bitmapped images. This parameter has no effect when the user uses other printers. The last two parameters tell the print handler that each printed page should be the same size.

With these few simple steps, your program will handle multiple-page text and graphics printing.

## ▶ Summary

In this chapter, we have looked at the basic MacApp view architecture and the relationships among windows and views. We have looked at the methods and instance variables that are central to a proper display of information in a view so that a user can see it and make use of it.

Chapter 14 continues our examination of views by looking at the alternative method of creating them using ViewEdit and view resources.

# 14 ▶ View Resources

This chapter discusses how to use the ViewEdit utility program to create complex windows in MacApp and describes a sample program that uses 'view' resources created with ViewEdit.

## ▶ ViewEdit

ViewEdit is a highly interactive tool for building MacApp views without the necessity of writing C++ code. The program, which comes with MacApp (and was written using MacApp), enables you to define views using normal Macintosh user interface techniques and to include the views' description directly in your MacApp programs without writing any complex code.

As an introduction to ViewEdit, we will walk through an example of creating a window with many subviews and show how to incorporate that complex window into a MacApp program.

## ▶ Using 'view' Resources

Figure 14-1 shows the window we will create in the VRes sample program. Imagine the work it would take first to create all these subviews procedurally and then to establish the necessary subview/superview relationships. It would probably take hours and a few pages of source code. It would also be terribly slow and frustrating. ViewEdit provides an elegant solution to that problem.

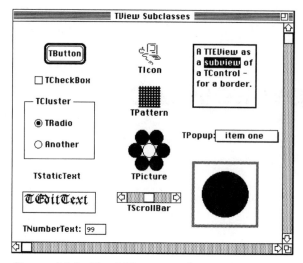

Figure 14-1. The VRes sample program

## ▶ The Advantages

By using ViewEdit you gain some significant advantages. First, you need only a single resource of type 'view' to define a window and all of its subviews, regardless of how many views it contains or how complex any or all of them may be. Second, ViewEdit's convenience allows you to draw the views with the mouse, so you don't have to estimate screen-coordinate locations for objects within the window. Finally, creating a 'view' resource means you can create and initialize a window with a single call to the MacApp utility function NewTemplateWindow. Using this one-line call is far easier than creating and initializing each view and window individually with new, FailNIL, and initialize routines.

This approach, then, saves time in design, time in programming, time in debugging, and runs more efficiently in the bargain. It's no wonder that we recommend this method of view creation and initialization for all but the simplest of views.

## ▶ The VRes Sample Program

To create the VRes sample program, we will create a 'view' resource describing the window and subviews shown in Figure 14-1 and write the code summarized by the class diagram in Figure 14-2. We will define an application class, **TVResApplication**, that can create the desired window, and a custom view class, **TMyControl**, to show how to deal with a custom view class in ViewEdit. This custom view appears in the lower-right corner of the window in Figure 14-1.

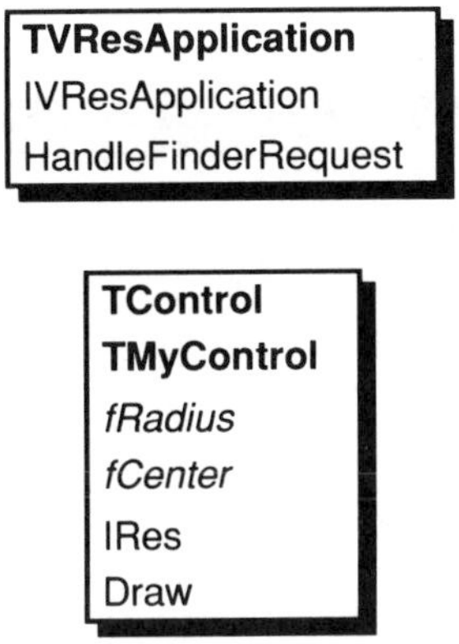

```
TVResApplication
IVResApplication
HandleFinderRequest
```

```
TControl
TMyControl
fRadius
fCenter
IRes
Draw
```

Figure 14-2. The class diagram for VRes

The first steps in creating the sample involve using ViewEdit to design the window and its subviews.

## ▶ Creating 'view' Resources Using ViewEdit

To create a new view resource in ViewEdit, follow these steps:

1. Launch ViewEdit from the Finder, which produces an empty window display, as shown in Figure 14-3.

2. From the Edit menu, select Create Resource...

3. Set the resource ID values in the dialog box. Your resource IDs should range from 1000 to 32767 (MacApp reserves IDs from 1 to 999). We recommend that you enter the optional resource name in this dialog, as it reduces confusion in programs that use more than one view resource. Then click the OK button.

4. An icon representing the view will appear in the Untitled -1 window. Double-click on the icon to open the view editing window, as shown in Figure 14-4.

5. Select the type of view you wish to draw from the View: popup menu. We want the window contents to be scrollable in the VRes sample, so we choose the subview of the window to be an instance of **TScroller**.

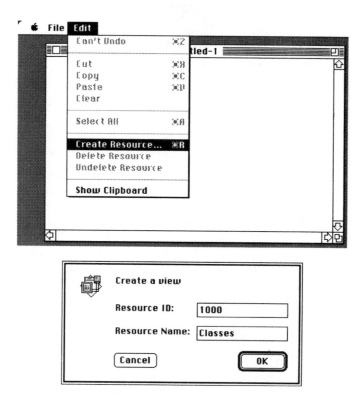

Figure 14-3. Starting the ViewEdit program

6. Draw the size and location of this view using the mouse, as shown in Figure 14-5.

7. Double-click on the newly created view to open a modal dialog for setting the initial properties for that view, as shown in Figure 14-6. For our scroller, we use the default setting, which includes both horizontal and vertical scrollbars. We also use the default settings of *sizeRelSuperView* as horizontal and vertical sizeDeterminers, since we want the scroller to resize with its enclosing window. Note that we have not yet defined that enclosing window. We will do that step after we define the window contents.

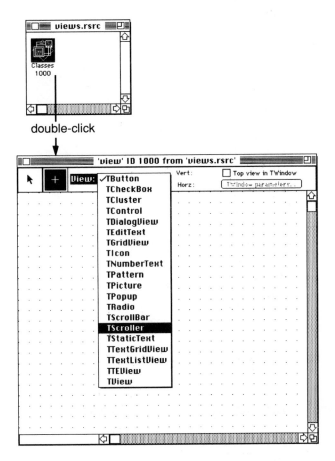

Figure 14-4. ViewEdit's view editing window

You need to choose an easy-to-remember view identifier for each view. In this case we choose 'sc01.' You will often need to use these IDs in your program, so note your choices. ViewEdit's default identifiers are 'VW01,' 'VW02,' and so forth, which are hard to remember.

8. Repeat steps 5 through 7 until the view is completely defined the way you want it. In our example, we drew a large instance of **TDialogView** to hold the other subviews, after which we drew instances of **TButton**, **TCheckBox**, and so on.

9. Request that the views be placed in a window by selecting the Top view in TWindow check box in the upper-right corner of the view editing window.

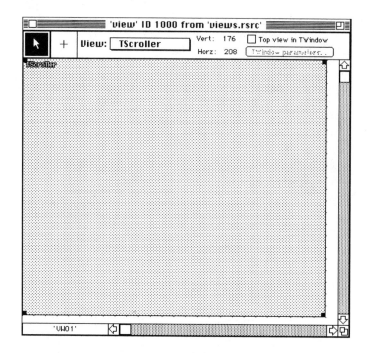

Figure 14-5. Drawing a view in the editing window

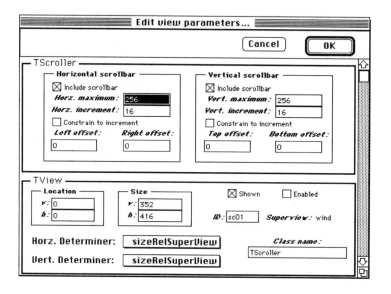

Figure 14-6. Setting the scroller's initial properties

10. Set the window parameters by clicking the TWindow parameters... button in the upper-right corner. This will display the dialog shown in Figure 14-7. In this dialog, be sure to set the Window title to the string you desire, or leave the default <<<>>> when defining windows that will be created by a document. In the latter case, MacApp will use the document title as the window title.

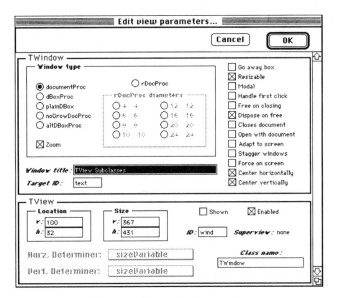

Figure 14-7. Setting the window parameters

Be sure to set the Target ID to be the ID of the view in your window that should be set to *gTarget* by MacApp when the window is activated. In our example, we set the target to be 'text', the ID of the view in the upper-right corner, so that the instance of **TTEView** in the upper-right corner of our window will get **DoIdle** and **DoKeyCommand** messages.

Finally, set the window size you need. In the VRes sample, we have a scroller that should fill almost the whole window, leaving room only for the scrollbars. Scrollbars are 16 pixels wide, but they should overlap the window border by 1 pixel. By adding 15 to the scroller's width and height (shown in Figure 14-6), we can determine the size of the window. In this case, we arrive at the numbers 367 and 431 shown in Figure 14-7 as the window size.

11. Save the file. We usually use the file name views.rsrc , but you can choose almost any name you wish. The final layout is shown in Figure 14-8.

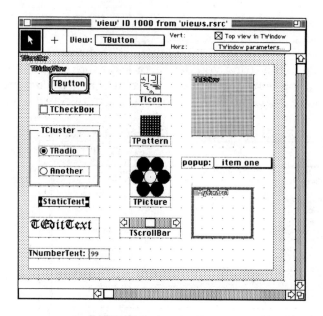

Figure 14-8. VRes's final 'view' resource number 1000

▶ Making a "Default" Button

Figure 14-9 shows how to set the properties for a default button, using an RRect adornment flag, a control inset of (4, 4, 4, 4), and a pen size of (3, 3).

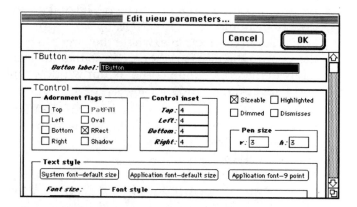

Figure 14-9. Making a default button

## ▶ Making a Custom View

Figure 14-10 shows how to define a custom view — that is, one that does not appear in ViewEdit's popup menu. In the VRes class diagram, you saw a new class, **TMyControl**. This will be defined in the code that follows as a subclass of **TControl**. Therefore, you can initially draw that view as a **TControl** and double-click on it to display the modal dialog shown in Figure 14-10. You first set the desired properties to be inherited from the **TControl** class by filling in the dialog items. You then tell ViewEdit that the class name you want to associate with this view is the string TMyControl. To do this you fill in the edit text item on the bottom-right of Figure 14-10. When the program executes, the **New-TemplateWindow** function used to create the window will make that view an instance of whatever class name was entered.

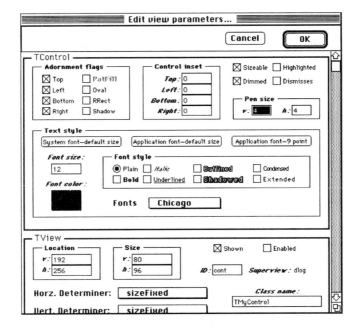

Figure 14-10. Defining a custom view

## ▶ Using the View Resource File

You are now nearly ready to use the resource file created with View-Edit directly in the C++ program. You need to do three things first:

1. Create the usual VRes.r file. This will be similar to the VProc.r file used in the VProc sample, except that no WIND resource is needed.

2. Add the following line to the VRes.r file to insure that the new 'view' resource(s) are included as part of the final application.

```
include "views.rsrc"
```

3. Create a new file, VRes.MAMake, as shown in Listing 14-1. You will need an MAMake file when you use any files beyond the standard set of four files (for example, MVRes.cp, UVRes.cp, UVRes.h, and VRes.r) we have described previously. Be sure that the makefile suffix includes the letters MA; otherwise, the MPW build scripts will not treat your program as a MacApp program.

Listing 14-1. The VRes.MAMake file

```
 1: #------------------------------------------------------------
 2: AppName = VRes
 3:
 4:
 5: #------------------------------------------------------------
 6: #  List resource files that the Rez file includes if you want
    to include
 7: #  more or less than the standard set
 8: OtherRsrcFiles = ∂
 9:    "{MAObj}Printing.rsrc" ∂
10:    "{SrcApp}views.rsrc"
```

Once you create a view using ViewEdit, you can include it in your MacApp code with a single call to the **NewTemplateWindow** function. This method has the same basic use and effect as the **NewSimpleWindow** function we saw in Chapter 13, but it works with view resources rather than with procedurally defined views and windows, and it creates all the views in that window.

## ▶ The Main Program

Listing 14-2 shows a relatively standard main program file. The only addition to the MVProc.cp file seen in the last chapter are lines 14 and 15. The Init UTEView() function should be used whenever you create instances of TTEView in your view resources. The Init UDialog() function should be called when your view resources include dialog items such as buttons, check boxes, etc.

Listing 14-2.  Main program for the VRes sample

```
 1: #ifndef __UVRes__
 2:     #include "UVRes.h"
 3: #endif
 4:
 5: TVResApplication    *gVResApplication;
 6:
 7: #pragma segment Main
 8:
 9: void main()
10: {
11:     InitToolBox();
12:     if (ValidateConfiguration(&gConfiguration)){
13:         InitUMacApp(8);
14:         InitUTEView();
15:         InitUDialog();
16:
17:         gVResApplication = new TVResApplication;
18:         FailNIL(gVResApplication);
19:         gVResApplication->IVResApplication();
20:         gVResApplication->Run();
21:     }
22:     else
23:         StdAlert(phUnsupportedConfiguration);
24: }
```

▶ The Class Definitions

Listing 14-3 shows the UVres.h header file that defines the two new classes.

Listing 14-3. The UVRes.h header file that defines the classes

```
 1: #ifndef __UVRes__
 2: #define __UVRes__
 3:
 4: #ifndef __UMacApp__
 5:     #include <UMacApp.h>
 6: #endif
 7:
 8: #ifndef __UDialog__
 9:     #include <UDialog.h>
10: #endif
11:
```

```
12: //============================================================
13: class TVResApplication : public TApplication {
14: public:
15:     pascal virtual void IVResApplication();
16: };
17:
18: //============================================================
19: class TMyControl : public TControl {
20: private:
21:     short    fRadius;
22:     short    fCenter;
23: public:
24:     pascal virtual void IRes(TDocument *itsDocument,
25:                              TView *itsSuperView,
26:                              Ptr *itsParams);         //override
27:     pascal virtual void Draw(Rect *area);            //override
28: };
29:
30: #endif __UVRes__
```

The macros on lines 1, 2, and 30 allow other files that include this file to test against __UVRes__ so that this file will not be included more than once in the compile process. Lines 8-10 conditionally include the header file that defines the dialog classes. We need this since we use the **TControl** class as a superclass on line 19.

The **TVResApplication** class adds only a new initialization method, as shown on line 15. The **TMyControl** class is defined on lines 19-28 to override two view methods, **IRes** and **Draw**. The **IRes** method is the standard way to initialize template views (i.e., those defined in view resources). We will describe its use below. The new **Draw** method is used to draw the filled circle in the lower-right corner of Figure 14-1.

▶  The Methods

The methods are defined in the UVRes.cp file shown in Listing 14-4.

Listing 14-4. The UVRes.cp file that implements the methods

```
1: #ifndef __UVRes__
2:     #include "UVRes.h"
3: #endif
4:
5: //============================================================
6: const OSType kFileType        =   '????';
```

```
 7: const short kClassesWindowID   =   1000;
 8:
 9: //=============================================================
10: #pragma segment AInit
11: pascal void
12: TVResApplication::IVResApplication()
13: {
14:     this->IApplication(kFileType);
15:     fLaunchWithNewDocument = false;        // default is true
16:
17:     if (gDeadStripSuppression) {
18:         TMyControl  *aMyControl = new TMyControl;
19:     }
20:
21:     TWindow* aWindow = NewTemplateWindow
            (kClassesWindowID, NULL);
22:     aWindow->Open();
23: }
24:
25: //=============================================================
26: #pragma segment AOpen
27: pascal void
28: TMyControl::IRes(TDocument *itsDocument,
29:                             TView *itsSuperView, Ptr *itsParams)
30: {
31:     inherited::IRes(itsDocument, itsSuperView, itsParams);
32:     fRadius = 35;
33:     fCenter = 50;
34: }
35:
36: //-------------------------------------------------------------
37: #pragma segment ARes
38: pascal void
39: TMyControl::Draw(Rect*  area)             //override
40: {
41:     Rect    circleRect;
42:
43:     inherited::Draw(area);
44:     PenNormal();
45:     ForeColor(magentaColor);
46:     SetRect(&circleRect, fCenter - fRadius, fCenter - fRadius,
47:                         fCenter + fRadius, fCenter + fRadius);
48:     PaintOval(&circleRect);
49:     ForeColor(blackColor);
50: }
```

The **IVResApplication** method shown on lines 11-23 has a number of interesting features. The application object is initialized on lines 14 and 15. Setting the *fLaunchWithNewDocument* variable to false on line 15 prevents the **TApplication::HandleFinderRequest** method from trying to open an Untitled document. We must do this since this program does not support documents.

| By the Way ▶ | Another way to prevent an Untitled document from being opened is to override the **HandleFinderRequest** method as we did in the VProc sample in the last chapter. The alternate way shown in this VRes sample is generally easier. Using *fLaunchWithNewDocument* is definitely preferred when you want to allow the user to open existing documents from the Finder. |
|---|---|

The window containing all the interesting subviews is created on line 21 using the MacApp utility function, **NewTemplateWindow**. This is the function (not a method) we will always use to create windows defined using view resources. It takes two arguments: a 'view' resource ID and a reference to the document that created the view, if any.

**NewTemplateWindow** creates a complex window with these three steps:

1. It creates an unitialized view for each view defined in the resource by first getting the class name as a string from the resource. It then uses the MacApp utility function **NewObjectByClassName** to create an instance of that class. This is done for the window object and for each of its subviews.

2. The data in the 'view' resource is then used to initialize each view.

3. Further initialization is performed by sending each view the **IRes** message. An example of an **IRes** method is shown on lines 27-34 of the listing. In your **IRes** method, you should always call the superclass's **IRes** method, as shown on line 31. You can then perform further initialization as shown on lines 32 and 33.

The **NewTemplateWindow** function always creates the window to be invisible, so it can be moved and resized as necessary before the user sees it. When a window is created by a document object, the document will generally then make the window visible to the user. Since we created this window ourselves, we will send it the Open message to make it visible, as shown on line 22.

## ▶ Deadstrip Suppression

We have just described a system for displaying a window defined by a 'view' resource. Unfortunately, the code as described so far would lead to a system crash when the window was opened. We must add one more trick to protect ourselves, represented by the strange code on lines 17-19. The problem this solves is that the **NewTemplateWindow** function creates views using the **NewObjectByClassName** function — which does not use C++'s new operator (or Object Pascal's NEW procedure). Since these are not called, the MPW Linker would normally assume that we never made an instance of the class **TMyControl**, and would dead strip (i.e., remove) all the methods for that class — in order to make the program smaller. We use the code in lines 17-19 to fool the Linker into thinking we will create an an instance of the class, and the methods will not be stripped. This trick works even though MacApp defines the global variable *gDeadStripSuppression* to always be false, so the code on line 18 will never execute. The threat is sufficient.

You must deadstrip suppress any custom view classes to be created from view resources — otherwise the non-debug version of your program will crash, and you will be very upset. You do not need to deadstrip suppress the standard **TView**, **TWindow**, and **TScroller** classes, as the MacApp initialization code takes care of those. The InitUTEView and InitUDialogView functions called from the main program are used to deadstrip suppress classes such as **TTEView**, **TControl**, **TButton**, **TDialogView**, etc.

The final part of the listing is the **TMyControl::Draw** method shown on lines 38-50. Line 43 calls the **TControl::Draw** method that adorns the view with a rectangular border. We designated this adornment in the **TControl** dialog box in ViewEdit, as shown in Figure 14-10.

## ▶ Looking at the Resources

You will seldom have a need to manipulate 'view' resources outside of ViewEdit, but if such a need arises it is possible to do so. Simply use the MPW DeRez tool to convert the resource file to a text file, then edit the resulting text file. (See Chapter 11 for a discussion of DeRez and other MPW tools for MacApp programming.) You can convert the 'view' resource to a text file named views.r by executing the following MPW statement:

```
DeRez views.rsrc  "{MARIncludes}ViewTypes.r" "Types.r" > views.r
```

▶ **Summary**

This chapter has described how to use ViewEdit to create complex views and windows. It has described ViewEdit's basic use and has discussed how to make flexible use of the resource file created by the ViewEdit program.

You also learned in this chapter how to use the **NewTemplateWindow** function to create a window based on a resource template created using ViewEdit.

Chapter 15 begins the construction of a text-editing sample program, showing you how to create a window for a specific application using ViewEdit and 'view' resources.

# 15 ▶ Creating a Text Editing Window

In this chapter, we will review the code involved in creating a text editing window from a 'view' resource template. The program is called Text. It implements styled text editing based on the MacApp TTEView class, which is based on the routines in the Macintosh Toolbox.

In an instance of the class **TTEView**, each character can have its own font, size, style, and, on color systems, its own color. Each view can contain a maximum of 32,767 characters. Tabs are not supported in views of this type in MacApp 2.0, but are expected to be supported in MacApp 2.1. Because instances of the class **TTEView** maintain their own data structures, they do not require an associated document object to store the data. Our sample program will also (automatically) use the command objects in the unit UTEView so that it can support Undo.

## ▶ The Application

Figure 15-1 shows the appearance of the window in this sample program, while Figure 15-2 shows the spartan class diagram. The window contains a scroller with associated scrollbars and an instance of the class **TTEView** as a subview to the scroller. As you will see, we do not need to define any new view classes or methods for our sample program. We can use the class **TTEView** exactly as it is supplied by MacApp and provide a great deal of functionality to our users. This is one of the most directly usable concrete classes in MacApp.

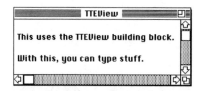

Figure 15-1.  Output of Text sample

Figure 15-2.  Class diagram of Text sample

## ▶ The Program

As with most small MacApp programs, Text consists of four basic files:

- UText.h, which contains the interface
- UText.cp, where the implementation is stored
- UText.r, including the resource definitions
- MText.cp, the main program

We will discuss these modules in the order given.

### ▶ UText.h, the Header File

Listing 15-1 contains the few lines of code required for the class definition, in the U'Text.h header file.

Listing 15-1.  Text interface code

```
 1: #ifndef __UText__
 2: #define __UText__
 3:
 4: #ifndef __UMacApp__
 5:     #include <UMacApp.h>
 6: #endif
 7:
 8: #ifndef __UPrinting__
 9:     #include <UPrinting.h>
10: #endif
11:
```

```
12: #ifndef __UTEView__
13:     #include <UTEView.h>
14: #endif
15:
16: // ============================================================
17: class TTextApplication : public TApplication {
18: public:
19:     pascal virtual void ITextApplication();
20: };
21:
22: #endif  __UText__
```

Notice in line 13 that we include the UTEView.h header file so that we can use its **TTEView** command and view classes.

## ▶ UText.cp, the Implementation

Listing 15-2 is the program code for the implementation portion of Text.

### Listing 15-2. Text implementation

```
 1: #ifndef __UText__
 2:     #include "UText.h"
 3: #endif
 4:
 5: //============================================================
 6: const OSType kFileType  = '????';
 7: const short  kWindowID  =  1001;
 8:
 9: //============================================================
10: #pragma segment AInit
11: pascal void
12: TTextApplication::ITextApplication()
13: {
14:     this->IApplication(kFileType);
15:     fLaunchWithNewDocument = false;
16:
17:     TWindow* aWindow = NewTemplateWindow(kWindowID, NULL);
18:     aWindow->Open();
19:
20:     TView* aView = aWindow->FindSubView('text');
21:     TStdPrintHandler* aStdHandler = new TStdPrintHandler;
22:     FailNIL(aStdHandler);
23:     aStdHandler->IStdPrintHandler(NULL,    // document
24:                                   aView,   // view to be printed
```

```
25:                          !kSquareDots,   // kSquareDots = bitMaps
26:                          kFixedSize,     // horizontal page size
27:                          !kFixedSize);   // vertical page size
28:
29: }
```

All of the work in this sample is done in the **ITextApplication** method.
Line 14 calls the initialization method **IApplication**, inherited from
the superclass, **TApplication**.

Line 17 calls **NewTemplateWindow** to create whatever window and
views were designed in ViewEdit. Figures 15-3 and 15-4 show details of
that design.

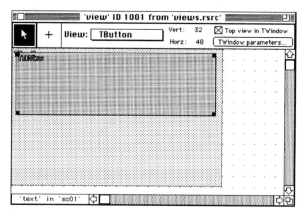

Figure 15-3. Screen design using ViewEdit

Notice in Figure 15-4 that the text edit view parameters included choosing 'text' as the view identifier, and *sizeFillPages* as the vertical size determiner. This last choice sets the initial view height to be the size of one
printed page. If the user types more text that that, the size will increase
to exactly two full pages, then three, and so forth. Remember that you
can only choose *sizeFillPages* or *sizePage* for views that are to be printed
— that is, for views that have an associated print handler object.

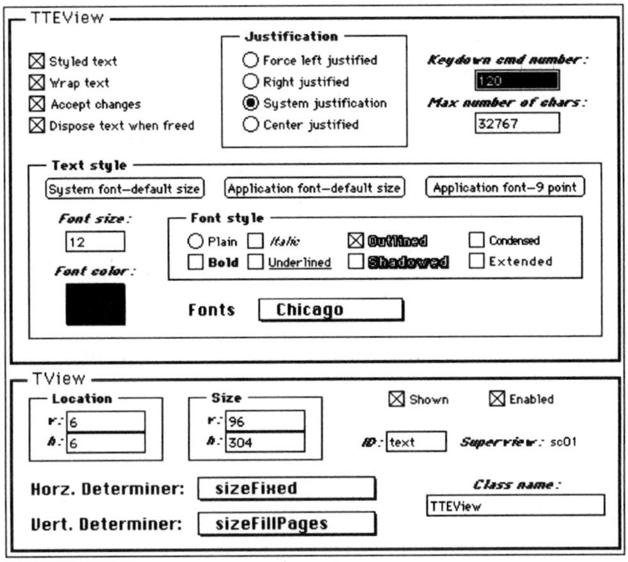

**TTEView**

Justification

☒ Styled text
☒ Wrap text
☒ Accept changes
☒ Dispose text when freed

○ Force left justified
○ Right justified
● System justification
○ Center justified

*Keydown cmd number:*
120

*Max number of chars:*
32767

**Text style**

[ System font—default size ] [ Application font—default size ] [ Application font—9 point ]

*Font size:*
12

**Font style**
○ Plain ☐ *Italic* ☒ Outlined ☐ Condensed
☐ **Bold** ☐ Underlined ☒ Shadowed ☐ Extended

*Font color:*
■

Fonts [ Chicago ]

**TView**

**Location**
r: 6
h: 6

**Size**
r: 96
h: 304

☒ Shown  ☒ Enabled

*ID:* text    *Superview:* sc01

Horz. Determiner: [ sizeFixed ]
Vert. Determiner: [ sizeFillPages ]

*Class name:*
TTEView

Figure 15-4. Setting the TTEView parameters

Figure 15-5 shows that we set the Target ID of the window to be 'text', the ID for the text view. This crucial step insures that each time the window is activated, MacApp's global variable *gTarget* will point to the text view. Should you forget to do this, the text view will not receive **DoIdle** messages to blink the insertion point cursor. Worse yet, the text view will not be sent **DoKeyCommand** messages when the user is typing. If you ever create a text view that seems "dead," check to see if it is the target view for that window.

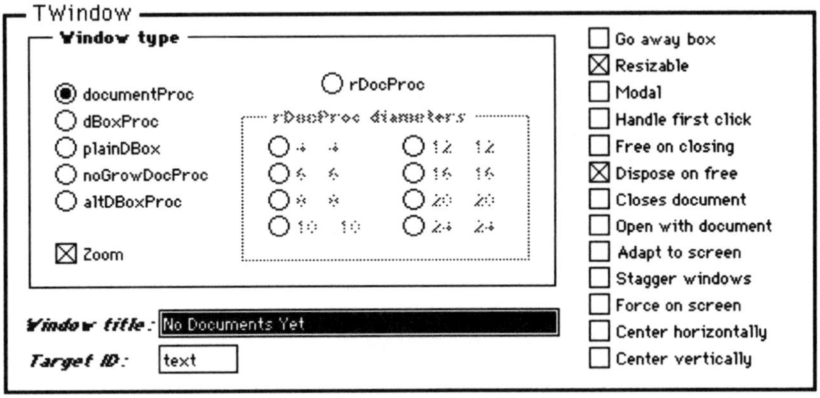

**TWindow**

**Window type**

● documentProc          ○ rDocProc
○ dBoxProc          *rDocProc diameters*
○ plainDBox        ○ 4  4      ○ 12 12
○ noGrowDocProc    ○ 6  6      ○ 16 16
○ altDBoxProc      ○ 8  8      ○ 20 20
                   ○ 10 10     ○ 24 24
☒ Zoom

☐ Go away box
☒ Resizable
☐ Modal
☐ Handle first click
☐ Free on closing
☒ Dispose on free
☐ Closes document
☐ Open with document
☐ Adapt to screen
☐ Stagger windows
☐ Force on screen
☐ Center horizontally
☐ Center vertically

*Window title:* No Documents Yet
*Target ID:* text

Figure 15-5. Making the TTEView the target

Line 20 of Listing 15-2 uses the **TTEView**'s ID of 'text' to get a reference to that view by sending the **FindSubView** message to the window object. This view reference is then passed to the print handler in line 24. We will use this FindSubView method whenever we need a reference to a subview of a window, since the NewTemplateWindow function returns only a reference to the window object.

Lines 21-27 create and initialize a standard print handler object. The parameters are described below.

Line 23 sets the document reference to NULL, since this program uses no documents.

Line 24 designates the view to be printed.

Line 25 designates that by default an ImageWriter dot matrix printer should not use the "tall adjusted" mode. This parameter should be set to *kSquareDots* when printing bit-mapped views.

Line 26 means that each printed page should have the same width.

Line 27 means that pages may vary in height, in order that page breaks will not occur in the middle of a line of text.

Line 18 makes the window visible on the screen. You will not need to do this explicitly in succeeding programs in this book, because the windows will be created and opened by document methods.

## ▶ UText.r, the Resources

The code in Listing 15-3 is the resource file (with the .r extension) that defines the resources included in the finished program.

Listing 15-3. Text resource file code

```
 1: // ================================================================
 2: #ifndef __TYPES.R__
 3:    #include "Types.r"                  // SIZE, WIND, STR  , MBAR etc.
 4: #endif
 5:
 6: #ifndef __SYSTYPES.R__
 7:    #include "SysTypes.r"               // needed for version resource
 8: #endif
 9:
10: #ifndef __MacAppTypes__
11:    #include "MacAppTypes.r"            // cmnu, etc.
12: #endif
13:
14: #ifndef __ViewTypes__
15:    #include "ViewTypes.r"              // view resources
```

```
16: #endif
17:
18: #if qDebug
19:    include "Debug.rsrc";                // always include
20: #endif
21:
22: include "MacApp.rsrc";                   // always include
23: include "Printing.rsrc";
24:
25: include $$Shell("ObjApp")"Text" 'CODE'; // from your app
26: include $$Shell("SrcApp")"views.rsrc";  // compiled resources
27:
28: =============== optional includes ==========================
29: include "Defaults.rsrc" 'SIZE' (-1);    // 534, 246; 384, 96 KB
30: include "Defaults.rsrc" 'ALRT' (phAboutApp); // About... window
31: include "Defaults.rsrc" 'DITL' (phAboutApp); // About... contents
32: include "Defaults.rsrc" 'vers' (1);     // application version
33: include "Defaults.rsrc" 'vers' (2);     // overall package
34: include "Defaults.rsrc" 'cmnu' (mApple); // default Apple menu
35: include "Defaults.rsrc" 'cmnu' (mEdit);  // default Edit menu
36:
37: // =========================================================
38: resource 'cmnu' (2) {
39:    2,
40:    textMenuProc,
41:    0x7FFFFBBB,
42:    enabled,
43:    "File",
44:      {
45:        "Close", noIcon, noKey, noMark, plain, cClose;
46:        "-", noIcon, noKey, noMark, plain, nocommand;
47:        "Page Setup...", noIcon, noKey, noMark, plain, cPageSetup;
48:        "Print One", noIcon, "P", noMark, plain, cPrintOne;
49:        "Print...", noIcon, noKey, noMark, plain, cPrint;
50:        "-", noIcon, noKey, noMark, plain, nocommand;
51:        "Quit", noIcon, "Q", noMark, plain, cQuit
52:      }
53: };
54:
55: resource 'MBAR' (kMBarDisplayed,
56: #if qNames
57: "Text",
58: #endif
59:    purgeable) {
60:    {mApple; 2; mEdit;}
61: };
```

The contents of this file are for the most part self-explanatory since the file is essentially the same as those shown in earlier chapters.

Two significant additions are needed to support printing of the text edit view. First, you must include the resources that MacApp's printing code uses, as shown on line 23. Then you must, of course, add the standard print items to the File menu, as shown on lines 47-49. The **DoSetupMenus** and **DoMenuCommand** methods provided with the class **TStdPrintHandler** will automatically handle the *cPageSetup, cPrintOne,* and *cPrint* command numbers used in those items.

## ▶ MText.cp, the Main Program

Finally, Listing 15-4 is the main program itself. As is always the case, it is short and simple.

Listing 15-4. MText.cp program code

```
 1: #ifndef __UText__
 2:     #include "UText.h"
 3: #endif
 4:
 5: TTextApplication    *gTextApplication;
 6:
 7: #pragma segment Main
 8: void main()
 9: {
10:     InitToolBox();
11:     if (ValidateConfiguration(&gConfiguration)){
12:         InitUMacApp(8);
13:         InitUPrinting();
14:         InitUTEView();
15:
16:         gTextApplication = new TTextApplication;
17:         FailNIL(gTextApplication);
18:         gTextApplication->ITextApplication();
19:         gTextApplication->Run();
20:     }
21:     else
22:         StdAlert(phUnsupportedConfiguration);
23: }
```

Other than the initialization code that concerns itself with machine independence, which we discussed briefly in Chapter 13, there is nothing particularly startling about the code in Listing 15-4.

## ▶ Summary

As you can see from the very straightforward code in the listings in this chapter, defining and using a TextEdit view in an application is simple. Because MacApp's definitions for the class **TTEView** are so well thought out and well integrated, you don't need to create any new classes or methods. You override only one method, **HandleFinderRequest**, and for the most part you simply use all of the supporting structure furnished by MacApp without having to think much about it. Yet we have created a text-editing application that supports full editing, cut, copy, and paste, and allows the user to undo changes to the text's contents.

In Chapter 16, we will look at a more complete application and at how to keep track of data in documents and in disk files. In particular, we will expand our Text program to be able to read and write ordinary text files.

# 16 ▶ Storing Data in Documents

You will probably want much of the information displayed in the views we have been discussing for the last few chapters to end up stored in a disk file as a Macintosh document. In this chapter, we will examine the class **TDocument** to see how it allows us to manage such documents. Along the way, we will also

- briefly examine the issue of document file formats
- see how to create documents in MacApp
- examine a sample text editing program that handles documents

## ▶ Documents: An Overview

Documents are instances of the class **TDocument** or one of its subclasses from MacApp's perspective. They have four primary purposes:

- They provide the means for storing data in RAM.
- They generally are the means by which views and windows that display their data are created.
- They are responsible for reading and writing data to and from document files on disk.
- They manage certain menu items.

More importantly, the documents are often the primary focus of the Macintosh user interface. We have described views and windows as being the visible portion of the interface but from the user's perspective, it is the document's data represented in these views that make up the most important part of your MacApp application. When a window is updated, its views usually access the document to determine what needs to be drawn on the screen. Furthermore, when the user enters or modifies data in a window or view, the resulting command objects send the new data to the document object and then force an update event, which results in the screen being redrawn to reflect the new document contents.

Of course, a document is never seen directly in a Macintosh application; a document's contents are interpreted, or translated, through views into that document. As you can see, the relationships between views, windows, and documents are intimate and important.

## ▶ Documents and File Formats

The format in which data are stored in RAM in an instance of a **TDocument** sub-class is generally not the same as the format in which the same data are stored on the disk when it is saved there. There is nothing to prevent the two from being identical but because they are often put to different uses they are usually quite different.

As you know, a Macintosh disk file is divided into two forks: a data fork and a resource fork. Either of these forks may be empty in a particular document's file. There are numerous ways the forks can be used in combination to store the data and information about the data that make up a document.

For example, an application whose contents are never stored on the disk but rather printed using some special formatting options might have only print information stored on disk. This print information might be stored in the data fork, while the resource fork would be empty. On the other hand, a document used in another application that takes advantage of standard printing functions might store its raw text in the data fork and have an empty resource fork.

Most applications, however, use information in both forks. Typically, a text-based document will store its raw content in the data fork and store support data such as print information, text specifications, and style descriptions in the resource fork. A graphics program might store its shapes in the data fork, perhaps along with print information (that is, the information set by the user in the Page Setup... dialog), while keeping other information such as window and scrollbar locations in the resource fork.

# ▶ The Class TDocument

All document objects in MacApp are instances of subclasses of the class **TDocument**. This powerful class encompasses a large number of instance variables and methods. In this section, we will look at the important variables and methods you need to understand to work with documents effectively.

## ▶ TDocument Variables

Table 16-1 summarizes ten important instance variables of the class **TDocument**.

Table 16-1. Variables of class TDocument

| Variable | Definition/notes |
| --- | --- |
| fWindowList | A list of windows belonging to the document. |
| fViewList | A list of views belonging to the document. |
| fChangeCount | A long integer that records the number of changes that have been made to the document since the last time it was saved. |
| fSavePrintInfo | If true, print information for the document is saved in the data fork of the disk file. If false, print information is not being retained in the disk file. |
| fFileType | A four-character code defining the document's file type. |
| fCreator | A four-character code identifying the application that created the document. |
| fUsesDataFork | If true, MacApp will open the data fork of the file for reading and writing. If false, fork is not opened. |
| fUsesRsrcFork | If true, MacApp will open the resource fork of the file for reading and writing. If false, fork is not opened. |
| fDataOpen | If true (which is recommended for multi-user applications), the data fork of the file is always open as long as the file is open. If false, the data fork is closed between file accesses. |
| fRsrcOpen | If false (which is recommended), the resource fork of the file is closed between file accesses. If true, the fork is always kept open as long as the file is open. |

Six of the variables shown in Table 16-1 are used in initializing a document. The interface for document initialization looks like this:

```
virtual pascal void IDocument(OSType itsFileType, OSType itsCreator,
                  Boolean usesDataFork, Boolean usesRsrcFork,
                  Boolean keepsDataOpen, Boolean keepsRsrcOpen);
```

## ▶ TDocument Methods

Of the many methods implemented by the class **TDocument**, the following prove to be most useful in day-to-day programming with MacApp. Three of these methods relate to initializing and freeing documents. We have already looked at the **IDocument** method, which you will call when you wish to initialize a document. The **Free** method releases all of the views and windows associated with the document and then frees the document itself. You will often override this method to dispose of any data structures on the heap used by your documents. The interface looks like this:

```
pascal void TDocument::Free();
```

Your application generally overrides the **FreeData** method if it allows for a Revert command selection. It frees all of the data objects that should be freed when reverting to the most recently saved version of the document. Its interface looks like this:

```
pascal void TDocument::FreeData();
```

Four of the important **TDocument** methods relate to opening documents. The first, **DoInitialState**, must be overridden if you wish to undertake any initialization that isn't handled by the default behavior of the **IDocument** method described earlier. For example, you might want to set up a default font for your document. If you don't override the method, it does nothing. Its interface looks like this:

```
pascal void TDocument::DoInitialState();
```

Your application must always override the **DoMakeViews** method of the class **TDocument** to create the windows and views for a document. We will have more to say about this procedure in the next section when we discuss how to create documents. The interface to this method is:

```
pascal void TDocument::DoMakeViews(Boolean forPrinting);
```

You will need to override the **DoMakeWindows** method if you create windows and/or views procedurally, but if you use the **NewTemplate-Window** function to create views and windows, you can ignore this method. Its interface looks like this:

```
pascal void TDocument::DoMakeWindows();
```

The **DoRead** method in the class **TDocument** is also usually overridden. By default, it results in the document's print record being read from the disk file if the value of the instance variable *fSavePrintInfo* is true; otherwise, this method does nothing. Your override of the **DoRead** method should read all other data from the file. The interface to **DoRead** looks like this:

```
pascal void Document::DoRead(short aRefNum,
                Boolean rsrcExists, Boolean forPrinting);
```

Two of the **TDocument** methods with which you will often work relate to the saving of data on the disk. **DoNeedDiskSpace** determines how much disk space is needed to store the document in its current state, including its data and resource fork requirements. If you don't override this method, only enough disk space to save the document's print information will be calculated (which will happen only if the instance variable *fSavePrintInfo* is true). Its interface looks like this:

```
pascal void Document::DoNeedDiskSpace(
                long *dataForkBytes, long *rsrcForkBytes);
```

MacApp uses the number of bytes calculated by your **DoNeedDisk-Space** method to see if there is room on the disk for the file the user wants to save. If there is, then the file is opened by MacApp, after which your **DoWrite** method is called. If there is not room on the disk, then MacApp asks the user if he or she wants to delete the original copy of the file before saving the revised version.

Here's what the interface to the **DoWrite** method looks like:

```
Pascal void TDocument::DoWrite(short aRefNum, Boolean  makingCopy);
```

If the user has not previously named the file, MacApp will call the **RequestFileName** method. This call will put up the standard Macintosh file dialog box and handle the user's input correctly.

After the **TDocument::Save** method calls your **DoWrite** method, it closes the file and flushes the disk cache. You only need to get the data written correctly; MacApp handles the rest.

As you will see in Chapter 18, there are two methods for handling menus that you usually must override: **DoSetupMenus** and **DoMenuCommand**. The default versions for the **TDocument** class handle the Save and Save As... menu items from the File Menu. You generally will not have to be concerned with these items, since MacApp handles them well.

## ▶ Creating Documents

The process through which MacApp goes to create a document in RAM that can then be seen through your application's views depends on whether the document is an existing one to be read from the disk or a new one being created by the user.

### ▶ New Document

If users launch your application by opening it from the Finder or if they choose the New item from the File menu when the application is running, MacApp makes a call to **TApplication**'s **OpenNew** method. You do not need to write this method since it works fine as supplied with MacApp. The **OpenNew** method, written in Object Pascal, simply calls, in order:

1. SELF.**DoMakeDocument**, which assigns its function result to a variable (we'll use the variable name *aDocument* here).

2. *aDocument*.**DoInitialState**, which sets the document's state to a new, untitled document.

3. *aDocument*.**DoMakeViews**, which creates any views the document needs to display representations of its data.

4. *aDocument*.**DoMakeWindows**, which creates the windows to contain the document's views.

(You must write the third method only if you are using **NewSimpleWindow** to create the windows in your application and are building your views procedurally. If you are using templates and the **NewTemplateWindow** function for this purpose, you will create views and windows at the same time in your **DoMakeViews** method.)

### ▶ Existing Document

If the user launches your application by opening a document from the Finder or if the Open item from the file menu is chosen, a new step is inserted between the first and third steps described in the preceding section. This step is executed by **TApplication**'s **OpenOld** method, which is called by MacApp whenever the user signals a desire to open an existing document with your application.

In this event, the four-step process for creating the document will be:

1. SELF.**DoMakeDocument**, which assigns its result to a variable (aDocument).

2. *aDocument*.**DoRead**, which reads the document's data from the disk.

3. *aDocument*.**DoMakeViews**, which creates any views the document needs.

4. *aDocument*.**DoMakeWindows**, which creates the windows to contain the document's views if you are using procedural methods to create them.

## ▶ Order of Creation

Regardless of whether **OpenOld** or **OpenNew** is used to create the document, you should by now recognize the order in which objects are created in your MacApp application:

1. Documents are created and initialized.
2. The document's data is initialized, or read from disk.
3. Views are created.
4. Windows are created (views and windows are created together when using 'view' resources).
5. The creation of the windows generates an update event that MacApp responds to by calling each view's **Draw** method. This makes the document's data appear in the windows on the display.

## ▶ Building a Simple Text Editor

Let's clarify the process of creating and dealing with documents by enhancing the Text sample built in Chapter 15. This new application is shown in Figure 16-1.

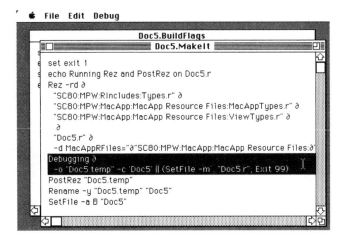

Figure 16-1. The enhanced Text sample

This application uses the TTEView building block (from Chapter 15) and associated command objects to support Undo for typing, Cut, Copy, and Paste. Views and windows are created from 'view' resources and **NewTemplateWindow**. With the new version of this example, the user can open multiple documents, each of which has its own view and window objects. If the user saves one of these documents, the characters are stored in a generic TEXT file, but its print information is not stored.

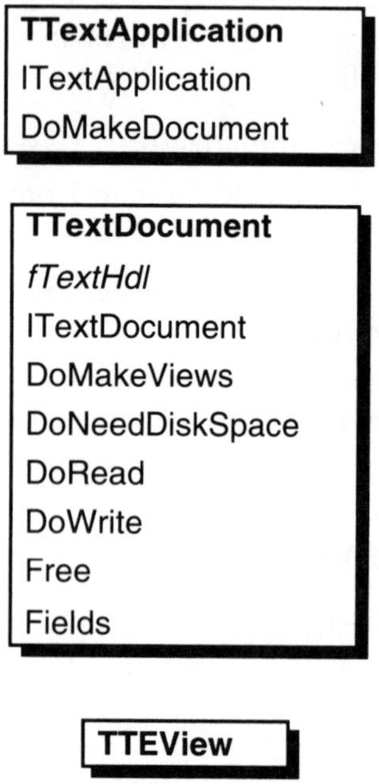

```
┌─────────────────────┐
│ TTextApplication    │
│ ITextApplication    │
│ DoMakeDocument      │
└─────────────────────┘

┌─────────────────────┐
│ TTextDocument       │
│ fTextHdl            │
│ ITextDocument       │
│ DoMakeViews         │
│ DoNeedDiskSpace     │
│ DoRead              │
│ DoWrite             │
│ Free                │
│ Fields              │
└─────────────────────┘

      ┌─────────────┐
      │ TTEView     │
      └─────────────┘
```

Figure 16-2. Text class diagram

Figure 16-2 is the class diagram for this example.
Let's examine the code modules that make up this program.

## ▶ MText.cp, the Main Program

Listing 16-1 contains the main program listing for the Text application. Be sure to call InitUTEView() if you are using 'view' resources, as we will in this sample.

Listing 16-1. Text program code

```
 1: #ifndef __UText__
 2:     #include "UText.h"
 3: #endif
 4:
 5: TTextApplication    *gTextApplication;
 6:
 7: #pragma segment Main
 8:
 9: void main()
10: {
11:     InitToolBox();
12:     if (ValidateConfiguration(&gConfiguration)){
13:         InitUMacApp(8);
14:         InitUPrinting();
15:         InitUTEView();
16:
17:         gTextApplication = new TTextApplication;
18:         FailNIL(gTextApplication);
19:         gTextApplication->ITextApplication();
20:         gTextApplication->Run();
21:     }
22:     else
23:         StdAlert(phUnsupportedConfiguration);
24: }
```

## ▶ UText.h, the Header File

Listing 16-2 shows the class definitions in the UText.h header file.

Listing 16-2. Text interface code

```
 1: #ifndef __UText__
 2: #define __UText__
 3:
 4: #ifndef __UMacApp__
 5:     #include <UMacApp.h>
 6: #endif
 7:
 8: #ifndef __UPrinting__
 9:     #include <UPrinting.h>
10: #endif
11:
12: #ifndef __UTEView__
13:     #include <UTEView.h>
14: #endif
```

```
15:
16: // ==========================================================
17: class TTextApplication: public TApplication{
18: public:
19:     virtual pascal void ITextApplication();
20:     virtual pascal TDocument *DoMakeDocument(
21:                 CmdNumber itsCmdNumber);     // override
22: };
23:
24: // ==========================================================
25: class TTextDocument: public TDocument{
26: private:
27:     Handle  fTextHdl;
28:     TTEView *fTEView;
29: public:
30:     virtual pascal void ITextDocument();
31:     virtual pascal void DoMakeViews(Boolean forPrinting);
32:                             // override
33:     virtual pascal void DoNeedDiskSpace(long *dataForkBytes,
34:                                long *rsrcForkBytes);
35:                             // override
36:     virtual pascal void DoRead( short aRefNum,
37:                         Boolean rsrcExists,
38:                         Boolean forPrinting);
39:                         // override
40:     virtual pascal void DoWrite(short aRefNum,
41:                         Boolean makingCopy);
42:                         // override
43:     virtual pascal void Free();                     // override
44:     virtual pascal void FreeData();                 // override
45:     virtual pascal void ShowReverted();             // override
46:     virtual pascal void StuffTheText();
47:     virtual pascal void Fields(pascal void (*DoToField)
48:                         (StringPtr fieldName,
49:                         Ptr fieldAddr, short fieldType,
50:                         void *DoToField_StaticLink),
51:                         void *DoToField_StaticLink);
52: };
53:
54: #endif  __UText__
```

Note that in lines 27 and 28 we define two instance variables called *fTextHdl* and *fTEView*, which will be used later in the program. Note, too, that in lines 31-44 we override the **TDocument** methods we discussed earlier: **DoMakeViews, DoNeedDiskSpace, DoRead, DoWrite, FreeData** and **Free**. In lines 47-51, we define an override for the **Fields** method used by the MacApp debugging code.

## ▶ UText.cp, the Application

The method implementation file, UText.cp, is shown in Listing 16-3 and discussed in some detail following the listing.

Listing 16-3. Text's methods

```
 1: #ifndef __UText__
 2:     #include "UText.h"
 3: #endif
 4:
 5: const OSType    kFileType   =   'TEXT';
 6: const OSType    kSignature  =   'doc1';     // Creator name
 7: const short     kWindowID   =   1001;       // view 1001
 8: const ResType   kTextID     =   'text';     // from view 1001
 9:
10: //============================================================
11: #pragma segment AInit
12: pascal void
13: TTextApplication::ITextApplication()
14: {
15:     this->IApplication(kFileType);
16: }
17:
18: //------------------------------------------------------------
19: #pragma segment AOpen
20: pascal TDocument*
21: TTextApplication::DoMakeDocument(CmdNumber /*itsCmdNumber*/)
    //override
22: {
23:     TTextDocument *aTextDocument = new TTextDocument;
24:     FailNIL(aTextDocument);
25:     aTextDocument->ITextDocument();
26:     return aTextDocument;
27: }
28:
29: //============================================================
30: #pragma segment AOpen
31: pascal void
32: TTextDocument::ITextDocument()
33: {
34:     fTextHdl = NULL;
35:     this->IDocument(kFileType,        // 'TEXT' file
36:                     kSignature,       // creator name
37:                     kUsesDataFork,    // store text in data fork
38:                     ! kUsesRsrcFork,  // nothing in resource fork
```

```
39:                 ! kDataOpen,              // close after read or write
40:                 ! kRsrcOpen);            // close after read or write
41:        fSavePrintInfo = false;          // can't clutter data fork
42:        Handle aTextHdl = NewPermHandle(0);   // put text here later
43:        FailNIL(aTextHdl);               // in case out of memory
44:        fTextHdl = aTextHdl;             // save this handle
45: }
46:
47: //------------------------------------------------------------
48: #pragma segment AClose
49: pascal void
50: TTextDocument::Free()          //override
51: {
52:     DisposIfHandle(fTextHdl);    // Delete text and block on heap
53:     inherited::Free();
54: }
55:
56: //------------------------------------------------------------
57: #pragma segment ARes
58: pascal void
59: TTextDocument::FreeData()          //override
60: {
61:     SetPermHandleSize(fTextHdl, 0); // Delete text for Revert
62: }
63:
64: //------------------------------------------------------------
65: #pragma segment ARes
66: pascal void
67: TTextDocument::ShowReverted()          //override
68: {
69:     this->StuffTheText();
70:     inherited::ShowReverted();          // for Revert
71: }
72:
73: //------------------------------------------------------------
74: #pragma segment ARes
75: pascal void
76: TTextDocument::StuffTheText()
77: {
78:     fTEView->StuffText(fTextHdl); // Make TEView use
         document text
79: }
80:
81: //------------------------------------------------------------
82: #pragma segment AOpen
83: pascal void
84: TTextDocument::DoMakeViews(Boolean /* forPrinting */)//override
85: {
```

```
86:      TWindow *aWindow = NewTemplateWindow(kWindowID,
            this);
87:      TTEView *aTEView = (TTEView *)
            (aWindow->FindSubView(kTextID));
88:      fTEView = aTEView;
89:      this->StuffTheText();
90:
91:      TStdPrintHandler *aStdHandler = new TStdPrintHandler;
92:      FailNIL(aStdHandler);
93:      aStdHandler->IStdPrintHandler(NULL,     // document
94:              aTEView,        // view
95:              !kSquareDots,   // kSquareDots = bitMaps
96:              kFixedSize,     // horizontal page size
97:              kFixedSize);    // vertical page size
98: }
99:
100:
101: //------------------------------------------------------------
102: #pragma segment AWriteFile
103: pascal void
104: TTextDocument::DoNeedDiskSpace(long *dataForkBytes, long
     *rsrcForkBytes)
105: {                                                    //override
106:     inherited::DoNeedDiskSpace(dataForkBytes, rsrcForkBytes);
107:     *dataForkBytes += GetHandleSize(fTextHdl);
108: }
109:
110: //------------------------------------------------------------
111: #pragma segment AWriteFile
112: pascal void
113: TTextDocument::DoWrite(short aRefNum, Boolean makingCopy)
        //override
114: {
115:     inherited::DoWrite(aRefNum, makingCopy);
116:     long dataBytes = GetHandleSize(fTextHdl);
117:     FailOSErr(FSWrite(aRefNum, &dataBytes, *fTextHdl));
         // write text
118: }
119:
120: //------------------------------------------------------------
121: #pragma segment AReadFile
122: pascal void
123: TTextDocument::DoRead(short aRefNum,                  //override
124:                 Boolean rsrcExists, Boolean forPrinting)
125: {
126:     long    dataBytes;
127:
```

```
128:        inherited::DoRead(aRefNum, rsrcExists, forPrinting);
129:        FailOSErr(GetEOF(aRefNum, &dataBytes));
              // bytes of file data
130:        SetPermHandleSize(fTextHdl, dataBytes);
              // heap space for text
131:        FailOSErr(FSRead(aRefNum, &dataBytes, *fTextHdl));
132: }
133:
134: //------------------------------------------------------------
135: #pragma segment AFields
136: pascal void
137: TTextDocument::Fields(pascal void (*DoToField)(StringPtr
     fieldName,
138:                         Ptr fieldAddr, short fieldType,
139:                         void *DoToField_StaticLink),
140:                         void *DoToField_StaticLink)
141: {
142:     (*DoToField)("\pTTextDocument", NULL, bClass,
            DoToField_StaticLink);
143:     (*DoToField)("\pfTextHdl", (Ptr)&fTextHdl, bHandle,
144:                                     DoToField_StaticLink);
145:     (*DoToField)("\pfTEView", (Ptr)&fTEView, bObject,
146:                                     DoToField_StaticLink);
147:     inherited::Fields(DoToField, DoToField_StaticLink);
148: }
```

## ▶ Initializing the Document

Documents are usually created by the application's **DoMakeDocument** method. Our latest version is shown on lines 20-27 of Listing 16-3. This is what the method looks like in most programs, with the standard four lines of code. These lines create a document object on line 23, check to make sure there was enough memory with FailNIL on line 24, initialize it on line 25, and return a pointer to it as a function result on line 26.

**By the Way ▶** Notice that we commented out the name of the function's one argument on line 21. This is optional, but should be done for any arguments that you do not use inside the body of the function. If you forget to do this, your MPW worksheet window will be cluttered by warnings about unused arguments from the CFront preprocessor during the build process.

In lines 34 and 44 of Listing 16-3, notice that we use the *fTextHdl* variable declared in the class definition in Listing 16-1. We assign it a value of NULL in line 34 so that it will have some non-random value, enabling our **Free** method (shown in lines 49-54) to work properly. This is important in case **Free** gets called in response to an error executing **IDocument**. An example of such an error would arise from the **IDocument** method trying to allocate memory and failing because memory was full. This would cause MacApp's error-handling routines to send the **Free** message to the document.

Line 41 insures that we avoid cluttering up the data fork with print information by setting *fSavePrintInfo* to false.

In line 42, we use the MacApp function NewPermHandle(0) to allocate a handle to the variable *aTextHdl*, but we don't do anything with the handle at the moment. Later (see lines 130-131) we read text into this handle directly from disk. Note, too, that in line 44, we store this newly created handle in the instance variable *fTextHdl*, which we earlier initialized to NULL while we waited to see if we could allocate a handle to it.

Notice that we allocated memory on the heap by using the MacApp function NewPermHandle rather than the Toolbox call NewHandle. This allocates space on the heap from permanent memory, making sure that sufficient temporary memory is reserved for your CODE segments.

| By the Way ▶ | MacApp divides the available heap space into these two kinds of memory. *Permanent memory* is the space occupied by data and objects allocated by your program. *Temporary memory* is available for your program's CODE segments. Resources or other memory demands of the Toolbox for temporary use by the Macintosh Toolbox can also be satisfied in the temporary memory area, which is allocated with the NewHandle Toolbox call. Objects, data structures, and other less transient items your program creates should normally be placed in permanent memory with the NewPermHandle call in MacApp. In fact, this routine is used by the new operator that creates handle-based objects. For more detail on this important subject, you should read Curt Bianchi's article entitled "Memory Management with MacApp," published in *Dr. Dobb's Macintosh Journal*, Fall 1989. |
|---|---|

Our **Free** method in lines 49-54, uses the built-in MacApp routine DisposIfHandle to free the handle to the text in our document before calling the inherited **Free** method in the class **TDocument**. This procedure confirms that the handle refers to a valid block on the heap before calling the Toolbox DisposHandle routine.

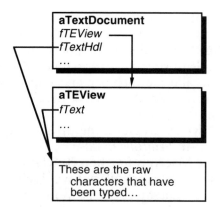

Figure 16-3. Document and View objects referencing raw text

To be sure the view uses the same text that we have stored in memory and that it is pointed to by the handle now stored in the instance variable *fTextHdl*, we send the message **StuffTheText** at line 69 to the method **StuffTheText**. This routine calls the **TTEView** method **StuffText** on line 78.

The interrelationships among *fTextHdl*, the view, and the text characters the raw text, are depicted in Figure 16-3.

Look at lines 103-108, where the **DoNeedDiskSpace** method is defined. Notice that it works by first calling the inherited method so that it can find out how much data would be needed to store the Print Record on the disk. In this example, we do not store the Print Record but we leave this call in place for future compatibility. Then the method calculates the number of bytes needed in the data fork by using the Toolbox call **GetHandleSize**. MacApp uses the result of this calculation to determine if room exists for the file to be written to disk. If it does, then your document will be sent the **DoWrite** message.

Lines 112-118 implement the **DoWrite** method. Notice that in line 116 we assign the size of the handle *fTextHdl* to the variable dataBytes and then use that variable in line 117 when we call the Toolbox function FSWrite. This is a mandatory step; the FSWrite routine insists that the second parameter passed to it be a pointer, not an actual number or constant. The third parameter must be a pointer to the data. We get this by dereferencing *fTextHdl*. This is safe since the Toolbox routine FSWrite does not cause a heap compaction.

The **DoRead** method (lines 122-132) uses two MacApp error-handling routines, **FailOSErr** and **FailMemError**. You should use these routines because they handle errors related to disk files and memory management in a user-friendly manner. Notice, too, that although our **DoRead** method does not explicitly check to see if the file has more than 32K characters, your program should do so since an instance of class **TTEView** cannot hold more than 32,767 characters. You can probably tell that the inherited **DoRead** method in our **DoRead** method does nothing, but we put it there for future MacApp compatibility.

▶ Supporting Revert

A typical File menu is shown in Figure 16-4. We have described the code you must write to support the New, Open..., and Save menu items, but have not yet discussed the code to support Revert. Revert works in one of two modes. If the user chooses Revert but has never saved the current document to disk, then all the characters that the user has typed should be deleted. If the file does exist on disk, then the last-saved version of that file should be read from disk and the view should be reinitialized appropriately. MacApp supports both of these cases, provided you override the methods **FreeData** and **ShowReverted**.

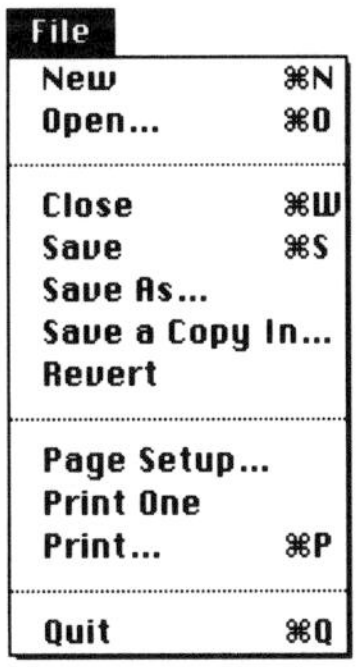

```
┌─────────────────────┐
│ File                │
├─────────────────────┤
│ New            ⌘N   │
│ Open...        ⌘O   │
├─────────────────────┤
│ Close          ⌘W   │
│ Save           ⌘S   │
│ Save As...          │
│ Save a Copy In...   │
│ Revert              │
├─────────────────────┤
│ Page Setup...       │
│ Print One           │
│ Print...       ⌘P   │
├─────────────────────┤
│ Quit           ⌘Q   │
└─────────────────────┘
```

Figure 16-4. The File menu

The **FreeData** method shown in lines 58-62 of Listing 16-3 merely gets rid of any text typed by the user. This prepares the document for reverting to the previous state. In our Text sample program, we also need to restore the size of the view to its previous state. To do this, we provide the **ShowReverted** method of lines 66-71. Line 69 insures that the reverted data from an existing disk file is used by our text view. Line 70 calls **TDocument's** standard **ShowReverted** method which requests each of the document's views to restore their size, and so forth to the correct state.

If you review the code necessary to support these text files on disk, you will see that less than 150 lines of code in a MacApp program can provide a surprising amount of functionality.

## ▶ Summary

In this chapter, you have learned how to work with documents. You have seen that documents are the data associated with views and windows and that the windows are generally created in response to the creation of a document. We have examined the important variables and significant methods of the class **TDocument**. Finally, we have looked closely at an example text editor using these techniques to create, read, and save text files.

In Chapter 17, we will discuss using lists to track and manage multiple objects in an application. By using lists of objects in your document, you can write much more interesting and complex programs.

# 17 ▶ Using Lists

This chapter discusses the use of *lists* in your MacApp applications. They are quite common in object programming environments where these lists are used to keep track of a collection of objects to be displayed.

After an overview of list objects, we will examine the class **TList**, which is MacApp's most important collection object. We will examine this class's important instance variables and methods. Finally, we will look at a small sample program that uses a list to keep track of objects drawn in a window.

## ▶ Lists: An Overview

It is important at the outset that we are clear about one thing lists are not. They are not visible, scrolling lists of items from which users make selections. In other words, don't confuse lists with the lists associated with the Macintosh List Manager in the Toolbox. A list object is simply a dynamic list of other objects; your application uses it to keep track of such objects and to send them messages when appropriate.

MacApp lists are really lists of object reference variables. This means that only objects can be stored in these lists, not strings, numbers, records, or any other kinds of data. In an accounting package, for example, you might store customer objects in a list. In a CAD/CAM application, a list could be used for shapes, or you might put chess pieces in a list in a game program. In the sample program we will examine later in this chapter, we use a list to keep track of icons being drawn in a window. It is not necessary that all of the objects in a list be homogeneous; such lists often contain mixed items belonging to an abstract superclass.

All MacApp lists are instances of the class **TList** but the objects in the list are not. We will examine some of **TList's** important instance variables and methods later in this chapter.

From a programmer's perspective, lists are much like one-dimensional dynamic arrays. When you create them, they have a size of zero. Then you add elements to them as they are needed during program execution. Each element of the list is accessed using an index number.

Instances of the class **TList** have methods associated with them that allow you to

- add and delete objects
- access individual objects
- perform some operation on all objects in the list

The class **TList** has one subclass, **TSortedList**, in which objects are sorted. You may also want to use the class **TDynamicArray** (the superclass of **TList**) to manage a collection of things that are not objects.

## ▶ The Class TList

The interface for the class **TList** is in the file UList.h. There are no instance variables in this class with which you need to be concerned. We will look briefly at some thirteen programming methods and one debugging-related method connected to the class **TList**.

To create a new instance of the class **TList**, you do not need to use the usual **new** operator to which you have by now become accustomed. Instead, MacApp defines a global function called NewList that is used only for this purpose. This function creates an object of type **TList**, calls the initialization method **IList** to initialize it, and then returns the object.

MacApp supplies many methods for accessing the contents of a list and modifying them, including **AtPut**, **InsertFirst**, **InsertLast**, **At**, **First**, and **Last**. The **AtPut** method places an item into a list. It is typically used to place a new object in the list at some point other than the beginning or end, since there are specific methods to put objects in those two places.

The interface to this method looks like this:

```
virtual pascal void AtPut(ArrayIndex index, TObject *newItem);
```

When you call this method, you supply the index position in the list at which you want the newItem to be placed.

To put a new object at the head of an existing list, you should call the **InsertFirst** method. Similarly, the **InsertLast** method will put a new object at the end of an existing list. The interfaces to these two methods are identical except for the method names:

```
virtual pascal void InsertFirst(TObject *item);
virtual pascal void InsertLast(TObject *item);
```

Retrieving objects from a list requires the use of methods with names parallel to those used to add new objects. To retrieve an object based on its position in the list, for example, use the **At** method, whose interface looks like this:

```
virtual pascal TObject *At(ArrayIndex index);
```

Similarly, retrieving the first or last object in a list requires the use of the **First** and **Last** methods:

```
virtual pascal TObject *First(void);
virtual pascal TObject *Last(void);
```

The three most powerful methods you will use in conjunction with lists in MacApp are collectively referred to as iterator methods because they cause an operation to be performed on all or selected members of the list. The most general of these is the **Each** method. Its interface looks like this:

```
virtual pascal void Each(pascal void (*DoToItem)
    (TObject *item, void *DoToItem_StaticLink),
    void *DoToItem_StaticLink);
```

This method carries out the function supplied as an argument once for each element of the list, in the order in which they are stored. We will show how to use the weird parameters shortly.

Sometimes you want to find an object that meets some test criteria. In those cases, you can use the MacApp methods **FirstThat** and **LastThat**. Here is the interface to the **FirstThat** method:

```
virtual pascal TObject *FirstThat(pascal Boolean (*TestItem)
    (TObject *item, void * TestItem_StaticLink),
    void *TestItem_StaticLink);
```

The first parameter to **FirstThat** is a function that is called once for each object in the order in which they are stored in the list until the TestItem function returns a value of true. It then returns a reference to the object that satisfied the test. If none of the objects in the list satisfies the criterion, the **FirstThat** method returns a value of NULL.

The **LastThat** method is analogous except that it returns the last element in the list that matches the criterion. Its interface looks like this:

```
virtual pascal TObject *LastThat(pascal Boolean (*TestItem)
    (TObject *item, void * TestItem_StaticLink),
    void *TestItem_StaticLink);
```

When you need to know how many objects are in a list, you can use the **GetSize** method inherited from **TDynamicArray**. Its interface is quite simple:

```
virtual pascal ArrayIndex GetSize(void);
```

This function returns the number of objects in the list.

To manage the memory associated with your lists correctly, MacApp supplies methods that include: **Delete**, **DeleteAll**, **FreeAll**, and **FreeList**.

**By the Way ▶**

While the Macintosh handles most memory management for you and while this is even more true of MacApp applications, there is a fundamental rule of Macintosh programming you must follow. If your program creates special objects about which MacApp does not know, then you have an obligation to free them when you are finished using them.

The **Delete** method deletes a specific object reference from the list but does not free it (that is, it does not release its associated memory). In other words, it reduces the size of the list by one and makes that object disappear from the list perspective, but it does not result in any memory being freed. Its interface looks like this:

```
virtual pascal void Delete(TObject *item);
```

To delete all of the elements of the list, still without freeing the memory associated with them, use the **DeleteAll** method. Its interface looks like this:

```
virtual pascal void DeleteAll(void);
```

MacApp includes methods that correspond to these two but which release the memory associated with the deleted objects. You will generally only free the objects; you will delete them only when the program is still running but the current contents of the list have become invalid or are no longer needed. The **FreeAll** method frees the memory associated with each object in the list but leaves the list itself accessible in memory so that you can add new items to it. It essentially facilitates the destruction and reconstruction of a list. Its interface looks like this:

```
virtual pascal void FreeAll(void);
```

The **FreeList** method, on the other hand, frees each object in the list and then frees the memory associated with the list as well, making the list disappear. Its interface is also quite simple:

```
virtual pascal void FreeList(void);
```

Finally, there is one debugging-oriented method associated with the class **TList**. It is called **SetEltType** (for set element type) and is needed so that the MacApp Inspector can display the class of objects kept in a particular list. Its interface looks like this:

```
virtual pascal void SetEltType(StringPtr toClass);
```

# ▶ An Example Using Lists

The Bird sample program we will build is a simple application that draws a funny-looking little bird (shown in Figure 17-1) in a window anyplace the user clicks the mouse. We use a list to keep track of all the birds so they can be redrawn in response to a window update event, or printed. Each bird object has a **DrawBird** method so it knows how to draw itself.

## ▶ The Bird Icon

The visual appearance of each bird is defined by 'ICON' resource number 1000. If you wish to follow along with the development of this example, you can do one of two things: You can create your own new icon (or use an existing one and either renumber it or change the resource ID in the example to reflect the icon's number), or draw the icon as we've used it. If you wish to draw the icon, you can use any of several techniques. If you own MPW, you already have ResEdit. Figure 17-2 shows the finished bird icon in a ResEdit window being used to edit or create an icon.

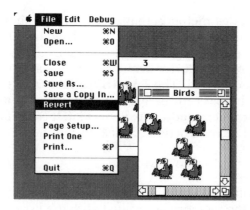

Figure 17-1. The Bird sample program

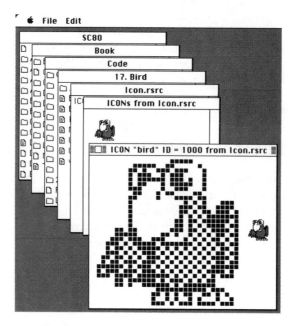

Figure 17-2. ResEdit window showing bird ICON

This is the first sample program where you will be including a file that is not expected by the MABuild process. The file containing the icon — which we've arbitrarily called Icon.rsrc — must be known to MABuild or it will not be included in the build process carried out when you compile your application. To handle this situation, you must put a reference to this file in two places: the resource (or .r) file... and a new file that must be named after your application with the suffix .MAMake — in this case, we're calling the application Bird, so the file is called Bird.MAMake.

In the resource file, you need only an *include* statement to make Rez place the ICON resource in your final application. The necessary line in Bird.r looks like this:

```
include "Icon.rsrc";
```

The file Bird.MAMake is shown in Listing 17-1. This file provides extra information used by the MABuild tool. It ensures that MABuild will call Rez to compile Bird.r if you make changes to any of the files on lines 10-12.

Listing 17-1. Bird.MAMake

```
 1: #----------------------------------------------------------
 2: #  List here the Application's Name
 3: AppName = Bird
 4:
 5:
 6: #----------------------------------------------------------
 7: #  List resource files that the Rez file includes if you
 8: #  want to include more or less than the standard set
 9: OtherRsrcFiles =   ∂
10:      "{MAObj}Printing.rsrc"  ∂
11:      "{SrcApp}Icon.rsrc"  ∂
12:      "{SrcApp}Views.rsrc"
```

Notice the MPW shell variables used on lines 10-12. These are defined as follows:

{MAObj} — path name to the folder containing the compiled MacApp libraries.

{SrcApp} — path name to the folder containing the source code files for your application.

| By the Way ▶ | We have to take these additional descriptive steps here because we added a resource file to the list of things about which MABuild needs to know before it can compile our code. But we would have to take the same steps if we added any file — a resource file, code file, or any other kind of file — to the program. MABuild is aware of the existence of the following files (assuming your application is called MyApp): |
|---|---|

- **MMyApp**.cp
- **UMyApp**.h
- **UMyApp**.cp
- **UMyApp**.r

Any other file you want included when your program is built must be referenced in the MAMake file.

## ▶ The Sample Application

Figure 17-3 is a class diagram for the example program Bird. In addition to the usual application, document, and view classes, there is also the new class TBird.

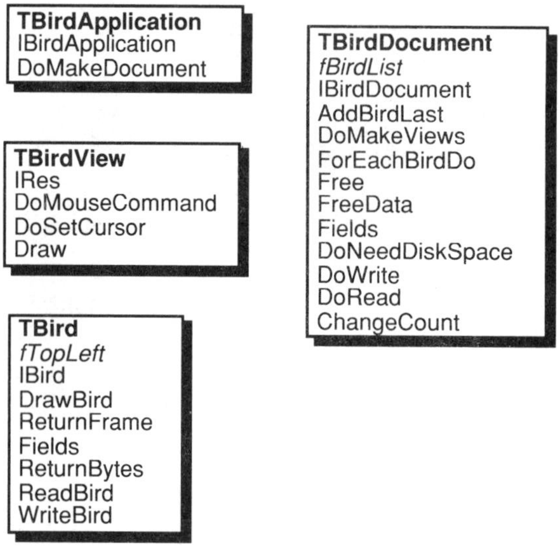

```
TBirdApplication
IBirdApplication
DoMakeDocument
```

```
TBirdView
IRes
DoMouseCommand
DoSetCursor
Draw
```

```
TBird
fTopLeft
IBird
DrawBird
ReturnFrame
Fields
ReturnBytes
ReadBird
WriteBird
```

```
TBirdDocument
fBirdList
IBirdDocument
AddBirdLast
DoMakeViews
ForEachBirdDo
Free
FreeData
Fields
DoNeedDiskSpace
DoWrite
DoRead
ChangeCount
```

Figure 17-3. Bird class diagram

Let's turn our attention now to the sample program code itself. (This time we will not look at the code file by file but rather purpose by purpose. We will not even reproduce the listing for the main program, since that process simply duplicates what we have done in previous examples.)

## ▶ The Application Class

Listing 17-2 shows the code in the file UBird.h needed to define the application class with which we will be working. All we need are methods to initialize our application object and to create document objects on demand.

Listing 17-2. UBird.h application class declaration

```
1:   class TBirdApplication: public TApplication {
2:   public:
3:      virtual pascal void IBirdApplication();
4:      virtual pascal TDocument *DoMakeDocument(CmdNumber
         itsCmdNumber);
5:   };
```

## ▶ The Document Class

Listing 17-3 contains the code from UBird.h that defines the document class for our application.

Listing 17-3. UBird.h document class

```
1: typedef pascal void (*DoToABirdProc)(TBird *aBird, void
   *params);
2:
3: class TBirdDocument: public TDocument {
4: private:
5:    TList   *fBirdList;
6: public:
7:      virtual pascal void IBirdDocument();
8:      virtual pascal void Free();                  //override
9:      virtual pascal void FreeData();              //override
10:     virtual pascal void AddBirdLast(TBird *aBird);
11:     virtual pascal void ForEachBirdDo(DoToABirdProc DoToABird,
12:                              void *DoToBird_StaticLink);
13:     virtual pascal void DoMakeViews(Boolean forPrinting);
                                                     //override
14:     virtual pascal void DoNeedDiskSpace(long *dataForkBytes,
15:                              long *rsrcForkBytes); //override
```

```
16:     virtual pascal void DoWrite(short aRefNum,
17:                           Boolean makingCopy);     //override
18:     virtual pascal void DoRead(short aRefNum, Boolean
        rsrcExists,
19:                           Boolean forPrinting);     //override
20:     virtual pascal void Fields(pascal void (*DoToField)
                                                      //override
21:       (StringPtr fieldName, Ptr fieldAddr, short fieldType,
22:       void *DoToField_StaticLink), void *DoToField_StaticLink);
23: };
```

In line 5 of Listing 17-3, we define an instance variable to hold the contents of our list, called *fBirdList*. Note that this object is of class **TList**, not **TBird**. The objects in the list will be of type **TBird**, however. The **AddBirdLast** message described in line 10 will, as we will see shortly, add the next bird to *fBirdList*.

As you would expect, we define an initialization method called **IBirdDocument** on line 7. This method will create an empty list of birds. We therefore need a corresponding **Free** method, defined on line 8, that will dispose of the list and its associated bird objects when the document is closed. We also define a **FreeData** method on line 9 that is used when the user chooses Revert from the File menu.

The most interesting method is the **ForEachBirdDo** iterator function defined on lines 11-12. We will use this method whenever we need to carry out some operation on each bird in the list. We will use it to tell each bird to draw itself in the view, and to read and write its data to disk.

Notice the strange argument list to this method on lines 11 and 12. The first argument is named DoToABird, which is of type DoToABird-Proc. This DoToABirdProc type is defined in the typedef statement on line 1 to be a pointer to a function that has two arguments: a pointer to a bird object and an untyped pointer to some data. You might want to read the last two sentences again, slowly. They mean that the first argument to our **ForEachBirdDo** method must be a function with two parameters: a pointer to a bird and a pointer to some associated data. The result of this will be that the DoToABird function will be called repeatedly, passing each bird in the list as its first argument. In this way, we can send a message to each bird to draw itself, for example. This will probably not be clear yet, so we will show you exactly how we do this later in the chapter.

Notice the second argument to **ForEachBirdDo** is defined on line 12 to be another untyped pointer. This is a minor detail related to the fact that the implementation of our method will use the **TList::Each** method. This method was actually written in MacApp as a Pascal procedure, and the Pascal calling conventions require the extra parameter. If you are interested in all the gory details of static links, be sure to read Keith Rollin's excellent treatise in Apple's Macintosh Technical Note #265, entitled "Pascal to C: PROCEDURE Parameters."

We will discuss the methods shown on lines 14-19 for reading and writing disk files later in this chapter.

## ▶ The View Class

Next, look at the code in Listing 17-4, which defines the view class associated with our sample application. Like the code in the preceding two listings, this code is stored in the UBird.h file of our sample application.

Listing 17-4. UBird.h view class definition

```
 1: class TBirdView: public TView {
 2: private:
 3:     TBirdDocument    *fBirdDocument;
 4: public:
 5:     virtual pascal void IRes(TDocument *itsDocument, //override
 6:                         TView *itsSuperView, Ptr *itsParams);
 7:     virtual pascal TCommand* DoMouseCommand(Point *theMouse,
                                                         //override
 8:                                     EventInfo *info,
 9:                                     Point *hysteresis);
10:     virtual pascal Boolean DoSetCursor(Point localPoint,
                                                         //override
11:                                 RgnHandle cursorRgn);
12:     virtual pascal void Draw(Rect *area);           //override
13: };
```

Notice in lines 7-9 of Listing 17-4 that we override the **DoMouse-Command** method in the class **TView** to enable our application to draw a bird each time the mouse is clicked. The **Draw** method in line 12 is also an overridden method; as we have mentioned, this is usually the case. Here, the **Draw** method will be used to draw all the birds when necessary.

## ▶ The Bird Class

The last class we must define in the header file UBird.h is the class **TBird**. The code in Listing 17-5 accomplishes this task.

Listing 17-5. UBird.h TBird class definition

```
 1: class TBird: public TObject {
 2: private:
 3:     Point fTopLeft;
 4: public:
 5:     virtual pascal void IBird(const Point corner);
 6:     virtual pascal void DrawBird();
 7:     virtual pascal Rect ReturnFrame();
 8:     virtual pascal long ReturnBytes();
 9:     virtual pascal void ReadBird(short aRefNum);
10:     virtual pascal void WriteBird(short aRefNum);
11:     virtual pascal void Fields(pascal void (*DoToField)
                                                    //override
12:      (StringPtr fieldName, Ptr fieldAddr, short fieldType,
13:       void *DoToField_StaticLink), void *DoToField_StaticLink);
14: };
```

The **TBird** class is a simple subclass of **TObject** that defines only one instance variable, *fTopLeft*. This is all that differentiates one bird from another in this simple example, since all birds are drawn with the same icon and the same width and height. In later chapters, we'll show how to have each bird maintain its own bounding rectangle and color. You could easily add further variables so that each instance of **TBird** could be drawn with its own icon, for example.

The messages defined for the **TBird** class include:

**IBird** — initialize the bird location

**DrawBird** — draw the bird icon at the specified location

**ReturnFrame** — return a rectangle that defines where the bird will be drawn

**Fields** — display the current value of *fTopLeft* in the MacApp debugger

**ReturnBytes**, **ReadBird**, and **WriteBird** — used to read and write disk file data

In line 3 of Listing 17-5, we define an instance variable for the class **TBird** to hold the upper-left corner of the icon being drawn. We then define the messages, including: **DrawBird**, which will actually draw each icon, and **ReturnFrame**, which enables us to obtain the rectangle enclosing each icon. This information will be used when the view needs to be redrawn.

## ▶ Creating the Bird List

We will create our list of birds in the **IBirdDocument** method in the implementation file UBird.cp. Listing 17-6 shows the code for this.

Listing 17-6.  Code to create list of birds

```
1: #pragma segment AOpen
2: pascal void
3: TBirdDocument::IBirdDocument()
4: {
5:     fBirdList = NULL;                          // if IDocument fails
6:     this->IDocument(kFileType, kSignature, kUsesDataFork,
7:             !kUsesRsrcFork, !kDataOpen, !kRsrcOpen);
8:     fSavePrintInfo = true;                     // save print record
9:     TList *aList = NewList();
10:     fBirdList = aList;
11:     fBirdList->SetEltType("\pTBird");     // for Inspector
12: }
```

This method is surprisingly similar to the ITextDocument method described in Chapter 16. Again, we set the document's instance variable to NULL on line 5, in case the **IDocument** method on line 6 should fail. If that were to happen, our document's **Free** method shown below could safely handle the *fBirdList* variable.

| By the Way ▶ | Notice that we use two lines (9 and 10) to create the new list and place it into the instance variable *fBirdList*. You may wonder why we don't handle this all in one statement:

```
fBirdList=NewList();
```

The problem with that approach is that we would be storing the new list object directly in the instance variable of our document object. Now consider what that means. The compiler interprets .fBirdList as (**this).fBirdList in reality. In other words, "this" is a handle to a relocatable block on the heap, and the *fBirdList* reference becomes the actual address of that storage location inside this relocatable block. When we call the NewList function, the code that executes will allocate a new structure on the heap for the new list object. Allocating memory on the heap means that our document object, referenced by "this" in this method, may be moved in memory, changing the address of the *fBirdList* instance variable.

We may therefore be trying to save the reference to the new object where the document used to be located, but not where it is after it has moved. To be safe, we'll use a temporary variable, *aList*, to receive the result of the NewList function call. We know this is safe since the *aList* local variable is allocated on the stack and will therefore not move.

▶ Freeing the Bird List

Listing 17-7 presents the code we use to free the bird list when it is no longer needed.

Listing 17-7. Code to free the list

```
1: #pragma segment AClose
2: pascal void
3: TBirdDocument::Free()              // override
4: {
5:     if (fBirdList != NULL)
6:         fBirdList->FreeList();  // free Birds and List
7:     inherited::Free();
8: }
```

Notice that in line 6 of Listing 17-7 we use the **TList::FreeList** method to free the objects in the display list and the display list itself. Then we call the inherited **Free** method to release memory used by our document object itself.

| By the Way ▶ | You may think it odd for an object to free itself. All this means is that the **Free** method, located in a CODE resource, disposes of the object's data storage, which is on the heap in a different block. That instance of the class **TBirdDocument** is disposed of, but the methods remain in memory, since they belong to the class as a whole, not just to one object. |
| --- | --- |

▶ Adding a Single Bird to the List

Now that we've defined the classes and created the list in which we'll store all of our bird objects, we're ready to examine the meat of our sample program: four methods that add a new bird to the list when the user clicks the mouse in our application's window. The process is driven by the **DoMouseCommand** method, which as you'll recall we defined in our view class as an override method. Listing 17-8 contains the code for this method.

Listing 17-8. DoMouseCommand method

```
1: #pragma segment ASelCommand
2: pascal TCommand*
3: TBirdView::DoMouseCommand(Point*      theMouse,        //override
4:                           EventInfo* /* info */,
5:                           Point*     /* hysteresis */)
6: {
7:     TBird *aBird = new TBird;
8:     FailNIL(aBird);
9:     aBird->IBird(*theMouse);
10:
11:     Rect birdRect = aBird->ReturnFrame();
12:     fBirdDocument->AddBirdLast(aBird);    // add bird to document
13:     fBirdDocument->SetChangeCount(1);     // data changed
14:     this->InvalidRect(&birdRect);         // update bird area
15:     return gNoChanges;                    // or NULL
16: }
```

Let's focus our attention on the main portion of Listing 17-8, lines 7-15. Line 7 uses the traditional MacApp method of creating a new instance of class **TBird** called aBird. Line 8 checks to be sure we were successful in allocating memory for this new object. Line 9 then calls the initialization routine IBird (see Listing 17-9). Line 12 calls the **AddBird-Last** method discussed below (Listing 17-10) to add the new bird to the list stored in *fBirdList*. Line 14 uses the view method **InvalidRect** to force an update event for an area the size of the bird. Notice that the bird area is determined on line 11. Finally, line 15 uses the built-in MacApp global *gNoChanges* to fulfill its obligation to return some command object as a function result from the **DoMouseCommand** method. If you prefer, return NULL instead of *gNoChanges*. In later chapters, we'll draw bird objects using real command objects, so we can undo their drawing.

Listing 17-9 shows the small routine that initializes each bird's location as it is created with a mouse click.

Listing 17-9. Initializing each bird

```
1: #pragma segment ASelCommand
2: pascal void
3: TBird::IBird(const Point corner)
4: {
5:     fTopLeft = corner;
6: }
```

Listing 17-10 reproduces the document method used to add a bird to the *fBirdList* list. Notice that it uses the **InsertLast** method of **TList** discussed earlier to put each new bird at the end of the list. The bird must be added at the end of the list so that it will be drawn on top of any previous birds in the list.

Listing 17-10. Adding a bird to display list

```
1: #pragma segment ASelCommand
2: pascal void
3: TBirdDocument::AddBirdLast(TBird *aBird)
4: {
5:     fBirdList->InsertLast(aBird);
6: }
```

The **ReturnFrame** method shown in Listing 17-11 used in the **DoMouseCommand** method (see Listing 17-8) to inform the MacApp **TView** method **InvalidRect** as to what portion of the window needs redrawing.

Listing 17-11. The ReturnFrame method

```
1: #pragma segment ASelCommand
2: pascal Rect
3: TBird::ReturnFrame()
4: {
5:    Rect      birdFrame;
6:
7:    birdFrame.top = fTopLeft.v;
8:    birdFrame.left = fTopLeft.h;
9:    birdFrame.bottom = birdFrame.top + kBirdHeight;
10:   birdFrame.right = birdFrame.left + kBirdWidth;
11:   return birdFrame;
12: }
```

Notice in lines 7 and 8 we use the value in the instance variable *fTop-Left*, stored here when the **DoMouseCommand** method called the **IBird** method, as an anchor point to calculate the size of the rectangle to return to the **InvalidRect** routine.

## ▶ Drawing All the Birds

The next routines we will examine are two that involve the drawing of all of the birds in the view. The method that is called when the view needs to be redrawn is the **Draw** method, shown in Listing 17-12. Remember that the area parameter on line 14 is the rectangle that encloses the update region, as determined by MacApp when it sends the Draw message to your view.

Listing 17-12. Draw method

```
 1: //------------------------------------------------------------
 2: #pragma segment ARes
 3: pascal void
 4: DrawABird(TBird *aBird, Rect *updateArea)
 5: {
 6:     Rect birdRect = aBird->ReturnFrame();
 7:     if (SectRect(&birdRect, updateArea, &birdRect))
 8:         aBird->DrawBird();
 9: }
10:
11: //------------------------------------------------------------
12: #pragma segment ARes
13: pascal void
14: TBirdView::Draw(Rect *area)           //override
15: {
16:     Rect     viewBorder;
17:
18:     PenNormal();                       // always do before drawing
19:     PenSize(2, 2);
20:     PenPat(qd.gray);
21:     this->GetQDExtent(&viewBorder);
22:     FrameRect(&viewBorder);            // a frame just for fun
23:
24:     fBirdDocument->ForEachBirdDo((DoToABirdProc) DrawABird,
        area);
25:
26:     PenNormal();                       // leave grafport normal
27: }
```

Lines 19-22 merely frame the view with a two-pixel-wide gray border, so we can see it for debugging purposes. The interesting work is done on line 24, where we send the **ForEachBirdDo** message. The method is defined to take two arguments: the first is a function (which we here call DrawABird), and the second is a pointer to some variable (here we pass a pointer to the area enclosing the region to be drawn). We pass this area so we can use it on line 7 of the DrawABird function to decide if a given bird intersects the area that needs to be drawn. Without this test, updating and scrolling are slower than they need to be.

Notice that the DrawABird function (not a method) shown on lines 3-9 takes a reference to a bird as its first parameter, but that parameter is not shown when we call the function on line 24. Remember to use that syntax when you write methods like these that take a function as an argument. The complete argument list of the DrawABird function must agree with the definition of DoToABirdProc defined on the header file, and shown below:

```
typedef pascal void (*DoToABirdProc)(TBird *aBird, void *params);
```

This code is odd-looking, but the result of using it is quite simple. When line 24 of listing 17-12 executes, the **DrawABird** method is called once for each bird in the list, passing that bird as an argument. The result is that each bird in the list is sent the DrawBird() message, hence each bird draws itself on the screen.

Listing 17-13. DrawBird method

```
1: #pragma segment ARes
2: pascal void
3: TBird::DrawBird()
4: {
5:     Handle aHandle = GetIcon(kIconID);
6:     FailNILResource(aHandle);
7:     Rect aRect = this->ReturnFrame();
8:     PlotIcon(&aRect, aHandle);
9: }
```

The **DrawBird** method is shown in Listing 17-13. In line 6 we use a MacApp routine called FailNILResource that checks for both Resource Manager errors (such as a missing ICON resource), and out of memory errors. Then in line 8, we use the Toolbox routine PlotIcon to draw the bird. Notice that we use the bird's **ReturnFrame** method again, to determine the location in the view to be occupied by the icon.

## ▶ Supporting Disk Files

This section discusses saving files to disk, opening existing files, and supporting the Revert operation.

## ▶ Saving Files

In Chapter 16, you saw how to save text files to disk. In this discussion, you will see how to handle saving files to disk when these documents contain non-textual information. As in Chapter 16, you will define a **DoNeedDiskSpace** method and a **DoWrite** method. Listing 17-14 shows the documents' **DoNeedDiskSpace** method, and the associated bird's **ReturnBytes** method.

Listing 17-14. Methods to compute disk space

```
 1: //------------------------------------------------------------
 2: #pragma segment AWriteFile
 3: pascal void
 4: TBirdDocument::DoNeedDiskSpace(long *dataForkBytes, long
    *rsrcForkBytes)                              // override
 5:     // File format:
 6:     // Print info
 7:     // Short - # Birds saved in the file
 8:     // Bird info #1
 9:     // Bird info #2
10:     // etc.
11: {
12:     inherited::DoNeedDiskSpace(dataForkBytes, rsrcForkBytes);
13:                                              // print info
14:     short numberOfBirds = fBirdList->GetSize();
15:     long numberOfBirdsBytes = sizeof(short);
16:     TBird *aBird = new TBird;
17:     FailNIL(aBird);
18:     long birdBytes = aBird->ReturnBytes();
19:     aBird->Free();
20:     *dataForkBytes += numberOfBirdsBytes + (birdBytes *
        numberOfBirds);
21: };
22:
23: //------------------------------------------------------------
24: #pragma segment AWriteFile
25: pascal long
26: TBird::ReturnBytes()
27: {
28:     return  sizeof(fTopLeft);
29: }
```

Lines 5-10 describe the file format. In this sample, all information will be stored in the data fork. Line 12 uses the inherited **DoNeedDisk-Space** method to compute the number of bytes needed for the print record. Each document can thus have its own page setup information, as chosen by the user. Lines 14 and 15 compute the amount of space needed in the file to store an integer indicating how many birds are in the document. Lines 25-29 calculate the number of bytes required by each bird's data. The bird object itself will not be written to disk; only sufficient data to describe the bird will be stored. Line 20 computes the total number of bytes needed for the file. (A more sophisticated form of data storage using streams is described in Chapter 24.)

The **DoWrite** method in Listing 17-15 is called to write the data to disk, using each bird's **WriteBird** method to write out that bird's data.

Listing 17-15. Methods to write the birds to disk

```
 1: //------------------------------------------------------------
 2: #pragma segment AWriteFile
 3: pascal void
 4: WriteABird(TBird *aBird, short *fileRefNumPtr)
 5: {
 6:     aBird->WriteBird(*fileRefNumPtr);
        // each bird writes out itself
 7: }
 8:
 9: //------------------------------------------------------------
10: #pragma segment AWriteFile
11: pascal void
12: TBirdDocument::DoWrite(short aRefNum, Boolean makingCopy)
    //override
13: {
14:     inherited::DoWrite(aRefNum, makingCopy);
          // write print info
15:     short numberOfBirds = fBirdList->GetSize();
16:     long  numberOfBirdsBytes = sizeof(numberOfBirds);
17:     FailOSErr(FSWrite(aRefNum,                // file number
18:                      &numberOfBirdsBytes,     // 2 bytes
19:                      (Ptr) &numberOfBirds));  // # of birds
20:     this->ForEachBirdDo((DoToABirdProc)WriteABird, // function
21:                      &aRefNum);                // * file number
22: };
23:
24: //------------------------------------------------------------
25: #pragma segment AWriteFile
```

```
26: pascal void
27: TBird::WriteBird(short aRefNum)
28: {
29:     long dataBytes = sizeof(fTopLeft);
30:     FailOSErr(FSWrite(aRefNum, &dataBytes, (Ptr) &fTopLeft));
31: }
```

As with the Draw method discussed above, this method will iterate over the list of birds. In this case the call to ForEachBirdDo requests each bird to write itself out to disk. The inherited::DoWrite call on line 14 writes the print record to the data fork of the file. Lines 15-19 write out the number of birds as a 16-bit integer, while lines 20 and 21 call the WriteABird function for each bird in the list. This function is shown on lines 3-7. It sends a message to each bird telling it to write itself to disk, passing a pointer to the reference number of the open file as a parameter.

| By the Way ▶ | It would be simpler if we could pass the **WriteBird** method as the argument to ForEachBirdDo(), but we cannot. The reason is that the compiler places the address of the function on the stack, and methods in general do not have an address defined at compile time (because of dynamic binding). |
|---|---|

## ▶ Opening Existing Files

Listing 17-16 shows the document's **DoRead** method, and the bird's **ReadBird** method which it uses.

Listing 17-16. Methods to read the birds from disk

```
1: //------------------------------------------------------------
2: #pragma segment AReadFile
3: pascal void
4: TBirdDocument::DoRead(                               // override
5:         short aRefNum, Boolean rsrcExists, Boolean forPrinting)
6:
7: {
8:     short   numberOfBirds;
9:     TBird   *aBird;
10:
11:     inherited::DoRead(aRefNum, rsrcExists, forPrinting);
        // print info
12:     long  numberOfBirdsBytes = sizeof(numberOfBirds);
13:     FailOSErr(FSRead(
```

```
14:         aRefNum, &numberOfBirdsBytes, (Ptr)&numberOfBirds));
15:
16:     for (short index = 0; index < numberOfBirds; index++){
17:         aBird = new TBird;              // create Bird
18:         FailNIL(aBird);                 // enough memory
19:         aBird->ReadBird(aRefNum);       // read its data from disk
20:         this->AddBirdLast(aBird);       // add it to the list
21:     }
22: }
23:
24: //------------------------------------------------------------
25: #pragma segment AReadFile
26: pascal void
27: TBird::ReadBird(short aRefNum)
28: {
29:     long dataBytes = sizeof(fTopLeft);
30:     FailOSErr(FSRead(aRefNum, &dataBytes, (Ptr) &fTopLeft));
31: }
```

The primary difference between writing birds individually to a disk file and reading those birds back in from the file is that you must create each bird before you ask it to read its data from the disk file, since you cannot send a message to a non-existent object. This is done in lines 17-19. In line 20, you must remember to add this newly created bird to the list of birds in the document.

▶  Supporting Revert

To support the ability of the user to revert to the most recently saved version of the document, you must override the **FreeData** method as shown in Listing 17-17.

Listing 17-17. The FreeData method

```
1: #pragma segment AClose
2: pascal void
3: TBirdDocument::FreeData()    // override
4: {
5:     fBirdList->FreeAll();    // for Revert: free Bird, not List
6: }
```

Line 5 frees each bird object in the list but leaves the empty list object in the document. The **FreeData** method will be called by MacApp when the user chooses Revert from the File menu.

## ▶ Summary

In this chapter, we have described lists and their use in MacApp. We have discussed the class **TList** and some of its most important methods. By examining a relatively complex program that uses lists to keep track of icons that need to be drawn in a window, we have seen a practical case of how to use lists. We have also seen how to support disk files and reverting.

Continuing with the Bird example of this chapter, we will see in Chapter 18 how to handle menu interaction in a MacApp program.

# ▶ Obtaining Information from the User

Part Four consists of three chapters that help you support user input of data and commands in your application.

▶ Chapter 18 shows you how to handle menu operations, including setting up the menus and implementing the Undo command with some kinds of operations the user might perform.

▶ Chapter 19 provides the basic methods and techniques involved in supporting mouse operations and drawing. It explains how a MacApp program responds to mouse presses, and shows how MacApp handles mouse tracking and supports Undo for drawing.

▶ Chapter 20 describes how to create and manage dialogs in your MacApp programs. It discusses how you can build modeless and modal dialogs with ViewEdit, and how you can manage such dialogs and the user's interaction with them.

# 18 ▶ Handling Menu Operations

In this chapter you will learn how to handle menu interaction in your MacApp applications. We will look at two menu-oriented extensions to the Bird application we started in Chapter 17. The first extension simply adds a custom menu to the program, and the second adds another custom menu item that is supported by Undo.

## ▶ General Menu Processing

As you develop your program — whether using MacApp or not — you must deal with menus in many ways, including these six:

- add a menu item to an existing menu
- add a new menu to the menu bar
- disable items that are not available
- enable items that are available
- place a checkmark next to an item that has been selected
- respond to the user's selection of a specific item

MacApp includes many routines that facilitate handling the last four run-time tasks.

When you develop your program, you will often want to add items or complete new menus. To add a menu item to an existing menu, all you have to do is add the item to an existing resource of the type 'cmnu' (about which we have more to say in the next section). Adding an entirely new menu to the menu bar requires two steps: defining a new 'cmnu' resource in the resource file and then adding this new 'cmnu' resource to the existing 'MBAR' resource. (Note that when we talk of adding an entirely new menu, we do not mean adding it dynamically while the program is running.)

You never have to disable any items explicitly; MacApp disables all menus (except the Apple menu) and menu items after each event. It then re-enables those that should be enabled as defined by your application. To enable a menu item, you write a **DoSetupMenus** method which calls MacApp's Enable routine. To place a checkmark next to a menu item, you call EnableCheck, another MacApp routine, rather than Enable.

Finally, to respond to a menu selection, you simply write a **DoMenu-Command** method that returns a command object (if the command supports Undo) or the special global *gNoChanges* (if the command is not undoable).

You may have noted that we have not discussed any specific class in which the menu operations are handled. This is because menus, unlike the other kinds of objects we've seen in MacApp, are not handled by a single class. Instead, their functionality is distributed throughout the event-handling classes, including your application, document, and view classes. This involves the target chain described in Chapter 8.

**DoSetupMenus** and **DoMenuCommand** methods are defined for these classes: **TEvtHandler, TApplication, TDocument, TView, TWindow, TStdPrintHandler, TTEView,** and **TEditText.** You will override these methods in many of your subclasses to handle menu items unique to your program.

## ▶ The Enhancements

Figure 18-1 shows a Color menu we will add to the Bird sample first and a Delete menu that will be added later in the chapter. The items in the Color menu set a mode — the color in which succeeding birds will be drawn.

By its nature, this menu operation need not be undoable; it is easy for the user to select a different color if he or she selects a wrong one. When you have finished adding both menus to be described in this chapter, the Bird sample will look something like Figure 18-2.

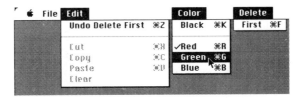

Figure 18-1. Bird sample added menus

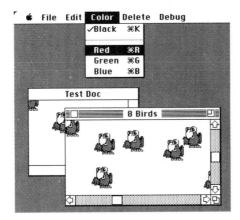

Figure 18-2. Bird sample with color menu and birds

Figure 18-3 shows a class diagram of the Bird sample with these enhancements. A new command object, **TDeleteCmd**, is shaded to indicate that it is a new class, added since the last chapter. The *fColorArray* variable of the **TBirdDocument** class is underlined to show it is a static variable shared by all instances of the class. This will be discussed below.

## ▶ Coloring the Birds

First, you'll add the menu and associated commands to permit the user to pick a color for each bird before it is drawn. By designing the new capability so that it alters only subsequently drawn birds, we are avoiding the necessity of supplying a command object with which the operation can be undone. This is because this operation does not have any effect on existing data. Listing 18-1 is the portion of the resource file that defines the 'cmnu' resource to create the menu we will be adding.

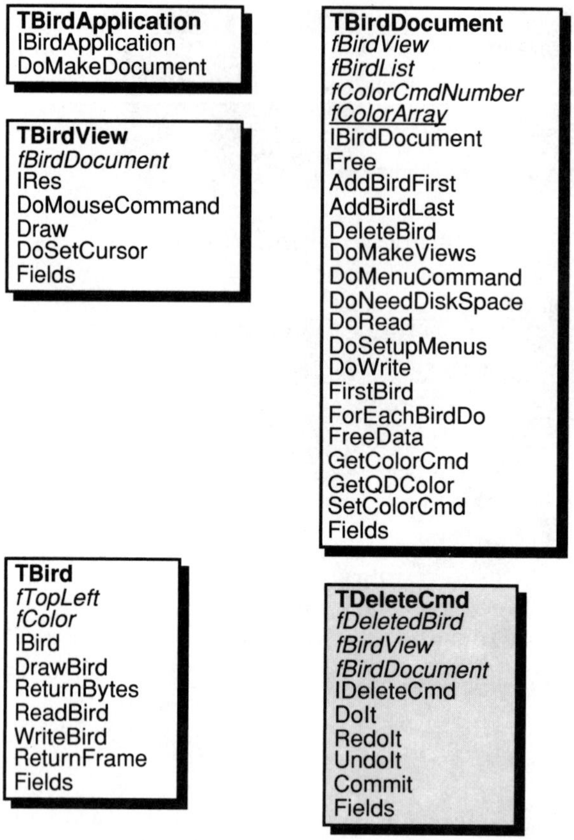

```
TBirdApplication
IBirdApplication
DoMakeDocument
```

```
TBirdView
fBirdDocument
IRes
DoMouseCommand
Draw
DoSetCursor
Fields
```

```
TBirdDocument
fBirdView
fBirdList
fColorCmdNumber
fColorArray
IBirdDocument
Free
AddBirdFirst
AddBirdLast
DeleteBird
DoMakeViews
DoMenuCommand
DoNeedDiskSpace
DoRead
DoSetupMenus
DoWrite
FirstBird
ForEachBirdDo
FreeData
GetColorCmd
GetQDColor
SetColorCmd
Fields
```

```
TBird
fTopLeft
fColor
IBird
DrawBird
ReturnBytes
ReadBird
WriteBird
ReturnFrame
Fields
```

```
TDeleteCmd
fDeletedBird
fBirdView
fBirdDocument
IDeleteCmd
DoIt
RedoIt
UndoIt
Commit
Fields
```

Figure 18-3. Class diagram of revised Bird sample

Listing 18-1. Defining 'cmnu' resources

```
1: #define cBlack        2001
2: #define cRed          2002
3: #define cGreen        2003
4: #define cBlue         2004
5:
6: include"Defaults.rsrc"'cmnu'(mApple);
7: include"Defaults.rsrc"'cmnu'(mFile);
8: include"Defaults.rsrc"'cmnu'(mEdit);
9:
10: resource 'cmnu' (4) {
11:     4,
12:     textMenuProc,
13:     0x7FFFFFFF,
```

```
14:      enabled,
15:      "Color",
16:        {
17:          "Black", noIcon, "K", noMark, plain, cBlack;
18:          "-", noIcon, noKey, noMark, plain, nocommand;
19:          "Red", noIcon, "R", noMark, plain, cRed;
20:          "Green", noIcon, "G", noMark, plain, cGreen;
21:          "Blue", noIcon, "B", noMark, plain, cBlue;
22:        }
23: };
24:
25: resource'MBAR'(kMBarDisplayed,
26: #if qNames
27: "Bird",
28: #endif
29:      purgeable){
30:      {mApple; mFile; mEdit; 4;}
31: };
```

This resource description creates a new menu called Color, which has
entries for the colors black, red, green, and blue. Notice the second entry in the menu, where a hyphen appears and is associated with the
global special constant *nocommand*. This construct results in a disabled
dashed line being placed in the menu.

Any new menu you create must be added to the 'MBAR' resource so
that it will appear on the menu bar. We handle this step on line 30.

Listing 18-2 is the portion of the class definitions for **TBirdDocument**
and **TBird** needed to handle this added menu. You will generally need
to add a document's methods any time you add new data to the document, as we do in this example to keep track of the currently selected
color. You also must add an instance variable to the **TBird** class, so that
each bird can store the color in which it is to be drawn. This color, as
you will see, will be determined when each bird is created and
initialized.

Listing 18-2. Modified document and bird class definitions

```
1: //=========================================================
2: const CmdNumber cBlack     =    2001;
3: const CmdNumber cRed       =    2002;
4: const CmdNumber cGreen     =    2003;
5: const CmdNumber cBlue      =    2004;
6: const short     cFirst     =    cBlack;
7: const short     cLast      =    cBlue;
8:
```

```
 9: //===========================================================
10: class TBirdDocument: public TDocument {
11: private:
12:     TList           *fBirdList;
13:     TBirdView       *fBirdView;
14:     short           fColorCmdNumber;
15:     static short    fColorArray[cLast - cFirst + 1];
16: public:
17:     virtual pascal void IBirdDocument();
18:     virtual pascal void Free ();                      //override
19:     virtual pascal void FreeData();                   //override
20:     virtual pascal void SetColorCmd(CmdNumber aCmdNumber);
21:     virtual pascal CmdNumber GetColorCmd();
22:     virtual pascal short GetQDColor();
23:     virtual pascal void AddBirdFirst(TBird *aBird);
24:     virtual pascal void AddBirdLast(TBird *aBird);
25:     virtual pascal void DeleteBird(TBird *aBird);
26:     virtual pascal TBird* FirstBird();
27:     virtual pascal void ForEachBirdDo(DoToABirdProc DoToABird,
28:                              void *DoToBird_StaticLink);
29:     virtual pascal void DoMakeViews(Boolean forPrinting);
        //override
30:     virtual pascal void DoNeedDiskSpace(long *dataForkBytes,
31:                              long *rsrcForkBytes); //override
32:     virtual pascal void DoWrite(short aRefNum,
33:                     Boolean makingCopy);          //override
34:     virtual pascal void DoRead(short aRefNum, Boolean
        rsrcExists,
35:                         Boolean forPrinting);     //override
36:     virtual pascal void DoSetupMenus();           //override
37:     virtual pascal TCommand* DoMenuCommand(
38:                     CmdNumber aCmdNumber);   //override
39:     virtual pascal void Fields(pascal void (*DoToField)
                                                    //override
40:        (StringPtr fieldName, Ptr fieldAddr, short fieldType,
41:         void *DoToField_StaticLink), void *DoToField_StaticLink);
42: };
43:
44: //===========================================================
45: class TBird: public TObject {
46: private:
47:     Point   fTopLeft;
48:     short   fColor;   // classic QuickDraw colors: redColor,…
49: public:
50:     virtual pascal void IBird(const Point corner, short
        theQDColor);
51:     virtual pascal void DrawBird();
52:     virtual pascal Rect ReturnFrame();
```

```
53:    virtual pascal long ReturnBytes();
54:    virtual pascal void ReadBird(short aRefNum);
55:    virtual pascal void WriteBird(short aRefNum);
56:    virtual pascal void Fields(pascal void (*DoToField)
       //override
57:      (StringPtr fieldName, Ptr fieldAddr, short fieldType,
58:        void *DoToField_StaticLink), void *DoToField_StaticLink);
59: };
```

Notice the constants defined on lines 2-7. These correspond to the menu command numbers defined for the Color menu in the Bird.r resource file. You could even use the same #define statements that we used in the Bird.r file but, as we have pointed out, const declarations are safer to use in your C++ code, since they provide type-checking support.

## ▶ Two Types of Color Numbers

The **TBirdDocument** class is defined on lines 10-42. This definition is similar to the one we saw in the last chapter, but we have added a few variables and methods to support color. Color must be supported in two ways, which complicates the code a bit. The constants defined above represent menu command numbers, which in this example were arbitrarily chosen to be consecutive integers from 2001 through 2004. These are the numbers used in the **DoSetupMenus** and **DoMenuCommand** methods defined on lines 36-38, which we will examine shortly. However, when it is time to use the QuickDraw graphics routines in the Macintosh Toolbox for drawing, we are going to use color constants defined in Volume 1 of *Inside Macintosh*. The eight classic QuickDraw color constants are predefined to be blackColor, whiteColor, redColor, greenColor, blueColor, cyanColor, magentaColor, and yellowColor. These are non-consecutive integers like 33, 30, 205, and so forth. We therefore need to map from menu command numbers for items chosen by the user to QuickDraw constants that can be used to draw colored birds.

The *fColorCmdNumber* variable defined on line 14 stores the Color menu's currently selected color. The **SetColorCmd** and **GetColorCmd** methods on lines 20 and 21 are accessors for this variable. We will use the currently selected color in the **DoSetupMenus** method to checkmark the correct menu item. The mapping to QuickDraw color numbers is done using the static variable *fColorArray* defined on line 15. The method **GetQDColor** defined on line 22 will return the color number corresponding to the selected menu item.

## ▶ Static Members

Perhaps you are wondering why the *fColorCmdNumber* variable is defined normally, while the *fColorArray* is defined as a static variable, with a related method **GetQDColor** to access it. In this example, each document stores its own currently selected color, so that each window activated by the user can have its own color checkmarked. Therefore, the currently selected color is stored in a normal instance variable.

On the other hand, static variables provide a mechanism for sharing a single variable among all instances of a class, as we discussed in Chapter 6. Since the color mapping from a menu number to a Quick-Draw number is the same for every document, it would be wasteful to use a normal instance variable, so we use a static variable.

| By the Way ▶ | In Object Pascal, you cannot define static variables in a class. When we wrote the Object Pascal version of the Bird sample for the other version of this book, we used a simple global variable for the color-mapping array. The disadvantage of this variable is that the global array can be seen and accessed by all the methods of any class defined in that file, which can lead to less maintainable code. In general, we recommend avoiding globals whenever possible, and using static variables instead. |
|---|---|

## ▶ Adding fcolor

The **TBird** class is defined on lines 45-59 to be a simple extension of the one defined in the last chapter. We merely add the *fColor* instance variable to store the color of each bird, and extend the **IBird** initialization method on line 50 to accept a QuickDraw color as an argument.

Listing 18-3 shows the **DoSetupMenus** method in our sample.

Listing 18-3. The DoSetupMenus method

```
1: #pragma segment ARes
2: pascal void
3: TBirdDocument::DoSetupMenus()                    //override
4: {
5:     inherited::DoSetupMenus();                    // always do this
6:     for (short colorIndex = cFirst; colorIndex <= cLast;
    colorIndex++)
7:         EnableCheck(colorIndex,                    // menu item
8:             true,                                  // enable
9:             (this->GetColorCmd() == colorIndex));  // check
10: }
```

Line 5 is required so that other event handlers in the target chain can enable their menu items. Otherwise, for example, the Quit option on the File menu would not be enabled. Lines 6-9 cycle through all of the items on the color menu, calling the MacApp utility procedure **Enable-Check**. The constants cFirst and cLast are defined in Listing 18-2. Line 7 passes the menu item's command number, line 8 enables each item, and line 9 places a checkmark next to the item that corresponds to the currently selected color, at the same time removing any checkmarks from other choices.

Listing 18-4 shows the **DoMenuCommand** method associated with this version of Bird. We will add a case to the switch statement later in this chapter.

Listing 18-4. The DoMenuCommand method

```
1 #pragma segment ASelCommand
2 pascal TCommand*
3 TBirdDocument::DoMenuCommand(CmdNumber aCmdNumber)    //override
4 {
5     if (aCmdNumber >= cFirst && aCmdNumber <= cLast) {
6         this->SetColorCmd(aCmdNumber);
7         return gNoChanges;
8         }
9     else {
10        switch (aCmdNumber){
11
12            default:
13                return inherited::DoMenuCommand(aCmdNumber);
14
15        }  // switch
16    }   // else
17 }
```

Notice that **DoMenuCommand** is a function that must return a command object. You may either return a real command object or the global dummy command object *gNoChanges* (see line 7).

Lines 5-16 use an if-else construct with two components. The first is executed if the argument passed by **DoMenuCommand** is one of those defined as 2001-2004. If that is the case, the **DoMenuCommand** method sends its document the **SetColorCmd** message to set the value of the *fColorCmdNumber* instance variable in the document. Then it returns the *gNoChanges* global variable from the **DoMenuCommand** method. The default construction at line 12 handles all other menu situations — that is, those not involving the Color menu — simply by calling the inherited version of the method.

These modifications prepare our revised application to use the new menu called Color, but the menu is not yet functional. We need to define two methods for setting and changing the color of a bird we are about to draw and we must modify the Draw routine so that it uses a color pen. Listing 18-5 shows the three methods needed to access the currently selected color in the document.

Listing 18-5. Methods to set and get current color

```
1: //===============================================================
2: short TBirdDocument::fColorArray[cLast - cFirst + 1] =
                                              {blackColor,
3:                                            redColor,
4:                                            greenColor,
5:                                            blueColor};
6:
7: //===============================================================
8: #pragma segment ASelCommand
9: pascal void
10: TBirdDocument::SetColorCmd(CmdNumber aCmdNumber)
11: {
12:     fColorCmdNumber = aCmdNumber;
13: }
14:
15: //---------------------------------------------------------------
16: #pragma segment ASelCommand
17: pascal CmdNumber
18: TBirdDocument::GetColorCmd()
19: {
20:     return fColorCmdNumber;
21: }
22:
23: //---------------------------------------------------------------
24: #pragma segment ASelCommand
25: pascal short
26: TBirdDocument::GetQDColor()
27: {
28:     return fColorArray[this->GetColorCmd() - cFirst];
        // QD color
29: }
```

Both the **SetColorCmd** and the **GetColorCmd** methods are associated with the **TBirdDocument** object. Each is a one-line method. **Set-ColorCmd** assigns the value of the color command number generated by the **DoMenuCommand** method to the instance variable *fColorCmd-Number* as shown on line 12. **GetColorCmd** merely retrieves the value of that instance variable, as shown on line 20.

The static variable *fColorArray* defined for the **TBirdDocument** class is shared by all instances of the class. The unusual consequence of this is that no instances of the class allocate memory for static variables. Instead, you must have a separate allocation statement in your .cp file, such as the one shown on lines 2-5 to allocate the color array. The **GetQDColor** method on lines 25-29 then uses this array to return the correct QuickDraw color for the selected menu item.

Next, you will need to write some code to deal with the situation when the user wants to draw the next bird. Recall from Chapter 17 that the user draws a bird by clicking in the window, and that the drawing is managed by the **DoMouseCommand** method. You must now do a little more work when the user clicks the mouse, as you can see from Listing 18-6.

Listing 18-6. The DoMouseCommand method

```
1: #pragma segment ASelCommand
2: pascal TCommand*
3: TBirdView::DoMouseCommand(Point *theMouse,          //override
4:                 EventInfo* /*info*/, Point* /*hysteresis*/)
5: {
6:     short birdColor = fBirdDocument->GetQDColor();
7:     TBird *aBird = new TBird;
8:     FailNIL(aBird);
9:     aBird->IBird(*theMouse, birdColor);
10:
11:     Rect birdRect = aBird->ReturnFrame();
12:     fBirdDocument->AddBirdLast(aBird);  // add bird to document
13:     fBirdDocument->SetChangeCount(1);   // data changed
14:     this->InvalidRect(&birdRect); // force update for bird area
15:     return gNoChanges;                  // or return NULL or nil
16: }
```

The only changes to this method are in lines 6 and 9. In Line 6 you get the currently selected color for a bird from the document and put it into the variable *birdColor*. Then in line 9 you initialize the bird with this color.

You must also make some simple changes to the **IBird** method. The revised method is shown in Listing 18-7.

Listing 18-7. The IBird method

```
1: #pragma segment ASelCommand
2: pascal void
3: TBird::IBird(const Point corner, short theQDColor)
4: {
5:     fTopLeft = corner;
6:     fColor = theQDColor;
7: }
```

## ▶ Drawing the Birds

The **DoMouseCommand** method in Listing 18-6 forces a window up-date event by invalidating the view. In response to that, MacApp sends our view the **Draw** message. Listing 18-8 shows the **Draw** method of the view.

Listing 18-8. The view's Draw method

```
1: //------------------------------------------------------------
2: #pragma segment ARes
3: pascal void
4: DrawABird(TBird *aBird, Rect *updateArea)
5: {
6:     Rect  birdRect = aBird->ReturnFrame();
7:     if (SectRect(&birdRect, updateArea, &birdRect))
8:         aBird->DrawBird();
9: }
10:
11: //------------------------------------------------------------
12: #pragma segment ARes
13: pascal void
14: TBirdView::Draw(Rect *area)     //override
15: {
16:     Rect     viewBorder;
17:
18:     PenNormal();                    // always do this before drawing
19:     PenSize(2, 2);
20:     PenPat(qd.gray);
21:     this->GetQDExtent(&viewBorder);
22:     FrameRect(&viewBorder);     // a frame just for fun
23:     fBirdDocument->ForEachBirdDo((DoToABirdProc) DrawABird,
            area);
24:     ForeColor(blackColor);     // grafPort back to normal
25:     PenNormal();
26: }
```

Because we are using each bird's **DrawBird** method (discussed next) to draw each bird in the chosen color, we can get by with only a single change to this method. That change takes place at line 24, where we make sure the grafPort's foreground color is returned to its normal default setting of black so that views will not draw in color.

Listing 18-9 shows the modified **DrawBird** function that draws the bird in its own color.

Listing 18-9. Drawing each bird in color

```
 1: //-------------------------------------------------------------
 2: #pragma segment ARes
 3: pascal void
 4: TBird::DrawBird()
 5: {
 6:     Handle aHandle = GetIcon(kIconID);
 7:     FailNILResource(aHandle);
 8:     Rect aRect = this->ReturnFrame();
 9:     ForeColor(fColor);
10:     PlotIcon(&aRect, aHandle);
11: }
```

Only line 9 has been added to the old **DrawBird** method to handle color drawing. It sets the foreground color to be used for the **PlotIcon** call to match the value of the instance variable *fColor*.

In the **TBirdDocument::IBirdDocument** method, we should add a line that sets the color to black during initialization as well. That line would look like this:

```
this->SetColorCmd(cBlack);
```

You have now done all that you need to do to convert your drab black-and-white Bird application into a colorful Bird application. It is worth pausing for a moment here to reflect on how relatively easy and painless the process was, thanks to object-oriented programming and MacApp's help.

You defined a new resource and made only minor modifications to six existing methods: **IBirdDocument, DoSetupMenus, DoMenuCommand, DrawBird**, and the view's **Draw** and **DoMouseCommand** methods. You only had to write two new methods — **SetColorCmd** and **GetColorCmd** — each of which consists of only one line of code. The rest of the application was untouched; as a result, you can be sure it all works as expected. This encapsulation advantage recurs every time you start with an existing application you are sure works and make even fairly radical changes to its behavior.

## ▶  Deleting Birds: An Undoable Menu Operation

Now let's take a look at what further modifications you need to make to create another new menu called Delete. This menu will have one option, enabling you to delete the first bird in the current list of birds. (It would be an easy extension — and one you might find enjoyable to write — to add another option to delete all of the birds.) Because a deletion affects the contents of the document, Apple's *Human Interface Guidelines* suggest it should be an undoable operation, so we will make it so.

Although it is obviously true that the order in which we do things is not, for the most part, significant, we will stay with the order of programming we've been following in this chapter. First, we'll modify the resource file to include the new menu. Second, we'll modify the **DoSetupMenus** and **DoMenuCommand** methods to deal with the new menu's operations. Third, we'll make other programming changes needed to incorporate the new menu fully into the application. Finally, we'll define any new methods we need.

Listing 18-10 shows the resource file entries that define the new menu called Delete.

Listing 18-10.  Delete menu resource description

```
 1: #define cDeleteFirst     3001
 2: #define cDeleteFirstMsg 3101
 3:
 4: //=============================================================
 5: resource 'cmnu' (5) {
 6:     5,
 7:     textMenuProc,
 8:     0x7FFFFFFF,
 9:     enabled,
10:     "Delete",
11:       {
12:         "First", noIcon, "F", noMark, plain, cDeleteFirst;
13:       }
14: };
15:
16: resource'MBAR'(kMBarDisplayed,
17: #if qNames
18: "Bird",
19: #endif
20:     purgeable) {
21:     {mApple; mFile; mEdit; 4; 5; }
22: };
23:
```

```
24: //============================================================
25: resource 'cmnu' (128) {
26:     128,
27:     textMenuProc,
28:     allEnabled,
29:     enabled,
30:     "Buzzwords",
31:      {
32:         "Page Setup Change", noIcon, noKey, noMark, plain,
            cChangePrinterStyle;
33:         "Delete First", noIcon, noKey, noMark, plain, cDelete-
            FirstMsg;
34:      }
35: };
```

In lines 1 and 2 we define two new constants to deal with deletion. These become menu command numbers. In lines 5-14, we define this new menu as menu number 5. Notice, then, that on line 21, we must add menu 5 to the 'MBAR' resource.

Recall that in Figure 18-1, the Undo entry in the Edit menu that is supplied by MacApp is Undo Delete First. MacApp's default behavior is to take the name of the menu choice and append it to the word Undo when you create a command object to handle a menu item. In this case, then, we would expect MacApp to label this menu choice Undo First after the user chooses First from the Delete menu. So how did MacApp come up with the wording Undo Delete First for this option? The answer lies in lines 30-34 in Listing 18-10. There, we define a menu called Buzzwords that we will not display (notice that it is not added to the 'MBAR' resource). This menu contains two entries, one for undoing page setup changes and one for undoing a deletion. The latter, on line 33, is associated with the command number *cDeleteFirstMsg*. Keep this in mind. We'll explain shortly how we make use of this special menu to force MacApp to word its Undo menu entry the way we want.

Enabling this new Delete menu requires a simple addition to the **DoSetupMenus** method:

```
if (this->FirstBird() !=NULL)
   Enable(cDeleteFirst, true);
```

We check to see if there is a bird in the list at all using a new method (which we'll examine shortly) called **FirstBird**. If there is at least one entry in the list, we enable the menu command *cDeleteFirst* which we have associated with the menu called Delete in our resource file (Listing 18-10).

The change to the **DoMenuCommand** method is only slightly more complex. Listing 18-11 shows the few lines of code on lines 12-16 that you need to add to the existing method to manage the new menu item.

Listing 18-11. Additions to DoMenuCommand method

```
 1: #pragma segment ASelCommand
 2: pascal TCommand*
 3: TBirdDocument::DoMenuCommand(CmdNumber aCmdNumber)    //override
 4: {
 5:     if (aCmdNumber >= cFirst && aCmdNumber <= cLast) {
 6:         this->SetColorCmd(aCmdNumber);
 7:         return gNoChanges;
 8:         }
 9:     else {
10:         switch (aCmdNumber){
11:
12:             case cDeleteFirst:
13:                 TDeleteCmd* aDeleteCmd = new TDeleteCmd;
14:                 FailNIL(aDeleteCmd);
15:                 aDeleteCmd->IDeleteCmd(fBirdView, this);
16:                 return aDeleteCmd;
17:
18:             default:
19:                 return inherited::DoMenuCommand(aCmdNumber);
20:
21:         } // switch
22:     }
23: }
```

We must add another case to the switch statement. Notice that in line 13 we define a new local variable called *aDeleteCmd* that is an instance of the class **TDeleteCmd**. This defines a variable to hold a new command object. (Notice that since a command object is, like any other object, subject to memory allocation problems, we call FailNIL in line 14 after we create it to ensure that we were successful in doing so.) In line 15, we call the initialization routine for the command object, **IDeleteCmd**. We define the class **TDeleteCmd** as a subclass of the predefined MacApp class **TCommand**. Its definition, found in UBird.h, is shown in Listing 18-12.

Listing 18-12. The TDeleteCmd class definition

```
1: class TDeleteCmd: public TCommand {
2: private:
3:     TBird          *fDeletedBird;
4:     TBirdView      *fBirdView;
5:     TBirdDocument  *fBirdDocument;
6: public:
7:     virtual pascal void IDeleteCmd(TBirdView *itsView,
8:                            TBirdDocument *itsDocument);
9:     virtual pascal void DoIt();                    //override
10:    virtual pascal void RedoIt();                  //override
11:    virtual pascal void UndoIt();                  //override
12:    virtual pascal void Commit();                  //override
13:    virtual pascal void Fields(pascal void (*DoToField)
                                                   //override
14:        (StringPtr fieldName, Ptr fieldAddr, short fieldType,
15:        void *DoToField_StaticLink), void *DoToField_StaticLink);
16: };
```

The code in Listing 18-12 is typical of the way you will define a command object. It includes three instance variables (lines 3-5) that refer to a bird that has just been deleted (so you have it when the user wants to undo a deletion), the view, and the document. It then defines five non-debugging procedures in addition to the usual **Fields** method for debugging purposes. The five methods your command objects will usually define are initialization (in this case, **IDeleteCmd**), **DoIt**, **RedoIt**, **UndoIt**, and **Commit**. Listing 18-13 reproduces the code for the **IDeleteCmd** method.

Listing 18-13. Initializing the command object

```
1: #pragma segment ASelCommand
2: pascal void
3: TDeleteCmd::IDeleteCmd(TBirdView *itsView,
4:                         TBirdDocument *itsDocument)
5: {
6:     fBirdView = itsView;
7:     fBirdDocument = itsDocument;
8:     fDeletedBird = itsDocument->FirstBird();
9:     TScroller* aScroller = itsView->GetScroller(true);
10:    this->ICommand(cDeleteFirstMsg,  // itsMenuNumber
11:                   itsDocument,
12:                   itsView,
13:                   aScroller);       // for autoscrolling later
14: }
```

The interface to the **IDeleteCmd** method requires that you pass it the name of the view and document associated with the command object. The main part of the method, in lines 6-13, initializes three instance variables and then calls the inherited MacApp method **ICommand** to initialize the variables we inherit from **TCommand**. Notice that on line 10 we use the constant *cDeleteFirstMsg*, which we associated earlier with the Buzzwords menu. This causes MacApp to use the string Delete First after the word Undo to create the first entry in the Edit menu.

The **FirstBird** method referred to on line 8 of Listing 18-13 is shown in Listing 18-14.

Listing 18-14. FirstBird method

```
1: #pragma segment ASelCommand
2: pascal TBird*
3: TBirdDocument::FirstBird()
4: {
5:     return (TBird *) fBirdList->First();
6: }
```

We use the method **TList.First** to retrieve the first bird and type cast it to be of class **TBird** on line 5.

▶ ## Handling the Deletion

After we return an initialized instance of **TDeleteCmd** from our **Do-MenuCommand** method, MacApp sends our command object the message **DoIt**. In Listing 18-15, we reproduce the **DoIt**, **UndoIt**, and **RedoIt** methods. They are, as you can see, quite similar to one another.

Listing 18-15. Three methods to support Undoing bird deletions

```
 1: //-----------------------------------------------------------
 2: #pragma segment ADoCommand
 3: pascal void
 4: TDeleteCmd::DoIt()                                //override
 5: {
 6:     fBirdDocument->DeleteBird(fDeletedBird);
 7:     Rect birdRect = fDeletedBird->ReturnFrame();
 8:     fBirdView->InvalidRect(&birdRect);       // force update
 9: }
10:
11: //-----------------------------------------------------------
```

```
12: #pragma segment ADoCommand
13: pascal void
14: TDeleteCmd::RedoIt()                            //override
15: {
16:     this->DoIt();
17: }
18:
19: //------------------------------------------------------------
20: #pragma segment ADoCommand
21: pascal void
22: TDeleteCmd::UndoIt()                            //override
23: {
24:     fBirdDocument->AddBirdFirst(fDeletedBird);
25:     Rect birdRect = fDeletedBird->ReturnFrame();
26:     fBirdView->InvalidRect(&birdRect);          // force update
27: }
```

The first of these methods carries out the deletion of the first bird on the list. As you can see from lines 6-8, it carries out the deletion simply by calling the **DeleteBird** method (which we'll see in a moment) and then using the **ReturnFrame** to identify the region of the view that needs redrawing. We use this information to invalidate the view (line 8) and force an update event. **InvalidRect** is a method of class **TView**. It focuses on our view with the **Focus** method of **TView** and then calls the Toolbox routine InvalRect.

The **UndoIt** method in lines 21-27 requires further explanation. This method is called when the user chooses Undo Delete First from the Edit menu. In essence, it is the reverse of the **DoIt** method. It calls the **AddBirdFirst** method with the instance variable *fDeletedBird* as an argument so that the most recently deleted bird is put back at the beginning of the bird list. It then invalidates the area where the bird is to be redrawn and sends the view the **InvalidRect** message to force the Macintosh to redraw the display at that point. The **RedoIt** command in lines 13-16 is self-explanatory.

The **DeleteBird** method called by the **DoIt** method is shown in Listing 18-16.

### Listing 18-16. DeleteBird method

```
1: #pragma segment ASelCommand
2: pascal void
3: TBirdDocument::DeleteBird(TBird *aBird)
4: {
5:     fBirdList->Delete(aBird);
6: }
```

This method simply uses the **TList::Delete** method to remove the first bird from the bird list.

The **UndoIt** method in Listing 18-15 sends the document the message **AddBirdFirst**, which is reproduced in Listing 18-17.

Listing 18-17. Adding the bird back to the list

```
1: #pragma segment ASelCommand
2: pascal void
3: TBirdDocument::AddBirdFirst(TBird *aBird)
4: {
5:     fBirdList->InsertFirst(aBird);
6: }
```

## ▶ Making the Operation Permanent

MacApp keeps track of the last command object using the **TApplication** variable *fLastCommand*. This command object allows the user to alternate between Undo and Redo of the last operation that changed the data. There are, of course, circumstances for which MacApp must make that operation permanent. These include the relevant document being saved to disk, or the creation of a new command object to support a different Undoable operation. In these cases, the **TApplication:: PerformCommand** method will check the command object's *fCmdDone* Boolean instance variable to see if the user has left the command "done" or "undone". If the command has been done, the command object will be sent the message **Commit** to make the change permanent, followed by the message **Free** to delete the old command object. If the command has been undone, just the Free message will be sent.

Listing 18-18 shows the **Commit** method for our **TDeleteCmd** class of command objects. This method merely deletes the bird object that has already been deleted from the document, using MacApp's FreeIfObject routine. Remember that the **Commit** method will not be called if the command object has been left in the UndoIt state.

Listing 18-18. Making a Change Permanent with Commit

```
1: #pragma segment AClose
2: pascal void
3: TDeleteCmd::Commit() // o'ride - called if fCmdDone = true
4: {
5:     FreeIfObject(fDeletedBird);
6: }
```

# ▶  Summary

In this chapter, you have learned how to define and use menus in your MacApp applications. This was done by extending the Bird application of Chapter 17, adding two new menus. The first simply permits the user to select a color to be used to draw the next bird. It is not an undo-able operation. As you saw, adding such capability to a MacApp program is relatively simple and straightforward.

The second menu allows the user to delete the first bird in the current bird list. This menu option has to be undoable since it affects the document's contents, so we created a new class, **TDeleteCmd**, to serve as the basis for the command objects that make such actions undoable.

# 19 ▶ Managing Mouse Operations

This chapter discusses how to handle mouse events in your MacApp programs. As with menu-management techniques discussed in Chapter 18, mouse operations fall into two categories: those that do not use command objects and those that require the use of such objects. Mouse events that involve no tracking of the mouse location — relatively simple situations where you are concerned only with a mouse-click — do not need to create and manage command objects. Any mouse event that involves tracking — including mouse dragging — would benefit from using command objects. Of course, command objects also allow the user to undo a mouse-driven operation.

We will begin with a general discussion of mouse operations and their management in MacApp programs. We will then look at two examples that extend the Bird application of Chapter 18 to demonstrate how to handle mouse operations in MacApp. The first extension incorporates a palette view from which the user can make the color selection that we associated with a menu in Bird. The second enhancement involves creating a new command object that will allow us to draw birds of any size rather than having the application choose a default size for the icon object. Because this involves keeping track of the mouse starting point and the size of the rectangle created by the mouse-dragging operation, we need a command object to handle this mouse operation.

## ▶ General Mouse Operations

In virtually all Macintosh applications, the first place a mouse event gets trapped and examined is in the main event loop. When you use MacApp, the same is true. MacApp includes in a **HandleMouseDown** method the class **TApplication.**

### ▶ HandleMouseDown

The following pseudo-code contains a skeleton of this method's code. This is shown in Object Pascal, since MacApp is written in that language. Of all the methods called by MacApp in this method, you only have to be concerned with a few: **DoMouseCommand** (which we've seen before), **TrackMouse**, and some related tracking methods. All the others are handled automatically by MacApp.

```
1: TApplication.HandleMouseDown
2:   CASE
3:     inMenuBar:
4:         SELF.SetupTheMenus;
5:         SELF.MenuEvent;
6:
7:     inDrag: aWindow.MoveByUser;
8:
9:     inGrow: aWindow.ResizeByUser;
10:
11:    inGoAway: aWindow.GoAwayByUser;
12:
13:    inZoom: aWindow.ZoomByUser;
14:
15:    inDesk: ;
16:
17:    inContent:
18:        aWindow.Focus
19:        aWindow.HandleMouseDown;
20:            aView.HandleMouseDown;
21:                aCmd := SELF.DoMouse Command;
22:        IF aCmd <> gNoChanges THEN aCmd.TrackMouse;
```

In line 21, notice that the **HandleMouseDown** method calls the **DoMouseCommand** method in the application. If the **DoMouseCommand** method returns any value other than *gNoChanges*, that indicates a command object has been created and must be managed, so line 22 calls the **TrackMouse** method.

## ▶ DoMouseCommand

The **DoMouseCommand** method is one we've seen before, but in this discussion we need to look at it more closely. The general form of this method is

```
virtual pascal TCommand* TView::DoMouseCommand(Point *theMouse
                                EventInfo *info
                                Point *hysteresis);
```

The arguments to this method have the following meanings:

- *theMouse* provides the location, in view coordinates, where the mouse was pressed.
- *info* is event information, including both keyboard and click-count data.
- *hysteresis* is the amount of slack the user has in dragging the mouse. It defaults to 4 pixels horizontally and 4 pixels vertically. If the mouse moves less than that amount, MacApp assigns the value of FALSE to the parameter mouseDidMove, which we'll see used in other mouse tracking methods.

The **DoMouseCommand** function, as we said earlier, must return a value. It either returns a real command object or the special global dummy command object *gNoChanges*.

## ▶ EventInfo

Table 19-1 shows the format of the very convenient EventInfo record. You will most often be concerned with the five modifier key fields and the field called *theClickCount* when managing mouse operations in your MacApp programs.

Table 19-1. EventInfo record format

| Field | Type | Meaning |
|-------|------|---------|
| thePEvent | PEventRecord | Pointer to Toolbox Event Record. |
| theBtnState | Boolean | Modifiers field for an Event Record. |
| theCmdKey | Boolean | Was Command key depressed? |
| theShiftKey | Boolean | Was the Shift key depressed? |
| theAlphaLock | Boolean | Was the Alpha Lock key depressed? |
| theOptionKey | Boolean | Was the Option key depressed? |
| theControlKey | Boolean | Was a Control key depressed? |
| theAutoKey | Boolean | TRUE if event involves a repeating key press. |
| theClickCount | Short | Number of clicks within time set by Control Panel. (If event is not a mouse down, this field = 0.) |
| affectsMenus | Boolean | Do menus need to be set up as a result of event? |

## ▶ Bird Sample Application

Figure 19-1 shows what the Bird application will look like when we are finished. Notice the horizontal palette across the top of the window, where the user can select the color to use to draw the next bird. (Because the book is in black and white, you can't, of course, see the actual colors. In the real application, however, the palette contains four separate color swatches from which the user can select a color. This color then correlates to the menu selections so that they stay synchronized. A change in one affects the other.)

Figure 19-2 is a class diagram for this application so that you can see where the methods and variables we discuss through the rest of this chapter fit. The classes added in this chapter are shaded.

To build the extensions to Bird to handle the palette, you must do the following:

1. Design the palette view using ViewEdit and modify the program to be aware of the new palette view that is part of the window.
2. Write the **DoMouseCommand** method.
3. Write selected action methods that work with the **DoMouseCommand** method to highlight a particular location on the palette and update the color and menu information related to it.

Let's take a look at how each of these tasks is carried out.

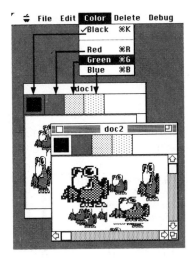

Figure 19-1. Bird application

## ▶ Creating and Describing the Palette

To create a palette, you need to define a new class, **TPaletteView**, which is a subclass of **TView**. Its complete definition appears in Listing 19-1.

Listing 19-1. TPaletteView class definition

```
1: class TPaletteView: public TView {
2: private:
3:           TBirdDocument    *fBirdDocument;
4:     static   Rect            fRectArray[cLast - cFirst + 1];
5: public:
6:     virtual pascal void IRes(TDocument *itsDocument, //override
7:                      TView *itsSuperView, Ptr *itsParams);
8:     static void InitRectArray();
9:     virtual pascal void ChangeSelection(CmdNumber
                   newColorNumber);
10:     virtual pascal TCommand *DoMouseCommand(Point *theMouse,
11:           EventInfo *info, Point * hysteresis);   //override
12:     virtual pascal void DoHighlightSelection(HLState fromHL,
13:                                   HLState toHL); //override
14:     virtual pascal void Draw(Rect *area);          //override
15:     virtual pascal void Fields(pascal void (*DoToField)
                                            //override
```

```
16:             (StringPtr fieldName, Ptr fieldAddr, short fieldType,
17:        void *DoToField_StaticLink), void *DoToField_StaticLink);
18: };
```

The class includes these methods:

**ChangeSelection** on line 9 forces the palette view and the Color menu to show the currently selected color.

**DoMouseCommand** on lines 10-11 handles mouse clicks in the palette view and finds the color rectangle in which the user clicked.

**TBirdApplication**
IBirdApplication
DoMakeDocument

**TBirdView**
*fBirdDocument*
IRes
DoMouseCommand
Draw
DoSetCursor
Fields

**TPaletteView**
*fBirdDocument*
*fRectArray*
IRes
InitRectArray
ChangeSelection
DoHighlightSelection
DoMouseCommand
Draw
Fields

**TBirdDocument**
*fBirdView*
*fPaletteView*
*fBirdList*
*fColorCmdNumber*
*fColorArray*
IBirdDocument
Free
AddBirdFirst
AddBirdLast
DeleteBird
DoMakeViews
DoMenuCommand
DoNeedDiskSpace
DoRead
DoSetupMenus
DoWrite
FirstBird
ForEachBirdDo
FreeData
GetColorCmd
GetQDColor
SetColorCmd
Fields

**TBird**
*fTopLeft*
*fColor*
IBird
DrawBird
ReturnBytes
ReadBird
WriteBird
ReturnFrame
Fields

**TSketcher**
*fBird*
*fBirdView*
*fBirdDocument*
ISketcher
TrackMouse
DoIt
RedoIt
UndoIt
Free
Fields

**TDeleteCmd**
*fDeletedBird*
*fBirdView*
*fBirdDocument*
IDeleteCmd
DoIt
RedoIt
UndoIt
Commit
Fields

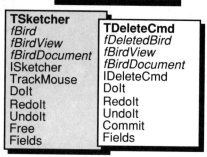

Figure 19-2. Bird class diagram

**DoHighlightSelection** on lines 12 and 13 must highlight the selected color in the palette view with a 4-pixel-wide box. It is the only method used in any of this book's samples which is called by both our code (to selected the current color) and by MacApp (when windows are activated or deactivated).

**Draw** on line 14 draws the color rectangles in the palette view.

Notice that this class uses a static variable, similar to one we described in the last chapter. In this case, the **fRectArray** variable is used to store an array of rectangles that define the color squares used in each window's color palette. Since the rectangles are the same in each window, it is best for each instance of TPaletteView to share the array. The **Draw** method will use this array to draw the palette.

The static method **InitRectArray** defined on line 8 will be used to initialize the array of rectangles. Since it is defined as a static method, it cannot access normal instance variables or methods of the **TPalette-View** class (the pointer "this" is undefined in static methods). It can, however, access the static variables.

## ▶ Creating a Palette View

Figure 19-3 shows the modified window, as designed in ViewEdit. The main **TBirdView** is moved down 32 pixels to make room for the new **TPaletteView**. The new view is initially drawn as an instance of **TView**, and then declared to be an instance of **TPaletteView** by modifying the class name in the "Edit view parameters..." dialog window. Notice in the figure that we set the horizontal view size of the palette to be *sizeSuperView*, that is, the size of the window itself. We also set the view identifier to be 'pall', which we'll use in the C++ code to get a reference to this view.

Before you can use the new **TPaletteView** class, however, you must define an instance of it. As you might expect, this definition will take place in the **DoMakeViews** method of the class **TBirdDocument**. You will use type casting, as you have seen it used before, to get a reference to this subview of the window.

```
TPalleteView* aPaletteView =
    (TPaletteView *) aWindow->FindSubView('pall');
```

You then set an instance variable in the document called *fPaletteView* to hold a reference to this view:

```
fPaletteView = aPaletteView;
```

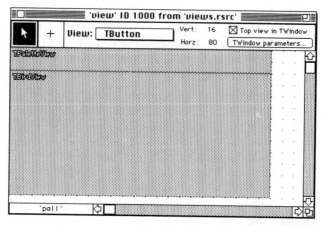

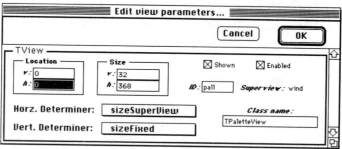

Figure 19-3. Designing the palette view in ViewEdit

Once the palette view is created and initialized by **NewTemplate-Window**, we need a method to draw it. This method is shown in Listing 19-2, along with the code to create an array of rectangles that is used by the **Draw** method.

Listing 19-2. Drawing the palette view

```
 1: //=============================================================
 2: Rect TPaletteView::fRectArray[cLast - cFirst + 1];
 3:
 4: //=============================================================
 5: #pragma segment AInit
 6: pascal void
 7: TBirdApplication::IBirdApplication()
 8: {
 9:     this->IApplication(kFileType);
10:     if (gDeadStripSuppression) {
11:         TBirdView *aBirdView = new TBirdView;
12:         TPaletteView* aPaletteView = new TPaletteView;
13:     }
```

```
14:      TPaletteView::InitRectArray();
15: }
16:
17: //============================================================
18: #pragma segment AInit
19: void
20: TPaletteView::InitRectArray()
21: {
22:    for (short iconIndex = cFirst; iconIndex <= cLast;
       iconIndex++)
23:        SetRect(&fRectArray[iconIndex - cFirst],
24:             kIconWidth * (iconIndex - cFirst),       // left
25:             0,                                       // top
26:             kIconWidth * (iconIndex - cFirst + 1),   // right
27:             kIconWidth);                             // bottom
28: }
29:
30: //------------------------------------------------------------
31: #pragma segment ARes
32: pascal void
33: TPaletteView::Draw(Rect*  /* area */)
34: {
35:    Rect     aColorRect;
36:    Rect     aFrame;
37:    Point    aPenSize;
38:
39:    for (short colorIndex = cFirst; colorIndex <= cLast;
          colorIndex++){
40:        ForeColor( fBirdDocument->CmdToQDColor(colorIndex) );
41:        aColorRect = fRectArray[colorIndex - cFirst];
42:        PaintRect(&aColorRect);
43:    }
44:    ForeColor(blackColor);
45:    this->GetQDExtent(&aFrame);
46:    SetPt(&aPenSize, 1, 1);
47:    this->Adorn(&aFrame, aPenSize, adnLineBottom);
48: }
```

The **Draw** method is shown on lines 32-48. The majority of the work involves drawing four colored squares with the loop shown on lines 39-43. For a *colorIndex* going from *cFirst* (2001) to *cLast* (2004), we set the grafPort's color on line 40, select the correct rectangle on line 41, and fill that rectangle with color on line 42. Lines 45-47 merely use MacApp's **TView::Adorn** method to place a horizontal line at the bottom of the palette view. This visually separates the palette from the bird view below.

Initializing the Static Variable

Before the **Draw** method can be used, however, we must initialize the array of rectangles that is kept in the palette view's static variable. The storage for this array is allocated at the beginning of the UBird.cp file, as shown in line 2 of Listing 19-2. The **InitRectArray** method that actually computes the rectangles is shown on lines 19-28. Where would you think that this method would be called? At first glance, you might think it should be called from the **TPaletteView::IRes** method that initializes the instance variables for the view. However, that is not a good choice because **IRes** is called each time another document window is opened. Since there is only one copy of the static variable, you want the array initialized only once. For this reason the array is initialized in the **IBirdApplication** method, as shown on line 14. Since it is a static method, it can be called by referencing the class name.

## ▶ Mouse Interaction Methods

The rest of the methods associated with this palette view involve the mouse and are triggered when the user clicks the mouse in the palette view. This activates the view's **DoMouseCommand** method, which in turn invokes the **ChangeSelection** method. This method in turn calls the **DoHighlightSelection** method. These three methods are reproduced in Listings 19-3 through 19-5.

Listing 19-3. DoMouseCommand

```
 1: #pragma segment ASelCommand
 2: pascal TCommand*
 3: TPaletteView::DoMouseCommand(Point*     theMouse,
 4:                             EventInfo* /* info */,
 5:                             Point*     /* hysteresis */)
 6: {
 7:     CmdNumber newColorCmd = (theMouse->h / kIconWidth) +
     cFirst;
 8:     if ((newColorCmd <= cLast))
 9:         this->ChangeSelection(newColorCmd);
10:     return gNoChanges;                            // or NULL
11: }
```

As we indicated earlier, **DoMouseCommand** is an overridden method. In line 7, the routine uses the mouse's horizontal location to determine where in the palette the mouse-click occurred. Line 8 checks to be sure that this location is within the bounds of the colored rectangles; obviously if the user has expanded the size of the window horizontally it would be possible to click the mouse in the palette and not be positioned over a color rectangle. If the click is within the range of color-selection icons, then the **ChangeSelection** method is called. This method appears in Listing 19-4.

Listing 19-4. ChangeSelection

```
 1: #pragma segment ASelCommand
 2: pascal void
 3: TPaletteView::ChangeSelection(CmdNumber newColorNumber)
 4: {
 5:     CmdNumber currentColorNum = fBirdDocument->GetColorCmd();
 6:     if (newColorNumber != currentColorNum){
 7:         if (Focus()) this->DoHighlightSelection(hlOn, hlOff);
                // old
 8:         fBirdDocument->SetColorCmd(newColorNumber);
 9:         if (Focus()) this->DoHighlightSelection(hlOff, hlOn);
                // new
10:     }   // if
11: }
```

This method is responsible for highlighting the last color palette icon chosen by the user. It receives the newly selected color's command number as an argument and first checks to be sure it is different from the currently chosen color. If they are equal, no action is needed and the method simply terminates. (If you did not include this test, the icon would blink when the user chose the currently selected color.) If, on the other hand, the colors are different, then line 7 turns off the highlighting of the currently highlighted icon, line 8 updates the current color in the *fBirdDocument* variable with the newly chosen color, and line 9 highlights the new color icon.

Notice that both lines 7 and 9 use the **DoHighlightSelection** method, passing it two arguments, which represent the state from which the selection should be changed and the state to which it should be changed. The **DoHighlightSelection** method is shown in Listing 19-5.

Listing 19-5. DoHighlightSelection

```
 1: #pragma segment ARes
 2: pascal void
 3: TPaletteView::DoHighlightSelection(HLState fromHL, HLState
    toHL)
 4: {
 5:     PenSize(4,4);
 6:     Rect aRect = fRectArray[fBirdDocument->GetColorCmd() -
        cFirst];
 7:     aRect.bottom--;                // protect bottom border
 8:     SetHLPenState(fromHL, toHL);   // MacApp global routine
 9:     FrameRect(&aRect);             // draw the highlighting
10:     PenNormal();
11: }
```

This method simply sets the pen size to 4 pixels by 4 pixels to highlight the icon. It then finds out what rectangle is highlighted with the **GetColorCmd** method sent to the document via the view's reference variable *fDocument*. It insets the bottom of the rectangle by one pixel (because there is already a one-pixel line drawn there with the **Adorn** call in the **TPaletteView::Draw** method) and then switches the pen's state as appropriate using the MacApp utility routine SetHLPenState. This routine automatically supports dim highlighting when the window is deactivated. The QuickDraw FrameRect call then draws a rectangle around the color icon rectangle in question.

The menu and the palette are kept synchronized by virtue of the fact that in the **TBirdDocument::DoMenuCommand** method, we add a line to update the palette view any time the user changes the color with the Color menu described in Chapter 18. The line looks like this:

```
fPaletteView->ChangeSelection(aCmdNumber);
```

The synchronization in the other direction — ensuring that the menu is updated when the user clicks on a palette color icon — takes place semi-automatically. The mouse-click is an event, which means that MacApp disables all menu items when it detects the event. The **SetColorCmd** method then updates the instance variable *fColorCmdNumber* in **TBirdDocument**. This value is in turn used in the **TBirdDocument::DoSetupMenus** method to ensure that the correct menu option is checked.

## ▶ Drawing a Bird with a Command Object

We have now successfully added mouse handling to our Bird sample application. The last thing we want to do with this sample application is add the ability to use the mouse to define a rectangle which will then be filled with the shape of our now-infamous bird. Because this involves not just intercepting a mouse-click but tracking where the mouse moves during the time it is held down, we need to create a command object. We also need the command object to support undo, since the operation will add data to the document.

### ▶ Defining and Creating the Class

You would think that a mouse-tracking command object would be radically different from a command object used to implement the undo capability of a menu. In actuality, the two have much in common. First, let's look at the class definition. Listing 19-6 reproduces the code.

Listing 19-6. The TSketcher class definition

```
 1: class TSketcher: public TCommand {
 2: private:
 3:     TBird           *fBird;
 4:     TBirdView       *fBirdView;
 5:     TBirdDocument *fBirdDocument;
 6: public:
 7:     virtual pascal void ISketcher(TBirdView *itsView,
 8:                             TBirdDocument *itsDocument);
 9:     virtual pascal TCommand *TrackMouse(TrackPhase aTrackPhase,
10:                         VPoint *anchorPoint,
11:                         VPoint *previousPoint,
12:                         VPoint *nextPoint,
13:                         Boolean mouseDidMove);     //override
14:     virtual pascal void DoIt();                    //override
15:     virtual pascal void RedoIt();                  //override
16:     virtual pascal void UndoIt();                  //override
17:     virtual pascal void Free();                    //override
18:     virtual pascal void Fields(pascal void (*DoToField)
                                                       //override
19:        (StringPtr fieldName, Ptr fieldAddr, short fieldType,
20:        void *DoToField_StaticLink), void *DoToField_StaticLink);
21: };
```

Notice that the sketcher command object needs reference variables to point to the document and the view so that it can add a bird to the document and invalidate the view to force an update and redraw of the view. We will discuss the **TrackMouse** method defined in lines 9-13 shortly.

The actual creation of the command object with which we will be working takes place in the view's **DoMouseCommand** method. Listing 19-7 reproduces this method.

Listing 19-7. DoMouseCommand

```
 1: #pragma segment ASelCommand
 2: pascal TCommand*
 3: TBirdView::DoMouseCommand(Point* /* theMouse */,      //override
 4:                           EventInfo* /*info*/,
 5:                           Point* /*hysteresis*/)
 6: {
 7:     TSketcher* aSketcher = new TSketcher;
 8:     FailNIL(aSketcher);
 9:     aSketcher->ISketcher(this,               // itsView
10:                     fBirdDocument);          // itsDocument
11:     return aSketcher;
12: }
```

As you can see in lines 9 and 10, this method calls the initialization routine for the sketcher command object passing references to the view and the document. This method is shown in Listing 19-8.

Listing 19-8. Initializing sketcher

```
 1: #pragma segment ASelCommand
 2: pascal void
 3: TSketcher::ISketcher(TBirdView *itsView, TBirdDocument
    *itsDocument)
 4: {
 5:     fBird = NULL;
 6:     fBirdView = itsView;
 7:     fBirdDocument = itsDocument;
 8:     TScroller* aScroller = itsView->GetScroller(true);
 9: this->ICommand(cSketcher,        // itsCmdNumber
10:                itsDocument,      // itsDocument
11:                itsView,          // itsView
12:                Scroller);        // itsScroller
13: fConstrainsMouse = false; // do not call TrackConstrain
14: }
```

▶ Initializing the Sketcher

Lines 5-7 initialize the variables we defined for our **TSketcher** class, while lines 9-12 initialize the variables inherited from its superclass, **TCommand**. Remember to *always* call your superclass's initialization method as part of initializing your subclass. In this case, the **ICommand** message requires four parameters.

Line 9 passes a menu command number, *cSketcher*, defined in our Buzzwords menu. MacApp will then append the word(s) defined in that menu item to the word Undo in the Edit menu. This is a small touch that allows users to work with more confidence, because they know what operation can be undone.

Lines 10 and 11 pass references to the document and the view, while line 12 passes a reference to the bird view's scroller. This is needed by MacApp to support autoscrolling as the user drags the mouse to the borders of the window. All you need to do to support autoscrolling is to provide this scroller reference, which you get by sending the view the **GetScroller** message on line 8.

Line 13 sets the value of an instance variable of **TCommand** called *fConstrainsMouse* to be false. This variable is used by MacApp to determine whether the **TrackConstrain** method of the command object should be called during mouse tracking. When it is false, the mouse motion will still be constrained to the view's border. If you set it to be true, you could further constrain the mouse motion with **TrackConstrain** to be limited, for example, to one part of the view.

Once you've created a command object for mouse tracking, it has a number of variables associated with it. These variables are summarized in Table 19-2.

Table 19-2. Mouse tracking variables

| Variable | Type | Use or meaning |
|----------|------|----------------|
| fCmdNumber | CmdNumber | Command number associated with current operation. |
| fChangedDocument | TDocument | Document that's being changed. |
| fTarget | TEvtHandler | Target before **UndoIt** or **RedoIt**. |
| fCmdDone | Boolean | Last message = **DoIt** or **RedoIt**. |
| fCanUndo | Boolean | Defaults to true. If false, Undo on the Edit menu will be disabled. You might use this for scrolling with a hand tool in a graphics program, for example. |
| fCausesChange | Boolean | Does operation change document? Default is true, which causes the fChangeCount field of the document to be incremented by **DoIt**. |
| fChangesClipboard | Boolean | Does operation change clipboard contents? Default is false. |
| fView | TView | View where tracking occurs. |
| fConstrainsMouse | Boolean | Constrain mouse movement to window by calling TrackConstrain? Default is false. |
| fViewConstrain | Boolean | Constrain mouse movements to limits of view? Default is true. |
| fTrackNonMovement | Boolean | Track mouse when it is not moving? Default is false. |
| fScroller | TScroller | Scroller object responsible for handling autoscrolling. |

## ▶ Tracking the Mouse

You can think of the mouse-tracking operations in MacApp as dividing the mouse's activities into three phases: the initial mouse-press; the continued holding down of the mouse button, usually but not always during mouse movement; and the release of the mouse button. These three phases are defined by the MacApp type TrackPhase and are called *trackPress*, *trackMove*, and *trackRelease*.

In operation, once you have created a command object and returned it via the **DoMouseCommand** method, MacApp then tracks the mouse automatically by repeated calls to your **TrackMouse, TrackConstrain,** and **TrackFeedback** methods. Depending on what action you want to take based on mouse movement during its tracking, you may or may not override the **TrackFeedback** method. If you don't override it, the default behavior is to call **TView::TrackFeedback** which simply draws a temporary gray rectangle anchored at the point where the mouse was pressed. This is often the only behavior you need during mouse movement; it clearly is sufficient in our Bird sample application.

Listing 19-9 shows the **TrackMouse** method for our sample application.

Listing 19-9. TrackMouse

```
 1: #pragma segment ARes
 2: pascal TCommand*
 3: TSketcher::TrackMouse(TrackPhase aTrackPhase,
 4:                       VPoint*  anchorPoint,
 5:                       VPoint*  /* previousPoint */,
 6:                       VPoint*  nextPoint,
 7:                       Boolean  /* mouseDidMove */)
 8: {
 9:    Rect            birdRect;
10:
11:    if (aTrackPhase == trackRelease){
12:      Point birdTL = fBirdView->ViewToQDPt(anchorPoint);
13:      Point birdBR = fBirdView->ViewToQDPt(nextPoint);
14:      Pt2Rect(birdTL, birdBR, &birdRect);
15:      short birdColor = fBirdDocument->GetQDColor();
16:      TBird* aBird = new TBird;
17:      FailNIL(aBird);
18:      aBird->IBird(&birdRect, birdColor);
19:      fBird = aBird;
20:    }  // if (trackRelease
21:    return this;
22: }
```

The variables *birdTL* and *birdBR* defined in lines 15 and 16 represent, respectively, the top-left and bottom-right corners of the rectangle in which the bird will be drawn. Notice that on line 18 we define a variable, *birdColor*, to represent the color, which is the QuickDraw color associated with the chosen color's menu item.

Our **TrackMouse** method does not need to do anything special with mouse tracking until the user releases the mouse. This, in fact, is frequently the case. The if construct in lines 11-20 handles the case when the user releases the mouse, that is, when the **TrackMouse** method's *aTrackPhase* argument is *trackRelease*. Lines 12 and 13 use the **TView** method **ViewToQDPt** to convert the top-left and bottom-right corners of the rectangle drawn by the user into QuickDraw coordinates. The results of these conversions are then used in line 14 in conjunction with the Macintosh Toolbox routine Pt2Rect to create a rectangle from the two points. Line 15 gets the current color with the **GetQDColor** method, and then line 16 creates a new bird. Line 18 initializes the bird's rectangle and color and line 19 updates the command object's instance variable *fBird* to point to the newly created bird. This reference to the newly created bird must be saved for later, in case the user selects Undo and then Redo.

## ▶ Doing the Command

As you would expect, given our previous experience with command objects, we will define **DoIt, UndoIt, RedoIt,** and **Free** methods for the new sketcher command object we have created in this final extension to the Bird sample application. Listing 19-10 reproduces these four methods.

Listing 19-10. DoIt, UndoIt, RedoIt, and Free

```
1:   #pragma segment ADoCommand
2:   pascal void
3:   TSketcher::DoIt()
4:   {
5:       fBirdDocument->AddBirdLast(fBird);
6:       Rect birdRect = fBird->ReturnFrame();
7:       fBirdView->InvalidRect(&birdRect);        // force update
8:   }
9:
10:  //-----------------------------------------------------------
11:  #pragma segment ADoCommand
12:  pascal void
13:  TSketcher::RedoIt()
14:  {
15:      this->DoIt();
16:  }
```

```
17:
18:   //-------------------------------------------------------
19:   #pragma segment ADoCommand
20:   pascal void
21:   TSketcher::UndoIt()
22:   {
23:       fBirdDocument->DeleteBird(fBird);
24:       Rect birdRect = fBird->ReturnFrame();
25:       fBirdView->InvalidRect(&birdRect);      // force update
26:   }
27:
28:   //-------------------------------------------------------
29:   #pragma segment AClose
30:   pascal void
31:   TSketcher::Free()
32:   {
33:       if (!fCmdDone)
34:           FreeIfObject(fBird);
35:       inherited::Free();
36:   }
```

With the exception of **Free**, the methods shown in Listing 19-10 should be familiar to you by now. For the **Free** method, lines 33 and 34, we use a built-in MacApp routine called FreeIfObject if the user has undone the drawing. We test the **TCommand** instance variable *fCmdDone*, which will be true if the last message was DoIt or RedoIt but false if the last message was UndoIt. This is a little tricky, because we want to keep the bird object if the command has been done, but we want to free it otherwise. Remember, the command object will be freed when the next command object is created (for example, when the next bird is drawn).

## ▶ Summary

In this chapter, you have learned how to handle mouse operations of two types: those that are simple mouse-clicks, such as in a palette view where the user is simply selecting an option, and those that require tracking of the mouse's movements and operations, as in drawing with the mouse. We have seen how mouse operations are generally handled and we have extended the Bird sample of Chapter 18 to include a palette view from which the user can select a color for the bird and methods for drawing a bird of arbitrary size.

# 20 ▶ Handling Dialogs

This chapter concludes our discussion of accepting user input by examining another way in which a user enters information into a Macintosh application: modal and modeless dialogs. We will begin with a brief discussion of the types of dialogs and the role they play in Macintosh applications. We will then describe how to create a modeless dialog that has been designed in ViewEdit and how to manage the response to the user's interaction with that dialog. Finally, we will discuss how to display and handle a modal dialog.

## ▶ Dialogs: An Overview

Macintosh applications can use one of two kinds of dialogs: modeless and modal. A modeless dialog is presented in a window that can be used and then placed behind other windows. A modal dialog on the other hand is one to which the user must respond in some way and explicitly dispose of before he or she can continue running the application. This mandatory response is the only difference between modeless and modal dialogs that is of any interest to us.

**By the Way ▶** Apple's *Human Interface Guidelines* discourage modal dialogs and encourage modeless ones, since modeless dialogs allow the user much more flexibility. You will often find that you could use a modeless dialog in place of the modal dialog that was your first choice. Remember, modes are usually bad.

There is no fundamental difference between dialogs and windows. This is particularly true when you are using MacApp to build your applications because MacApp deliberately blurs the lines of distinction between dialogs and windows. A dialog is basically a window with some control elements (such as buttons) added to it so that the user can, or must, interact with it.

## ▶ Creating a Dialog Using ViewEdit

ViewEdit is the only practical way to define complex dialog boxes for MacApp applications. If you use ViewEdit to define and create your dialog, you will find the process is nearly identical to the process you use for creating any other kind of view. The primary difference is that the main view of the window will usually be an instance of **TDialogView** or a sub-class of it. Inside this view, then, will typically be one or more controls, all of which are instances of class **TControl** or of one of its subclasses. These subclasses include most of the views in the VRes sample program we described in Chapter 14, shown in Figure 14-1. In that chapter, you learned how to create windows full of controls. In this chapter, you will see how to write a small program called Dialogs that can respond when the user clicks the mouse on a control.

## ▶ The Dialogs Sample

Figure 20-1 shows the modal and modeless dialogs created in our sample application, Dialogs. The modeless dialog is always visible, while the modal dialog is displayed when the user chooses the Name... item from the Special menu.

The class diagram for this program is shown in Figure 20-2.

The application methods include

- **IDialogsApplication** — initialize the application, and create the modeless dialog window
- **HandleFinderRequest** — insure that no documents are created
- **DoSetupMenus** — enable the Name... menu item
- **DoMenuCommand** — respond to the Name... item by displaying the modal dialog
- **ShowModalDialog** — display the window and manage it

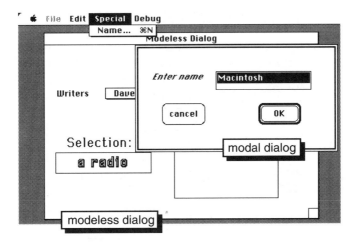

Figure 20-1. The Dialogs sample program

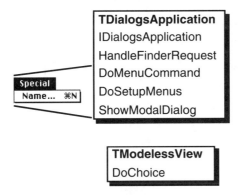

Figure 20-2. The class diagram for the Dialogs sample

The single method necessary to manage the items in the modeless dialog is a unique method called **DoChoice**. This overridden method is implemented in our new class **TModelessView**, which is a subclass of **TDialogView**. You will see its use in the following section.

## ▶ Handling Modeless Dialog Items

The arrangement of the views in the modeless window is shown at the top of Figure 20-3, as is the appearance in ViewEdit.

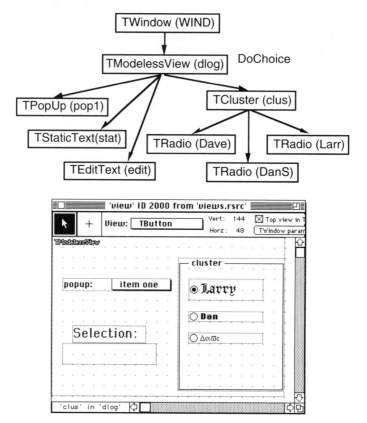

Figure 20-3. Creating the modeless window in ViewEdit

This 'view' resource number 2000 consists of

- **TWindow** — the root view class
- **TModelessView** — the view that encloses all the items that follow
- **TStaticText** — the label Selection:
- **TPopupMenu** — popup menu associated with the label Writers:

- **TEditText** — text-editing rectangle beneath static label Selection:
- **TCluster** — rectangle surrounding three radio buttons at right of view
- **TRadio** — three radio buttons labeled Larry, Dan, and Dave

The schematic diagram of these views in Figure 20-3 includes the four-letter identifiers (called IDs) by which each item in the view is referred in the code. You will see these view identifiers used to refer to a particular subview of the window.

## ▶ Interacting with a Dialog

The user can interact with this modeless dialog in two ways: by clicking on the pop-up menu and selecting one of the writers' names from the list that appears and by clicking on one of the radio buttons. This turns the selected button on (if it isn't already) and turns off any other button that might be on at the time (this is handled automatically by the cluster object).

Once a dialog has been defined and displayed, the user's interaction with it is managed in your code by means of the MacApp method **DoChoice**. You will frequently override this method for modeless dialogs. Its interface looks like this:

```
virtual pascal void DoChoice(TView *origView, short itsChoice);
```

Most of MacApp's controls call **DoChoice** in response to being clicked. The **DoChoice** method implemented in MacApp's **TView** class simply sends its superview the message **DoChoice**. Therefore, when the user selects any control in our window, the control will send the **DoChoice** message up the view hierarchy, eventually calling our new version of **DoChoice**. It passes two parameters: *itsChoice*, which contains an integer defining the type of object that has been activated (hit) by the user; and *origView*, which is the reference (that is, the handle) to the view selected by the user. This information enables our **DoChoice** method to react appropriately to each user action.

## ▶ Dialogs Sample Code

We need concern ourselves with only two parts of the file UDialogs.cp to understand how the program deals with the user's actions. The first part is shown in Listing 20-1.

Listing 20-1.  Initializing the Application

```
1: #pragma segment AInit
2: pascal void
3: TDialogsApplication::IDialogsApplication()
4: {
5:     this->IApplication(kFileType);
6:
7:     if (gDeadStripSuppression) {
8:         TModelessView *aModelessView = new TModelessView;
9:     }
10:
11:     TWindow *aWindow = NewTemplateWindow(kModelessID, NULL);
12:     aWindow->Open();
13: }
```

In lines 11 and 12 we create the dialog using the **NewTemplateWindow** method we have seen before. We make the window visible by sending it the Open message. In the previous two chapters, we did not have to send our windows the Open message, because the document did that for us.

Listing 20-2 contains the code for the **DoChoice** method that handles the user's interaction with the dialog.

Listing 20-2.  The DoChoice method

```
1: //=========================================================
2: #ifndef __STRINGS__
3:     #include <Strings.h>    // for string copy
4: #endif
5:
6: extern "C" char* memcpy(void*, void*, int);
7: #define pstrcpy(p,q)  memcpy(p, q, q[0]+1)
8:
9: //=========================================================
10: #pragma segment ARes
11: pascal void
12: TModelessView::DoChoice (TView *origView, short itsChoice)
    //override
```

```
13: {
14:     Str255      menuText;
15:     Str255      displayText;
16:
17:     pstrcpy(displayText, "\p");
18:
19:     switch (itsChoice){
20:         case mPopupHit:
21:             short menuItem = ((TPopup *) origView)->
                GetCurrentItem();
22:             ((TPopup *)origView)->GetItemText(menuItem,
                menuText);
23:             pstrcpy(displayText, menuText);
24:             break;
25:
26:         case mRadioHit:
27:             pstrcpy(displayText, "\pa radio button");
28:             if (origView == (TRadio *) this->FindSubView
                ('Larr'))
29:                 pstrcpy(displayText, "\pLarry");
30:             break;
31:     }
32:
33:     TEditText *anEditText = (TEditText *) this->FindSubView
        ('edit');
34:     anEditText->SetText(displayText, kRedraw);
35: }
```

The **DoChoice** method determines the general category of control selected by the user with a switch statement based on the integer *itsChoice*.

If the user selects a popup menu item, we use the **GetCurrentItem**
and **GetItemText** methods of **TPopup** to grab the string from the menu
item, as shown on lines 20-24. This string is copied into the variable *displayText* using the pstrcpy function defined on line 7. This function is
based on the memcpy function defined in the Strings.h header file that
comes with MPW C, as shown on lines 2-6. The argument *origView* is
passed to our **DoChoice** method as a pointer to the particular view
which the user selected with the mouse. Since it is defined to be a
pointer to a TView, we typecast it on line 22 to be a pointer to an instance of **TPopup**, so we can use methods for that class.

If the user selects any radio button, then the code on lines 26-30 uses
the **TView::FindSubView** method to determine whether the radio button was selected that has the four-letter identifier 'Larr' defined in its
'view' resource. Other radio buttons could be dealt with in a similar way.

Lines 33 and 34 place the *displayText* string into the editText view in
the dialog, by sending the SetText message to that view.

## ▶ A Modal Dialog

Figure 20-4 provides a ViewEdit look at the modal dialog used in The Dialogs Sample program.

As you can see, this view is created in ViewEdit in the same manner as the modeless view. Because the dialog is modal it has no go-away box; instead, the box will be dismissed by the user clicking on the OK button (or pressing the Return or Enter key), or by clicking the Cancel button (or pressing the Escape key or Command-period). Notice that in a typical modal dialog, you do not have to respond immediately to the user action — you can be patient and wait for the user to select OK or cancel. Therefore, you do not need to provide the **DoChoice** method used to respond to items in a modeless dialog.

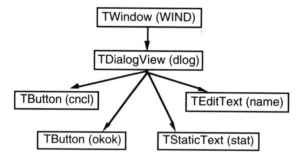

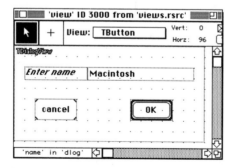

Figure 20-4. Designing the modal dialog in ViewEdit

Listing 20-3 is the **ShowModalDialog** method that would result in this dialog being displayed, dealt with, and disposed of. This method would be called from the point in your application where it was needed — from a menu, as in this example, from another dialog, or from any of a number of other places.

Listing 20-3. The ShowModalDialog method

```
1: #pragma segment ASelCommand
2: pascal void
3: TDialogsApplication::ShowModalDialog()
4: {
5:     const IDType kDialogView    = 'dlog';   //  dialog view id
6:     const IDType kName          = 'name';   //  edit text id
7:     const IDType kOK            = 'okok';   //  OK button id
8:     const IDType kCancel        = 'cncl';   //  Cancel button id
9:
10:    Str255      userName;
11:
12:    TWindow *aWindow = NewTemplateWindow(kModalID, NULL);
13:    TDialogView *aDialogView = (TDialogView *)
14:                        aWindow->FindSubView(kDialogView);
15:    IDType dismisser = aDialogView->PoseModally();
16:
17: #if qDebug
18:    if (dismisser == kOK) {
19:        TEditText *anEditText = (TEditText *)
20:                                aWindow->FindSubView(kName);
21:        anEditText->GetText(userName);
22:        printf("The user typed %P in the box\n", userName);
23:        };
24:    if (dismisser == kCancel)
25:        printf("The user cancelled the box\n");
26: #endif
27:    aWindow->Close();           // dispose of the dialog window
28: }
```

This window is still created by the MacApp utility function **New-TemplateWindow** in line 12. In lines 13 and 14 we find a reference to the enclosing dialog view object and then send it the message **PoseModally** in line 15. This standard method of the **TDialogView** class causes the dialog to remain displayed until it is properly dismissed. The dismisser will be set to the four-letter ID of the button that dismisses the dialog. In designing this view in ViewEdit, we set both the OK and Cancel buttons to be dismissers.

Lines 17-26 show a useful debugging technique using the printf() function. If you are debugging the application, then this line will put the user's entry into the MacApp Debugger window. This enables you to be sure that the user's entry is in fact being assigned to the proper variable when the dialog is dismissed. In line 27, we dispose of the dialog window by sending it the **Close** message.

▶ **Summary**

In this brief chapter, you have seen how to design, build, and handle simple modeless and modal dialogs in a MacApp program. You have seen that a dialog is very much like a window and that it can be designed in ViewEdit. You have also learned to deal with various user interactions in a modeless dialog using a Switch statement in your **Do-Choice** method. However, in a modal dialog you will send the dialog view that contains your dialogs items the message **PoseModally**. In this way, you do not have to subclass any of the classes used in the window. (If you want to study the code for a much more complex set of dialogs, you should look at the DemoDialogs sample program shipped as part of MacApp.)

This chapter ends our discussion of user interaction in a MacApp program. At this point, we have discussed many of the common parts of Macintosh applications, including how to

- provide a Main Event Loop by using an application object
- display complicated windows with many views and scrollbars
- display and handle menu items
- select and draw with the mouse
- support Undo
- read and write disk files
- handle text editing with Cut, Copy, Paste, and Undo

In Part 5, we will turn our attention to some more advanced design issues and considerations for more complex and realistic MacApp programs.

# PART FIVE

# ▶ Constructing a Real-World Application

In this concluding part of our exploration of MacApp, we will make two important shifts of focus. First, we will move beyond the simple programs we've been building so far and focus on the design and implementation of a more elaborate sample program. Second, we will concentrate more of our time on design issues that are important when we create building blocks to be reused by other programmers. By making these changes in emphasis, we will be able to reinforce the concepts we have studied so far while spending more time and energy pointing out design decisions and trade-offs.

As you build up libraries of reusable code like those discussed in the next five chapters, you will find that putting together new applications can be nearly as easy as plugging together existing libraries.

Throughout these chapters, we will describe the thought process that went into implementing the sample program as well as some of the design trade-offs we made. You will probably face similar choices as you build your real-world MacApp programs.

▶  Chapter 21 begins by discussing the central concept of code reusability and how it should be taken into account when designing an application to be subclassed and used by others.

▶  Chapter 22 describes how to use streams for general-purpose input and output in your MacApp programs. It explores the issues involved when you need to store objects in a file.

**437**

▶ Chapter 23 outlines the architecture for a graphic building block that forms the visible core of the application. It discusses how shapes are drawn and what classes are needed to facilitate their use.

▶ Chapter 24 teaches you how to create the interactive portion of a complex application involving extensive use of the mouse. It describes how to build MacApp routines to sketch, select, and drag shapes.

▶ Chapter 25 concludes by focusing on three important application features. It describes how to use low-level methods for reading and writing documents in addition to using filters in commands and implementing cut, copy, and paste operations.

# 21 ▶ Designing Code for Reusability

In this chapter, we will begin designing a reasonably robust sample application by thinking about the issue of code reusability. We will examine the main advantages and techniques involved in reusable code construction. Then we'll take a look at some rules of thumb that may help you decide when you should define new classes as opposed to subclassing existing classes and simply creating or overriding methods.

We'll also present some suggestions that, if you follow them, will make your code easier for you and others to reuse. Chief among these considerations are the issues of constants and variables, whose proper use can make a significant difference in reusability.

## ▶ Reasons for Reusability

The purpose of designing reusable modules (or *building blocks*) is to reduce the time necessary to create a new application. Instead of implementing all the details of your application each time, you can simply plug in an existing building block. Designing a useful building block requires a little more thought than designing a module for one particular purpose. You have to anticipate how other programmers might want to use your building block and provide ways they can customize it.

In traditional programming environments, reusability is achieved by providing subroutine libraries. In fact, the Macintosh ROM is an example of such a library. The ROM contains hundreds of useful routines that you can use to implement a Macintosh program. Rather than defining your own implementation of windows or menus, for example, you can take advantage of the implementations provided in ROM. This saves programming time and helps ensure that windows, menus, and other elements in different applications look the same.

Unfortunately, with a simple subroutine library, there isn't much flexibility in customizing how a subroutine works unless you can modify its source code. About all you can do is pass a subroutine different parameters. Otherwise you must completely rewrite it from scratch, which isn't always possible.

Object programming, however, can change this. If the library contains class definitions instead of plain subroutines, then users of the library can create subclasses of the library classes and override methods. If the library is designed properly, then you can make substantial changes to its behavior without modifying the source code, or even having access to it.

MacApp is just such a library. Recall from our discussion in Chapter 2 that using MacApp in your application saves time compared to calling the ROM routines directly, since MacApp implements the standard parts of your application. In the same way, a building block that you implement for one program will save time when developing the next application that needs the same capabilities.

The only difference between MacApp itself and one of your building blocks is that MacApp is the basic framework used in any program, while a building block is optional. The MacApp release comes with a number of optional building blocks; UTEView and UGridView are two of them. Some MacApp developers have written other building blocks that are available from the MacApp Developers Association.

The issues involved with designing a useful building block are slightly different from those involved with designing code that will be used in a single application. For a building block to be useful, it must be adaptable to different situations. The whole purpose of using a building block is to reduce implementation time the next time it is used. This purpose will be defeated if large parts of your building block have to be rewritten for each new application.

On the other hand, you shouldn't be discouraged if you don't get the design of your building block right the first (or even the second) time; like anything else, it takes some practice. If you were to look at MacApp version 1.0, you would find many places where the original version of MacApp was not as reusable as it could have been. Many of these problems were fixed in MacApp 2.0.

# ▶ Rules of Thumb

As the designer of a building block, you must put yourself in the place of the programmers using your work. You need to think about what they want your building block to do and how they might want to customize it. There are no hard and fast rules that you can use to design a building block. The best we can do is to offer some rules of thumb to guide your design. As you read the following discussion, remember that they are only guidelines; there will likely be cases where violating one of the rules will result in a better design.

In the following sections we use examples from a structured graphics building block we are building. By structured graphics we mean an application in which each shape has its own identity, as opposed to a painting program which deals with individual pixels. In Chapter 23 we will examine the structured graphics building block in more detail.

There are two distinct groups of users that you (as a building block writer) have to keep in mind. One is the programmers who will be incorporating your building block into their programs. The other is the end users who will use those programs. In the following sections, we will refer to the programmer as the building block *client* and the end user as simply the *user*. (You can imagine that the programmer has hired you as a consultant to write the building block, which would make him or her your client.)

## ▶ When to Define New Classes

When creating an object-oriented building block, you must first determine the conceptual model your client must have to use the building block. Often, there will be more than one way to approach the problem you are trying to solve. Once you choose a conceptual model, then you must define a set of classes that describe that model. Sometimes programmers define the classes first and then construct a conceptual model that fits the implementation. Unfortunately, if the conceptual model you construct is very different from the one your client uses, then your client will have a difficult time using the building block.

Usually the conceptual model and the corresponding set of classes will be evident. As we mentioned in Chapter 4, the nouns inherent in your problem are modeled as classes. In the case of the graphics building block, there are different kinds of shapes. It makes sense to define one class for each kind of shape in the building block; for example, a **TLine** class and a **TRectangle** class.

Even shapes as different as a line and a rectangle share some properties. For example, both can be dragged and both can be drawn (although with different QuickDraw calls). One way to capture these similarities in the building block is to define a generic shape class. The **TShape** class would define the properties common to all shapes, even if it couldn't implement all these properties. Then you can make the **TRectangle** and **TLine** classes subclasses of **TShape** and define the unique properties of each shape in the subclass.

A class that exists only to define the common properties of its subclasses is called an *abstract* class. Other classes are known as *concrete* classes. You will never create an object of an abstract class, only of a concrete class. This is because an abstract class does not implement all the methods it defines; some of those methods are implemented only in concrete classes.

It is not possible to write one function that can operate on a **TLine** object as well as a **TRectangle** object, because **TLine** and **TRectangle** are different types. This limitation is a result of the type-checking inherent in the C++ language.

It *is* possible to write a function that operates on **TShape** objects. Since **TLine** and **TRectangle** are subclasses of **TShape**, that function can operate on line and rectangle objects, as well as other kinds of shapes. Because **TLine** is a subclass of **TShape**, it inherits all the properties of **TShape** and can be used in any situation that calls for a shape object.

Our graphics building block contains a number of other classes in addition to the abstract **TShape** class and its concrete subclasses. Most of these additional classes are dictated by MacApp. For example, to manipulate the shapes, we must include several command classes, including those to sketch new shapes and to implement copy and paste. We can summarize this rule of thumb as:

**Important ▶** The classes in your building block should correspond with the conceptual model of the problem. Use abstract classes to define properties common to two or more concrete classes.

## ▶ When to Define New Methods

When using an object-oriented building block, your client can do some customization by varying the parameters you pass to the various methods. This is especially true of the methods that initialize a new object, since those methods determine how the object will behave later.

This kind of customization is not very different, however, from that provided by a library of ordinary subroutines. The real power of an object-oriented building block comes from the ability to subclass one of its classes and override one or more methods. Your client doesn't even need the original source code to do this. Therefore, it is usually advantageous to add methods to a class, since each method provides another opportunity to customize the building block.

When your clients override one of your methods, they can still call your original implementation. They cannot, however, invoke only part of the inherited method. If the method performs two separate functions and your clients need to change one of these, then they will have to override the method and copy half of the code from the old to the new method (assuming that the source code is available). On the other hand, if the method calls other methods to do its job, then your client can selectively override methods to suit the application.

In our example, the graphics building block, all shapes have an interior and a frame. Instead of drawing both the interior and frame in a single **Draw** method, you can define separate **DrawInterior** and **DrawFrame** methods, which gives you two advantages. The abstract class **TShape** can actually implement the **Draw** method, because it can call the **DrawInterior** and **DrawFrame** methods. The concrete classes would then implement the **DrawInterior** and **DrawFrame** methods. Also it is possible to draw only the shape's frame, without its interior, which can be useful for providing feedback when the user is dragging or creating shapes.

Notice that by following this rule we have implemented methods at two levels of detail. There is the general **Draw** method, which in turn calls the specific **DrawInterior** and **DrawFrame** methods. The latter methods implement the two parts of the entire drawing process. If your clients need to customize the drawing process in this building block, they have a choice of three places to do so.

In most cases, you would carry this design rule to more than two levels. For example, one way to implement the **DrawFrame** method is shown in Listing 21-1.

Listing 21-1. DrawFrame

```
1:  pascal void TRectangle::DrawFrame(void)
2:  {
3:    PenPat(&fPenPattern);
4:    PenSize(fFrameSize.h, fFrameSize.v);
5:    FrameRect(&fBoundsRect);
6:  }
```

But suppose you need to draw a rectangle with a gray frame when you are dragging it. With the implementation just given, you would have to change the *fPenPattern* field before calling **DrawFrame**. If we add more methods, then we could implement **DrawFrame** as as shown in Listing 21-2.

Listing 21-2. DrawFrame modified

```
1:  pascal void TRectangle::DrawFrame(void)
2:  {
3:    this -> SetupFrameStyle();
4:    this -> DoFrame();
5:  }
```

The **SetupFrameStyle** method, called on line 3, would set the pen pattern and size, while the **DoFrame** method (line 4) would only need to call **FrameRect**. Other parts of the building block can then call **DoFrame** with a different pen pattern or size. The **SetupFrameStyle** method could even be implemented in the **TShape** class and inherited in all the concrete shape classes. We can summarize this rule of thumb as:

| Important ▶ | Each method should have a single purpose. If a method does more than one thing, it should be divided into separate methods, or it should call other methods to implement the different parts. |

## ▶ Creating Objects Within a Building Block

Sometimes a method in a building block needs to create another object. For example, most commands in a MacApp program are handled by creating a command object and returning it to MacApp. If the building block is to handle commands, which it should, then it will be responsible for creating the appropriate command objects. In our example, the graphics building block defines a **TShapeDragger** class. The method in the building block that handles a mouse press needs to create an object of this class and return it to MacApp.

How do you furnish a mechanism for clients to customize this? Suppose a client creates a subclass of **TShapeDragger**, and wants to use an instance of that class instead. There are several ways to provide for this. First, we can apply the previous rule of thumb and define a method whose single purpose is to create the object. Other methods in the building block would call this method whenever they needed a particular kind of object. In the case of **TShapeDragger**, the result is shown in Listing 21-3.

Listing 21-3. A method to create the object

```
1:  pascal TCommand* TShapeView::DoMouseCommand(...)
2:  {
3:    ...
4:    TShapeDragger* aShapeDragger = NewShapeDragger(...);
5:    ...
6:  }
7:
8:  pascal TShapeDragger* TShapeView::NewShapeDragger(...)
9:  {
10:   TShapeDragger* aShapeDragger = new TShapeDragger;
11:     FailNIL(aShapeDragger);
12:     aShapeDragger -> IShapeDragger(...);
13:   return aShapeDragger;
14:  }
```

Now it is easy for your client to override the **NewShapeDragger** method and create a special kind of object.

Another way to create a brand new object is to copy an existing object. In MacApp, class **TObject** implements a method called **Clone** that does this for you. Since every class descends from **TObject** (with only rare exceptions), every class has a **Clone** method. Instead of defining a **NewShapeDragger** method, you could write the **DoMouseCommand** method as shown in Listing 21-4.

Listing 21-4. DoMouseCommand

```
1:  pascal TCommand* TShapeView::DoMouseCommand(...)
2:  {
3:    ...
4:    TShapeDragger* aShapeDragger =
5:              (TShapeDragger*)(fExampleDragger -> Clone());
6:    ...
7:  }
```

The *fExampleDragger* field used on line 5 would normally refer to a **TShapeDragger** object. Your client could, however, initialize the field with a customized shape-dragger object, and **DoMouseCommand** would then use the custom dragger command instead of the standard command.

It is important to ensure that the objects you intend to clone properly implement the **Clone** method. **TObject** provides a default implementation that makes an exact copy of the object. If the object contains fields that refer to other objects, the clone will refer to those same objects. This might not be the behavior you want; in that case, you will have to override the **Clone** method and clone those other objects.

Finally, MacApp provides a useful extension to Object Pascal, called **NewObjectByClassName**, which allows you to create an object by specifying the name of its class as a string. (This mechanism, incidentally, is used for creating views from 'view' resource templates.) Your client can simply supply the name of the class that the building block should create. This approach, by the way, only works for subclasses of Pascal Object. (See Listing 21-5.)

Listing 21-5. Using NewObjectByClassName

```
1:   pascal TCommand* TShapeView::DoMouseCommand(...)
2:   {
3:     ...
4:     TShapeDragger* aShapeDragger =
5:         (TShapeDragger*)(NewObjectByClassName(fDraggerClass));
6:     ...
7:   }
```

This is similar to the previous approach using **Clone**. In this case, however, *fDraggerClass* contains a string identifying the class. The primary advantage of this approach is that the class name string can be initialized in a variety of ways; for example, it could be read from a document file. Also, since no example object need be created, this approach usually requires less memory.

To summarize the preceding discussion: If a building block needs to create an object, there should be a mechanism for the client to substitute a custom version of that object. You can:

1. define a method responsible for creating the object,
2. clone an example object supplied by the client, or
3. create the object using NewObjectByClassName and the object's class name.

Which alternative you choose depends on the situation.

For example, providing a separate method has the advantage that your clients can dynamically decide whether to create their own kind of object or the one you specified. In the example in Listing 21-3, your client can override the **NewShapeDragger** method and either create a custom **TShapeDragger** object or call inherited **NewShapeDragger** to create an actual **TShapeDragger** object, depending on the circumstances.

Another way of achieving the same thing is to combine the first and third mechanisms. You could create the object from its name, but call a method to get the name of the class (for example, **GetShapeDragger-Class**). **GetShapeDraggerClass** would normally return the appropriate field, but your client can override it to return a different class name.

**By the Way ▶** An advantage of using class names is that they can be stored in resources, which makes them easy to change. Also, MacApp defines a class **TAssociation** which maps a key string to a value string. You can use an instance of **TAssociation** to map a key such as "dragger" to the name of the dragger command class.

## ▶ Constants

Another thing to watch out for is the use of constants in a building block. Constants, by definition, can't be changed. It is good programming style to define symbolic names for constants that you use, so that changing the constant definition affects all the places the constant is used. (Notice, though, that this does require changing the source code.)

Using constants within a building block is not necessarily bad, but you should be aware when you use them. This leads to the following rule:

**Important ▶** Examine places where you use constants, since they can't be changed by clients of your building block.

A specific case where constants are often used is defining command numbers. A building block might handle certain menu commands itself, or it might create command objects. When you create a command object, you have to supply a command number. If you were to use constants in your building block you risk having a conflict between the command objects used in your building block and those used in another building block. A client who needed to use both building blocks would be in trouble.

Another use of constants is in defining such characteristics as the font number and size used to draw text and the pen size or pattern used to draw graphics. The solution in these cases is to use variables instead of constants. This adds a tiny bit of overhead to the final application, since constants are evaluated at compile time. In exchange, you gain more flexibility. You should generally provide default values for these variables, so your clients only need to change them when necessary.

▶ Global Versus Local Variables

The previous rule of thumb can also be applied to global variables:

| Important ▶ | Examine places where you use global variables and make sure that they are truly global. |
| --- | --- |

When you use a global variable instead of an instance variable, you are assuming that your client will only need one instance of that piece of data. Again, you gain generality by using an instance variable, at the expense of a little extra overhead. (Accessing an object's variable takes an extra machine instruction or two.)

Sometimes, you only reference variables of the active view. In that case, you can move the instance variables into global variables when the view is made active. You end up caching the instance variables in global variables, from which they can be accessed more quickly. You would override the **TView.Activate** method to do this. Although this technique works, it can be tricky to debug if something goes wrong. You have to ensure that the global variables always correspond to the variables of the active view.

▶ Good Design and Documentation

Following the above guidelines will help you design reusable building blocks, but it does not guarantee that the code you write will be reusable. You must still follow good programming and design principles.

If you expect other people to use your building block, it should be well documented. This is true even if your clients have access to the source code. Programmers should not have to dive into the details of your implementation if all they want to do is use it. It also helps to provide examples that show how to use and customize your building block.

Above all, try to imagine yourself as a client of your own building block. Try to anticipate the questions and problems your clients might have and address these in your documentation or your code. Where possible, include consistency checks that will prevent client mistakes and reduce debugging time. (These checks can be included only in debugging versions of a program, which means they do not have to slow down the final application.)

## ▶ Putting the Principles to Work

In the rest of the book, we are going to design and implement a complete MacApp program. In the process of doing this, you will see how the principles described above are used in a real example. We also hope to give you a feeling for the kinds of issues and tradeoffs you will have to make when you use MacApp for your own work.

The program is ExampleDraw, a simple graphics editor similar to the DrawShapes example program shipped with MacApp. It supports rectangles, ovals, and lines. The user can create new shapes, move them around, and change their styles. In addition, the user can cut and paste shapes from one document to another and from an ExampleDraw document to other applications (a word processor that supports graphics or another graphics program, for example).

Since this is intended to be a more serious application than the DrawShapes sample, it will manipulate shapes in a more precise manner. For example, DrawShapes detects whether the user clicked a particular shape (known as *hit detection*) by comparing the mouse position against the shape's bounding box. Although this is easy to implement, the results are very imprecise.

Figure 21-1 shows the difference between using the actual shape and its bounding box for testing. The difference is especially noticeable for lines. Example Draw will perform hit detection based on the actual shape rather than its bounding box.

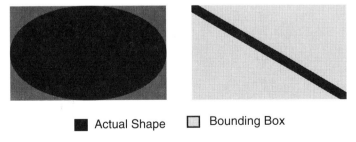

■ Actual Shape    ☐ Bounding Box

Figure 21-1.  Hit detection

The second difference has to do with the way shapes are drawn. Consider drawing a line on a blueprint. You place your pen on one endpoint of the line and draw to the other endpoint. If you use a thick pen, the resulting line would be centered on the two endpoints. If you then draw a rectangle enclosing the line, the sides of the rectangle would line up nicely with the line itself, as shown in Figure 21-2.

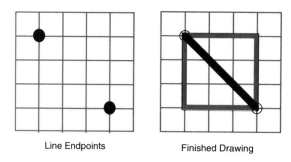

Line Endpoints                Finished Drawing

Figure 21-2. Centered drawing model

DrawShapes uses QuickDraw, which has a particular model for drawing shapes. A line is drawn by dragging a rectangular pen from the beginning to ending point, with the pen hanging below and to the right of the points. Rectangles are drawn just inside their boundaries. If we draw the picture shown in Figure 21-2 using QuickDraw's model, the results would be as shown in Figure 21-3.

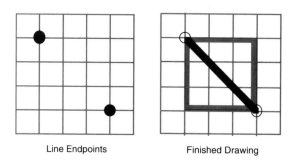

Line Endpoints                Finished Drawing

Figure 21-3. QuickDraw drawing model

Notice that the diagonal line extends outside the rectangle and that the rectangle frame is not centered on the grid lines. To produce the first, more accurate drawing, ExampleDraw will have to account for QuickDraw's drawing model when drawing shapes.

▶ **Summary**

The design of ExampleDraw has been broken down into four parts, corresponding to the next four chapters. In Chapter 22, we implement the concept of a *stream*, which is an abstract sequences of bytes. Streams will be important in ExampleDraw, as well as other MacApp programs, because they allow us to implement document and Clipboard reading and writing with the same application code.

In Chapter 23 we describe the basic architecture of the graphics building block. The graphics building block is a reusable set of classes that implements the data structures and code for manipulating a list of shape objects. ExampleDraw then becomes a very simple application for testing the building block. In Chapter 24 we implement three simple mouse commands that select, sketch, and drag shapes. We also develop a framework for dealing with mouse actions in the building block.

Finally, in Chapter 25 we implement three more complicated features of the building block: document reading and writing, filtering, and Clipboard support. Filtering is a technique for implementing Undo which greatly reduces the memory requirements.

For space reasons, we don't show the full source code for ExampleDraw in this book. The full source code is available on diskette. Some versions of this book include the diskette; others include a coupon that you can use to order the diskette.

# 22 ▶ Input/Output with Streams

This chapter describes how to implement general purpose input/output (I/O) routines that can read and write both files and handles. It begins by explaining the concept of a stream and its importance in programming. Then it describes the design and implementation of an abstract class and three concrete subclasses to handle stream I/O in MacApp. With that background, the chapter delves into the more complex issue of reading and writing objects rather than bytes or simple data structures. The chapter closes with a brief discussion of four implementation issues that are not completely addressed in this explanation, but which may prove significant in some kinds of I/O routines you might write.

## ▶ The Problem

When you think of input/output on the Macintosh, you probably think of reading and writing files on the disk. Most applications read and write files when they open and save documents. But file I/O is not the only kind of I/O we need in our applications. Reading and writing the Clipboard, for example, is also a kind of I/O.

The Macintosh Scrap Manager uses handles to store information on the Clipboard. When you copy a piece of data, the application creates a handle containing a representation of the data. In many applications, the same representation is used for writing data to the Clipboard as for writing data to a file. This is certainly the most convenient way to handle both tasks, since it allows us to reuse the same I/O code for both functions. A problem arises, however, because a disk file and a handle (destined for the Clipboard) are different storage media. More importantly, you read and write them differently, which makes it difficult to use the same I/O code for both.

Other domains have no trouble dealing with different media; there is no problem hooking up a cassette player and a compact disk player to the same stereo, for example. The reason is that there is a standard interface between the players and the stereo in terms of the connectors, impedance, and so forth. It should be possible, then, to define a standard I/O mechanism that is general enough to encompass both file I/O and handle I/O. In the rest of this chapter, we will implement such a mechanism, called a *stream*.

## ▶ What Is a Stream?

Streams are not a new concept in software engineering. Many computer systems provide an implementation of a stream. At the lowest level, a stream is a sequence of bytes. At any point in time, therefore, the stream has a definite size, and programs can read or write bytes to the stream. Some streams allow both reading and writing; others may allow only one kind of access.

Viewed at a slightly higher level, a stream contains a sequence of data values. For example, a stream might contain a Point, a Rectangle, and a String. The order of the values within the stream is important. Programs that read and write the same stream must agree on the order in which the values are stored or must store a tag for each value that indicates its data type.

Some streams allow random access, which means the program can read or write at any position in the stream. A random-access stream maintains the current position within the stream. Programs read and write data at the stream's current position and can get or set the current position. Other streams provide only sequential access. An example of a stream that is not random-access would be a serial I/O stream; once you write a character to a serial communications line, that value is sent to its destination.

To summarize, a stream has several attributes:

• It contains a sequence of bytes at the lowest level.

• It has a certain size at any point in time.

• At a higher level it contains a sequence of data values.

• If it is a random-access stream, it has a current position, which can be examined and changed.

If you look at the operations provided by the Macintosh File Manager (or any other computer system's file manager), you will see that the above stream attributes correspond closely to those of a file. The only difference is that the File Manager has no calls to read or write higher level data; it deals only with bytes. What about handles? A handle also contains a sequence of bytes and is a definite size. To read or write the contents of a handle we can simply access the memory it occupies. (We can use the ROM routine BlockMove to move bytes around in memory.) There is no concept, however, of a current position within a handle.

Other Macintosh features can also fit into the stream model. As we mentioned, the serial port can be viewed as a stream. Similarly, there are network protocols (for example, AppleTalk Data Stream Protocol) that implement streams. These two kinds of streams are not random-access, however.

In the rest of this chapter we will only consider file and handle streams, since they can be used in almost every application. We will also implement a third kind of stream, called a counting stream, that you might not immediately consider, but which will be very useful for MacApp programs.

## ▶ Stream Classes

The class hierarchy for the stream classes is shown in Figure 22-1.

The classes **TFileStream** and **THandleStream** are necessary because of the differences in the way in which you read and write files and handles. There are two reasons for implementing the superclass **TStream**. First, there is code that is common to both kinds of streams. We can take advantage of this and implement the code once in **TStream**, where it can be inherited by **TFileStream** and **THandleStream**.

The second reason has to do with C++'s type checking. Our goal is to write functions that read and write data, without knowing whether the data are stored in a file or in a handle. C++, however, requires that we declare the types of all values. For these data handling functions to accept either a **TFileStream** or a **THandleStream** as a parameter, there must be a common ancestor class for **TFileStream** and **THandleStream** (that is, **TStream**). Since **TFileStream** and **THandleStream** inherit all the characteristics of **TStream**, C++ will allow us to use instances of those classes anywhere a **TStream** object could be used.

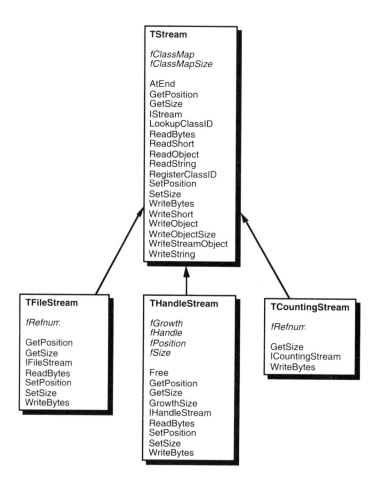

Figure 22-1. Stream class hierarchy

So our data handling functions can be written to accept a **TStream** object as a parameter, and at runtime we can pass either a **TFileStream** or a **THandleStream** object. Of course, the functions can only call methods that have been defined in the **TStream** class.

Not every method defined in the **TStream** class can be implemented in that class. For example, it defines low-level methods to read and write bytes, but the implementations of these methods differ with the type of stream involved. These methods cannot be implemented in the abstract class; each concrete subclass must override them.

C++ provides a way to force programmers to override such methods. If you follow the example of Listing 22-1 in the way it defines TStream::ReadBytes as a pure virtual function (by adding =0 at the end), then all subclasses of your defined class (in this case TStream) must override ReadBytes. If a subclass fails to override such a method, the C++ compiler will generate an error at compile time.

Another way C++ ensures that users of such classes will override them is by treating any class that contains one or more pure virtual methods as an abstract class. Since it is illegal to create an instance of an abstract class, the only way to use such methods is to override them.

It is important for you to anticipate common programming mistakes and warn programmers when they occur rather than allowing these mistakes to become runtime problems. This practice will help reduce the time spent debugging. MacApp, for example, contains many such checks in its source code. Where possible, you should use C++ language features like pure virtual functions that will catch mistakes at compile time. If this isn't possible, you should consider adding code to your programs to perform these checks at runtime. Be sure to use conditional compilation if you take this approach so the extra code is included only in debugging versions. The conditional code looks like this:

```
#if qDebug
 <code to check for mistakes>
#endif
```

Listing 22-1. Ensuring Overrides

```
1: class TStream: public TObject {
2: ...
3:   pascal void ReadBytes(void* p, long count) = 0;
4: ...
5: };
```

## ▶ TStream Design

Our first step is to design and implement **TStream**, since it defines the protocol all streams must follow. Then we can implement subclasses of **TStream**. As a starting point in the design, we can look back at the stream requirements described earlier. At its lowest level, a stream contains a sequence of bytes. Although the mechanism for reading and writing bytes is dependent on the kind of stream, once we have that mechanism, we can read or write higher-level data, such as a Point, by treating such data as a series of bytes.

The core of the **TStream** class, then, are the methods **ReadBytes** and **WriteBytes**. Each method has two parameters: a pointer to the bytes and a count of the number of bytes to read or write.

▶ Two Key Decisions

At this point, we must make two decisions. First, should the byte count parameter be a short or a long int? To answer this question, we need to consider the needs of the concrete stream classes. In this case, the sizes of files and handles are defined by long values, so we will also use a long in **TStream**.

The second decision is how to handle errors. (Note that there is no doubt that we will get errors — a program can have a bug in it, a file can become corrupted, or you can run out of disk or heap space while writing.) There are two alternatives. The first is to return an error code, in the same way that all the File Manager I/O calls return an error code. The second alternative is to use the MacApp failure mechanism to signal a failure if an error occurs.

Returning an error code makes it easier for the calling method to handle special errors such as reaching the end of the stream. On the other hand, it clutters up the code, since the returned error codes have to be dealt with. We will choose the second alternative, since making the code easier to read is a significant advantage. It is unlikely that clients would want to check for specific errors in any case. (Clients who want to catch these errors can establish a custom exception handler in their methods. See Listing 25-1 for an example of a custom exception handler.)

The two methods end up with the following interfaces:

```
pascal void TStream::ReadBytes(void* p, long count)
pascal void TStream::WriteBytes(const void* p, long count)
```

The keyword const indicates that **WriteBytes** does not change the data pointed to by the pointer p.

There are two differences between this interface specification and the one provided by the Macintosh File Manager for reading and writing files. First, the File Manager returns an error code as the function result. Second, the File Manager uses the count parameter to return to the calling routine the number of bytes read or written. This parameter will normally become significant only when an error arises and fewer bytes than expected are read or written. Since we don't expect clients to examine the error code itself, this parameter would be of questionable utility or value. Making this parameter one that need not be specifically examined simplifies the implementation of other **TStream** methods.

## ▶ Handling Higher-Level Data

The next step in designing **TStream** is to implement methods that read and write higher-level data structures. There is a wide range of data structures that we could handle in these methods. To keep the task manageable, however, we will implement methods for types (char, short, long, string), as well as the QuickDraw types Point and Rect. For example, the methods to read and write integers are shown in Listing 22-2.

**By the Way** ▶

The stream methods that handle higher-level data are oriented towards Pascal data types, since the interface to the Macintosh Toolbox is defined in a Pascal-like way.

Keep in mind the two key differences:
- the C++ type "short" corresponds to "integer" in Pascal
- the methods **ReadString** and **WriteString**, described below, handle Pascal strings

Listing 22-2. ReadShort and WriteShort

```
 1: pascal short TStream::ReadShort()
 2: {
 3:  short data = 0;
 4:  this -> ReadBytes(&data, sizeof(short));
 5:  return data;
 6: }
 7:
 8: pascal void TStream::WriteShort(short data)
 9: {
10:  this -> WriteBytes(&data, sizeof(short));
11: }
```

These methods simply call the low-level, byte-oriented methods to handle the actual I/O. Even though the methods **TStream::ReadBytes** and **TStream::WriteBytes** do nothing, we can still call those methods from **ReadShort** and **WriteShort**. It is unnecessary for **TStream** subclasses to override high-level methods (such as **ReadShort**) provided they implement the low-level methods (such as **ReadBytes**).

One thing to notice is that **ReadShort** and **WriteShort** don't have to worry about errors at all, since if an error occurs it will be signaled by **ReadBytes** or **WriteBytes**, respectively. Also, since **ReadBytes** and **WriteBytes** don't modify the byte count, we can directly pass the value sizeof(short) to them. You can see how the decisions we made earlier simplify the implementation here. If we had decided to return error codes, these methods would have had to pass along the error code from the byte-oriented methods on lines 4 and 10. Had we passed the byte count as a modifiable parameter we would have had to declare a local count variable, and assigned the result of sizeof to that variable.

The methods that read and write the other data types have similar structures. The exceptions are **ReadString** and **WriteString**, which read and write a Pascal string. Rather than reading and writing the maximum string length (255 bytes), these methods read and write exactly the number of characters in the string. Also, these methods take a pointer to the string as a parameter, rather than the string itself. (See Listing 22-3.)

Listing 22-3. ReadString and WriteString

```
1: pascal void TStream::ReadString(StringPtr data, short maxSize)
2: {
3:  this -> ReadBytes(data, 1);              /* Read length byte. */
4:
5:  if (Length(data)+1 > maxSize)
6:      FailOSErr(paramErr);                 /* Too many bytes. */
7:  else
8:      this -> ReadBytes(data+1, Length(data));
9: }
10:
11: pascal void    TStream::WriteString(StringPtr data)
12: {
13:  this -> WriteBytes(data, Length(data)+1);  /* +1 for length */
14: }
```

Both **ReadString** and **WriteString** take a pointer to the string, rather than the actual string value. This allows us to read or write a string of any length.

We require that the programmer pass to **ReadString** the total size of the memory available for storing the string. If the string in the stream is longer than this, then we signal an error (line 6). (We chose paramErr as the error code because the File Manager returns this error if the byte count is invalid.) The **ReadString** method reads the length byte from the stream (line 3), and if the string fits in the available space, it reads the characters that make up the string (line 8). The **WriteString** method does the opposite, making sure to write out the initial length byte as well as all the characters.

The final parts of the **TStream** design are the methods that deal with the size of the stream and the current position within the stream. There are four methods in all: **GetPosition**, **SetPosition**, **GetSize**, and **Set-**

**Size**. As with **ReadBytes** and **WriteBytes**, these methods can't be implemented in **TStream**. Once we have these methods defined, we can implement one last utility method, **TStream::AtEnd**, which returns true if the current position is at the end of the stream. This is intended for clients who are reading a stream, so they can detect the end of the data. The code for **TStream::AtEnd** is as follows:

```
1: pascal Boolean TStream::AtEnd() const
2: {
3:   return (this -> GetPosition()) >= (this -> GetSize());
4: }
```

**By The Way ▶**

The word "const" in the definition of **AtEnd** indicates that it is a constant method. A constant method is one that does not change the object receiving the message.

In C++, you can declare a variable that refers to a constant object by including the "const" keyword as in this example:

```
const TStream* aConstantStream;
```

C++ will generate a warning if you use a constant object to call a method that is not constant. For example, this code would cause a compiler warning, assuming that **TStream** had been defined as a constant object as above:

```
aConstantStream -> WriteInteger(X);
```

because **WriteInteger** is not a constant method.

C++ will generate a compile-time error if you try to change an instance variable of a constant object or attempt to assign a constant object to a non-constant variable.

## ▶ TStream Subclasses

Now that we have a complete design for **TStream**, we can implement the two subclasses **TFileStream** and **THandleStream**. In each case, we need to override the six methods of **TStream** that could not be implemented in the abstract class: **ReadBytes**, **WriteBytes**, **GetPosition**, **SetPosition**, **GetSize**, and **SetSize**. We also need a representation for the stream itself.

▶ TFileStream

**TFileStream** is very easy to implement, since **TStream** was modeled after the interface provided by the File Manager. A client method that creates a **TFileStream** will pass a File Manager refnum (reference number) to the initialization method. **TFileStream** stores that refnum in its *fRefnum* instance variable. There is a one-to-one correspondence between the methods we have to implement in **TFileStream** and File Manager calls:

| | |
|---|---|
| **ReadBytes** | FSRead |
| **WriteBytes** | FSWrite |
| **GetPosition** | GetFPos |
| **SetPosition** | SetFPos |
| **GetSize** | GetEOF |
| **SetSize** | SetEOF |

Since each of these File Manager calls returns an error code, we will use the MacApp routine FailOSErr to signal a failure if they return a nonzero error. To illustrate what we mean, Listing 22-4 shows the implementation of **GetPosition**.

Listing 22-4. GetPosition

```
1: pascal long TFileStream::GetPosition() const
2: {
3:   long x;
4:
5:   FailOSErr(GetFPos(fRefnum, &x));  /* Call the File Manager */
6:   return x;
7: }
```

The implementations of the other **TFileStream** methods are similar.

▶ THandleStream

**THandleStream** is a bit more complex, because there are no existing calls in the Toolbox that provide the stream functions we need to implement. In addition to an instance variable to store the handle (*fHandle*), we also need instance variables to record the current stream position (*fPosition*) and the current size (*fSize*). We'll see below why we need to keep track of the stream size separately from the handle size.

There is also an instance variable, *fGrowthRate*, in **THandleStream**. This variable is used to control how much the handle grows when data are added to it. It would be inefficient to increase the handle size each time some piece of data was written; potentially each write operation could require moving heap blocks around. Instead, we will increase the handle size in larger increments to reduce the number of times the handle is grown. The incremental growth means the handle size (as far as the Memory Manager is concerned) is usually larger than the number of bytes written to the stream, which is why we add a separate *fSize* field to **THandleStream**.

The implementations of **ReadBytes** and **WriteBytes** call the Toolbox utility BlockMove to copy the data between the handle and the buffer area passed to the methods by the client. Both methods must ensure that they do not run past the end of the stream. This is shown in Listing 22-5.

Listing 22-5. ReadBytes and WriteBytes

```
 1: pascal void THandleStream::ReadBytes(const void* p, long count)
 2: {
 3:   OSErr err;
 4:
 5:   long  available = fSize - fPosition;     /* Bytes available */
 6:
 7:   if (available < count) {      /* Reading past end of stream */
 8:       count = available;
 9:       err = eofErr;
10:   }
11:   else
12:       err = noErr;
13:
14:   if (count > 0) {                         /* Move the bytes */
15:       BlockMove( (Ptr)((char*)(*fHandle) + fPosition),
16:               (Ptr)p,  count);
17:       fPosition = fPosition + count;
18:   }
19:   else if (count < 0)
20:       err = paramErr;              /* Negative request count */
21:
22:   FailOSErr(err);
23: }
24:
25: pascal void THandleStream::WriteBytes(const void* p, long
        count)
26: {
27:   if (count < 0)
```

```
28:        FailOSErr(paramErr);               /* Negative request count */
29:
30:    long available = fSize - fPosition;        /* Bytes available */
31:
32:    if (available < count)                     /* Grow the handle */
33:        SetSize(fSize + GrowthSize(count - available));
34:
35:                                               /* Move the bytes. */
36:    BlockMove((Ptr)p, (Ptr)((char*)(*fHandle)+fPosition), count);
37:    fPosition = fPosition + count;
38:
39:    if (fPosition > fSize)                     /* Adjust the size */
40:        fSize = fPosition;
41: }
```

If **ReadBytes** reaches the end of the stream, it signals a failure; the local variable *err* is set to eofErr at line 9. **WriteBytes**, however, attempts to grow the handle to create extra space in which to store the data. It calls the method **GrowthSize** to determine how much to expand the handle. **GrowthSize** simply returns the maximum of the stream's *fGrowthRate* variable and the number of bytes needed. Our method here allows clients to override the default behavior, if necessary. The code for **GrowthSize** is:

```
1: pascal long THandleStream::GrowthSize(long needed) const
2: {
3:    return Max(fGrowthSize, needed);
4: }
```

Accessing or changing the current stream position involves simply accessing or changing the *fPosition* field. The implementation of **SetPosition** signals an error if the new position is smaller than zero or larger than the current stream size. This is shown in Listing 22-6.

Listing 22-6. GetPosition

```
1: pascal long THandleStream::GetPosition() const
2: {
3:    return fPosition;
4: }
5:
6: pascal void THandleStream::SetPosition(long newPosition)
7: {
```

```
 8:    OSErr err;
 9:
10:    if (newPosition < 0)
11:        FailOSErr(posErr);
12:
13:    else if (newPosition > fSize) {          /* End of stream */
14:        newPosition = fSize;                 /* Position to end */
15:        err = eofErr;
16:    }
17:    else
18:        err = noErr;
19:
20:    fPosition = newPosition;
21:    FailOSErr(err);
22: }
```

Similarly, the **GetSize** and **SetSize** methods simply return or set the
*fSize* field. As with **SetPosition**, **SetSize** does consistency checking. It
also will adjust the *fPosition* field if the size of the stream is made
smaller than the current position. (See Listing 22-7.)

Listing 22-7. GetSize and SetSize

```
 1: pascal long THandleStream::GetSize() const
 2: {
 3:   return fSize;
 4: }
 5:
 6: pascal void THandleStream::SetSize(long newSize)
 7: {
 8:   SetHandleSize(fHandle, newSize);
 9:   FailMemError();
10:
11:   if (newSize < fPosition)              /* Adjust the position */
12:        fPosition = newSize;
13: }
```

The FailMemError function used on line 9 is a MacApp routine that
checks to see if there is a Memory Manager error, such as we would
have if there was not enough memory for proper execution of SetHan-
dleSize on line 8.

▶ TCountingStream

There is one other subclass of **TStream** that will be very useful in MacApp applications. That is **TCountingStream**. The purpose of **TCountingStream** is to accumulate the number of bytes written to it. This is useful in MacApp because the **TDocument** class requires that you override the **DoNeedDiskSpace** method and tell MacApp how much disk space your document needs.

Rather than trying to estimate this value or write extra code to compute it, you can use the same code that saves the document. In your **DoNeedDiskSpace** method, you create an instance of **TCounting-Stream**. You then pass this stream to your standard document-saving code. **TCountingStream** keeps track of the number of bytes that would be written into the file, but performs no actual file output. When your document-saving code finishes execution, you can call the **TCounting-Stream::GetSize** method to find out how many bytes your document needs. **TCountingStream** requires two variables to hold its current size (*fSize*) and position (*fPosition*). It needs to remember its position because it implements a random-access stream. Listing 22-8 shows the **TCountingStream::WriteBytes** method.

Listing 22-8. TCountingStream

```
 1: pascal void TCountingStream::WriteBytes(const void* p,
       long count)
 2: {
 3:   if (count < 0)
 4:       FailOSErr(paramErr);                  /* Invalid count */
 5:
 6:   fPosition = fPosition + count;            /* Advance position */
 7:
 8:   if (fPosition > fSize)                     /* Expand the size */
 9:       fSize = fPosition;
10: }
```

Notice that **WriteBytes** keeps track of the current stream position and only increases the size when the client program writes past the end of the stream (lines 8 and 9).

Also, **TCountingStream** cannot be used for reading, since it contains no data to read. This restriction means that clients can't use a document-saving algorithm that requires access to bytes that have already been written to the disk. For example, they could not use an algorithm that writes a document header and later reads that same header.

To warn programmers who might attempt to read from a **TCountingStream**, we override TStream::ReadBytes and make a call to the MacApp delbugging routine **ProgramBreak**. If **ProgramBreak** is called, MacApp will display a message in its debugging window and stop in the debugger. The client programmer can immediately see the problem and correct it.

# ▶ Object I/O

When we designed **TStream**, we did not implement a method for reading and writing objects. Object I/O is more difficult to implement, for two reasons. First, consider how you would write an object to a stream. One possibility is to write all of the object's instance variables. The problem with this approach is that objects usually contain references to other objects; in MacApp programs, these references are normally implemented as handles, which are pointers within the application's heap. In general, those same pointers won't be valid when read back from the stream, especially if different programs read and write the data. Even if there aren't any pointers, writing out the entire data block may not be the best way to save an object to a stream. Ideally, we should call a method of that object and let the object write itself to the stream.

Second, consider reading an object from a stream. If we call a method to write an object to the stream, then we should call another method to read the object back into memory. The problem is that making a method call requires an object, so we have to create an uninitialized object first. How will the reading method know what kind of object is in the stream? It may know that the object is a view, for example, but it could be any subclass of **TView**. The reading method must be able to create an object of the correct class, which means the class name or ID must be stored in the stream. If we tag each object with its class, then we can read the class information first, create an object of the specified class, and then call a method to have the object read the rest of itself from the stream.

The second problem is relatively easy to solve, because MacApp provides procedures and methods to get information about an object. First, however, we need to discuss in more detail how objects are implemented.

## ▶ How Pascal Objects Are Implemented

From the point of view of the Macintosh, an object is just a block of data. The key difference between an object and an ordinary block of data is that the object contains information identifying its class. Each object contains a class ID; in MacApp, there is a method **TObject::GetClass**, which returns the object's class ID. (There are other methods that return additional information about the object, such as its superclass and the size of an instance.)

A class ID is valid only for one version of the program. If you rebuild your program, it is possible that the ID for a particular class will be different. If you use the same class in another program, it is very likely that its ID will be different. Using the class ID as an object's tag, then, limits the programs that are able to read those objects.

Fortunately, there is a more universal representation for a class — its name. MacApp also implements a method **TObject::GetClassName**, which returns the object's class name as a string. The name of a class never changes, even if you rebuild your application or use the class in another program. MacApp also provides a global function, NewObject-ByClassName, that creates an object given the name of the class.

**By the Way ▶**

The preceding discussion applies only to classes descended from MacApp's TObject class. General C++ classes (that is, any class not descended from TObject) don't provide methods such as GetClass-Name, which means they can't be written into streams. In our MacApp sample programs, we use classes that are descended from MacApp's TObject class, which makes them compatible with Object Pascal. This allows us to mix Object Pascal and C++ classes freely.

A main drawback of working toward Object Pascal compatibility, however, is that you cannot use some features of C++. Features like multiple inheritance that aren't supported by Object Pascal must be avoided. It is possible, however, to define "native" C++ classes that don't descend from TObject but which provide access to the complete language. You can use both kinds of classes in the same program, but they can't inherit from one another.

## ▶ First Attempt at Object I/O

With this approach, which we will refine in subsequent sections, we can implement **TStream::ReadObject** and **TStream::WriteObject** as shown in Listing 22-9.

Listing 22-9.  TStream.ReadObject and TStream.WriteObject

```
 1: pascal TObject* TStream::ReadObject()
 2: {
 3:   MAName className;
 4:   this -> ReadString(&className, sizeof(MAName));
 5:   TObject* data = NewObjectByClassName(className);
 6:   FailNIL(data);                      /* Fail if out of memory. */
 7:
 8:   return data;
 9: }
10:
11: PROCEDURE TStream.WriteObject(const TObject* data);
12: {
13:   MAName className;
14:   data -> GetClassName(className);
15:   this -> WriteString(&className);
16: }
```

(The type MAName in line 3 is used in MacApp to represent a string that contains a class name.)

Note that these methods are only the first steps in reading or writing an object. **ReadObject** only creates an uninitialized object of the correct class (line 5) and **WriteObject** just writes the name of the class (line 15). The code that calls these methods, must then read or write the specific data of the object, usually by calling one of the object's methods.

This approach to object I/O makes inefficient use of space, since we write out the class name with every object. If you had a hundred objects of class **TRectangle**, the class names alone would require 1,000 bytes. The first enhancement we will make is to reduce the space required to store objects in a stream.

## ▶ First Improvement: Efficient Memory Use

The way we will do this is by tagging only the first object of a given class with its name. Subsequent objects of the same class will be tagged with their class IDs, which are much shorter than the class name. To solve the problem of class IDs changing, which we mentioned above, we will also map the class IDs stored in the stream to the corresponding class IDs used in the program. The stream object will build the mapping table incrementally, as it reads or writes objects. The new implementation of **ReadObject** is shown in Listing 22-10.

Listing 22-10. TStream.ReadObject enhanced

```
 1: pascal TObject* TStream::ReadObject()
 2: {
 3:    TObject* data;                        /* return result */
 4:    ObjClassID currentID;                 /* Class ID in program */
 5:
 6:    ObjClassID streamID;                  /* Class ID in stream  */
 7:    this -> ReadBytes(&streamID, sizeof(ObjClassID));
 8:
 9:    MAName className;
10:    this -> ReadString(&className, sizeof(MAName));
11:
12:    if (Length(className) == 0)           /* Lookup the currentID */
13:        currentID = this -> LookupClassID(streamID)
14:
15:    else {                    /* Get ID from name and register */
16:        currentID = GetClassIDFromName(className);
17:        this -> RegisterClassID(streamID, currentID);
18:    }
19:
20:    if (currentID == kNilClass)           /* Don't know the class */
21:        return NULL;
22:
23:    else {                                /* Create the object */
24:        data = NewObjectByClassID(currentID);
25:        FailNIL(data);        /* Fail if we run out of memory */
26:        return data;
27:    }
28: }
```

You will notice that this method deals with two different class IDs. The *streamID* variable contains the class ID found in the stream, which is the ID of the class when the object was written. This may be different from the currentID, which is the ID of the same class in the current program. The link between these two IDs is their common class name. The calls **LookupClassID** and **RegisterClassID** are new methods in **TStream**. The first searches a table for the given stream class ID and returns the corresponding current class ID. **RegisterClassID** adds a new entry to the table, given the stream and current IDs.

The **ReadObject** method reads both a class ID and a class name from the stream (lines 7 and 10). The class name will be empty if this is not the first object of the given class, in which case, **ReadObject** calls **LookupClassID** to find the current ID of the class (line 13). If the class name is present, then **ReadObject** calls the MacApp routine GetClassID-

FromName (line 16) to get the corresponding class ID. It also registers the mapping from the stream ID to the current class ID (line 17), in case there is another object of the same class in the stream.

At this point, **ReadObject** has the current class ID of the object it needs to create. If the ID is kNilClass, then this program doesn't have the class linked into it, and we can't create the object. In that case we return NULL (line 21). (If the class isn't linked into the program, then there aren't any methods for manipulating the object. In particular, we won't be able to call the method that reads the rest of the object from the stream.) Otherwise, we call the MacApp routine NewObjectByClassID (line 24) to create the object and signal failure (line 25) if we run out of memory while doing so. Unlike the first version of **ReadObject**, this version can detect the difference between running out of memory and trying to read a class that the program can't understand. (The first version would signal a failure in both cases.)

The corresponding implementation of **WriteObject** is shown in Listing 22-11.

### Listing 22-11. WriteObject enhanced

```
 1: pascal void TStream::WriteObject(const TObject* data);
 2: {
 3:   MAName className;
 4:
 5:   ObjClassID streamID;
 6:   if (data != NULL)
 7:       streamID = data -> GetClass();
 8:   else
 9:       streamID = kNilClass;
10:                                   /* Write the class ID */
11:   this -> WriteBytes(&streamID, sizeof(ObjClassID));
12:
13:   if ( (data != NULL) &&
14:       (this -> LookupClassID(streamID) == kNilClass))
15:
16:   {                  /* This is the first object of the class. */
17:       data -> GetClassName(className);
18:
19:       this -> RegisterClassID(streamID, streamID);
20:           /* Register the ID, to avoid writing the class name
21:              the next time.  The second parameter can be
22:              anything except kNilClass. */
23:   }
```

```
24:  else
25:      *className = '\0';      /* Assign an empty Pascal string */
26:
27:  this -> WriteString(&className);
28: }
```

**WriteObject** first writes out the object's class ID (line 11). Then it checks whether an object of this class has been written out already (line 14). If not, it gets the name of the class (line 17), which it writes out on line 27, and registers the class ID (line 19). Otherwise, it writes an empty string (lines 25 and 27). In ReadObject, the empty class name is a signal to look up the class ID (see line 13 of Listing 22-10). Note that when registering the class ID it doesn't matter what we use for the second parameter.

## ▶ Final Improvement: Error Recovery

There is one last enhancement to these methods. As we mentioned above, the second version of **ReadObject** will return a NULL object if the program can't understand a particular class. For example, suppose the stream contains a series of shape objects (TRectangle, TOval, TPolygon), but the current program only implements TRectangle and TOval. If the program encounters a TPolygon object, **ReadObject** will return NULL instead of an object.

The question is what the program will do next. Since the program doesn't understand anything about polygons, it can't interpret the polygon data in the stream. Therefore, it isn't capable of recovering and skipping over the polygon data. We need to make it possible for a program to read objects from a stream and simply skip any it doesn't understand. To do this, however, we need to add the size to each object in the stream. **ReadObject** can use the size to skip over the object if it doesn't understand the particular type of object.

Since **TStream::WriteObject** doesn't know how big the object will be when written into the stream, it can't write the size at the same time as it writes the rest of the data. It can only leave a space for the size, which will be filled in later. The code that writes the object itself will then have to call a method of **TStream** to fill in the size, after the entire object is written out. The final implementation of object I/O is shown in Listing 22-12.

## Listing 22-12. Final version of TStream::ReadObject

```
 1: pascal TObject* TStream::ReadObject(Boolean& known)
 2: {
 3:    ObjClassID currentID;        /* Class ID in program. */
 4:    ObjClassID streamID;         /* Class ID in stream. */
 5:    TObject* data;              /* result */
 6:                                         /* Read class ID */
 7:    this -> ReadBytes(&streamID, sizeof(ObjClassID));
 8:
 9:        /* Read object size and remember the current position. */
10:    long sizePosition = this -> GetPosition();
11:    long objectSize = this -> ReadLong();
12:
13:    MAName className;                        /* Read its name. */
14:    this -> ReadString(className, sizeof(MAName));
15:
16:    if (Length(className) == 0)        /* Already seen this class,
17:                                          lookup the currentID. */
18:       currentID = this -> LookupClassID(streamID);
19:
20:    else {            /* Get ID from name and register the IDs */
21:       currentID = GetClassIDFromName(className);
22:       this -> RegisterClassID(streamID, currentID);
23:    }
24:
25:    if (currentID == kNilClass) {
26:       data = NULL;
27:              /* if (streamID == kNilClass) then object is NULL,
28:                  which is a known object, otherwise the class
29:                                      isn't available. */
30:       known = (streamID == kNilClass);
31:
32:                              /* Skip over the object's data. */
33:       this -> SetPosition(sizePosition + objectSize);
34:    }
35:
36:    else {                              /* Create the object. */
37:       data = NewObjectByClassId(currentID);
38:       FailNIL(data);
39:       known = TRUE;
40:    }
41:
42:    return data;
43: }
44:
45: pascal void TStream::WriteObject(const TObject* data,
46:                                          long& sizePosition)
47: {
```

```
48:    ObjClassID streamID;
49:    MAName className;
50:
51:    if (data != NULL)
52:        streamID = data -> GetClass();
53:    else
54:        streamID = kNilClass;
55:                                        /* Write the class ID. */
56:    this -> WriteBytes(&streamID, sizeof(ObjClassID));
57:
58:    sizePosition = this -> GetPosition(); /* Remember position */
59:
60:    this -> WriteLong(LONG_MAX);          /* Write a dummy size */
61:
62:    if ((data != NULL) &&
63:            (this -> LookupClassID(streamID) == kNilClass)) {
64:
65:    /* Got an object to write, and it is the first of its class */
66:        data -> GetClassName(className);
67:
68:        this -> RegisterClassID(streamID, streamID);
69:        /* Register ID, so we don't write the class name again */
70:    }
71:    else
72:        *className = '\0';
73:
74:    this -> WriteString(className);        /* Write class name */
75: }
76:
77: pascal void TStream::WriteObjectSize(long sizePosition)
78: {
79:    long currentPosition = GetPosition();
80:    this -> SetPosition(sizePosition);
81:
82:    this -> WriteLong(currentPosition - sizePosition);
83:
84:    this -> SetPosition(currentPosition);
85: }
```

This version of **ReadObject** reads the size of the object (line 11) after reading its class ID. It also remembers the position of the object size within the stream (line 10). The object size is used on line 33 to skip the rest of the object's data, if **ReadObject** does not understand the object's class ID. **ReadObject** returns NULL in two cases: when the object's class is unknown or when the value is NULL. The caller of **ReadObject** can distinguish these cases by examining the Boolean parameter *known*. If the object's class is unknown this variable will be set to false (line 30).

The parameter *known* is a reference to a Boolean variable. Using a reference parameter allows **ReadObject** to modify the variable passed by the caller. It is similar to a pointer, except that the caller treats it as a normal parameter.

The corresponding version of **WriteObject** reserves space in the stream for the object's size by writing LONG_MAX as the object's size (line 60). We chose this value as a precaution; if **ReadObject** uses this value as the size of the object, it will skip to the end of the stream. We cannot calculate the actual size of the object until the data specific to the object are written into the stream. **WriteObject** does return the stream position of the object's size (in the variable sizePosition), which is used in the **WriteObjectSize** method (line 77). **WriteObject** also handles the case where the object being written is NULL. In that situation, it writes kNilClass as the object's ID (line 54) and the empty string as its class name. Figure 22-2 depicts five objects written into a stream (two rectangles, a polygon, an oval, and another rectangle).

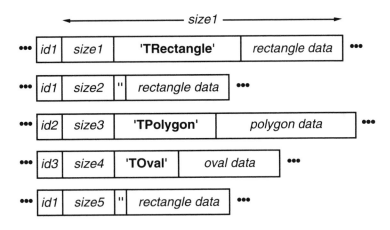

Figure 22-2. Format of objects in a stream

You can see that the size of the object is written to the stream immediately after the class ID, before the class name. (Note that in the diagram, we are assuming that the size of each object can be different. Usually, however, all the objects of a given class will have the same size.) This size is defined to be the total size of the object (in bytes), including the size field itself but not the class ID. If **ReadObject** can't create the object because its class is unknown, it skips over the object by calling **SetPosition**. For example, if TPolygon is unknown, **ReadObject** will skip over the polygon data field and continue by reading the oval next.

To write an object to a stream, a program must follow these steps:

1. Call TStream.WriteObject to write out the object's class information and the dummy size. Save the value returned in the sizePosition parameter.
2. If the object is not NULL, call a method of the object to write the specific object data to the stream.
3. Call **TStream::WriteObjectSize** to fill in the correct object size.

To read an object from a stream, a program first calls **TStream:: ReadObject** to create an uninitialized object of the proper class. If the resulting object is not NULL, the program then calls a method of the object to initialize itself based on the data in the stream. If **ReadObject** returns NULL, then either the class of the object is unknown or the object itself is NULL. (In the former case, **ReadObject** will skip the private data of the object.)

## ▶ The TStreamObject class

The processes of reading and writing an object involve calling methods of the object to read and write its private data. We can simplify these processes by defining a class called **TStreamObject**. **TStreamObject** is an abstract subclass of **TObject** that defines two new methods: **ReadFrom** and **WriteTo**. We can add methods to **TStream** that deal specifically with instances of **TStreamObject**. (See Listing 22-13.)

Listing 22-13. TStreamObject methods

```
 1: pascal TStreamObject* TStream::ReadStreamObject(Boolean&
    known)
 2: {
 3:                            /* Create an uninitialized object. */
 4:    TStreamObject* newObject =
 5:                  (TStreamObject*)(this -> ReadObject(known));
 6:
 7:    if (newObject != NULL)                /* Initialize object */
 8:        newObject -> ReadFrom(this);
 9:
10:    return newObject;
```

```
11: }
12:
13: pascal void TStream::WriteStreamObject(const TStreamObject*
    data)
14: {
15:   long sizePosition;
16:                                /* Write the object header. */
17:   this -> WriteObject(data, sizePosition);
18:
19:   if (data != NULL)            /* Write the private data. */
20:       data -> WriteTo(this);
21:
22:   this -> WriteObjectSize(sizePosition);  /* Write its size. */
23: }
```

You can see that **ReadStreamObject** and **WriteStreamObject** follow the steps for reading and writing an object that we described above. But since they deal with instances of **TStreamObject**, they can call **ReadFrom** and **WriteTo** to process the object's private data. If you define a class as a subclass of **TStreamObject** (instead of **TObject**), you will reduce the process of reading or writing instances of that class to one step: a call to **ReadStreamObject** or **WriteStreamObject**. Of course the classes defined in MacApp still inherit from **TObject**. If you define a subclass of a MacApp class, or any other class descended from **TObject**, then you cannot use the **ReadStreamObject** or **WriteStreamObject** methods. In those cases, you will have to use the multistep processes that work with any kind of object.

## ▶ Implementation Issues

There are four implementation issues that we will mention here but not describe in great detail. (We'll leave their implementation as an exercise for you.)

### ▶ TFileStream Performance

The first is a performance issue involving **TFileStream**. **TFileStream**, as we implemented it, makes one call to the Macintosh File Manager each time the program calls **ReadBytes** or **WriteBytes**. **ReadBytes** and **WriteBytes**, in turn, are called (at least once) by each higher level I/O method. You may find that the overhead of making one File Manager call each time is significant. For example, opening and saving a document may be unacceptably slow. The solution is to add an additional memory buffer and only call the FileManager when that buffer needs to be read or written. One way to do this is to change the implementation of **TFileStream**. A better way is to make a new subclass of **TFileStream**, called **TBufferedFileStream**.

Rather than trying to implement a memory buffer from scratch, **TBufferedFileStream** can simply use an instance of **THandleStream** to manage the buffer. **TBufferedFileStream** would call methods of **THandleStream** to transfer data into or out of the buffer. In **TBufferedStream::WriteBytes**, if the size of the buffer reaches a certain point, the methods call inherited **WriteBytes** to transfer the data from the buffer to the disk file, and then they call **THandleStream::SetPosition** to reset the current position within the buffer. When the buffered stream was freed, it would also have to flush the remaining buffer to disk.

To implement a buffered read operation, we would read as many bytes as possible from the buffer (using **THandleStream** methods). If we needed to read additional bytes, we would refill the buffer with a call to inherited **ReadBytes**, which in turn would call the File Manager. In addition, **TBufferedFileStream** would have to override **GetPosition**, **SetPosition**, **GetSize**, and **SetSize**. These methods would have to take into account the fact that part of the stream data is stored in the file and part in the buffer.

## ▶ Improving Use with DoNeedDiskSpace

The second implementation issue is also related to performance. Implementing **TCountingStream** makes it easier for us to implement the **DoNeedDiskSpace** method, since the same code that writes the document to the file is used to compute the needed disk space. The problem is that this approach requires us to make two passes through the document's data structures: once with an instance of **TCountingStream** and once with an instance of **TFileStream**, which isn't very efficient.

One solution is to use an instance of **THandleStream** for **DoNeedDiskSpace**. After **DoNeedDiskSpace** makes its pass through the document, it will not only know the amount of disk space needed, but it will also have collected the bytes that need to be written in a handle. The **DoWrite** method can then write out the document in a single write call.

Clearly, the disadvantage of this approach is that you need memory space to store the entire document in a handle. If your application can write very large documents, this may not be a viable option. But if the size of your documents on disk is generally small, then this approach could improve performance. A compromise approach would be to accumulate data in a handle until some limit is reached. If the entire document can fit in the handle, then the document's **DoWrite** method simply writes the data from the handle to the file. Otherwise, **DoWrite** makes a second pass through the data structures.

One way to implement this is to define a subclass of **TCounting-Stream** and add an instance of **THandleStream** as a field. All the bytes written to the stream would be saved in the handle by calling **THandleStream::WriteBytes**. Rather than imposing an arbitrary maximum on the handle size, you could check the amount of space left in the heap. If that space becomes too small, then the handle stream would be freed. If the handle stream is still allocated at the end of **DoNeedDiskSpace**, then **DoWrite** can write the contents of the handle.

## ▶ Object Conversions

The third issue involves converting objects when they are read in. For example, in Chapter 23 we will define the class **TRectangle** as part of the graphics building block. Suppose you create the class **TShadowedRectangle**, which inherits from **TRectangle**, and then you use **TShadowedRectangle** in a program. If another program tried to read one of your documents, it would skip over the instances of **TShadowedRectangle**.

It would be more desirable, however, if the other program converted all instances of **TShadowedRectangle** into instances of **TRectangle** and ignored the extra information specific to the former class. To do this, **TStream** would have to be enhanced to include information about the class hierarchy in the stream. When the stream failed to find the **TShadowedRectangle** class, it would test whether the superclass (**TRectangle**) was known. In this case, the test would succeed and the stream could create an instance of **TRectangle**. After the new rectangle object read its private data, the stream would have to skip any private data specific to **TShadowedRectangle**. This is easily done, since the size of each object is written to the stream.

You would have to define the extent to which the stream can convert objects. For example, the class **TObject** is available in every program; therefore, any object in the stream can be converted to an instance of **TObject**. This conversion doesn't make sense, however, since **TObject** is an abstract class.

## ▶ Handling Shared References

The final design issue concerns shared references. Earlier, we mentioned that one reason for not writing out the instance variables "as is" is that they are likely to contain references to other objects. We never addressed this issue directly but said that the object is responsible for reading and writing itself to disk. So how would an object read and write itself if it contains references to other objects?

If the referenced object was a subclass of **TStreamObject**, it would call **ReadStreamObject** and **WriteStreamObject**. Otherwise, it would follow the multistep processes we described above. The problem occurs when two objects each contain references to a third object, as shown in Figure 22-3.

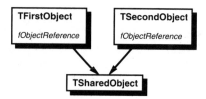

Figure 22-3. Shared references

Both of the first two objects would write the shared object to the stream. The stream would contain two copies of the shared object. If you then read the objects from the same stream, you would read the first object, and it would read the shared object. Then you would read the second object, and it would also read the shared object. The resulting structure is shown in Figure 22-4.

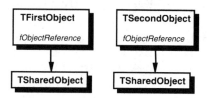

Figure 22-4. Lost sharing

In this case, the sharing between the objects has been lost; the problem is that the sharing was not represented in the stream. The solution to this problem is conceptually simple, although its implementation is not.

The stream keeps track of all the objects that have been written to it. The first time a particular object is written, the stream assigns it a number and writes the number as part of the data describing the object. If the same object is written a second time, only the number is written, along with an indication that the object was shared.

When reading from the stream, the reverse procedure is followed. The first time the object is read, the stream allocates the object and saves the object's number in a table. The next time the same object is read, the stream notices that it is shared. Instead of allocating a new instance, it returns a reference to the existing object. (It is important to note that a shared object is only initialized the first time it is read from the stream. In the current implementation of **TStream**, **ReadObject** would have to return a Boolean value to indicate if the object needs to be initialized or not. This could be handled automatically for objects descended from **TStreamObject**.)

## ▶ Summary

In this chapter, we have looked closely at how to use streams in MacApp to perform general-purpose I/O. After examining the basic concept of a stream, we described how we would implement a **TStream** class to handle I/O for our **ExampleDraw** application.

We then designed the class and its subclasses **TFileStream** and **THandleStream**. Then we turned our attention to the special problems involved in storing and retrieving objects rather than text or other data structures.

Finally, we looked at four design issues that could serve as points at which you might wish to improve our design of the **TStream** class and its methods.

In Chapter 23, we will describe the architecture of the graphics building block component of our sample application as we near its completion.

# 23 ▶ Graphics Building Block Architecture

This chapter discusses the design and implementation of a reusable set of classes that can create and manipulate graphic objects. It begins by discussing the problems caused by the lack of standardized code for creating and manipulating graphic objects in the Macintosh and MacApp. Then it describes the anatomy of shapes in general.

With this background, the chapter walks through the process of designing and creating the **TShape** class and its subclasses. The chapter closes with a discussion of how to implement a list of graphic shapes, and how a client might make use of the **TShape** class.

## ▶ The Problem

Graphics are an important part of most Macintosh applications. Many programs provide features that create and manipulate a collection of shapes. These include applications whose primary function is to create drawings, as well as applications with other primary functions, to which graphics are secondary. For example, many presentation graphics and page layout programs provide simple drawing capabilities. Unfortunately, there isn't any standard code in either the Macintosh Toolbox or MacApp to implement structured graphics. The result is that there are subtle differences between applications in how the user manipulates shapes.

One solution to this problem, for MacApp applications, is to implement a standard graphics building block that can be used in any application that manipulates shapes. The graphics building block would define the user interface for manipulating shapes once and for all, resulting in more consistency among these applications and less programmer effort to create them.

The graphics building block should be usable in a variety of applications. This requires that it handle different kinds of shapes. It also requires that the building block provide hooks for customizing and extending the way shapes are manipulated. The approach we will take is to implement the building block as a library of object classes that programmers can subclass as needed. (This parallels MacApp's approach to writing Macintosh applications.)

As we present the design, we will describe the various alternative ways it could be approached. Inevitably, when you start designing your own MacApp programs, you will face some of the same design alternatives. We hope we will give you a feeling for dealing with the tradeoffs involved with each choice to help make your decisions easier.

## ▶ The Anatomy of a Shape

An important goal of the graphics building block is that it supports many kinds of shapes. It should be able to handle simple shapes, such as lines and rectangles, as well as more complicated shapes, such as polygons or the class description diagrams we have used in this book. To accomplish this goal, we need to think about the abstract concept of a shape and figure out what characteristics objects such as lines, rectangles, and class diagrams have in common.

First, each kind of shape has a geometric description. For example, QuickDraw defines a line with two Point structures, a rectangle or oval with a Rect structure, and a polygon with a PolyHandle structure. Although the geometric description of these shapes varies, we can compute the rectangular bounding box of the shape, which can prove useful for some operations.

Second, shapes are displayed on the screen and printed. When drawn, a shape has two visual components: an interior and a frame of a certain thickness. Each of these components is drawn in a certain pattern or color or is transparent. In addition, when a shape is selected it is highlighted; this is usually done by drawing small rectangles on the edge of the shape.

There are many possibilities for determining a shape's interior and frame styles. One reason for the multiplicity of choices is that Quick-Draw draws shapes in several ways. All Macintosh computers support black-and-white patterns. Color machines can also draw with colored versions of these patterns (substituting any two colors in place of black and white), as well as solid colors, and arbitrary pixel patterns.

Beyond these basic choices, at least three different user models can be implemented. One simple model is to have a fixed palette of black-and-white patterns and arbitrary foreground and background colors. One advantage to this approach is that we can show these displays effectively on black-and-white machines. The MacApp DrawShapes sample uses this approach.

Another model is to define a palette of patterns that the user can change, either by adding, removing, or editing a pattern. You also have a choice of what happens when the user edits a pattern — whether the shapes that were drawn with that pattern change or not. If they do change, then we have a kind of graphics style sheet. If they don't change, then the shapes need to have their own copy of the pattern.

A third model is one in which the user can select a color or gray value according to the percentages of its component colors. This might be percentages of red, green, and blue, or of cyan, magenta, yellow, and black. The former is used internally in Color QuickDraw, the latter is used in the publishing industry. This differs from the first two models, because there is a large (potentially infinite) number of styles.

In the graphics building block we will use the second alternative and give each shape its own copy of the patterns.

## ▶ The TShape Class

We need to implement the concept of a shape in the graphics building block. Our approach is to define an abstract class called **TShape**. (**TShape** inherits from **TStreamObject**, because in Chapter 25 we will implement methods to read and write shapes to a stream.) **TShape** will have instance variables and methods that correspond to the general characteristics we described above. We will also define concrete subclasses of **TShape** to implement specific kinds of shapes.

Once we have implemented **TShape**, we can implement the rest of the building block using its instance variables and methods. This makes the design of the **TShape** object crucial to the success of the graphics building block. We must anticipate what functions are needed in the building block and provide the appropriate methods in the **TShape** class.

As we mentioned, there are two aspects to a shape: its geometric definition and its visual attributes. The implementation of **TShape**, therefore, has instance variables and methods dealing with both of these. **TShape** won't include instance variables that define the shape's geometry, since there is not a single geometric definition that applies to all shapes. Instead, each concrete subclass of **TShape** will implement its own representation. We will, however, define methods to access and manipulate the representation.

One such method is **TShape::GetGeometricBounds**, which returns the smallest rectangle that completely encloses the shape (also known as its bounding box). Since **TShape** has no implementation for the shape's representation, this method must also be overridden in every subclass of **TShape**.

**By the Way ▶**

We could have made the bounding box a field of **TShape**, and caused **GetGeometricBounds** simply to return that instance variable. Some shapes — for example polygons and regions — contain their own bounding box which would have made the variable redundant. We would have to ensure that the bounding box instance variable was in sync with the polygon or region structure at all times.

At this point, we have to make a fundamental decision about whether to represent shapes using the 16-bit QuickDraw coordinates, or the 32-bit coordinates supported by MacApp. The advantage of using 32-bit coordinates is that we can use the graphics building block in extremely large views. (Note that each shape must be smaller than 32,767 pixels in size, since we still need to draw it with QuickDraw. Using 32-bit coordinates simply allows us to position the shape anywhere within a 32-bit view.) Using 32-bit coordinates requires more work, because you have to call MacApp methods to convert these coordinates to the 16-bit coordinates that QuickDraw can deal with. Also, 32-bit coordinates require twice as much space as 16-bit coordinates for storage. To keep things simple in this example, we will use 16-bit coordinates.

In addition to its geometric bounds, a shape also has a bounding rectangle when drawn on the screen. As we mentioned in Chapter 21, the drawing bounds are different from the geometric bounds. This is computed by the method **TShape::GetDrawingBounds** because we want the frame to be drawn centered on the shape's geometric bounds.

Fortunately, there is a simple conversion from the geometric to the drawing bounds; simply take the geometric bounds and expand them by half the frame thickness. You can verify this formula by noting that if the frame is centered on the geometric bounds, half of it lies inside and half outside the lines. Assuming that we define a method **TShape::GetFrameSize**, which returns the frame thickness, then we can implement **GetDrawingBounds** as shown in Listing 23-1.

Listing 23-1. GetDrawingBounds

```
1: pascal Rect TShape::GetDrawingBounds() const
2: {
3:   Rect r = this -> GetGeometricBounds();
4:   this -> Geometric2DrawingBounds(r, this -> GetFrameSize());
5:   return r;
6: }
```

This implementation assumes that **TShape** also has a method **Geometric2DrawingBounds** (line 4), which takes a rectangle and a point representing the frame size and expands the rectangle by half the size.

This is a typical example of the power of object programming. Even though we don't know how the shape is actually defined, we can still implement **GetDrawingBounds** in such a way that it applies to every kind of shape. We did this by noting that **GetDrawingBounds** needs two pieces of information — the geometric bounds and the frame size — and defining methods that return that information. **GetDrawingBounds** doesn't know, and doesn't care, how the specific shape object computes these values.

We already know that the **GetGeometricBounds** methods must be overridden in each subclass of **TShape**. What about the **GetFrameSize** method? Since the frame size is a characteristic of every shape, we will represent it with a field in the **TShape** class. The **TShape::GetFrameSize** method will simply return that field, and the companion method **TShape::SetFrameSize** will set the value of that field.

As you know, you can easily define any field of any object in C++ to be private. This prohibits direct access to such fields and enforces the strong object programming emphasis on encapsulation.

It is usually best to ignore performance issues when you are starting a design and to concentrate on the correct architecture instead. Once you have your program working correctly, then you can make performance measurements to determine whether these method calls are performance problems. In the graphics building block, we have defined methods to get and set fields of an object, so that clients need not access the fields directly. (In Chapter 25, we will change these methods so that they do more than just return the corresponding field. Because clients do not access the fields directly, this change will be very easy to make.)

▶  **Styles for Shapes**

Just as the frame size is part of every shape, so are the frame and interior styles. As we did with the frame size, we can implement these attributes with additional fields in **TShape**. But what should these fields contain? To answer this question, we need to consider the user model we want to implement. There are four issues to consider.

1. Does the program support more than one kind of pattern; that is, plain black-and-white patterns as well as full color patterns?

2. Is the set of patterns used in a document fixed or variable? If the user pastes a shape into a document, and that shape uses a special pattern, is the special pattern preserved? Can the user create additional shapes with that pattern?

3. How many different patterns does the program support? If the number is small (less than a hundred), then we would use a different implementation than if the number is large (say sixteen million). Does the program support every possible pattern?

4. Are the pattern data shared among all the shapes that use the pattern? Suppose the user edits a pattern; do we want all the shapes using that pattern to change?

These issues are not independent of one another. For example, if the pattern data are not shared among the shapes, then it really doesn't matter how many different patterns the program supports. If the program supports every possible pattern, then there is no issue when pasting a shape containing a custom pattern.

Since the graphics building block is intended to support a variety of applications, we want to make it as flexible as possible. Because of this goal, we will support any kind of pattern that QuickDraw supports. Doing this is not as difficult as it sounds, because we can use an object-oriented design.

There are two ways to use objects in our design. The first is to define an abstract **TQuickDrawPattern** class and concrete subclasses for each kind of pattern. (Like **TShape**, **TQuickDrawPattern** inherits from **TStreamObject**.) Then a shape object can contain references to two objects that define its interior and frame patterns. We can share pattern objects among the shapes, provided the total number of patterns is small; we can't create one object to represent each pattern if there are millions of possible patterns.

The second approach is to model the palette of patterns, rather than the individual patterns. We would refer to an individual pattern by an index into the palette. This approach automatically promotes sharing the pattern data among shapes. (Shapes using the same index share the same shape in the palette.) It can also handle a large number of patterns, since the individual patterns need not be stored separately. For example, a 3-byte index can be interpreted by the palette object as a 24-bit color value; the palette itself needs no data storage for each pattern.

Implementing a single palette object also makes it easier to read and write shapes to a stream. We can simply read and write the palette object, and then each shape can read and write the indices of the patterns it uses. If we try to implement sharing with individual pattern objects, we run into the problems we mentioned at the end of Chapter 22.

This gives three implementation alternatives, as shown in Table 23-1.

Table 23-1. Alternative implementations for patterns

1.  Individual pattern objects, with no sharing
    *Advantages:*       Easy to implement; easy to read and write
                        Can support more different pattern classes in one program
                        Can support large numbers of patterns
                        Easy to read and write patterns; each object writes itself
    *Disadvantage:*     Uses more storage than sharing

2.  Individual pattern object, with sharing
    *Advantages:*       Uses less memory, due to sharing
                        Can support more different pattern classes in one program
    *Disadvantages:*    Difficult to support large numbers of patterns
                        Tricky to read and write shared pattern objects

3.  Pattern palette object
    *Advantages:*       Uses less memory, due to sharing
                        Can support large numbers of patterns
                        Easy to read and write patterns (as indices)
    *Disadvantages:*    Difficult to support different kinds of patterns in one program
                        Need a reference to palette in each shape *or*
                        Need to use a global variable for the palette object
                        Must be shared between shapes

Since the purpose of this book is to explain MacApp and object-oriented design, we will choose the first alternative. The only real disadvantage of this approach is that it requires more storage than the others, which might be a problem if we wanted to deal with thousands of shapes. It has the advantage of being easy to implement in a clean object-oriented style.

The class **TQuickDrawPattern** needs a method to set up the current pen pattern in the current grafPort. Subclasses of **TQuickDrawPattern** will override this method and call the appropriate QuickDraw routine (PenPat for black-and-white patterns, PenPixPat for color patterns, and so forth).

## ▶ Drawing Shapes

The next step in designing **TShape** is implementing the methods that draw the shape in a MacApp view. The natural place to start is with a **Draw** method in **TShape**. Then each view's **Draw** method can sequence through a list of shapes and call each shape's **Draw** method. (Note that the **TShape::Draw** method is totally unrelated to MacApp's **TView::Draw** method, although both involve drawing.)

At first, you might think that each subclass of **TShape** would have to define its own **Draw** method. The process of drawing a shape, however, has several steps, each of which can be implemented by a method in **TShape**. We can implement **TShape::Draw** to call these other methods. First, you have to collect all the information needed to draw the shape: the drawing bounding box, the interior and frame patterns, and the frame size.

Once you have this information, you use it to draw the shape. First, draw the interior of the shape and then its frame, skipping either step if the corresponding pattern is transparent. Each drawing step involves setting up the QuickDraw pen state (that is, calling a method of **TQuickDrawPattern**) and then making the appropriate QuickDraw call.

Recall the design principle from Chapter 21 that says each method should have only one function. If we follow this principle, then we need the following distinct methods:

1. **TShape::Draw** — computes the bounds, patterns, and frame size and then passes them to DrawUsing.
2. **TShape::DrawUsing** — sets up the interior pattern in the current grafPort, and calls **DrawInterior**. It does the same thing for the frame, by calling **DrawFrame**.

3. **TShape::DrawInterior** — draws the interior using the current pen. It must be overridden by subclasses.

4. **TShape::DrawFrame** — draws the frame using the current pen. It must be overridden by subclasses.

This gives us three distinct levels of drawing methods: **TShape::Draw** draws the shape with its assigned styles. **TShape::DrawUsing** draws the shape with a certain set of attributes. **TShape::DrawInterior** and **TShape::DrawFrame** draw parts of the shape using the attributes of the current QuickDraw grafPort.

Because each drawing method in **TShape** has a specific function, programmers who subclass **TShape** have the advantage of knowing exactly which methods they need to override. Another advantage is that other parts of the program can call methods at any level. The methods themselves look like those in Listing 23-2.

Listing 23-2. TShape.Draw methods

```
 1: pascal void TShape::Draw() const
 2: {                                       /* Collect the attributes. */
 3:    Rect bounds = this -> GetDrawingBounds();
 4:    Point size = this -> GetFrameSize();
 5:    const TQuickDrawPattern* interiorPat =
 6:                            this -> GetInteriorPattern();
 7:    const TQuickDrawPattern* framePat = this ->GetFramePattern();
 8:
 9:    this -> DrawUsing(bounds, size, interiorPat, framePat);
10: }
11:
12: pascal void TShape::DrawUsing(const Rect& bounds, Point
    frameSize,
13:                   const TQuickDrawPattern* interiorPat,
14:                   const TQuickDrawPattern* framePat) const
15: {
16:    interiorPat -> SetPen();
17:    this -> DrawInterior(bounds);
18:
19:    framePat -> SetPen();
20:    PenSize(frameSize.h, frameSize.v);
21:    this -> DrawFrame(bounds);
22: }
```

Note that we were able to implement **Draw** and **DrawUsing** without knowing what kind of shape is being drawn. All the work is handled in the methods **DrawInterior** and **DrawFrame**. These methods are defined as pure virtual functions in the **TShape** class, which forces each subclass of **TShape** to override them.

We saw this technique in Chapter 22. It is particularly important to use this approach when creating a building block because it catches errors in the way clients use the building block and gives them compile-time warnings of potential problems.

**By the Way ▶**

Another useful technique is to perform consistency checking in the code itself. For example, you might check the parameters passed to a method to ensure they are within required limits. Such code only needs to appear in debugging versions of the code; as a result, there is no penalty in the final version either in terms of memory usage or in terms of performance.

Although the preceding sentence is true in theory, the presence of debugging code does change the program, which means it may not behave the same way when the debugging code is removed. For example, the debugging code increases the size of code segments, which may affect the program's memory requirements. In most cases, however, the differences do not affect how the program works.

Let's review the process we have gone through thus far in designing **TShape**. We first chose a particular action, in this case, drawing, and defined a method that carries out the action. Then we divided this action into two steps (drawing the interior, followed by the frame) and defined a method for each step (**DrawInterior** and **DrawFrame**). We further refined the process by introducing an intermediate method. As we continue with the design, you will see this refining process repeated again. (We should point out that the original design of **TShape** didn't include **DrawUsing**. It was added after we started implementing various features of the building block and example program. This shows that it isn't possible to anticipate all possible features right at the beginning; designs always evolve over time.)

# ▶ Concrete Shape Classes

We now have a basic design for the abstract class **TShape**, although we will be adding more to **TShape** later. Earlier, we defined an abstract class as one that defines the general behavior of its subclasses; a program never creates any instances of an abstract class. Now it is time to define several concrete subclasses of **TShape**. Programs do create instances of these classes. Each of these subclasses will have to define a representation for the shape geometry and override the methods in **TShape** that cannot be implemented (such as **GetGeometricBounds** and **DrawInterior**).

## ▶ TLine

The first subclass we will build is **TLine**. A line in QuickDraw is defined by its two endpoints, and we will use this as **TLine's** internal representation. Computing the geometric bounds of the line is simple; we can use the QuickDraw routine Pt2Rect. Since a line has no interior, the **DrawInterior** method for **TLine** is empty. We still need to have an implementation, because **DrawInterior** will still be called for line objects. The implementation does nothing.

The **DrawFrame** method of **TLine** will simply draw the line. **Draw-Frame** will ignore the rectangle that is passed as a parameter and use its point fields for drawing. We can't use those points directly, however, because we need to account for the QuickDraw drawing model. QuickDraw draws lines with a pen that hangs below and to the right of the path between the points. If we shift the entire line up and to the left by half the line thickness, then the line will be centered on the endpoints. **TLine::DrawFrame** does this.

## ▶ TRectangle and TOval

For this example, we will define two other subclasses of **TShape**: **TRectangle** and **TOval**. Rectangles and ovals in QuickDraw are very similar. Both are defined by a rectangle; about the only difference is the Quick-Draw call you use to draw them. We can take advantage of these similarities by defining another abstract class called **TAbstractRectangle**, which represents a shape that is defined by a QuickDraw rectangle. It has a single variable, *fBounds*, which is the rectangle. It overrides **Get-GeometricBounds** and returns a copy of that field.

We do the drawing in subclasses of **TAbstractRectangle**, namely **TRectangle** and **TOval**. These classes are very simple and only need to override the **DrawInterior** and **DrawFrame** methods to do the actual drawing. By adding the **TAbstractRectangle** class, we save the work of duplicating the same **GetGeometricBounds** method in **TRectangle** and **TOval**. This may not seem like much of a saving. But as we will see in Chapter 24, there are other similarities between rectangles and ovals (for example, the way they are highlighted when selected) that make **TAbstractRectangle** worthwhile. Also, it would be very simple to add other subclasses of **TAbstractRectangle**, such as **TRoundedCornerRectangle**.

| | |
|---|---|
| **By the Way** ▶ | Adding **TRoundedCornerRectangle** introduces a slight problem. To draw a rounded-corner rectangle you need to supply the corner radius. If you want to allow the user to modify the radius, you need to implement a method to set the radius. The problem with this is that the rest of the graphics building block deals exclusively with **TShape** objects. If you add the **SetRadius** method to **TRoundedCornerRectangle**, the graphics building block won't be able to call it. |

You would either have to distinguish rounded-corner rectangles from other shapes or define the **SetRadius** method in **TShape**. (That method wouldn't do anything, of course, but **TRoundedCornerRectangle** would override it.) It is probably better to choose the latter approach, because it is more object oriented. If you find later that another kind of shape requires a corner radius, the **SetRadius** method in **TShape** will be available. Object programming's advantages aren't always immediately apparent; further down the line you may appreciate having made the object oriented choice.

Figure 23-1 shows the class hierarchy for the shape classes we have defined so far.

## ▶ Other Subclasses of TShape

As an exercise, you might consider how you would implement other kinds of shape classes. An interesting possibility would be a class that defines a shadowed rectangle, like the one we used in the class diagrams throughout this book. Although it could be a subclass of **TShape**, it makes more sense for it to inherit from **TRectangle**. Alternatively, we might decide that shadowing is a general property of all shapes. In that case, we would modify **TShape** to support shadowing. One way to do this would be to add a third pattern object to represent the shadow pattern and a **DrawShadow** method. The rest of our design would be modified accordingly.

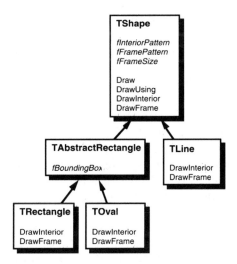

Figure 23-1. Shape class hierarchy

▶ ## TShapeList: A Collection of Shapes

You can use individual **TLine**, **TRectangle**, and **TOval** objects in a simple program. Most programs, however, deal with collections of shapes, rather than isolated shapes. In this section, we will describe the implementation of a **TShapeList** class that implements a collection of shapes and the code to manipulate them.

The first question you might ask is why define a new class at all? After all, MacApp contains a **TList** class, which implements a list of any kind of object. We could store the shapes in an instance of **TList** and write routines that operate on the elements of the list. By now you should recognize this as the old, procedural approach to writing a program, in which we define a data structure and the routines that operate on the data structure. Since we are convinced that an object-oriented approach is more flexible and easier to extend, we will reject the procedural approach.

So now we need to decide what the superclass of **TShapeList** should be. The obvious possibility is **TList**. A list of shapes seems to be a specialization of a list of any object. The problem is that if **TShapeList** is a subclass of **TList**, then we expect that a **TShapeList** object can be used in any situation that expects a **TList** object. This isn't true, however. A shape list is supposed to contain only **TShape** objects. Also, we don't want **TShapeList** to support all the methods that **TList** defines. For example, **TList** allows us to insert an element anywhere within the list; when we add a new shape to the list, we only want to add it to the end, so it will appear in front of the other shapes. (The shapes are drawn in the same order in which they appear in the list. This means the last shape in the list is the one that appears frontmost on the screen, since it is drawn over all the other shapes.)

For these reasons, we will make **TShapeList** a subclass of **TStream-Object** rather than of **TList**. **TShapeList** will contain an instance variable referring to a **TList** object. Another advantage of this approach is that we can change the internal implementation of **TShapeList** without affecting the class' clients. We could not do that if **TShapeList** was a subclass of **TList**.

**TShapeList** defines only those methods we want clients to use. These methods, in turn, call methods of the class **TList**. For example, Listing 23-3 shows the implementation of two **TShapeList** methods.

Listing 23-3. AddShape and EachShapeDo

```
1: pascal void TShapeList::AddShape(TShape* newShape)
2: {
3:   fList -> InsertLast(newShape);
4: }
5:
6: typedef pascal void (*EachProcPtr)(TObject*, void*);
7: typedef pascal void (*DoToShapeProc)(TShape*, void*);
8:
9: pascal void TShapeList::EachShapeDo(DoToShapeProc DoToShape,
10:                         void* DoToShape_StaticLink) const
11: {
12:   fList -> Each((EachProcPtr)DoToShape, DoToShape_StaticLink);
13: }
```

In Chapter 24, we will expand the implementation of **AddShape** to maintain a count of the number of selected shapes, and in Chapter 25, we will add filtering to the **EachShapeDo** method.

By the Way ▶

You might wonder why we don't make **TShapeList** a subclass of **TDocument** instead of **TStreamObject**. After all, **TDocument** is supposed to be where the data of the application are stored. The main reason not to do this is flexibility. It is possible that you would want to display a collection of shapes in a dialog box, which doesn't have its own document. Also, a client of the building block may be using a specific document class already and couldn't switch to using a special **TShapeDocument** class. Finally, **TShapeList** is intended to be a simple data structure and doesn't require the additional methods defined in **TDocument**.

It is sometimes difficult to decide which class to subclass. In this case, we had a choice of making **TShapeList** a subclass of **TList**, or including a **TList** field in **TShapeList**. This is the typical choice you will face: making a subclass of an existing class or using an instance of that class as a field. There is a strong temptation to take advantage of inheritance as much as possible, to maximize code reuse and minimize total code size. For example, if **TShapeList** was a subclass of **TList**, then there would be no need for the methods shown in Listing 23-3.

It is always better to develop the best architecture first, rather than trying to optimize your implementation. Your class hierarchy should model your problem domain, rather than provide a way to save lines of code. One test to apply is to ask whether the subclass and the superclass have a relationship *in your application*; if the answer is no, then they should not be related in your class hierarchy.

The **TShapeList** class models a specific concept in the graphics building block. Clients using **TShapeList** need not know nor care how the implementation works. **TShapeList** could even change its implementation dynamically, based on the number of shapes it contains. Such a change would be impossible if **TShapeList** descended from **TList**.

At this stage in our design, there isn't very much to implement in **TShapeList**. That is not necessarily bad; it is usually better to have several classes with small implementations than one large class with a hundred methods. (In fact, our original design of **TShapeList** was one of those monstrous classes. As the implementation evolved, we divided it into three simpler classes.) **TShapeList** will have the usual methods to add and remove shapes from the list, sequence through all the shapes, and so forth. In the next chapter, we will add the concept of *selection*, and **TShapeList** will be enhanced to track the current selection.

## ▶ Using the Building Block

In its current state, the graphics building block doesn't do very much. We can create instances of concrete shape objects and add them to an instance of **TShapeList**, and we can remove shapes from the list. Still, it is useful to consider how the building block would be used in a MacApp program.

Earlier in the book, you learned that most MacApp programs define at least one subclass of **TDocument** and that an instance of this class contains the data for the document. Similarly, most MacApp programs define at least one subclass of **TView**, an instance of which displays the data and handles user interactions such as mouse clicks. The graphics building block includes a subclass of **TDocument** called **TShapeDocument** and a subclass of **TView** called **TShapeView**. In Chapter 25, we will see how instances of **TShapeView** are used to implement Cut and Copy.

Most clients of the building block will be able to use these classes directly in their programs, or they will define subclasses of them. But we don't want to require clients to use these classes; they should be free to use other document or view classes, if they choose. In such cases, however, the programmers should not have to reimplement all the functionality of **TShapeDocument** and **TShapeView**. Instead, we will define separate helper classes that make it easy for any kind of document and view to use the graphics building block. Any document or view subclass can make a few simple calls to these classes in order to use the graphics building block. **TShapeDocument** and **TShapeView** will serve as examples of how to use the helper classes as well as actual classes that can be used in an application.

The **TShapeList** class that we described can serve as the document helper class. We need to define another class, called **TShapeView-Helper**, to serve as the view helper class. Listing 23-4 shows one method in the **TShapeViewHelper** class.

Listing 23-4. TShapeViewHelper.Draw

```
1: pascal void DrawAShape(TShape* aShape, void* area)
2: {
3:   Rect shapeRect = aShape -> GetDrawingBounds();
4:   if (SectRect(&shapeRect, (Rect*)area, &shapeRect))
5:       aShape -> Draw();
6: }
7:
8: pascal void TShapeViewHelper::Draw(Rect* area)
9: {
10:    fShapeList -> EachShapeDo(&DrawAShape, area);
11: }
```

**TShapeViewHelper::Draw** is called from a client view's **Draw** method. (To reinforce the connection, we give the method in **TShape-ViewHelper** the same name and parameter as the one in **TView**.) It sequences through all the shapes in the list and calls **DrawAShape** on each (line 10). **DrawAShape**, in turn, tests whether the shape intersects the specified area (line 4), and if so, calls the shape's **Draw** method.

Notice that **DrawAShape** needs to access the *area* parameter of **TShapeViewHelper::Draw.** If we were working in Object Pascal, we would use a nested procedure that could access *area* directly. C++ does not, however provide for nested procedures, so we need an alternative approach.

The parameter to **EachSampleDo** is declared as a procedure in Pascal. If we pass a nested procedure, however, Pascal passes an additional parameter. This hidden value is a pointer to the enclosing procedure's stack frame. The nested procedure uses the pointer to access the other procedure's variables.

In C++, we can still pass the link pointer to **EachShapeDo** since it doesn't care what the pointer is. It simply passes the pointer to the procedure parameter. In this case, we pass along to **EachShapeDo** a pointer to *area*, and **DrawAShape** uses the pointer to access *area*.

Note that area is declared as an untyped pointer (void*), which means we must type cast it to a Rect* before using it.

Using these helper classes, the runtime structure of objects is as shown in Figure 23-2.

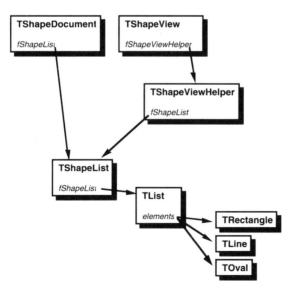

Figure 23-2. Graphics building block classes at runtime

## ▶ Summary

In this chapter, we have examined the design and implementation of the graphics building block and its architecture for our sample program. We have studied the anatomy of a shape object and then translated our findings into a design for the new class **TShape.** We discussed the relationship between styles (such as pattern or color) and objects to give you some insight into the trade-off decisions we made.

We implemented the **TShape** class and its several methods for storing and drawing the shapes. Along the way we saw how to create quite concrete classes from MacApp classes.

Finally, we discussed the use of a list to retain information about all of the shapes in our sample application's environment.

In Chapter 24, we will make our sample application more useful by adding selection and three mouse-driven commands.

(Note that we have not included complete program listings in this chapter. The full application, including source code, is available on the disk that accompanies this book or which may be purchased separately using the coupon in the back of the book.)

# 24 ▶ Three Mouse Commands

In Chapter 23 we laid the foundation of the graphics building block. In this chapter, we begin to build upon that foundation by implementing three mouse commands. The three kinds of commands are:

- creating or sketching a new shape
- selecting one or more shapes
- dragging the selected shapes

In each case, we want to implement the standard functionality that you would find in a Macintosh drawing program. For example, when you sketch a shape, holding down the Shift key should constrain rectangles to squares. Further, when you select shapes, the Shift key should add or remove shapes from the selection.

In addition, we need to develop a general framework for handling mouse actions in the building block. There are three kinds of command objects, and we need code that selects the correct command object in each circumstance. Most applications implement a palette of drawing tools. The current tool determines (in part) what happens when the user clicks the mouse.

As we design these commands, you will notice that we add fields and methods to the classes we implemented previously. Program designs always evolve as new features are added, and the graphics building block is no exception. Rather than simply present the final implementation, we want to give you a sense of how the design actually evolved so you will be able to see how object programming makes it easy to evolve programs.

## ▶ Creating a New Shape

The first command we will implement creates a new shape. This is an undoable command, which means we must define a subclass of **TCommand** and override the **DoIt, UndoIt,** and **RedoIt** methods. It is also a mouse command, which means we must override the **TrackMouse, TrackFeedback,** and **TrackConstrain** methods (also in **TCommand**).

## ▶ Tracking the Mouse

First, we will implement the mouse tracking portion of the command. It is possible that each kind of shape could require a separate subclass. Fortunately, however, most shapes are drawn by clicking the mouse at one corner and dragging to the opposite corner. This is true of the three kinds of shapes we implemented in Chapter 23, for example. Therefore, the same command class, **TShapeSketcher**, should be able to handle all of these shapes. (We'll come back to the question of other sketching commands later.) As users sketch the new shape, we want to give them feedback in the form of an outline of the new shape. We will use exclusive-or mode when drawing the outline so that it is easy to update the feedback.

Since **TShapeSketcher** is intended to be used with any kind of shape, it must contain a reference to the shape object it is sketching. As the user moves the mouse, **TShapeSketcher** will stretch the shape accordingly, and display the shape's outline as feedback. These two actions require two new methods in the **TShape** class: one to stretch a shape between two points and one to draw the appropriate feedback.

The method that stretches the shape is passed the position of the initial mouse click, called the *anchor point*, and the current mouse position. It must resize the shape to connect the points. We will call this method **TShape::Pt2Shape**, since it converts two points into the shape's bounds.

The second method is one that draws the feedback on the screen. We could avoid defining a new method by simply setting up the current QuickDraw port and calling **TShape::DrawFrame**. Although this would work, it would also prevent a particular shape class from implementing a custom form of feedback. Instead we will define a new method in **TShape** called **DrawFeedback**, shown in Listing 24-1.

Listing 24-1. DrawFeedBack

```
 1: pascal void TShape::DrawFeedback(Boolean /*turnItOn*/) const
 2: {                                    /* Collect the attributes. */
 3:     Rect bounds = this -> GetDrawingBounds();
 4:     Point size = this -> GetFrameSize();
 5:
 6:     if (size.h < 1) size.h = 1;      /* Frame size must be >= 1. */
 7:     if (size.v < 1) size.v = 1;
 8:
 9:           /* Draw the shape: transparent interior, XOR frame. */
10:     this -> DrawUsing(bounds, size,
11:                       gTransparentPattern, gFeedbackPattern);
12: }
```

The implementation of **DrawFeedback** is much like the implementation of **Draw**, in that both end up calling **DrawUsing** (lines 10 and 11). One difference is that **Draw** uses the interior and frame patterns stored in the shape object, while **DrawFeedback** uses two global pattern objects. The global variable *gTransparentPattern* refers to a pattern object that draws using QuickDraw's patOr mode with a white pen, which results in no change to the display on the screen. Similarly *gFeedbackPattern* refers to a pattern object that draws in exclusive-or mode with a black pen. These objects are instances of **TTransparentPattern** and **TFeedbackPattern**, respectively.

Another difference between **Draw** and **DrawFeedback** is that the latter forces the frame size to be 1 or greater (lines 6 and 7). This ensures that the user will get some feedback, even when drawing a shape that has no border. The end result is that **DrawFeedback** draws a shape with a transparent interior and some kind of frame, using exclusive-or mode. Note that we don't have to check the value of turnItOn in the **DrawFeedback** method. This is because we are using exclusive-or mode, in which the same drawing code that turns the feedback on also turns it off.

This gives us the methods we need to implement the tracking portion of **TShapeSketcher**. In MacApp, you implement a mouse-based action by overriding three methods of **TCommand**:

- **TrackMouse**
- **TrackFeedback**
- **TrackConstrain**

An instance of **TShapeSketcher** will contain a reference to the shape it is sketching in the variable *fNewShape*. Its implementation of **Track-Mouse** will call **Pt2Shape**, and its implementation of **TrackFeedback** will call **DrawFeedback**. Listing 24-2 shows the implementations of **TrackMouse** and **TrackFeedback**.

Listing 24-2. TrackMouse and TrackFeedback

```
 1: pascal TCommand* TShapeSketcher::TrackMouse(TrackPhase
    thePhase,
 2:               VPoint* anchorPoint, VPoint* /*previousPoint*/,
 3:               VPoint* nextPoint, Boolean mouseDidMove)
 4: {
 5:   if (thePhase == trackPress)
 6:       fAnchorPt = fView -> ViewToQDPt(anchorPoint);
 7:   Point nextPt = fView -> ViewToQDPt(nextPoint);
 8:
 9:   if (mouseDidMove)                     /* Stretch the shape */
10:       fNewShape -> Pt2Shape(fAnchorPt, nextPt);
11:
12:   if ( (thePhase == trackRelease) &&
13:        (EqualPt(fAnchorPt,  nextPt)))    /* Nothing sketched */
14:       return gNoChanges;
15:   else
16:       return this;                      /* Continue tracking */
17: }
18:
19:
20: pascal void TShapeSketcher::TrackFeedback(VPoint*/*anchorPt*/,
21:                   VPoint* /*nextPt*/,
22:                   Boolean turnItOn, Boolean mouseDidMove)
23: {
24:   if (mouseDidMove)
25:       fNewShape -> DrawFeedback(turnItOn);
26: }
```

The tracking methods use VPoints to indicate mouse positions. These are points that use 32-bit view coordinates. Since the graphics building block was designed for 16-bit (QuickDraw) coordinates, we have to convert the parameters by calling **TView.ViewToQDPt** (lines 6 and 7). Since the anchor point never changes, we perform this conversion once, saving the result in the command object (line 6). The methods also check that the mouse has actually moved before doing anything (lines 9 and 24). This is especially important in the **TrackFeedback** class, since it eliminates screen flashing when the user isn't moving the mouse.

Finally, on lines 12 and 13, **TrackMouse** tests whether the user released the mouse button without moving the mouse. In this case, it returns the pre-defined command object *gNoChanges* (line 14). This value tells MacApp that the command did not affect the document.

The other possible return value for **TrackMouse** is this (line 16). While MacApp is tracking the mouse, **TrackMouse** returns this to tell MacApp to continue tracking. When the user releases the button after moving the mouse, **TrackMouse** also returns this to indicate that the same command object should be used to carry out the command.

There is a third tracking method in **TCommand**, called **TrackConstrain**. The purpose of **TrackConstrain** is to adjust the actual mouse position before the other tracking methods see it. In effect, this constrains the mouse position (at least as far as the command object is concerned). We will override **TrackConstrain** in **TShapeSketcher**, to constrain the shape when the user holds down the Shift key. Rectangles and ovals, for example, should be constrained to have equal horizontal and vertical sizes. When drawing lines, however, the Shift key should constrain the line to horizontal, vertical, or 45 degrees. Since the type of constraint to apply varies with the shape class, we will add a new method to **TShape** called **ShiftConstrain**. Each subclass can override **ShiftConstrain** to provide its own constraint implementation.

The **TrackConstrain** method and an example of the **ShiftConstrain** method are shown in Listing 24-3.

Listing 24-3. TrackConstrain and one ShiftConstrain method

```
1: pascal void TShapeSketcher::TrackConstrain(VPoint*
   anchorPoint,
2:                                    VPoint* previousPoint,
3:                                    VPoint* nextPoint)
4: {
5:    Point anchorPt = fView -> ViewToQDPt(anchorPoint);
6:    Point prevPt = fView -> ViewToQDPt(previousPoint);
7:    Point nextPt = fView -> ViewToQDPt(nextPoint);
8:
9:    fNewShape -> ShiftConstrain(anchorPt, prevPt, nextPt);
10:
11:    fView -> QDToViewPt(nextPt, nextPoint);
12: }
13:
14: pascal void TAbstractRectangle::ShiftConstrain(Point anchorPt,
15:                              Point /*previousPt*/,
16:                              Point& nextPt) const
17: {
18:    Point delta = nextPt;       /* Compute the size */
19:    SubPt(anchorPt, &delta);
```

```
20:                                      /* Compute the maximum side */
21:    short maxDelta = (short)Max(abs(delta.h), abs(delta.v));
22:
23:        /* Adjust the deltas to be equal; retain the +/- sign. */
24:    delta.h = (delta.h < 0) ? -maxDelta : maxDelta;
25:    delta.v = (delta.v < 0) ? -maxDelta : maxDelta;
26:
27:    nextPt = anchorPt;            /* Compute the constrained point */
28:    AddPt(delta, &nextPt);
29: }
```

MacApp calls the **TrackConstrain** method only if the command object's *fConstrainsMouse* instance variable is set to true. The initialization method for **TShapeSketcher** sets the variable to true if the Shift key was pressed at the time of the mouse click.

Some programs allow the user to press (or release) the Shift key at any time during the sketching process. To implement that here, we would have to set *fConstrainsMouse* to true unconditionally and test the state of the Shift key in the **TrackConstrain** method.

### ▶ Performing the Command

Tracking the mouse is only part of the implementation of **TShape-Sketcher**. The other portion is adding the shape to the list of shapes and implementing Undo. In MacApp, this is done by overriding the **DoIt**, **UndoIt**, and **RedoIt** methods of **TCommand**. You will recall that each of these methods does two things: (1) modifies the data structures associated with the document and (2) invalidates the part of the view that needs to be redrawn.

In this case, modifying the data structures is as simple as calling the **AddShape** or **RemoveShape** method of **TShapeList**.

In **TShapeSketcher**, we want to invalidate the bounds of the new shape within a view. As before, we will define a new method in **TShape**, called **Invalidate**, for this purpose. **TShape::Invalidate** will call **GetDrawingBounds** to get the rectangle and **TView::InvalidRect** to invalidate the rectangle. We must now decide to which view to send the **InvalidRect** message. One solution would be to add an *fView* field to every shape object. Unfortunately, this would add extra storage to every shape. It would also make it difficult to display the same shapes in different views. Instead, we will pass the appropriate view as a parameter to **TShape::Invalidate**.

The implementations of **TShapeSketcher::DoIt** and **RedoIt** first call **TShapeList::AddShape** to add the new shape to the list and then **TShape::Invalidate** to invalidate the part of the view occupied by the shape. The **UndoIt** method calls **TShapeList::RemoveShape**, followed by **TShape::Invalidate**. This is shown in Listing 24-4.

Listing 24-4. TShapeSketcher.DoIt, UndoIt, and RedoIt

```
 1: pascal void TShapeSketcher::DoIt()
 2: {
 3:   fShapeList -> AddShape(fNewShape);
 4:   fShapeList -> SelectShape(fNewShape);
 5:   fNewShape -> Invalidate(fView);
 6: }
 7:
 8: pascal void TShapeSketcher::RedoIt()
 9: {
10:   fView -> Focus();        /* Make sure we're focused... */
11:   fShapeViewHelper -> Deselect();   /* ...before deselecting */
12:
13:   fShapeList -> AddShape(fNewShape);
14:   fShapeList -> SelectShape(fNewShape);
15:   fNewShape -> Invalidate(fView);
16: }
17:
18: pascal void TShapeSketcher::UndoIt()
19: {
20:   fView -> Focus();        /* Make sure we're focused... */
21:   fShapeViewHelper -> Deselect();   /* ...before deselecting */
22:
23:   fShapeList -> RemoveShape(fNewShape);
24:   fNewShape -> Invalidate(fView);
25: }
26:
27: pascal void TShapeSketcher::Commit()
28: {
29:   fNewShape = NULL; /* The shape was permanently added to the
30:                        list; set the variable to NULL so Free
31:                        won't free the new shape. */
32: }
33:
34: pascal void TShapeSketcher::Free() /* override */
35: {
36:   FreeIfObject(fNewShape);
37:   inherited::Free();
38: }
```

One tricky aspect of **TShapeSketcher** is managing the storage for the new shape. If the command is undone by the user, then the new shape must be freed along with the command object.

This is the function of the **Commit** and **Free** methods of Listing 24-4. The **Commit** method is called just before **Free**, but only if the command was done. In this case, the new shape has been added to the

shape list, and **Commit** sets its instance variable to NULL. The **Free** method frees the new shape if *fNewShape* is not NULL.

If the command is undone, **Commit** is not called and **Free** will free the new shape. Otherwise **Commit** sets *fNewShape* to NULL and the new shape won't be freed.

In general, it is a useful exercise to test your designs to see how well they can accommodate changes. This will help you determine if your design is general or not. In this case, a good question to ask is whether the architecture we have defined can support variations of the basic sketching operation.

One sketching variation that many programs implement allows the user to sketch shapes from the center to a corner, rather than from corner to corner. This could be done by modifying **TShapeSketcher. TrackMouse**. Instead of directly calling **Pt2Shape** with the anchor and current points, it would use the anchor point as the center, the current point as one corner, and compute the opposite corner. Then the two corner points could be passed to **Pt2Shape**. Alternatively, we could make a subclass of **TShapeSketcher** that overrides **TrackMouse** in this manner. Which design is better will depend on how we organize the mouse tracking commands in the building block, a topic we will discuss shortly.

What about shapes, such as polygons, or regions that aren't drawn by defining two corners (or the center and a corner)? These kinds of shapes don't fit into the model of dragging the mouse from one corner to the other, but they do involve modifying a prototype shape as the user moves the mouse.

Sketching a polygon is especially challenging to implement, because it requires several mouse actions. Each press of the mouse button defines another vertex. While the mouse button is up, the program tracks the mouse and draws a line from the current position to the last vertex. MacApp supports returning the same command object in successive mouse actions. So we could keep reusing the same command object until the user finished sketching the polygon. The command object could also track the mouse and provide feedback while the button was up. Handling this polygon sketcher object would require some special case code in the graphics building block, but would otherwise fit into the general sketching architecture.

As we can see, from this brief discussion, our architecture stands the test of supporting alternate methods of doing things.

## ▶ Basic Selection Design

Now that we have a command class that can create shapes, we can start implementing commands that operate on shapes. In the Macintosh user interface, however, the user first selects the objects and then issues a command that applies to those objects. Consequently, we need to implement a way for the user to select shapes.

There are two different ways to select shapes. In the first way, the user clicks on an individual shape to select that shape. As we mentioned in Chapter 21, the user must click on the actual shape and not simply within the shape's bounding rectangle. Also, if the interior of the shape is transparent, then clicking inside the shape should not select it. The second way of selecting shapes is to click in the space between shapes and drag the mouse to form a rectangle. All the shapes that lie within the rectangle are selected. This is known as an *area selection*.

Normally, when the user makes a selection we deselect all other shapes. By holding down the Shift key, however, the user can make incremental changes to the set of selected shapes. Combining the Shift key with either of the selection mechanisms toggles the selected state of the affected shapes.

Regardless of the mechanism used to select shapes, we need a way to implement the current selection. The easiest way to do this is to add a Boolean instance variable, *fIsSelected*, to **TShape**, along with methods to get and set the *fIsSelected* variable. The current selection, therefore, is represented by the set of shapes marked as selected.

The methods in **TShape** are used only to set the *fIsSelected* variable of a particular shape. **TShapeList** also has selection-related methods, which operate at a higher level of abstraction. First, **TShapeList** keeps track of the number of selected shapes in the instance variable *fNumSelected*. One use of this feature is to disable menu items when nothing is selected. Another is that it provides methods to select or deselect an individual shape and to deselect all the shapes. Finally, it provides a method to iterate over all the selected shapes. This is shown in Listing 24-5. The rest of the building block will use the higher-level methods in **TShapeList**, rather than the low-level method in **TShape**.

## Listing 24-5. TShape list methods

```
 1: pascal void TShapeList::DeselectShape(TShape* aShape)
 2: {
 3:   if (aShape -> IsSelected()) {
 4:       aShape -> SetSelection(false);
 5:       fNumSelected--;
 6:   }
 7: }
 8:
 9: pascal void DeselectAShape(TShape* aShape, void* aShapeList)
10: {
11:   ((TShapeList*)aShapeList) -> DeselectShape(aShape);
12: }
13:
14: pascal void TShapeList::Deselect()
15: {
16:   this -> EachShapeDo(&DeselectAShape, this);
17: }
18:
19: struct DoToShapeInfo {
20:   DoToShapeProc DoToShape;
21:   void*         DoToShape_StaticLink;
22: };
23:
24: pascal void ProcessShape(TShape* aShape, void* theInfo)
25: {
26:   DoToShapeInfo* info = (DoToShapeInfo*)theInfo;
27:
28:   if (aShape -> IsSelected())
29:       TShapeList::CallDoToShape( aShape,
30:                                  info -> DoToShape_StaticLink,
31:                                  info -> DoToShape);
32: }
33:
34: pascal void TShapeList::EachSelectedShapeDo(
35:                         DoToShapeProc DoToShape,
36:                           void* DoToShape_StaticLink) const
37: {
38:   DoToShapeInfo info;
39:   info.DoToShape = DoToShape;
40:   info.DoToShape_StaticLink = DoToShape_StaticLink;
41:
42:   this -> EachShapeDo(&ProcessShape, &info);
43: }
44:
45: pascal void TShapeList::SelectShape(TShape* aShape)
46: {
47:   if (! aShape -> IsSelected()) {
```

```
48:       aShape -> SetSelection(true);
49:       fNumSelected++;
50:   }
51: }
```

Note that **TShapeList::Deselect** and **TShapeList::EachSelectedShape-Do** pass a pointer to local data when calling **EachShapeDo** (lines 16 and 42). **EachSelectedShapedDo** needs to pass two variables, so it uses a struct (**DoToShapeInfo**).

The function **ProcessShape** is responsible for calling the function passed to it. To do this, it uses an inline function called **CallDoTo-Shape**. This function handles the details of calling a function parameter using the Pascal calling conventions.

## ▶ Highlighting the Selected Items

Not only do we need an internal representation of the current selection, we also need a visual representation so the user can tell which shapes are selected. Most drawing programs highlight the selection by drawing small squares around the selected shape(s). These "knobs" are selectable, and can be used to allow the user to stretch the shape. (We won't implement stretching in this book, however.) The number of knobs and their positions depend on the kind of shape. For example, a rectangle will have one knob at each corner, while a line has only two knobs, one at each end point.

This is another case where we need an additional method in **TShape**. This method will be called **Highlight**, and its parameters are the old and new highlight states. These are the same parameters passed to **TView::DoHighlightSelection** (see Chapter 13). Using the same design principles as in Chapter 23, we can break down **TShape::Highlight** into two steps: (1) set up the QuickDraw drawing state and (2) paint each knob.

The first step is accomplished by calling the MacApp global function **SetHLPenState**. This function sets the current pen pattern and drawing mode according to the old and new highlight states.

To paint each knob, we must compute the rectangular bounds of the knob and call the QuickDraw procedure PaintRect. Since the number and position of the knobs vary with the kind of shape, we can define a method in **TShape** called **EachKnob**, that iterates through all the knob rectangles. **TShape::EachKnob** is like the other iteration methods in MacApp. It takes a function as a parameter and repeatedly calls the function, passing it the rectangle representing a knob. The implementation of **TShape::Highlight** is shown in Listing 24-6.

Listing 24-6. TShape::Highlight

```
 1: pascal void PaintKnob(const Rect& r, void*)
 2: {
 3:   PaintRect(&r);
 4: }
 5:
 6: pascal void TShape::Highlight(HLState fromHL, HLState toHL)
    const
 7: {
 8:   SetHLPenState(fromHL, toHL);
 9:   this -> EachKnob(&PaintKnob, this);
10: }
```

With this implementation, each subclass of **TShape** must override **TShape::EachKnob**. But every implementation of **EachKnob** would have to compute the rectangles representing its knobs. The rectangles for each shape are the same size and only vary in position. This suggests that we define another method that enumerates the position of each knob. **TShape::EachKnob** can call this method and compute the proper rectangle for each position.

The method that iterates over knob positions is **TShape::EachKnobPt**. Again, this method takes a function as a parameter. **EachKnobPt** calls this function repeatedly, passing it the horizontal and vertical coordinates of the knob's center. **EachKnob** must be overridden by each subclass of **TShape**. One example, the implementation in **TAbstractRectangle**, is shown in Listing 24-7.

Listing 24-7. EachKnobPt

```
 1: typedef pascal void (*DoToKnobPtProc)(short, short, void*);
 2:
 3: pascal void TAbstractRectangle::EachKnobPt(
 4:                              DoToKnobPtProc DoToKnobPt,
 5:                              void* staticLink) const
 6: {
 7:   Rect r = this -> GetGeometricBounds();
 8:
 9:                            /* Place a knob at each corner. */
10:   CallDoToKnobPt(r.left, r.top, staticLink, DoToKnobPt);
11:   CallDoToKnobPt(r.right, r.top, staticLink, DoToKnobPt);
12:   CallDoToKnobPt(r.left, r.bottom, staticLink, DoToKnobPt);
13:   CallDoToKnobPt(r.right, r.bottom, staticLink, DoToKnobPt);
14: }
```

Using this method we can implement **TShape::EachKnob**. As you can see in Listing 24-8, we simply call **EachKnobPt**, passing it a function that computes the corresponding knob rectangle, by calling the method **TShape::MakeKnobRect**.

### Listing 24-8. EachKnob

```
 1: typedef pascal void (*DoToKnobProc)(const Rect&, void*);
 2:
 3: struct EachKnobInfo {
 4:    const TShape* theShape;
 5:    DoToKnobProc  DoToKnob;
 6:    void*         DoToKnob_StaticLink;
 7: };
 8:
 9: pascal void ComputeKnobRect(short hCoord, short vCoord,
10:                                      void* infoStruct)
11: {
12:    EachKnobInfo* info = (EachKnobInfo*)infoStruct;
13:    Rect knob = (info -> theShape) -> MakeKnobRect(hCoord,
       vCoord)
14:    CallDoToKnob( knob, info -> DoToKnob_StaticLink,
15:               info -> DoToKnob );
16: }
17:
18: pascal void TShape::EachKnob( DoToKnobProc DoToKnob,
19:                         void* staticLink) const
20: {
21:    EachKnobInfo info;
22:    info.theShape = this;
23:    info.DoToKnob = DoToKnob;
24:    info.DoToKnob_StaticLink = staticLink;
25:
26:    this -> EachKnobPt(&ComputeKnobRect, &info);
27: }
28:
29: pascal Rect TShape::MakeKnobRect( short hCoord,
30:                            short vCoord) const
31: {
32:    Rect r;
33:    SetRect(&r, hCoord-kHalfKnob, vCoord-kHalfKnob,
34:               hCoord+kHalfKnob, vCoord+kHalfKnob);
35:    return r;
36: }
```

It is difficult to understand the flow of control when **TShape::-Highlight** is called, because two iteration methods are involved. Figure 24-1 illustrates the process of highlighting a shape.

Since in MacApp the view is responsible for highlighting the selection, we will add the method **TShapeViewHelper::DoHighlightSelection**. This method sequences through the selected shapes and calls **Highlight** for each. This is shown in Listing 24-9. Any view that uses the graphics building block will call **TShapeViewHelper::DoHighlightSelection** from its own **DoHighlightSelection** method.

Listing 24-9. DoHighlightSelection

```
 1: struct HighlightInfo {
 2:   HLState fromHL;
 3:   HLState toHL;
 4: };
 5:
 6: pascal void HighlightShape(TShape* aShape, void*
    highlightStruct)
 7: {
 8:   HighlightInfo* info = (HighlightInfo*)highlightStruct;
 9:
10:   aShape -> Highlight(info -> fromHL, info -> toHL);
11: }
12:
13: pascal void TShapeViewHelper::DoHighlightSelection(
14:                       HLState fromHL, HLState toHL)
15: {
16:   HighlightInfo info;
17:   info.fromHL = fromHL;
18:   info.toHL = toHL;
19:
20:   fShapeList -> EachSelectedShapeDo(&HighlightShape, &info);
21: }
```

## ▶ Implementing Area Selections

Now that we have written the basic methods for managing selections, we can write the code that actually implements the interface for selecting shapes. We will start with the area selection command, since that is easier than individual selections. Making an area selection does not change the document. This means the area selection operation is not undoable and it does not commit the previous command. (In other words, the previous command is still undoable after making the area selection.)

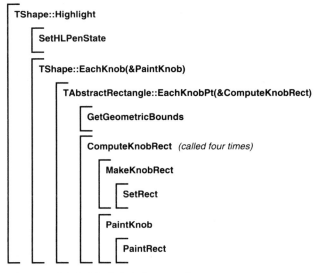

Figure 24-1. Highlighting a shape

Nevertheless, we will create a subclass of **TCommand** to track the mouse and modify the selection. This class is called **TShapeSelector**. Like all other mouse tracking commands it has two functions to track the mouse and to provide feedback.

The implementation of **TShapeSelector::TrackMouse** is shown in Listing 24-10.

Listing 24-10. TrackMouse

```
1: struct SelectInfo {
2:    TShapeViewHelper* fShapeViewHelper;
3:    Rect*            qdBounds;
4: };
5:
6: pascal void SelectInBounds(TShape* aShape, void* infoStruct)
7: {
8:    SelectInfo* info = (SelectInfo*)infoStruct;
9:    Rect shapeBounds = aShape -> GetDrawingBounds();
10:
11:           /* Select shapes inside; deselect shapes outside */
12:    if (RectsNest(info -> qdBounds, &shapeBounds))
13:       (info -> fShapeViewHelper) -> SelectShape(aShape);
14:    else
15:       (info -> fShapeViewHelper) -> DeselectShape(aShape);
16: }
17:                       /* Used if the Shift key was down */
```

```
18: pascal void Complement(TShape* aShape, void* infoStruct)
19: {
20:   SelectInfo* info = (SelectInfo*)infoStruct;
21:   Rect shapeBounds = aShape -> GetDrawingBounds();
22:
23:   if (RectsNest(info -> qdBounds, &shapeBounds))
24:       if (aShape -> IsSelected())
25:           (info -> fShapeViewHelper) -> DeselectShape(aShape);
26:       else
27:           (info -> fShapeViewHelper) -> SelectShape(aShape);
28: }
29:
30: pascal TCommand* TShapeSelector::TrackMouse(TrackPhase
    thePhase,
31:                                             VPoint* anchorPoint,
32:                                             VPoint* /*prevPoint*/,
33:                                             VPoint* nextPoint,
34:                                             Boolean /*mouseDidMove*/)
35: {
36:   if (thePhase == trackRelease) {     /* Change selection */
37:       VRect bounds;
38:       Rect qdBounds;
39:
40:       Pt2VRect(anchorPoint, nextPoint, &bounds);
41:       fView -> ViewToQDRect(&bounds, &qdBounds);
42:
43:       SelectInfo info;
44:       info.fShapeViewHelper = fShapeViewHelper;
45:       info.qdBounds = &qdBounds;
46:
47:       if (fShiftSelect)
48:           fShapeList -> EachShapeDo(&Complement, &info);
49:       else
50:           fShapeList -> EachShapeDo(&SelectInBounds, &info);
51:
52:       return gNoChanges;              /* No changes to document */
53:   }
54:
55:   else
56:       return this;            /* Track until button is released */
57: }
```

**TShapeSelector::TrackMouse** does nothing until the mouse is released. When the button is released, it computes the rectangle the user drew (lines 40 and 41) and sequences through the shapes, updating the current selection. How it updates the selection depends on whether or not the user held down the Shift key while making the selection. If the Shift key was not pressed, **TrackMouse** calls the function **SelectInBounds** (line 6) with each shape in turn as a parameter. **SelectInBounds** selects all the shapes within the rectangle and deselects the shapes outside. (It is important not to forget the shapes outside the rectangle in this case.) If the user held down the Shift key while making the selection, then **TrackMouse** uses the function **Complement** (line 18) instead. **Complement** changes the selection state of all the shapes in the rectangle and does nothing to shapes outside the rectangle.

In both cases, the implementation in Listing 24-10 calls the methods **TShapeViewHelper::SelectShape** and **TShapeViewHelper::DeselectShape** to change the actual selection. These methods (shown in Listing 24-11) change the highlighting on the screen and call the corresponding method of **TShapeList** to change the *fIsSelected* variable in the shape itself.

Listing 24-11. DeselectShape and SelectShape

```
 1: pascal void TShapeViewHelper::DeselectShape(TShape* aShape)
 2: {
 3:   if (aShape -> IsSelected()) {
 4:       fView -> Focus();                /* Establish focus */
 5:
 6:       aShape -> Highlight(hlOn, hlOff);
 7:       fShapeList -> DeselectShape(aShape);
 8:   }
 9: }
10:
11: pascal void TShapeViewHelper::SelectShape(TShape* aShape)
12: {
13:   if (! aShape -> IsSelected())  {
14:       fView -> Focus();                /* Establish focus */
15:
16:       aShape -> Highlight(hlOff, hlOn);
17:       fShapeList -> SelectShape(aShape);
18:   }
19: }
```

Providing the feedback while the user makes the selection is even easier. That's because the implementation of **TrackFeedback** in **TCommand** itself draws a gray rectangle between the point of the mouse click and the current mouse position. This is exactly the feedback we want in **TShapeSelector**, so it isn't necessary to override the **TrackMouse** method.

## ▶ Individual Shape Selection

The area selection is only one selection mechanism. The user can also click directly on a shape and select it. In most cases clicking on a shape is the start of a command that drags the selection. In this section we will implement methods that we can use to determine on which shape the user clicked. We will implement the shape-dragging command in the next section.

What we need is a method in **TShapeViewHelper** that, when given a mouse point, finds the shape object under that point. We will call this method **TShapeViewHelper::ShapeContainingPt**. We can't simply compare the point against the bounding rectangle of each shape, since that would not be exact. A diagonal line has a large bounding rectangle, but we want to detect clicks only on the line itself. Also, if a shape's interior is transparent, then users should be able to select other shapes they can see through it; to select the transparent shape they must click on the frame.

We really want to figure out whether the pixel under the mouse point would be touched in the course of drawing a particular shape. The last shape that touched the pixel would be the frontmost shape under the mouse, since the shapes are drawn from back to front. By *touched* we mean whether the shape drew that particular pixel. We can't simply look at the final result (as the user sees it) for the answer, since that won't allow us to distinguish a shape with a white interior from the white background of the view. We can, however, draw all the shapes using solid black, regardless of their true appearance. Then the pixel will be turned black if the shape touches the pixel.

Since it would be disconcerting to the user to see all the shapes change to black, we must do this drawing in an offscreen bitmap. Figure 24-2 shows the difference between drawing the shape normally (on screen) and drawing it with a black pattern (off screen).

Shape as shown on screen    Shape as drawn offscreen

Figure 24-2. Hit detection — normal versus offscreen drawing

**By the Way ▶** When you call a QuickDraw drawing routine, QuickDraw modifies a certain portion of memory. Normally, this memory is associated with the screen, so that the changes QuickDraw makes are visible to the user. It is possible, however, for QuickDraw to draw in any area of memory, even if it isn't associated with the screen. This is known (for obvious reasons) as offscreen drawing. To draw offscreen you must set up a Bitmap structure that refers to the area of memory, create a grafPort that uses the Bitmap, and make the grafPort the current QuickDraw port. Then, all drawing calls will result in changes to the designated area of memory. Drawing in color is similar, except that you create a Pixmap that refers to the offscreen memory and a color grafPort that refers to the Pixmap.

Because we are only interested in one particular pixel, we only need a 1-pixel size offscreen bitmap. QuickDraw doesn't allow a 1-by-1 bitmap, however; the minimum size is 16 pixels wide by 1 pixel high.

The basic technique used by **TShapeViewHelper::ShapeContainingPt** is diagrammed in Figure 24-3, and the actual implementation is shown in Listing 24-12.

Listing 24-12. ShapeContainingPt

```
 1: struct ShapeContainingInfo {
 2:    short   bits;
 3:    TShape* result;
 4: };
 5:
 6: pascal void TestShape(TShape* aShape, void* infoStruct)
 7: {
 8:    ShapeContainingInfo* info = (ShapeContainingInfo*)infoStruct;
 9:
10:    info -> bits = 0;                 /* Clear offscreen memory */
11:    aShape -> DrawSolid();                /* Draw the shape */
12:
13:    if ((info -> bits & 1) != 0)        /* It touched the pixel */
```

```
14:        info -> result = aShape;
15:
16: /* Note: the last shape touching the pixel becomes the result*/
17: }
18:
19: pascal  TShape* TShapeViewHelper::ShapeContainingPt(Point aPt)
20: {
21:   ShapeContainingInfo info;
22:
23:   info.result = NULL;                      /* Default return. */
24:
25:   GrafPtr oldPort;                         /* Save old port */
26:   GetPort(&oldPort);
27:
28:   GrafPort privatePort;                    /* Make a new port */
29:   OpenPort(&privatePort);
30:   PortSize(16, 1);
31:
32:   BitMap map;                    /* Set up the bitmap record */
33:   map.baseAddr = (Ptr)&info.bits;
34:   map.rowBytes = 2;
35:   SetRect(&map.bounds, 0, 0, 16, 1);
36:
37:   SetPortBits(&map);
38:
39:       /* Make aPt map to low-order bit of offscreen memory */
40:   SetOrigin(aPt.h - 15, aPt.v);
41:
42:   fShapeList -> EachShapeDo(&TestShape, &info);
43:
44:   SetPort(oldPort);                           /* Clean up. */
45:   ClosePort(&privatePort);
46:
47:   return info.result;
48: }
```

This method calls the **TShape::DrawSolid** method (line 11). **Draw-Solid** is similar to **TShape::Draw** and **TShape::DrawFeedback**. It computes the attributes of the shape and calls **DrawUsing**. By now you can probably see the value of implementing the **DrawUsing** method. We have used it not only for drawing the shape normally, but also for providing feedback when creating a new shape, and for selecting shapes. In this case, however, the attributes it uses define the selection area of the shape. This is shown in Listing 24-13.

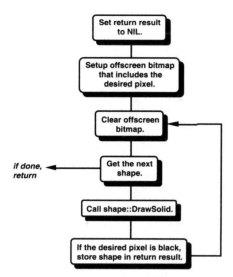

Figure 24-3. ShapeContainingPt flow of control

In Listing 24-12, the variable *bits* contains the offscreen memory. In lines 25 through 37, we set up an offscreen bitmap and a private Quick-Draw grafPort.

On line 40, we call **SetOrigin** so that the mouse point corresponds to the low-order bit of the off-screen memory. Then on line 13 we test that bit.

Listing 24-13. DrawSolid

```
1: pascal void TShape::DrawSolid() const
2: {
3:   Rect r = this -> GetDrawingBounds();
4:   Point size = this -> GetFrameSize();
5:   const TQuickDrawPattern* interiorPat =
6:                             this -> GetInteriorPattern();
7:   const TQuickDrawPattern* framePat = this-> GetFramePattern();
8:
9:   size.h += 2;                   /* Add a margin for error. */
10:   size.v += 2;
11:
12:   this -> DrawUsing( r, size,
13:                   interiorPat -> GetSolidPattern(),
14:                   gBlackPattern);
15: }
```

**DrawSolid** substitutes a solid black pattern for the normal interior pattern, using the call **TQuickDrawPattern::GetSolidPattern** (line 13). This method normally returns a pattern object that represents a solid black pattern; the class **TTransparentPattern** overrides **GetSolidPattern** and returns itself instead. The frame pattern is always black, which means the user can click on the frame of a shape, even if the frame is transparent. Finally, it uses a frame size that is two pixels larger than normal (lines 9 and 10). The larger frame size gives the user a small margin of error around the shape; a click one pixel outside the shape still selects it.

The technique we used to implement **ShapeContainingPt** will work regardless of how complicated the shape is. Of course, if all the shapes were simple, for example rectangles, then our algorithm is slightly less efficient than it could be. For the purposes of this program, however, this algorithm is fast enough. You could improve it a bit by testing whether the point of interest lies within the drawing bounds of the shape. You would have to allow for the margin of error and expand the drawing bounds by one pixel on each size.

## ▶ Dragging Shapes

Dragging a shape involves tracking the mouse, which means we must define a subclass of **TCommand**, in this case **TShapeDragger**, and override the mouse tracking methods. Dragging is an undoable operation, which means we must also override the **DoIt**, **UndoIt**, and **RedoIt** methods of **TCommand**.

We will design the **TrackFeedback** method first, since it influences the design of **TrackMouse**. There are two possible ways to provide feedback. First, we could draw outlines of all the shapes being dragged, using the **TShape::DrawFeedback** method. The disadvantage of this method is that when the user drags many shapes it will take longer to draw the feedback each time.

A faster algorithm is to draw only the outline of the shape in which the user clicked or the bounding rectangle of all the selected shapes if more than one is selected. This gives the user the ability to align precisely one particular shape with another, as well as to see an overview of everything being dragged. This algorithm requires drawing only two shapes to provide feedback, which makes it faster, although the user can't see the final result until the operation is completed.

Some programs provide both mechanisms, allowing the user to make the tradeoff between speed and accuracy. For example, the default might be to use the faster form of feedback, but to outline all the shapes if the user holds down the Command key. We will implement this dual form of feedback.

Since the feedback is the same each time and only changes position, we can improve performance by creating a QuickDraw picture that represents the feedback and drawing the picture at the desired position. This means we only have to sequence through the list of selected shapes once, when we create the picture. This is shown in Listing 24-14.

Listing 24-14. TrackFeedback

```
 1: pascal void TShapeDragger::TrackFeedback(VPoint*
                                    /*anchorPoint*/,
 2:                                 VPoint* /*nextPoint*/,
 3:                                 Boolean /*turnItOn*/,
 4:                                 Boolean mouseDidMove )
 5: {
 6:   if (mouseDidMove && (fFeedbackPicture != NULL)) {
 7:       Rect r = fPictureBounds;
 8:       DrawPicture(fFeedbackPicture, &r);
 9:   }
10: }
```

In this method, *fFeedbackPicture* is a QuickDraw picture that depicts the feedback, and *fPictureBounds* is the destination rectangle for drawing the picture. We copy the rectangle on line 7 to prevent an unsafe reference to the *fPictureBounds* instance variable. We will create the picture in the **TrackMouse** method shown in Listing 24-15, but only after the user has started moving the mouse. **TrackMouse** computes the destination rectangle as the user moves the mouse.

Listing 24-15. TrackMouse

```
 1: pascal TCommand* TShapeDragger::TrackMouse(
 2:                                 TrackPhase thePhase,
 3:                                 VPoint* anchorPoint,
 4:                                 VPoint* previousPoint,
 5:                                 VPoint* nextPoint,
 6:                                 Boolean mouseDidMove)
 7: {
 8:   if (mouseDidMove && (thePhase == trackMove)) {
 9:       if (fFeedbackPicture == NULL) {
10:                /* First mouse movement; create the picture */
11:
12:           Rect r = fShapeList -> SelectionBounds();
13:
14:           RgnHandle oldClip = MakeNewRgn(); /* MacApp utility */
15:           GetClip(oldClip);
16:
```

```
17:            fFeedbackPicture = OpenPicture(&r);
18:            ClipRect(&r);
19:
20:            this -> DrawFeedback(true);
21:
22:            ClosePicture();
23:
24:            fPictureBounds = r;
25:
26:            SetClip(oldClip);
27:            DisposeRgn(oldClip);
28:
29:            if (EmptyRect(&((*fFeedbackPicture) -> picFrame))) {
30:                KillPicture(fFeedbackPicture);
31:                fFeedbackPicture = NULL;
32:                Failure(memFullErr, 0);     /* Ran out of memory */
33:            }
34:        }
35:
36:        Point delta = fView -> ViewToQDPt(nextPoint);
37:        SubPt(fView -> ViewToQDPt(previousPoint), &delta);
38:
39:        OffsetRect(&fPictureBounds, delta.h, delta.v);
40:    } /* if mouse moved */
41:
42:
43:    if (thePhase == trackRelease) {
44:        Point delta = fView -> ViewToQDPt(nextPoint);
45:        SubPt(fView -> ViewToQDPt(anchorPoint), &delta);
46:
47:        fDelta = delta;
48:
49:        if ((delta.h == 0) && (delta.v == 0))
50:            return gNoChanges;
51:    }
52:
53:    return this;
54: }
```

The first time the user moves the mouse, **TrackMouse** will create a
QuickDraw picture containing the desired feedback. Notice that on line
18 we set the clipping to match the bounds of the picture. This ensures
that nothing in the picture gets clipped. If the picture frame is empty
(line 29), then QuickDraw ran out of memory creating the picture, so
we signal an error (line 32). Each time **TrackMouse** is called, it updates
the value of *fPictureBounds*; this instance variable is used in **TrackFeed-**

**back** (see Listing 24-14) when the picture is drawn. When the user releases the mouse button (line 43), **TrackMouse** computes the total distance the mouse moved (between the initial press and the release). This
distance is saved in the command object, where it can be used by the
**DoIt, UndoIt**, and **RedoIt** methods.

On line 49 we check to see if the user moved the selection at all. If not
then we return the pre-defined command object *gNoChanges*. This return value tells MacApp that the command made no changes to the
document.

The method **TShapeDragger::DrawFeedback** (shown in Listing
24-16) draws the two kinds of feedback, based on the setting of the variables *fFullFeedback* and *fShapeClickedIn*. These variables are initialized
when the command object is first created.

Listing 24-16. DrawFeedback

```
1: pascal void DrawShapeFeedback(TShape* aShape, void* turnItOn)
2: {
3:   aShape -> DrawFeedback(*(Boolean*)turnItOn);
4: }
5:
6: pascal void TShapeDragger::DrawFeedback(Boolean turnItOn)
7: {
8:   if (fFullFeedback || (fShapeClickedIn == NULL))
9:       fShapeList -> EachSelectedShapeDo( &DrawShapeFeedback,
10:                                 &turnItOn);
11:
12:   else {
13:       fShapeClickedIn -> DrawFeedback(turnItOn);
14:
15:       if (fShapeList -> NumberInSelection() > 1) {
16:           Rect bounds = fShapeList -> SelectionBounds();
17:           PenNormal();
18:           PenMode(patXor);
19:           FrameRect(&bounds);
20:       }
21:   }
22: }
```

**TShapeDragger::DrawFeedback** ends up calling **TShape::DrawFeed-
back** (lines 3 and 13), which is the same method we used earlier to provide feedback in **TShapeSketcher**.

Notice that the choice of feedback is made only once based on the
way in which the command object is initialized. Some programs, in
contrast, dynamically change the feedback method based on the cur-

rent state of the Command key. We can implement the same behavior here with a bit more work. First, MacApp does not pass the state of the modifier keys to the tracking methods, so those methods would have to test the Command key state themselves. Second, our current implementation creates the **QuickDraw** picture only once. We would either have to create the picture each time the state changed or create pictures for both kinds of feedback and simply display one or the other. Finally, we would have to be sure to use the same picture to turn off the feedback that we used to draw it.

The same work would be required if we wanted to implement the ability to constrain the shapes to move in a horizontal or vertical direction. In this case, we must also dynamically test the state of the Shift key, since the dragging operation starts by clicking within a shape. But holding down the Shift key while clicking within a shape deselects the shape. If we did not test for the Shift key dynamically, we would end up with a very awkward interface.

Notice also that while tracking the mouse we did not move any of the shapes. The shapes are moved by the method **TShapeDragger::MoveShapes**, shown in Listing 24-17.

Listing 24-17. MoveShapes

```
 1: pascal void MoveAShape(TShape* aShape, void* deltaPt)
 2: {
 3:   Point* pt = (Point*)deltaPt;
 4:   aShape -> OffsetBy(pt -> h, pt -> v);
 5: }
 6:
 7: pascal void TShapeDragger::MoveShapes(short deltaH, short
    deltaV)
 8: {
 9:     /* Turn off highlighting because we're changing the
10:        selection.  We need to focus before doing this. */
11:   if (fView -> Focus())
12:     fShapeViewHelper -> DoHighlightSelection(hlOn, hlOff);
13:   fShapeList -> RestoreSelection();
14:
15:   fShapeViewHelper -> InvalidateSelection();
16:
17:   Point deltaPt;
18:   SetPt(&deltaPt, deltaH, deltaV);
19:
20:   fShapeList -> EachSelectedShapeDo(&MoveAShape, &deltaPt);
21:
22:   fShapeViewHelper -> InvalidateSelection();
23: }
```

**MoveShapes** turns off the current selection highlighting (line 12) and selects the shapes that were originally moved (line 13). It sequences through the selected shapes and calls **TShape::OffsetBy** to move each shape (line 4). It also invalidates the selection before and after it is moved (lines 15 and 22). (**OffsetBy** is another method that must be overridden in each subclass of **TShape**. It moves the shape by the desired amount.)

How is the selection restored? Earlier we mentioned that each shape contains an instance variable that indicates if it is in the current selection. In order to remember the shapes a particular command modified, we must add another variable (*fWasSelected*) to record the selection at the time the command was done. The method **TShapeList::Remember Selection** saves the current selection, while the method **TShapeList::-RestoreSelection** restores it.

Each of these methods sequences through the list of shapes and calls the corresponding **TShape** method, which modifies the *fIsSelected* or *fWasSelected* instance variables. Listing 24-18 shows the implementation of **RememberSelection**; the implementation of **RestoreSelection** is analogous.

Listing 24-18. RememberSelection

```
 1: pascal void Remember(TShape* aShape, void* /*staticLink*/)
 2: {
 3:   aShape -> RememberSelection();
 4: }
 5:
 6: pascal void TShapeList::RememberSelection() const
 7:
 8: {
 9:   this -> EachShapeDo(&Remember, this);
10: }
11:
12: pascal void TShape::RememberSelection()
13: {
14:   fWasSelected = fIsSelected;
15: }
```

By the Way ▶ | The implementation of **TShapeDragger::MoveShapes** in Listing 24-17 sequences through the list of shapes five times — once each to turn off the highlighting, restore the selection, invalidate the old position of the shapes, move the shapes, and invalidate their new positions. For the purposes of this book, this implementation is adequate. If we wanted to improve the efficiency, however, we could sequence through the list of shapes once and perform the five steps on each shape in turn. The advantage of the implementation shown in Listing 24-17 is that it uses the existing methods for highlighting, invalidation, and so on, and therefore requires writing no new code.

The **DoIt**, **UndoIt**, and **RedoIt** methods are very short, since all the work is done by **MoveShapes**. This is shown in Listing 24-19.

Listing 24-19. TShapeDragger.DoIt, UndoIt, and RedoIt

```
1: pascal void TShapeDragger::DoIt()
2: {
3:   fShapeList -> RememberSelection();
4:   this -> MoveShapes(fDelta.h, fDelta.v);
5: }
6:
7: pascal void TShapeDragger::UndoIt()
8: {
9:   this -> MoveShapes(-fDelta.h, -fDelta.v);
10: }
11:
12: pascal void TShapeDragger::RedoIt()
13: {
14:   this -> MoveShapes(fDelta.h, fDelta.v);
15: }
```

The *fDelta* instance variable used in each method is the value that was computed in **TrackMouse** (see Listing 24-15) when the user released the mouse button.

## ▶ Putting It All Together

We have now implemented four basic capabilities in the graphics building block:

- sketching shapes
- making an area selection
- selecting individual shapes
- dragging shapes

What is still missing is the code that ties these actions together and decides which one the user wants to perform with a particular mouse click. The primary task is deciding which command object to create when the user clicks in the drawing view. We must also adjust the selection as the user clicks in individual shapes.

Earlier in the book (see Chapter 19) we said that when the user clicks in a view, the view's **DoMouseCommand** method is called. This method returns a command object, which MacApp uses to track the mouse and perform the command. A view that uses the graphics building block needs to implement the **DoMouseCommand** and create an instance of the appropriate command class. In the graphics building block, there are three classes from which to choose **TShapeSketcher**, **TShapeSelector**, and **TShapeDragger**.

There are two basic cases to consider: selecting one or more shapes and sketching a shape. To sketch a shape, we obviously must create an instance of **TShapeSketcher** and include in that object an instance of the shape object we want to sketch. As we mentioned in the discussion of **TShapeSketcher**, it is possible that certain shape classes will require a custom subclass of **TShapeSketcher**.

The flow of control is more complicated when the user is selecting shapes. There are two independent variables to consider: whether the user clicked within a shape and whether the user pressed the Shift key. If the user did not click in any shape, then we must begin an area selection by creating an instance of **TShapeSelector**. In this case, we create an instance of **TShapeSelector** whether the user is holding down the Shift key or not. When the user releases the button, the **TShapeSelector** command will select the desired shapes.

If the user clicked on a shape, then we first have to adjust the current selection. There are two possible scenarios. If the user is pressing the Shift key, then we complement the selection state of the shape the user clicked. Otherwise, the user isn't pressing the Shift key. If the checked shape is already selected, we do nothing. If it isn't selected, then we deselect all the shapes and select the clicked shape.

After we adjust the selection, we return an instance of **TShapeDrag-ger**, in case the user decides to drag the selection. There is one snag, however. Shift-clicking on an already selected shape deselects it. In this case, it doesn't make sense to begin a dragging operation, since the mouse is no longer within a selected shape. Therefore, before we create the **TShapeDragger** object, we check to see if the shape the user clicked on is still selected.

Figure 24-4 shows a flowchart of the selection and dragging process. The actual code is shown in Listing 24-20.

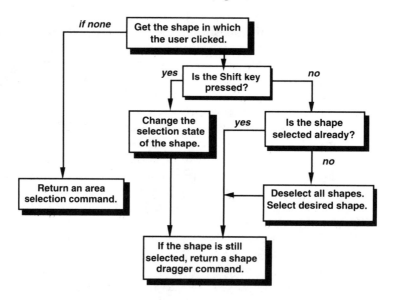

Figure 24-4. Shape selection and dragging

Next, we need a mechanism for the user to choose between selecting shapes and sketching a new shape. To sketch a shape, the user must select the kind of shape to create. In most drawing programs, there is a palette of tools from which the user can choose. The tool palette ge-nerally includes a selection tool and several sketching tools. We can define a **TShapePalette** class to represent the tool palette in our draw-ing program.

Next, we need to address how the **TShapePalette** class represents the individual tools. Since a tool's behavior is defined by the command ob-ject used to track the mouse, we can simply maintain a prototype com-mand object for each tool in the palette. When the program needs to use a particular tool, the **TShapePalette** object can supply a clone of the corresponding command object. It is the application's responsibility to register instances of the desired classes with the tool palette object.

| By the Way ▶ | We could also maintain the name of the appropriate class, instead of a prototype object. In this case, however, there are advantages to using prototype objects. First, we can share the same **TShapeSketcher** object among all the sketching tools that use that class. Second, the prototype objects can be initialized with the appropriate command numbers. To make the building block reusable, we should avoid using constants for the command numbers; instead, the command numbers will be stored in the prototype objects. |
| --- | --- |

For our sketching tools, we need to register not only the command object but also the shape that the command sketches. In most cases, the command object will be an instance of **TShapeSketcher**, but sometimes it will be an instance of a **TShapeSketcher** subclass. **TShapePalette** has a method called **RegisterSketcher** that takes as parameters a prototype sketcher object and a prototype shape object. It saves these objects in two separate **TList** instances.

The selection tool requires two separate entries in the tool palette, although the user will see only a single tool. One entry is for the area selection command object (usually an instance of **TShapeSelector**) and the other is for dragging the selection (usually an instance of **TShape-Dragger**). The client registers prototypes of these command classes when the tool palette object is initialized. It is not necessary to have a separate instance of **TShapePalette** for each document. All the documents of a given type can share the same object. (Some applications might support different kinds of documents, in which case, each kind of document could require a different instance of **TShapePalette**, containing a different set of command objects.)

Finally, we can put all the pieces together. Since we are dealing entirely with mouse commands, we will implement all the code for managing the tool palette in **TShapeViewHelper**. **TShapeViewHelper** has a variable that refers to the **TShapePalette** object for that collection of shapes. It also has a variable to indicate the currently selected tool.

**TShapeViewHelper** contains the methods **DoSelectShapes** to handle the selection tool (shown in Listing 24-20), and **DoSketchShape** to handle a sketching operation (shown in Listing 24-21).

Listing 24-20. DoSelectShapes

```
 1: pascal TCommand* TShapeViewHelper::DoSelectShapes(
 2:                                      Point* theMouse,
 3:                                      EventInfo* info,
 4:                                      Point* /*hysteresis*/)
 5: {
 6:                          /* Get the shape the user clicked in */
 7:   TShape* shape = this -> ShapeContainingPt(*theMouse);
 8:
 9:   if (shape == NULL)                       /* Area selection */
10:       return this -> NewSelector(info -> theShiftKey);
11:
12:   else {                                  /* Modify selection */
13:       if (info -> theShiftKey) {
14:           if (shape -> IsSelected())
15:               this -> DeselectShape(shape);
16:           else
17:               this -> SelectShape(shape);
18:       }
19:
20:       else if (! shape -> IsSelected()) {   /* Select 1 shape */
21:           this -> Deselect();
22:           this -> SelectShape(shape);
23:       }
24:
25:       /* At this point, we have modified the selection.  Next,
26:                           see if we should start dragging */
27:
28:       if (shape -> IsSelected())
29:           return this -> NewDragger(shape,
30:           info -> theCmdKey);
31:       else
32:           return gNoChanges;             /* Nope. Nothing to do */
33:   }
34: }
35:
36: pascal TCommand* TShapeViewHelper::NewSelector(Boolean
    shiftSel)
37: {
38:   return fShapePalette -> CloneSelector(this, shiftSel);
39: }
40:
41: pascal TCommand* TShapeViewHelper::NewDragger(TShape* clicked,
42:                                      Boolean fullFeedback)
43: {
44:   return fShapePalette -> CloneDragger(clicked,
45:                                      this, fullFeedback);
46: }
```

Listing 24-21. DoSketchShape

```
1: pascal TCommand* TShapeViewHelper::DoSketchShape(
2:                                    Point* /*theMouse*/,
3:                                    EventInfo* info,
4:                                    Point* /*hysteresis*/,
5:                                    short whichTool)
6: {
7:   this -> Deselect();
8:   return this -> NewSketcher(whichTool, info -> theShiftKey);
9:                    /* Clone the appropriate sketcher */
10: }
11:
12: pascal TCommand* TShapeViewHelper::NewSketcher(short
   whichTool,
13:                                    Boolean shiftConstrain)
14: {
15:   return fShapePalette -> CloneSketcher(whichTool,
16:                            this, shiftConstrain);
17: }
```

**DoSketchShape** calls the **NewSketcher** method (line 8) to create a new sketcher object. Defining this method allows the programmer to override **NewSketcher** and supply a sketcher object in a different way. Normally, however, we want to get a copy of the prototype sketcher object from the palette. **TShapePalette::CloneSketcher** retrieves the appropriate objects from the list of prototype commands and shapes, makes copies of the objects, and returns an initialize sketching command.

Last, we can implement **TShapeViewHelper::DoMouseCommand**, as shown in Listing 24-22. This is the method that the client's view object will call from its **DoMouseCommand**.

Listing 24-22. DoMouseCommand

```
1: pascal TCommand* TShapeViewHelper::DoMouseCommand(Point*
   theMouse,
2:                                    EventInfo* info,
3:                                    Point* hysteresis)
4: {
5:   if (fCurrentTool == kSelectTool)
6:       return this -> DoSelectShapes(theMouse, info,
       hysteresis);
7:   else
8:       return this -> DoSketchShape(theMouse, info,
9:                            hysteresis, fCurrentTool);
10: }
```

The instance variable *fCurrentTool* is an integer that records the selected tool in the current drawing. It is maintained in the **TShapeView-Helper** class because different windows might have different tools selected.

As you can see, all the work we put into defining mouse handling in the building block finally paid off in the form of a very short **DoMouse Command** method. In general, you will find that an object-oriented program will contain many small methods, rather than a few large ones. In fact, one might argue that the **DoSelectShapes** method we wrote is too large and should be broken into separate methods.

## ▶ Summary

In this chapter, we added three mouse-driven commands to the sample program. ExampleDraw can now create new shapes, select them, and move them around.

In Chapter 25, we finish the ExampleDraw program by adding support for documents, filtered commands and the Clipboard.

# 25 ▶ Documents, Filters, and the Clipboard

In the previous chapter, we implemented several commands in the graphics building block. Here, we will add the final features to the graphics building block. These features fall into three categories: reading and writing documents, command filtering, and Clipboard support.

## ▶ Reading and Writing Documents

Just as MacApp does not dictate how you represent your data in memory, it does not dictate how your data are saved into a disk file. This gives you the flexibility of choosing any disk format you like. Unfortunately, it also means you are totally responsible for writing the code to read and write that format. The general problem involves translating your data structures as they exist in memory to the desired disk format and back again. In the case of the graphics building block, the in-memory structure consists of a list of shape objects. Each shape consists of two pattern objects, a frame size, and other information specific to that kind of shape.

Our job is relatively easy for two reasons. First, in Chapter 22 we implemented the class **TFileStream**, which can write objects to a file and read them back again. Second, we decided to store copies of pattern objects in each shape, rather than sharing the pattern objects among all the shapes. The lack of shared data makes it easier to read and write the shape objects.

We use the same implementation strategy we have used before. **TShape** implements low-level reading and writing methods, which handle I/O for a single shape. **TShapeList** implements higher-level methods that handle the entire list of shapes. Since both **TShape** and **TShapeList** are subclasses of **TStreamObject**, the necessary methods (**ReadFrom** and **WriteTo**) are already defined; all that is necessary is to override them.

## ▶ Low-Level Methods

First, we will implement **ReadFrom** and **WriteTo** in class **TShape**. Each method has one parameter, which is a stream, and is responsible for reading or writing the data defined in **TShape**. These data consist of the interior and frame patterns and the frame size. Since the frame size is a Point, we can read and write it using the appropriate **TStream** method (either **ReadPoint** or **WritePoint**). The pattern fields are objects descended from **TStreamObject** and can be handled by the **TStream::Read-StreamObject** and **TStream::WriteStreamObject** methods. The implementations of **TShape::ReadFrom** and **TShape::WriteTo** are shown in Listing 25-1.

Listing 25-1. TShape::ReadFrom and WriteTo

```
 1: pascal void TShape::ReadFrom(TStream* aStream)
 2: {
 3:    fInteriorPattern = NULL;
 4:    fFramePattern = NULL;
 5:    TStreamObject* aPattern = NULL;
 6:
 7:    TRY {
 8:        Boolean known;
 9:
10:        aPattern = aStream -> ReadStreamObject(known);
11:        this -> SetInteriorPattern((TQuickDrawPattern*)aPattern);
12:                        /* Uses a default if passed NULL */
13:
14:        FreeIfObject(aPattern);    /* Shape made a private copy */
15:        aPattern = NULL;  /* So failure handler doesn't free it */
16:
17:        aPattern = aStream -> ReadStreamObject(known);
18:        this -> SetFramePattern((TQuickDrawPattern*)aPattern);
19:
20:        FreeIfObject(aPattern);
21:        aPattern = NULL;
22:
23:        Point frameSize = aStream -> ReadPoint();
```

```
24:        this -> SetFrameSize(frameSize);
25:
26:                          /* Initialize the other fields */
27:        this -> SetSelection(FALSE);
28:        this -> RememberSelection();
29:        this -> SetFilter(NULL);
30:        }
31:
32:    EXCEPT {
33:        FreeIfObject(aPattern);
34:        this -> Free();    /* Free the object so caller need not */
35:        }
36:
37:    ENDTRY
38: }
39:
40: pascal void TShape::WriteTo(TStream* aStream) const
41: {
42:    aStream -> WriteStreamObject(this -> GetInteriorPattern());
43:    aStream -> WriteStreamObject(this -> GetFramePattern());
44:    aStream -> WritePoint(this -> GetFrameSize());
45: }
```

One thing to note is that the **SetInteriorPattern** (line 11) and **Set-FramePattern** (line 18) methods make a copy of their parameters. Recall from Chapter 23 that each shape object contains private copies of its pattern objects. That is why **ReadFrom** frees *aPattern* on lines 14 and 20.

This is our first example of using a stream. We should note three things that apply to most uses of streams. First is the similarity between the **ReadFrom** and **WriteTo** methods; both process the fields in exactly the same order. It is important to keep the reading and writing methods synchronized so that the writer outputs the same data that the reader expects to input.

Second, notice how we handled the pattern objects to which the shape refers. The shape object is responsible for reading and writing the pattern objects to which it refers. In this case, **TQuickDrawPattern** is a subclass of **TStreamObject**, so the pattern instances are handled by calls to **ReadStreamObject** (lines 10 and 17) and **WriteStreamObject** (lines 42 and 43).

Finally, notice that the reader is responsible for initializing all the fields of the object. **TShape::ReadFrom** is called with a totally uninitialized object. Most of the fields are read from the stream, but some are initialized to standard values. In our program, shapes are initialized to be deselected. We could write the selection state into the stream as well, in which case the same shape would be selected when all the shapes were later read into memory.

Listing 25-1 also uses a private failure handler. You must define a private failure handler in methods that allocate memory; if an error occurs during the method's execution, the failure handler will be called and it can free any memory that was already allocated. In this case, the **Read-From** method allocates a pattern object that may need to be deallocated.

Failure handlers are set up using the macros TRY, EXCEPT, and ENDTRY. TRY establishes a failure handler. Then the statements after TRY are executed. If they succeed, control passes to the statement after ENDTRY.

If, however, the statements after TRY do not execute successfully, control passes to the statements folowing the label EXCEPT. These statements generally perform any necessary cleaning up, such as freeing allocated objects. When the EXCEPT clause finishes, the same failure is signalled and the next handler in the chain executes. Eventually, control reaches the main event loop, at which time MacApp displays an error message and continues.

**By The Way ▶**

The macros are defined so that they use MacApp's standard failure-handling mechanism. Normally, this mechanism requires that you use a nested procedure as the handler. Since nested procedures aren't supported in C++, these macros sidestep the problem. In the process, they make the code easier to read than if nested procedures were used.

The definitions of these macros are contained in the file Pascal.h, which is on the disk containing the ExampleDraw sources.

Listing 25-1 demonstrates two techniques you should use when writing your failure handlers. The first technique helps your failure handler determine what objects need to be freed. Notice that **TShape::ReadFrom** initializes the variable *aPattern* to NULL on line 5. The failure handler, called **HandleReadShape**, will free the object to which *aPattern* refers, provided it is not NULL (line 33). The MacApp utility procedure FreeIfObject is useful in this case. FreeIfObject tests whether its parameter is a valid object and, if so, frees it. (NULL is not a valid object.)

Also notice on lines 15 and 21 that **ReadFrom** sets *aPattern* back to NULL. This is necessary because it freed the pattern object on the previous lines, and we don't want the failure handler to attempt to free the object again.

By the Way ▶

Freeing an object twice is a common mistake in Macintosh programming. Normally, this results in a corrupted heap, which will eventually crash the application. Usually, the crash occurs some time after the heap is corrupted, which makes tracking down the problem especially difficult. A related problem occurs when one part of your program frees an object, but another part tries to use the now-freed object. Even though you may have freed an object, other parts of your program could still refer to the object. It is important to realize that freeing an object does not set all references to that object to NULL.

MacApp tries to catch this mistake at the time it occurs. When you build a debugging version of your program, MacApp performs an additional check each time you call a method. It checks that the object receiving the message is a valid object and that it has not been freed. If the object is invalid, MacApp will report an error in the debugging window. If you call the **Free** method with the same object twice, for example, the second method call will be reported as an error.

This doesn't completely eliminate the problem, however. The testing MacApp does is not foolproof. Also, if you free an object and then allocate a new object, the Macintosh Memory Manager may reuse the same memory space. If your program has mistakenly kept a reference to the old object, it will be confused when it tries to use that object. MacApp won't catch this mistake because the object will appear to be valid; it just won't be the object your program expects.

The second technique you should use when writing failure handlers is applicable to methods, such as **ReadFrom**, that initialize an object. By convention, objects you define should free themselves if their initialization method fails (line 34). This convention eliminates the need for the creator of the object to catch the failure. Since there are more places that create objects in a program than initialization methods, this convention also reduces the code size.

At the next level in the building block, we need methods to read and write the whole collection of shapes. In the same way that shape and pattern objects read and write themselves, instances of **TShapeList** should read and write themselves. The writing method is relatively simple, as you can see in Listing 25-2.

Listing 25-2. WriteTo

```
1: pascal void WriteShape(TShape* aShape, void* aStream)
2: {
3:   ((TStream*)aStream) -> WriteStreamObject(aShape);
4: }
5:
6: pascal void TShapeList::WriteTo(TStream* aStream) const
7: {
8:   aStream -> WriteLong(fNumShapes);
9:   this -> EachShapeDo(&WriteShape, aStream);
10: }
```

This method first writes the number of shapes (line 8) and then writes the individual shapes (line 9). The reason for writing the number of shapes is so that the output format does not rely on reaching the end of the stream to recognize the end of the shape list. This allows us the flexibility to write other data into the stream after the list of shapes.

Reading the shape list is complicated by the need to handle errors. If an error occurs, we want to restore the shape list to its original form. Listing 25-3 shows how to deal with this.

Listing 25-3. ReadFrom

```
1: void TShapeList::ReadFrom(TStream* aStream)
2: {
3:   ArrayIndex numberOfShapes;
4:   aStream -> ReadBytes(&numberOfShapes, sizeof(ArrayIndex));
5:
6:   ArrayIndex oldListSize = fNumShapes;
7:
8:   TStreamObject* newShape = NULL;
9:
10:   TRY {
11:       for (ArrayIndex i = 1; i <= numberOfShapes; i++) {
12:           Boolean known;
13:
14:             newShape = aStream -> ReadStreamObject(known);
15:           if (newShape != NULL)
16:               this -> AddShape((TShape*)newShape);
17:       }
18:   }
```

```
19:     EXCEPT {
20:         FreeIfObject(newShape);
21:                                 /* Free already-added shapes */
22:         if (oldListSize == 0)   /* Special case: free all shapes */
23:             this -> FreeData();
24:
25:         else {                          /* Free each shape we added. */
26:             ArrayIndex currListSize = this -> GetNumberOfShapes();
27:
28:             for ( ArrayIndex number = oldListSize+1;
29:                     number < currListSize;
30:                     number++ )
31:                 this -> RemoveShape((TShape*)(fList -> Last()));
32:         }
33:     }
34:     ENDTRY
35: }
```

There are two places where an error might occur. First, we could get an error from **ReadStreamObject** (line 14) trying to read the next shape object. Second, we could get an error trying to add the new shape to the list, in which case (line 16) the shape will have been created but not entered into the list. The only reference to the new shape will be through the variable *newShape*, which is why the exception handler frees that object (line 20).

If an error does occur, then the error handler frees the new shape, if necessary, and then frees the shapes that were already added to the list. **TShapeList::ReadFrom** optimizes the common case (line 22) where the shape list started out empty. It calls the method **TShapeList::FreeData**, which frees all the shapes. Otherwise, it deletes shapes from the end of the list, until the list returns to its original size (lines 26-31).

## ▶ DoRead, DoWrite, and DoNeedDiskSpace

The final step in our design is to implement the methods that call **TShapeList::ReadFrom** and **WriteTo**. In every MacApp program, three methods in **TDocument** are responsible for all document input/output. These are **DoRead**, **DoWrite**, and **DoNeedDiskSpace**. In the graphics building block, we will implement these functions in the **TShapeList** class. A program using the building block calls these methods from its corresponding document methods. Each of these methods has the same structure. It creates a stream object, calls either the **ReadFrom** or **WriteTo** method of **TShapeList**, and frees the stream object. (See Listing 25-4.)

Listing 25-4. DoRead, DoWrite, and DoNeedDiskSpace

```
 1: pascal void TShapeList::DoRead(short aRefnum)
 2: {
 3:   TFileStream* fileStream = new TFileStream;
 4:   FailNIL(fileStream);
 5:   fileStream -> IFileStream(aRefnum);
 6:
 7:   TRY
 8:       this -> ReadFrom(fileStream);
 9:   EXCEPT
10:       fileStream -> Free();
11:   ENDTRY
12:
13:   fileStream -> Free();
14: }
15:
16: pascal void TShapeList::DoWrite(short aRefnum) const
17: {
18:   TFileStream* fileStream = new TFileStream;
19:   FailNIL(fileStream);
20:   fileStream -> IFileStream(aRefnum);
21:
22:   TRY
23:       this -> WriteTo(fileStream);
24:   EXCEPT
25:       fileStream -> Free();
26:   ENDTRY
27:
28:   fileStream -> Free();
29: }
30:
31: pascal void TShapeList::DoNeedDiskSpace( long* dataForkBytes,
32:                                     long* /*rsrcForkBytes*/)
33: {
34:   TCountingStream* countingStream = new TCountingStream;
35:   FailNIL(countingStream);
36:   countingStream -> ICountingStream();
37:
38:   TRY
39:       this -> WriteTo(countingStream);
40:   EXCEPT
41:       countingStream -> Free();
42:   ENDTRY
43:
```

```
44:   dataForkBytes = dataForkBytes + countingStream -> GetSize();
45:
46:   countingStream -> Free();
47: }
```

In each method, we set up a failure handler to ensure that the stream is freed in the event of an error.

Notice that the implementation of **DoNeedDiskSpace** is very simple. You don't have to implement a special method to estimate the disk space required by the shapes because you can use the same method that **DoWrite** uses to save the shapes (**TShapeList::WriteTo**). Since the same method is used in both **DoNeedDiskSpace** and **DoWrite**, we can be sure that **DoNeedDiskSpace** computes the exact number of bytes needed.

## ▶ Filtered Commands

In Chapter 24, we implemented commands for sketching new shapes and moving one or more shapes. It was easy to undo each of these commands because their actions were reversible. In the first case, we removed the new shape from the collection of shapes; in the second, we moved the shapes the same distance in the opposite direction. Some commands, however, are not so easily reversible.

For example, consider the command that changes the interior pattern in the selected shapes. Reversing this change requires that we restore the original pattern in each shape. Since each shape may have started with a different interior, we would need to save the original pattern before making the change, in order to restore it. The amount of memory required to save all the patterns is unbounded and is proportional to the number of shapes in the selection. Another command that is not easy to reverse is the Bring to Front command, which positions the selected shapes in front of the other shapes. For this we need to remember the position of each selected shape within the list of shapes. Essentially, we would have to duplicate the entire list of shapes.

Both cases present the same problem. If we change the internal data structures to perform the command, it is difficult to restore the structures to their original form. Fortunately, we can use another technique, known as *filtering*, to implement this kind of command efficiently. Instead of changing the internal data structures, we simply draw the data as if the change had been made. Undoing the so-called change becomes simple, because the data structures were never changed.

For example, the command that changes the interior pattern will create a filter that applies to the selected shapes. Those shapes will be drawn using the new pattern instead of the pattern contained in the shape object. If the command is undone, then all we have to do is remove the filter and the shapes will be displayed with their original pattern. Think of the shape objects as 35mm slides and the view as a screen. The process of drawing the shapes in the view corresponds to projecting the slides on the screen. One way to change the appearance of the slide is to add a filter between the slide and the screen. To restore the original appearance, we simply remove the filter.

Let's look at a computer example. Suppose we have the two shape objects shown in the left half of Figure 25-1, which produce the display shown in the right half.

The user changes the shapes' interiors to white. Instead of changing the shape objects, we add a filter between the objects and the view, which makes the shapes look white in the view. This is shown in Figure 25-2.

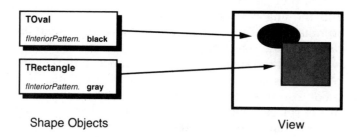

Figure 25-1. Two shapes without a filter

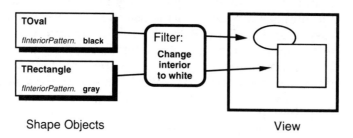

Figure 25-2. Filtering the shapes' interiors

To undo the change, all we have to do is remove the filter, which will result in the original situation shown in Figure 25-1. Here is another way to think of this technique. We fool the user into believing that the command was done. To the user, the shapes look changed, even though the internal objects are the same. We cannot keep up this charade indefinitely, however; at some point we have to change the shape objects. Since the purpose of the filter is to help us implement Undo, it follows that the filter is no longer needed when the command cannot be undone. This happens just before the next command is performed and is known as *committing* the command.

In our example, the Change to White command will be committed when it can no longer be undone. When this happens, the interior patterns in the shape objects will be changed to white and the filter will be removed. This result is shown in Figure 25-3. Notice that only the internal data structures change; the user sees the same image in the view.

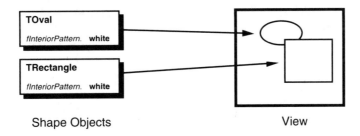

Shape Objects                              View

Figure 25-3. After committing the command

Filtering could apply as easily to the list of shapes as to the individual shape objects. For example, consider the implementation of the Bring to Front command. One approach is to rearrange the list at the time the command is performed. Undoing this command, however, would require remembering the exact position of each shape within the list.

With a filter, the implementation is much simpler. The Bring to Front command would set up a filter that modifies the way the shape list sequences through the list of shapes. Normally, the shapes are processed in order, with the frontmost shape processed last.

The Bring to Front filter would process the shapes unaffected by the command first and then the shapes affected by the command. Since the frontmost shapes are processed last, this produces the effect of the Bring to Front command.

## ▶ Filtering Shapes

Now we will show how to implement filtering, first for individual shapes. Any of the attributes of a shape are eligible for filtering including its interior and frame patterns, its frame size, and its geometric definition. We will define a **TShapeFilter** class, which can filter any of these attributes and subclasses of **TShapeFilter**, which implement particular kinds of filters.

**TShapeFilter** will have one method for each attribute that it can potentially filter. These methods are **FilterInteriorPattern**, **FilterFramePattern**, **FilterFrameSize**, and **FilterGeometricBounds**. Each of these methods has one reference parameter. The shape's attribute is passed to the method, which can modify the attribute if it wants to filter it. The implementations of these methods in the **TShapeFilter** class do nothing, which means no filtering occurs. Each subclass of **TShapeFilter** overrides the method corresponding to the attribute it is filtering. For example, the class **TInteriorFilter** overrides the **FilterInteriorPattern** method and substitutes the pattern in its *fNewPattern* instance variable for the parameter. This is shown in Listing 25-5, line 4.

Listing 25-5. Overriding FilterInteriorPattern

```
1: pascal void TInteriorFilter::FilterInteriorPattern(
2:              const TQuickDrawPattern*& interiorPattern) const
3: {
4:   interiorPattern = fNewPattern;
5: }
```

Since **TInteriorFilter** does not override any of the other filtering methods, it does not filter any of those attributes.

The filter must be applied when you access any attribute of **TShape**. You will recall from Chapter 23 that we defined methods in **TShape** to access its attributes and made the instance variables private to the class. Now you can see the value of this design decision.

To ensure that the filter object is available, we will add a field to **TShape** to contain the current filter. Although this adds 4 bytes to each shape object, it greatly simplifies the implementation.

<table>
<tr><td>**By the Way ▶**</td><td>There are other implementation alternatives. You can pass the filter object to any method that needs it, or you can use a global variable to refer to the filter. The first alternative clutters up the implementation, while the second makes it more difficult to handle multiple documents. You have to weigh these disadvantages and decide which alternative best suits your application.</td></tr>
</table>

Listing 25-6 gives the implementation of **TShape.GetInteriorPattern**.

Listing 25-6. GetInteriorPattern

```
1: pascal const TQuickDrawPattern* TShape::GetInteriorPattern
   () const
2: {
3:   const TQuickDrawPattern* pattern = fInteriorPattern;
4:
5:   if (this -> IsFiltered())                    /* Apply filter */
6:       fShapeFilter -> FilterInteriorPattern(pattern);
7:
8:   return pattern;
9: }
```

**GetInteriorPattern** calls the method **IsFiltered** on line 5. This method returns true if the last command affected this shape (that is, it was selected) and the shape has a filter. If the shape is being filtered, then we give the filter object a chance to change the pattern (line 6). The implementation of **TShape::IsFiltered** is as follows:

```
1: pascal Boolean TShape::IsFiltered() const
2: {
3:   return (this -> WasSelected()) && (fShapeFilter != NULL);
4: }
```

As we have said, when the user performs the next command, we have to commit the filtered command. This requires changing the shape objects and removing the filter. We will implement this with the **CommitFilter** method in **TShape**. The code for this is:

```
1: pascal void TShape::CommitFilter()
2: {
3:   if (this -> IsFiltered())                /* Change the shape */
4:       fShapeFilter -> CommitChangeTo(this);
5:
6:   fShapeFilter = NULL;                      /* Forget about filter */
7: }
```

Since the shape has no idea of what kind of filter it contains, **CommitFilter** must call a method of the filter object, **CommitChangeTo**, to apply the change to the shape. In the case of **TInteriorFilter**, this method simply sets the interior pattern with the following code:

```
1: pascal void TInteriorFilter::CommitChangeTo(TShape* aShape)
   const
2: {
3:   aShape -> SetInteriorPattern(fNewPattern);
4: }
```

We now have the mechanism to apply a filter to any set of shape objects. All that remains is to implement a command object that handles the filter. Since the filter object contains the knowledge of what attribute is being filtered, we only need a single command class to handle any kind of filter. The **TShapeChanger** class contains a reference to the filter object. To perform the command, it stores the filter in each affected shape object; to undo the command it removes the filter from the shapes. To commit the command, it calls **TShape::CommitFilter** for each shape in the list. The implementation of **TShapeChanger** is shown in Listing 25-7.

Listing 25-7. TShapeChanger

```
1: pascal void TShapeChanger::DoIt()
2: {
3:   fShapeList -> RememberSelection();
4:   if (fShapeFilter != NULL)
5:       this -> SetFilter(fShapeFilter);       /* Install filter */
6: }
7:
8: pascal void TShapeChanger::UndoIt()
9: {
10:   this -> SetFilter(NULL);                  /* Remove filter */
11: }
12:
```

```
13: pascal void TShapeChanger::RedoIt() /* override */
14: {
15:   if (fShapeFilter != NULL)
16:       this -> SetFilter(fShapeFilter);        /* Install filter */
17: }
18:
19: pascal void CommitAShape(TShape* aShape, void* /* unused */)
20: {
21:   aShape -> CommitFilter();
22: }
23:
24: pascal void TShapeChanger::Commit() /* override */
25: {
26:   if (fShapeFilter != NULL)
27:       fShapeList -> EachShapeDo(&CommitAShape, this);
28: }
29:
30: pascal void TShapeChanger::SetFilter(TShapeFilter*
   itsShapeFilter)
31: {
32: /* Turn off highlighting because we're changing the
   selection.
33:                           We need to focus before doing this. */
34:   if (fView -> Focus())
35:       fShapeViewHelper -> DoHighlightSelection(hlOn, hlOff);
36:   fShapeList -> RestoreSelection();
37:   fShapeViewHelper -> SetShapeFilter(itsShapeFilter);
38: }
```

The method **TShapeViewHelper::SetShapeFilter** (shown in Listing 25-8) changes the filter in each affected shape and invalidates those shapes so they'll be redrawn.

Listing 25-8. SetShapeFilter

```
1: struct SetShapeFilterInfo {
2:   TView*          fView;
3:   TShapeFilter*   newFilter;
4: };
5:
6: pascal void SetFilterInShape(TShape* aShape, void* infoStruct)
7: {
8:   SetShapeFilterInfo* info = (SetShapeFilterInfo*)infoStruct;
9:
10:                           /* Only process affected shapes */
```

```
11:    if (aShape -> WasSelected()) {
12:        aShape -> Invalidate(info -> fView);      /* Old position */
13:        aShape -> SetFilter(info -> newFilter);   /* Set filter */
14:        aShape -> Invalidate(info -> fView);      /* New position */
15:    }
16: }
17:
18: pascal void TShapeViewHelper::SetShapeFilter(
19:                                 TShapeFilter* newFilter)
20: {
21:    SetShapeFilterInfo info;
22:    info.fView = fView;
23:    info.newFilter = newFilter;
24:
25:    fShapeList -> EachShapeDo(&SetFilterInShape, &info);
26: }
```

Since **SetShapeFilter** cannot tell whether the filter affects the shape's bounds, it must invalidate the shape using both the old and new filters. Also note that we change the filter only in the shapes affected by the command. These are the shapes for which **WasSelected** returns true.

Using a shape filter in an application is fairly simple. If the user wants to change the interior pattern of the selection, we create instances of **TInteriorFilter** and **TShapeChanger**, and return the shape changer command to MacApp. MacApp will then call the methods **DoIt**, **UndoIt**, and so forth, as appropriate. To encapsulate this process in the building block, we will add a method to **TShapeViewHelper**, called **ChangeInteriorPattern**. This is shown in Listing 25-9.

Listing 25-9. ChangeInteriorPattern

```
 1: pascal TCommand* TShapeViewHelper::ChangeInteriorPattern(
 2:                         CmdNumber aCmdNumber,
 3:                         const TQuickDrawPattern* newInterior)
 4: {
 5:    TInteriorFilter* interiorFilter = new TInteriorFilter;
 6:    FailNIL(interiorFilter);
 7:    interiorFilter -> IInteriorFilter(newInterior);
 8:
 9:    return this -> CreateShapeChanger(aCmdNumber,
       interiorFilter);
10: }
11:
```

```
12: pascal TCommand* TShapeViewHelper::CreateShapeChanger(
13:                                     CmdNumber aCmdNumber,
14:                                     TShapeFilter* itsFilter)
15: {
16:    TShapeChanger* shapeChanger = NULL;
17:
18:    TRY {
19:       shapeChanger = new TShapeChanger;
20:       FailNIL(shapeChanger);
21:       shapeChanger -> IShapeChanger(aCmdNumber, this,
             itsFilter);
22:    }
23:    EXCEPT
24:       itsFilter -> Free();  /* Free filter so caller need not */
25:    ENDTRY
26:
27:    return shapeChanger;
28: }
```

**ChangeInteriorPattern** creates an instance of **TInteriorFilter** and calls **TShapeViewHelper::CreateShapeChanger** (line 9). **CreateShapeChanger** creates an instance of **TShapeChanger**, given the appropriate filter. It also handles the case where the command object can't be allocated (line 24). In that case it frees the filter object, so that the caller doesn't have to.

▶ Filtering the Shape List

In addition to filtering individual shapes, we also need a mechanism to filter the entire list of shapes. The purpose of the shape list filter is to change the order in which the shapes are processed. This is a simpler problem than filtering individual shapes, since there is only one attribute, the ordering of the list, being filtered. We will use the same design approach we used for filtering shapes. First, we will define the **TShapeListFilter** class. **TShapeListFilter** implements a method called **EachShapeDo**, which does the actual filtering. We use the filter in the implementation of **TShapeList::EachShapeDo**. (See Listing 25-10.)

Listing 25-10. EachShapeDo

```
1: pascal void TShapeList::EachShapeDo(DoToShapeProc DoToShape,
2:                                     void* staticLink) const
3: {
```

```
4:   if (fShapeListFilter != NULL)              /* Filter the list */
5:       fShapeListFilter -> EachShapeDo(DoToShape, staticLink);
6:
7:   else        /* Iterate over all the shapes without the filter */
8:       this -> UnfilteredEach(DoToShape, DoToShape_StaticLink);
9: }
```

If the filter is not NULL, **TShapeList** calls the filter to sequence through the list (line 5). Otherwise it calls the method **UnfilteredEach** (line 8), in order to sequence through the shapes in the list.

The default implementation of **TShapeListFilter.EachShapeDo** (see Listing 25-11) simply sequences through all the shapes, which results in no filtering. Later, we will define specific subclasses of **TShapeList-Filter** to override **EachShapeDo**. To implement these classes, **TShape-ListFilter** defines two utility methods, **AffectedShapesDo** and **Unaf-fectedShapesDo**. These methods sequence through the shapes affected or unaffected by the filter. The implementations of these methods are also shown in Listing 25-11.

Listing 25-11. TShapeListFilter.EachShapeDo

```
1: struct DoToShapeInfo {
2:   DoToShapeProc    DoToShape;
3:   void*            DoToShape_StaticLink;
4: };
5:
6: pascal void TShapeListFilter::EachShapeDo(DoToShapeProc
   DoToShape,
7:                                   void* staticLink) const
8: {
9:   fShapeList -> UnfilteredEach(DoToShape, staticLink);
10: }
11:
12: pascal void DoToAffectedShape(TShape* aShape, void* theInfo)
13: {
14:   DoToShapeInfo* info = (DoToShapeInfo*)theInfo;
15:   if (aShape -> WasSelected())
16:       TShapeList::CallDoToShape( aShape,
17:                               info -> DoToShape_StaticLink,
18:                               info -> DoToShape);
19: }
20:
21: pascal void TShapeListFilter::AffectedShapesDo(
22:                           DoToShapeProc DoToShape,
23:                           void* DoToShape_StaticLink) const
24: {
25:   DoToShapeInfo info;
26:   info.DoToShape = DoToShape;
```

```
27:    info.DoToShape_StaticLink = DoToShape_StaticLink;
28:
29:    fShapeList -> UnfilteredEach(&DoToAffectedShape, & info);
30: }
31:
32: pascal void DoToUnaffectedShape(TShape* aShape, void* theInfo)
33: {
34:    DoToShapeInfo* info = (DoToShapeInfo*)theInfo;
35:    if (! aShape -> WasSelected())
36:        TShapeList::CallDoToShape( aShape,
37:                                   info -> DoToShape_StaticLink,
38:                                   info -> DoToShape);
39: }
40:
41: pascal void TShapeListFilter::UnaffectedShapesDo(
42:                        DoToShapeProc DoToShape,
43:                        void* DoToShape_StaticLink) const
44: {
45:    DoToShapeInfo info;
46:    info.DoToShape = DoToShape;
47:    info.DoToShape_StaticLink = DoToShape_StaticLink;
48:
49:    fShapeList -> UnfilteredEach(&DoToUnaffectedShape, &info);
50: }
```

(Note that the structure DoToShapeInfo is the same as was shown in Listing 24-5.)

Notice that in lines 9, 29, and 49, the filter object calls the method **TShapeList::UnfilteredEach**. This method sequences through the actual shapes in the shape list without applying the filter. If instead we had called **TShapeList::EachShapeDo**, the result would be an infinite recursion. The filter would call **TShapeList::EachShapeDo**, which would call the filter, and so on.

Using these two utility methods you can implement a variety of filters. For example, we mentioned the Bring to Front command earlier in this section. A filter for this command would be implemented as shown in Listing 25-12.

## Listing 25-12. TFrontFilter

```
1: pascal void TFrontFilter::EachShapeDo( DoToShapeProc
   DoToShape,
2:                                        void* staticLink) const
3: {
4:    /* Process the affected shapes last to bring them forward */
5:    this -> UnaffectedShapesDo(DoToShape, staticLink);
6:    this -> AffectedShapesDo(DoToShape, staticLink);
7: }
```

The Send to Back command would use a similar filter (see Listing 25-13); the only difference is the order of the calls to **AffectedShapesDo** and **UnaffectedShapesDo**.

Listing 25-13. TBackFilter

```
1: pascal void TBackFilter::EachShapeDo( DoToShapeProc DoToShape,
2:                                   void* staticLink) const
3: {
4:   /* Process the affected shapes last to send them backward */
5:   this -> AffectedShapesDo(DoToShape, staticLink);
6:   this -> UnaffectedShapesDo(DoToShape, staticLink);
7: }
```

The final example is a filter that removes the selected shapes from view, which will be used in the next section to implement the Cut and Clear commands. Its code follows:

```
1: pascal void TClearFilter::EachShapeDo( DoToShapeProc
   DoToShape,
2:                                   void* staticLink) const
3: {
4:   this -> UnaffectedShapesDo(DoToShape, staticLink);
5: }
```

As with the shape filter, the shape list filter must commit the change when the user performs the next command. This is done by the method **TShapeListFilter::CommitChange**, which must be overridden by each list filter subclass. For example, to commit the Bring to Front command, we must move the affected shapes to the end of the list. (Remember that the shapes at the end of the list are closer to the front.) We will do this by removing the affected shapes and adding them to the end of the list as shown in Listing 25-14.

Listing 25-14. CommitChange

```
1: struct CommitInfo {
2:   TShapeList*     otherList;
3:   TShapeList*     fShapeList;
4: };
5:
6: pascal void RememberShape(TShape* aShape, void* theInfo)
7: {
8:   CommitInfo* info = (CommitInfo*)theInfo;
9:
```

```
10:    (info -> fShapeList) -> RemoveShape(aShape);
11:    (info -> otherList) -> AddShape(aShape);
12: }
13:
14: pascal void AddShape(TShape* aShape, void* fShapeList)
15: {
16:    ((TShapeList*)fShapeList) -> AddShape(aShape);
17: }
18:
19: pascal void TFrontFilter::CommitChange() const
20: {
21:    TShapeList* affectedShapes = new TShapeList;
22:    FailNIL(affectedShapes);
23:    affectedShapes -> IShapeList();
24:
25:    TRY {
26:        CommitInfo info;
27:        info.otherList = affectedShapes;
28:        info.fShapeList = this -> GetShapeList();
29:
30:            /* Move affected shapes from main to temporary list */
31:        this -> AffectedShapesDo(&RememberShape, &info);
32:
33:            /* Add affected shapes at the end of the main list */
34:        affectedShapes -> EachShapeDo( &AddShape,
35:                                        this -> GetShapeList());
36:    }
37:    EXCEPT
38:        affectedShapes -> Free();
39:    ENDTRY
40:
41:    affectedShapes -> RemoveAll();
42:    affectedShapes -> Free();
43: }
```

This method is a bit awkward, because **TShapeList** (and **TList**, which is used internally) does not provide an easy way to move list elements around in the list. Also, the iteration methods in **TList** (and therefore **TShapeList**) do not allow us to insert elements in the list while iterating through it. We can, however, delete elements from the list and add them to a temporary list (lines 6-12 and 31). Then we can iterate through the temporary list and add those shapes back to the original list (lines 14-17 and 34). It is important to call **RemoveAll** (line 41), otherwise the shapes in the temporary list will be freed when the list is freed (line 42).

The **TBackFilter::CommitChange** method simply moves the unaffected shapes to the end of the list, using the same technique above. The **TClearFilter::CommitChange** method just removes the affected shapes from the list.

We only need one command class (**TShapeListChanger**) to handle any kind of shape list filtering. The implementation is shown in Listing 25-15, along with the methods it calls. You will notice that the implementation is similar to that of **TShapeChanger** in Listing 25-7.

Listing 25-15. TShapeListChanger

```
 1: pascal void TShapeListChanger::DoIt()
 2: {
 3:    fShapeList -> RememberSelection();
 4:    if (fShapeListFilter != NULL)
 5:        this -> SetFilter(fShapeListFilter);  /* Install
           filter */
 6: }
 7:
 8: pascal void TShapeListChanger::UndoIt()
 9: {
10:    if (fShapeListFilter != NULL)
11:        this -> SetFilter(NULL);                  /* Remove filter */
12: }
13:
14: pascal void TShapeListChanger::RedoIt()
15: {
16:    if (fShapeListFilter != NULL)
17:        this -> SetFilter(fShapeListFilter); /* Install filter */
18: }
19:
20: pascal void TShapeListChanger::Commit()
21: {
22:    fShapeList -> CommitFilter();
23: }
24:
25: pascal void TShapeListChanger::SetFilter(
26:                             TShapeListFilter* newFilter)
27: {
28:    if (fView -> Focus())
29:        fShapeViewHelper -> DoHighlightSelection(hlOn, hlOff);
30:    fShapeList -> RestoreSelection();
31:    fShapeViewHelper -> SetShapeListFilter(newFilter);
32: }
```

```
33:
34: pascal void TShapeList::CommitFilter()
35: {
36:   if (fShapeListFilter != NULL) {
37:       fShapeListFilter -> CommitChange();
38:       this -> SetFilter(NULL);
39:   }
40: }
41:
42: pascal void TShapeViewHelper::SetShapeListFilter(
43:                                 TShapeListFilter* newFilter)
44: {
45:   this -> InvalidateSelection();        /* Invalidate before */
46:   fShapeList -> SetFilter(newFilter);   /* Change the filter */
47:   this -> InvalidateSelection();        /* Invalidate after  */
48: }
```

Finally, **TShapeViewHelper** will implement methods to handle the common commands we have discussed, such as Bring to Front, and Send to Back. One example is shown in Listing 25-16, along with the utility method **CreateShapeListChanger**.

Listing 25-16. BringToFront

```
1: pascal TCommand* TShapeViewHelper::BringToFront(
2:                                 CmdNumber aCmdNumber)
3: {
4:   TFrontFilter* frontFilter = new TFrontFilter;
5:   FailNIL(frontFilter);
6:   frontFilter -> IFrontFilter(fShapeList);
7:
8:   return this -> CreateShapeListChanger
     (aCmdNumber,frontFilter);
9: }
10:
11: pascal TCommand* TShapeViewHelper::CreateShapeListChanger(
12:                                 CmdNumber aCmdNumber,
13:                                 TShapeListFilter* itsFilter)
14: {
15:   TShapeListChanger* shapeListChanger = NULL;
16:
17:   TRY {
18:       shapeListChanger = new TShapeListChanger;
19:       FailNIL(shapeListChanger);
20:       shapeListChanger -> IShapeListChanger( aCmdNumber,
```

```
21:                                                  this,
22:                                                  itsFilter);
23:    }
24:    EXCEPT
25:        itsFilter -> Free();  /* Free filter so caller need not */
26:    ENDTRY
27:
28:    return shapeListChanger;
29: }
```

## ▶ Clipboard Support

We have saved Clipboard support for the end of this chapter, because
it depends on the methods we implemented for document reading and
writing as well as filtered commands. Clipboard support is divided
into two parts: implementing Cut and Copy and implementing Paste.

## ▶ Technical Overview

The Macintosh Clipboard contains one piece of information at a time. It
is possible, however, to store different representations of those data in
the Clipboard. Usually a program will store a private representation,
which only it can interpret, as well as a public representation, which
other programs can paste. Each representation is tagged with a four-
letter identifier. There are two universal representations: plain text
('TEXT') and a QuickDraw picture ('PICT').

When a program pastes data from the Clipboard, it chooses the representation that it can best handle. Usually, the private representations
contain a complete description of the data, while the public forms provide less information. For example, a word processor might use a private representation that includes font changes, margins, and tab stops,
while its public form would be just the text without style information.

MacApp also makes a distinction between a local and an external
Clipboard. When the data are first put into the Clipboard, they are
stored locally in the program. The local Clipboard is usually implemented with the same data structures used in the rest of the program.
The data are exported to the external Clipboard only when the user
switches to another program or to a desk accessory. At that time, the
program converts the local data to one or more external formats, which
are then stored in the Macintosh Clipboard, known as the Desk Scrap.
The Macintosh ROM contains routines to manage the system-wide
Clipboard; those routines expect the Clipboard data to be stored in a
handle. (There is a separate handle for each representation of the data.)

By the Way ▶ The distinction between a local and external Clipboard has two purposes. First, there is an efficiency gain, in that MacApp need not export the Clipboard until there is a chance it might be used in another program. This saves the cost of creating additional data representations for each cut or copy, and copying the data into the system Clipboard. Second, the ROM Clipboard routines do not implement Undo. MacApp solves this problem by keeping the Clipboard local to the program, where it can implement its own Undo.

In a MacApp program, a view object is responsible for most of the Clipboard implementation. To put data into the Clipboard, you create a view object that displays the data and install that view in the Clipboard. You might also create a document object, if the implementation of the Clipboard view requires one. One purpose of the view object is to display the contents of the Clipboard in a window. The view object also implements several other Clipboard-related methods. For example, there is a method **TView::GivePasteData**, which supplies the Clipboard data in a particular format. MacApp calls the method **TView::WriteToDeskScrap** to tell the view to export the Clipboard.

Internally, the graphics building block deals with objects. When it comes time to paste shapes into a shape list, for example, we will need a list of the shapes being pasted. The paste implementation will add those shape objects to the list. Externally, the Clipboard data are stored in a handle. This means that the graphics building block will have to convert the list of shapes to a handle when exporting data and recreate the shape object from a handle when pasting an external Clipboard. We will also store a picture representation of the data, in order to support applications that cannot handle shapes directly, but can paste standard pictures.

To minimize conversion between shape objects and shapes stored in a handle, the graphics building block will deal with both forms of data. We will prefer to manipulate the Clipboard as a list of shape objects, since that requires no conversion, but we will also accept a handle containing a sequence of exported shapes.

| By the Way ▶ | Handling both forms of data also simplifies the implementation. If the user switches into your MacApp program, and MacApp discovers that the Clipboard has changed, it calls the method of **TApplication::MakeViewForAlienClipboard**. The purpose of this method is to import an external Clipboard by creating an appropriate view object. The view not only imports the data, but also provides something to display in the program's Clipboard window.<br><br>The graphics building block does not have to override **MakeViewForAlienClipboard**, since it can accept shape objects stored in a handle. And since the building block exports a QuickDraw picture as well as the shapes, MacApp can display the Clipboard contents for us automatically. |
|---|---|

## ▶ Cut and Copy Implementation

The implementation of the Cut and Copy commands is nearly identical. The only difference is whether the selection is removed from the document or not. In the graphics building block, the difference in implementing Cut is using an instance of **TClearFilter** to filter the cut shapes from the list.

The view we put into the Clipboard will be an instance of **TShapeView**. (An instance of this class can also be used in a normal document window.) A **TShapeView** object contains a reference to an instance of **TShapeViewHelper**, which implements much of the functionality of the graphics building block. This object, in turn, refers to an instance of **TShapeList**, which contains the collection of shapes. We will also implement the Clipboard functionality in **TShapeViewHelper**.

The first step in implementing Cut and Copy is to define a command subclass; in this case, **TShapeCutCopyCmd**. Since the implementation of this command will use shape list filtering (in the case of Cut), this class will be a subclass of **TShapeListChanger**. When the command object is initialized, it will create the filter object in the case of a Cut command but not in the case of Copy. Also, since this command changes the Clipboard, it is important to set the variable *fChangesClipboard* to true in the initialization method, after calling **ICommand**. This tells MacApp that it should switch to the previous Clipboard data if the user selects the Undo command. In the case of the Copy command, the document is not changed; we inform MacApp of this by setting the variable *fCausesChange* to false, again after calling **ICommand**.

The **DoIt** method of **TShapeCutCopyCmd** does most of the work. It must clone the selected shapes, install them into an instance of **TShapeView**, and install that view into the Clipboard. (See Listing 25-17.)

Listing 25-17. TShapeCutCopyCmd::DoIt

```
 1: struct CutCopyInfo {
 2:   Rect*          selBounds;
 3:   TShapeList*     clipList;
 4: };
 5:
 6: pascal void CloneShape(TShape* aShape, void* infoStruct)
 7: {
 8:   TShape* newShape = (TShape*)(aShape -> Clone());
 9:   newShape -> SetSelection(false);
10:
11:   CutCopyInfo* info = (CutCopyInfo*)infoStruct;
12:
13:   newShape -> OffsetBy( 1 - (info -> selBounds) -> left,
14:                         1 - (info -> selBounds) -> top);
15:   (info -> clipList) -> AddShape(newShape);
16: }
17:
18: pascal void TShapeCutCopyCmd::DoIt()
19: {
20:   TShapeList* shapeList = this -> GetShapeList();
21:   Rect selBounds = shapeList -> SelectionBounds();
22:
23:                               /* Make the clipboard objects */
24:   TShapeList* clipList = NULL;
25:   TView* clipView = NULL;
26:
27:   TRY {
28:       clipList = new TShapeList;
29:       FailNIL(clipList);
30:       clipList -> IShapeList();
31:                               /* Create a view for clipboard */
32:       clipView = this -> NewClipboardView(clipList);
33:       shapeList -> RememberSelection();
34:
35:       CutCopyInfo info;
36:       info.selBounds = &selBounds;
37:       info.clipList = clipList;
38:                                   /* Clone the shapes */
39:       shapeList -> EachSelectedShapeDo(&CloneShape, &info);
40:       clipView -> AdjustSize();
41:                                   /* Store view in clipboard */
42:       gApplication -> ClaimClipboard(clipView);
43:   }
44:   EXCEPT {
45:       FreeIfObject(clipList);
```

```
46:        FreeIfObject(clipView);
47:    }
48:    ENDTRY
49:
50:    inherited::DoIt();                    /* Put filter into effect */
51: }
52:
53: pascal TView* TShapeCutCopyCmd::NewClipboardView(
54:                          TShapeList* itsShapeList) const
55: {
56:    TShapeView* shapeView = new TShapeView;
57:    FailNIL(shapeView);
58:    shapeView -> IShapeView( NULL, NULL, &gZeroVPt, &gZeroVPt,
59:                             sizeVariable, sizeVariable,
60:                             itsShapeList, NULL);
61:
62:    return shapeView;
63: }
```

If we were simply to clone the selected shapes, their positions within the Clipboard window would be the same as their positions in the document. This might result in a large amount of blank space in the Clipboard window, if the original shapes were not close to the top left of their original view. The call to OffsetBy on line 13 of the listing offsets the copied shapes to the top left of the view. (Actually, we allow a 1-pixel margin on the top left.) **TShapeCutCopyCmd::DoIt** calls **New-ClipboardView** (line 32) to create the view installed in the clipboard. We made this a method so that clients of the building block can create an alternate view object if needed.

It is not necessary to override the **UndoIt** or **RedoIt** methods, since we can inherit the implementations from **TShapeListChanger**. MacApp will take care of undoing or redoing the change to the Clipboard, since we indicated that the command changes the Clipboard. The only other effect of the command (in the case of Cut) is to show or hide the affected shapes, which will be handled by the **TShapeListChanger** methods.

**TShapeViewHelper** must implement three Clipboard-related methods. These methods will be called from the corresponding methods in **TShapeView**. The first is **ContainsClipType**. The purpose of this method is to tell MacApp what data representations the view can support. **TShapeViewHelper** supports only one representation: a list of shape objects. The four-character ID of this type will be stored as the *fShapeListClipType* instance variable of the shape view helper, in case the building block client needs to change its value. (Most clients will have no need to change the default value, however.)

The implementation of **ContainsClipType** is as follows:

```
1: pascal Boolean TShapeViewHelper::ContainsClipType(ResType
   aType)
2: {
3:   return (aType == fShapeListClipType);
4: }
```

The second Clipboard-related method is **TView::GivePasteData**, which complements **ContainsClipType**. Its purpose is to supply the actual Clipboard data in a specific form. In this case, we can provide a reference to **TShapeList**, which contains the Clipboard shapes. The implementation is shown in Listing 25-18.

Listing 25-18. GivePasteData

```
1: pascal long TShapeViewHelper::GivePasteData( Handle
   aDataHandle,
2:                                      ResType dataType)
3: {
4:   if (dataType == fShapeListClipType) {
5:                   /* We can satisfy the request */
6:       if (aDataHandle != NULL) {
7:           SetHandleSize(aDataHandle, sizeof(TShapeList*));
8:           **(HShapeList)aDataHandle = fShapeList;
9:       }
10:      return sizeof(TShapeList*);     /* Return size of data */
11:  }
12:
13:  else                          /* We don't support that type */
14:      return noTypeErr;
15: }
```

If MacApp asks for the Clipboard in the form of a shape list and the handle is not NULL (line 6), then we set the data handle (in line 7) to the size of an object reference, and store a reference to the shape list in the handle (line 8). The return value of **GivePasteData** is either the size of the Clipboard data or an error code, which is a negative number.

The third Clipboard-related method that must be implemented by **TShapeViewHelper** is **WriteToDeskScrap**. This method is called by MacApp to convert the local Clipboard into one or more external representations. The default implementation in **TView** stores a QuickDraw picture in the Clipboard; the implementation in **TShapeViewHelper** is responsible for storing the list of shapes in a handle. Fortunately, we have a method in **TShapeList** called **WriteTo**, which writes the shape to a stream, and we have a stream implementation that stores data in a handle. **WriteToDeskScrap**, therefore, only has to put the pieces together, as shown in Listing 25-19.

Listing 25-19. WriteToDeskScrap

```
 1: pascal void TShapeViewHelper::WriteToDeskScrap()
 2: {
 3:    Handle h = NULL;
 4:    THandleStream* handleStream = NULL;
 5:
 6:    TRY {
 7:        h = NewHandle(0);         /* Create a handle for writing */
 8:        FailNIL(h);
 9:
10:        handleStream = new THandleStream;
11:        FailNIL(handleStream);
12:        handleStream -> IHandleStream(h, 100);
13:
14:        fShapeList -> WriteTo(handleStream);
15:
16:
17:        handleStream -> Free();    /* This compacts the handle */
18:        handleStream = NULL;       /* So handler doesn't free it */
19:
20:                            /* Put the handle into the Clipboard */
21:        FailOSErr(PutDeskScrapData(fShapeStreamClipType, h));
22:        DisposHandle(h);
23:    }
24:    EXCEPT {
25:        DisposIfHandle(h);
26:        FreeIfObject(handleStream);
27:    }
28:    ENDTRY
29: }
30:
31: pascal void TShapeView::WriteToDeskScrap()
32: {
33:            /* Write the custom format then a QuickDraw picture */
34:    fShapeViewHelper -> WriteToDeskScrap();
35:    inherited::WriteToDeskScrap();
36: }
```

In line 21 we use the instance variable *fShapeStreamClipType*. This is the Clipboard type ID that indicates a list of shapes written to a stream. As before, we store this value in a field of **TShapeViewHelper**, in case the building block client wants to change it. (Changing this field prevents other clients of the graphics building block from recognizing and pasting your Clipboard format. For this reason, you should not change the value of this field unless you really want to keep your data private.)

Listing 25-19 also shows how **TShapeView** (or any view class that you might define) would use **TShapeViewHelper::WriteToDeskScrap**. In most cases, you will add to the Clipboard a QuickDraw picture that represents the copied shapes. The call to **inherited::WriteToDeskScrap** on line 35 shows how this would be done.

## ▶ Paste

To implement the Paste command, you simply define a **TShapePaste-Cmd** class. Rather than adding the pasted shapes to the main shape list and removing them to implement Undo, we will use another kind of filtering on the shape list. Therefore, you have to make **TShapePaste-Cmd** a subclass of **TShapeListChanger**. The filter object, called **TAdd-ShapesFilter**, contains an instance of **TShapeList**, which contains the shapes being pasted. Its **EachShapeDo** method processes these shapes after the existing shapes, as shown in Listing 25-20.

Listing 25-20. EachShapeDo

```
 1: pascal void TAddShapesFilter::EachShapeDo(
 2:                         DoToShapeProc DoToShape,
 3:                         void* DoToShape_StaticLink) const
 4: {
 5:                 /* Process old shapes first, then new shapes */
 6:    inherited::EachShapeDo(DoToShape, DoToShape_StaticLink);
 7:    fNewShapes -> EachShapeDo(DoToShape, DoToShape_StaticLink);
 8: }
 9:
10: pascal void AddShape(TShape* aShape, void* fShapeList)
11: {
12:    ((TShapeList*)fShapeList) -> AddShape(aShape);
13: }
14:
15: pascal void TAddShapesFilter::CommitChange() const
16: {
17:    fNewShapes -> EachShapeDo(&AddShape, this -> GetShapeList());
18:    fNewShapes -> RemoveAll();
19: }
```

(Note that the AddShape function is the same as was shown in Listing 25-14.)

**TAddShapesFilter** is not specific to the paste command. It can be used with any command that adds shapes, for example Duplicate. The **DoIt** method of **TShapePasteCmd** (as shown in Listing 25-21) will create a new instance of **TShapeList**, copy the shapes from the Clipboard to the new list, and create an instance of **TAddShapesFilter**.

Listing 25-21. TShapePasteCmd::DoIt

```
 1: pascal void FixupShapes(TShape* aShape, void* pasteOffset)
 2: {
 3:   aShape -> SetSelection(TRUE);
 4:   aShape -> OffsetBy( ((Point*)pasteOffset) -> h,
 5:                       ((Point*)pasteOffset) -> v );
 6: }
 7:
 8: pascal void TShapePasteCmd::DoIt() /* override */
 9: {
10:   TShapeList* pasteList = NULL;
11:   TShapeListFilter* pasteFilter = NULL;
12:
13:   TRY {
14:       pasteList = new TShapeList;
15:       FailNIL(pasteList);
16:       pasteList -> IShapeList();
17:
18:       TShapeViewHelper* shapeViewHelper =
19:                           this -> GetShapeViewHelper();
20:
21:       shapeViewHelper -> GetPastedShapes(pasteList);
22:
23:       pasteFilter = this -> CreatePasteFilter(pasteList);
24:       this -> InitializeFilter(pasteFilter);
25:
26:       Point pasteOffset = this -> GetPasteOffset(pasteList);
27:
28:       fView -> Focus() ;
29:       shapeViewHelper -> Deselect();
30:                                   /* Offset & select shapes */
31:       pasteList -> EachShapeDo(&FixupShapes, &pasteOffset);
32:
33:       pasteList -> RememberSelection();
34:   }
35:   EXCEPT {
```

```
36:         FreeIfObject(pasteList);
37:         FreeIfObject(pasteFilter);
38:     }
39:     ENDTRY
40:
41:     inherited::DoIt();                      /* Install filter */
42: }
43:
44: pascal TShapeListFilter* TShapePasteCmd::CreatePasteFilter(
45:                         TShapeList* pastedShapes) const
46: {
47:     TAddShapesFilter* addShapesFilter = new TAddShapesFilter;
48:     FailNIL(addShapesFilter);
49:     addShapesFilter -> IAddShapesFilter( this -> GetShapeList(),
50:                                 pastedShapes);
51:     return addShapesFilter;
52: }
53:
54: pascal Point TShapePasteCmd::GetPasteOffset(
55:                         TShapeList* pastedShapes) const
56: {
57:     TShapeList* theList = this -> GetShapeList();
58:     Rect bounds = theList -> SelectionBounds();
59:     if (EmptyRect(&bounds)) {          /* Nothing is selected */
60:         if (fView -> Focus())
61:             fView -> GetVisibleRect(&bounds);
62:     }
63:                             /* Get bounds of shapes to paste */
64:     Rect pasteBounds = pastedShapes -> TotalBounds();
65:
66:             /* Compute offset to paste at center of bounds. */
67:     Point pasteOffset;
68:     SetPt(&pasteOffset,
69:             ( (bounds.left+bounds.right) -
70:               (pasteBounds.left+pasteBounds.right) ) / 2,
71:             ( (bounds.top+bounds.bottom) -
72:               (pasteBounds.top+pasteBounds.bottom) ) / 2);
73:
74:     return pasteOffset;
75: }
```

**TShapePasteCmd::DoIt** starts by creating an instance of **TShapeList** to hold the pasted shapes (lines 14-16). It calls the method **TShape-ViewHelper::GetPastedShapes** to fill in that list (line 21).

Next, it creates a filter appropriate to the Paste command (line 23). The default is to create an instance of **TAddShapesFilter** (lines 47-51). The new filter is installed into the command object (line 24).

Next, **DoIt** computes the amount by which to offset the pasted shapes by calling **GetPasteOffset** (line 26). The default implementation of this method centers the shapes within the bounds of the currently selected shapes or, if nothing is selected, within the currently visible part of the view.

Finally, **DoIt** deselects the previous selection (lines 28-29), offsets and selects the pasted shapes (line 31), and calls **inherited::DoIt** to apply the filter (line 41).

As with the Cut/Copy command, the **UndoIt** and **RedoIt** methods of **TShapePasteCmd** are inherited from **TShapeListChanger**, since those methods need only remove and apply the filter.

Listing 25-22 shows the **TShapeViewHelper::GetPastedShapes** method.

### Listing 25-22. GetPastedShapes

```
 1: pascal void CopyShape(TShape* aShape, void* pastedShapes)
 2: {
 3:   ((TShapeList*)pastedShapes) -> AddShape(
 4:                           (TShape*)(aShape -> Clone()))
 5: }
 6:
 7: pascal void TShapeViewHelper::GetPastedShapes(
 8:                           TShapeList* pastedShapes)
 9: {
10:   Handle h = NULL;
11:   THandleStream* handleStream = NULL;
12:
13:   TRY {
14:       h = NewHandle(0);
15:       FailNIL(h);
16:
17:       ResType dataType;
18:       long dontCare =
19:               gApplication -> GetDataToPaste(h, &dataType);
20:
21:       if (dataType == fShapeStreamClipType) {
22:                       /* Read shapes from a handle stream */
23:           handleStream = new THandleStream;
24:           FailNIL(handleStream);
25:           handleStream -> IHandleStream(h, 0);
26:
27:           pastedShapes -> ReadFrom(handleStream);
```

```
28:
29:            handleStream -> Free();
30:            handleStream = NULL; */
31:        }
32:
33:    else {
34:            /* Copy shapes from list contained in Clipboard */
35:            TShapeList* clipList = **(HShapeList)h;
36:            clipList -> EachShapeDo(&CopyShape, pastedShapes);
37:        }
38:
39:        DisposHandle(h);
40:        h = NULL;
41:    }
42:    EXCEPT {
43:        DisposIfHandle(h);
44:        FreeIfObject(handleStream);
45:    }
46:    ENDTRY
47: }
```

**GetPastedShapes** calls the MacApp method **TApplication::GetData-ToPaste** (line 19) to get the data for the clipboard. There are two cases to consider.

First, the clipboard may contain a series of shapes that were written to a stream. In that case, we create an instance of **THandleStream** (lines 23-25) and use **TShapeList::ReadFrom** (line 27) to read the shapes.

Second, the clipboard might contain a **TShapeList** object. This would happen if the user has done a cut or copy, but the program hasn't converted the clipboard to its external form. In this case, we simply clone the clipboard shapes and copy them to our list of pasted shapes (lines 1-5 and 36).

There is still one thing missing from the implementation of paste. How does the **GetDataToPaste** method know which Clipboard representation to return? The answer is that the application tells MacApp the representations it can paste. To do this, you call the MacApp routine **CanPaste**, passing it the four-character ID of the data type the program can paste. You can call **CanPaste** several times; if you do that, you should use data types in descending order of preference.

The **CanPaste** routine should be called from an implementation of **DoSetupMenus**. MacApp will automatically enable the Paste menu command, if the Clipboard contains one of the data types the application can paste. In the case of the graphics building block, we will implement a short method in **TShapeViewHelper** to do this. Its code is as follows:

```
1: pascal void TShapeViewHelper::CanPasteShapes()
2: {
3:   CanPaste(fShapeListClipType);
4:   CanPaste(fShapeStreamClipType);
5: }
```

Since the building block deals with shape objects, it calls **CanPaste** with *fClipShapeList* first, which indicates its preference for pasting a list of shape objects. Its second choice, however, is to paste a stream containing shapes, in which case it will read the shape objects from the stream.

▶ ## Using the Graphics Building Block

We have completed the design and implementation of the graphics building block. The primary features it provides are

- sketching new shapes
- selecting shapes
- moving the selected shapes
- reading and writing shape documents
- changing the attributes of the selected shapes
- implementing Cut, Copy, and Paste commands
- implementing Bring to Front and Send to Back commands

As we discussed the design of each feature, we suggested how clients of the building block might use that feature in their programs. In general, for each feature we defined a method in either **TShapeList** or **TShapeViewHelper** that a client document or view object could call. In addition, the building block contains the **TShapeDocument** and **TShapeView** classes, which can be immediately used in a program.

Building a simple graphics editor that uses the building block is very easy. You must define a subclass of **TApplication** and implement the **DoMakeDocument** method of that class to create an instance of **TShapeDocument**. Your application also must create an instance of **TShapePalette** and register with the palette the sketching and selecting command objects it wants to use.

More importantly, the building block was designed to be extensible. For example, you can define new kinds of shape objects. We have also defined a filtering mechanism that you can use to implement new command objects.

We will not go into the design and implementation of any extensions in this book. The full source code for ExampleDraw shows examples of extending the building block with new shape classes and commands.

## ▶ Summary

This concluding chapter of our exploration of MacApp has put the finishing touches on a complex graphic editing example program. In it, you have learned to extend the user interface of a MacApp program to encompass the use of documents and disk files, filters on disk file retrieval, and the Clipboard for cut, copy, and paste operations.

You are now ready to tackle a MacApp project of your own with great confidence. We encourage you to do so, because the only certain way to learn MacApp well is to use it.

# Afterword

If you're like most prospective MacApp programmers, you were drawn to this book by a mixture of curiosity, excitement, fear, and hope. Curiosity comes from all the noise that's being made these days about object programming. The excitement is a by-product of our lightning-fast industry, in which there's always a shiny new toy to play with, especially if you're a Macintosh fan. The fear comes because object programming and C++ are radically different from the "old-fashioned" function-oriented way, and the learning curve often looks like that first big step out of the Grand Canyon. The feeling of hope, of course, stems from the desire to find out if this latest programmer's messiah can really live up to its claims.

In addition to all these strong feelings about MacApp, C++ has generated lots of strong opinions as well. It's become a blazingly hot topic in the Macintosh programming world lately, and it seems that everyone who has used it has a strong opinion about Dr. Stroustrup's little creation. As in any computer language debate, the best rule seems to be "the right tool for the job," rather than arguing about fine points of syntax or structure. C++ is already proving itself to be the right tool for many jobs.

After reading this book, I hope that you have a sharper focus on how MacApp and object programming in C++ can help you get your work and play done. The information in this book should help you set your expectations properly. For example, you've probably figured out by now that MacApp will not allow your younger brother to write a full-featured commercial-quality page layout/spreadsheet/communications program over the next weekend (unless, possibly, your younger brother is Andy Hertzfeld); at the same time, you should begin to realize that learning MacApp, even with C++, is not nearly as hard as determining the meaning of life.

You'd have a hard time finding a better trio of folks to tell you about MacApp. Dave Wilson has almost certainly taught more people more about MacApp (and Macintosh programming in general) than anybody else in the world during the years that he's been involved with the Macintosh. Dan Shafer knows a lot about a lot of things, as you can tell by examining the multitude of topics, from artificial intelligence to HyperCard, that he's written books about. Larry Rosenstein is no less than one of the principal inventors of MacApp and possibly Apple's leading object designer. If Bo Jackson ever decides to learn MacApp, these guys will be in the commercial.

The importance of object technology to Apple's future, and to the future of the whole industry, can't be overstated. You can find the following clear statement in Apple's February 1989 *developer* magazine: "If you don't learn object-oriented programming now, you will not be able to program the Macintosh later, and you will be months or years behind those who can." And please have no doubt that Apple means it.

With that having been said, welcome to the journey. I hope this book provided you with a nice way to get curious, excited, scared, and hopeful about what you can do with MacApp.

Scott Knaster
*Macintosh Inside Out* Series Editor

# Bibliography

1. Bianchi, Curt. *Memory Management with MacApp*, Dr. Dobbs Macintosh Journal, Fall 1989, pp. 23-29. (How to insure your program will not crash under low memory conditions).

2. Booch, Grady. *Object-Oriented Design*, Benjamin/Cummings Publishing, due in 1990. (Is expected to be an excellent book.)

3. "Class Diagrams: A Tool For Design, Documentation, and Teaching," *Journal of Object-Oriented Programming*, Jan./Feb. 1990.

4. Cox, Brad J. *Object Oriented Programming, An Evolutionary Approach*. Reading, Mass.: Addison-Wesley, 1986. (Good discussion of "Software ICs").

5. *Inside Macintosh*, volumes 1, 2, and 3. Reading, Mass.: Addison-Wesley, 1985. (The 64K ROM routines for Mac.)

6. *Inside Macintosh*, volume 4. Reading, Mass.: Addison-Wesley, 1986. (The 128K ROM routines for Mac Plus.)

7. *Inside Macintosh*, volume 5. Reading, Mass.: Addison-Wesley, 1988. (The 256K ROM routines for Mac SE and Mac II.)

8. Johnson, Ralph E. and Foote, Brian. "Designing Reusable Classes," *Journal of Object-Oriented Programming*, June/July 1988, pp. 22-35.

9. Kernighan, Brian W. and Ritchie, Dennis M., *The C Programming Language*, Prentice-Hall, 1978. (You must have this.)

10. Knaster, Scott. *How to Write Macintosh Software,* Hayden Book Co., Indianapolis, Ind.: 1986. (Memory management and debugging.)

11. Lippman, Stanley B. *C++ Primer*, Reading, Mass.: Addison-Wesley, 1989. (Covers AT+T Version 2.0)

12. Meyer, Bertrand. *Object-oriented Software Construction*, Prentice Hall, 1988. (O-O design, the Eiffel™ language)

13. Meyrowitz, Norman, ed. "OOPSLA '86 Conference Proceedings," special issue of *SIGPLAN Notices*, vol. 21, no. 11, November, 1986. (Order from ACM, 11 W. 42nd Street, New York, NY 10036, (212) 869-7440.)

14. Mullin, Mark. *Object Oriented Program Design With Examples in C++*, Reading, Mass.: Addison-Wesley, 1990 (The evolution of a corporate database program design)

15. Peterson, Gerald. *Tutorial: Object-Oriented Computing*, vol. 1, *Concepts; Tutorial: Object-Oriented Computing*, vol. 2, *Implementations*. Computer Society Press, (Telephone: (800) CSBooks; in California (714) 821-8380; $40 each, or $25 for IEEE members.)

16. Pizzuti, Louella, editor. "develop" (*The Apple Technical Journal*), Issue 2, April 1990, Cupertino, CA: Apple Computer. (Many good C++ and MacApp articles).

17. Stroustrup, Bjarne. *The C++ Programming Language*, Reading, Mass.: Addison-Wesley, 1987. (Covers version 1 by the creator of the language)

18. Schmucker, Kurt J. *Object-Oriented Programming for the Macintosh*. Hayden Book Co., Indianapolis, Ind.: 1986. (MacApp version of 1.0 beta, Smalltalk, Neon, Clascal)

19. West, Joel. *Programming with the Macintosh Programmer's Workshop*. New York, NY: Bantam Books, 1987. (A reference to MPW)

20. Wilson, Dave. "Programming in the Closet," *MacTutor*, July 1987.

21. Wilson, David A. Rosenstein, Larry S., and Shafer, Dan. *Programming With MacApp*, Addison-Wesley, 1990. (Using MacApp with Object Pascal)

22. Witten, Steve. "Programming in C++," *MacTech Quarterly*, Summer 1989, pp. 18-29. (Excellent concise review of the C++ language)

# Index

Disk to Accompany

## C++ Programming with MacApp®

The complete source code to twelve programs listed in **C++ Programming with MacApp** by David A. Wilson, Larry S. Rosenstein, and Dan Shafer is available on one 800K 3 1/2" disk.

Equipment you will need:

Hardware:    Macintosh® Plus, Macintosh SE, Macintosh Portable, members of Macintosh II family

Software:    To compile the source code: MacApp Version 2.0 and MPW™ Version 3.1, MPW C, and MPW C++ Compiler. Compiled versions of some of the applications are included for users who do not have a development system.

To order the disk, simply clip or photocopy this entire page and complete the coupon below. Enclose a check or money order for $20.00 in U.S. funds. California residents, add applicable state sales tax. (Please add $2.00 if you want overseas shipping.)

Mail to:    **Personal Concepts**
**635 Wellsbury Way**
**Palo Alto, CA 94306  USA**

— — — — — — — — — — — — — — — — — — —

Please send me _____(quantity) disks to accompany C++ *Programming with MacApp* by David A. Wilson, Larry S. Rosenstein, and Dan Shafer. I am enclosing a check or money order in the amount of $20.00 ($22.00 if I need overseas shipping) per disk in U.S. funds, plus California state tax if applicable.

Name:_____ Title:_____
Company (if applicable): _____
Address: _____
City:_____State/Province:_____Zip:_____
Country:_____

ISBN 0-201-57022-X